333.3550942

Lacock
Chippenham

ENGLAND'S RURAL REALMS

Dedicated to the memory of
The Rev John Aves (1951–2004)

ENGLAND'S RURAL REALMS

Landholding and the Agricultural Revolution

EDWARD BUJAK

Tauris Academic Studies
LONDON • NEW YORK

Published in 2007 by Tauris Academic Studies, an imprint of I.B.Tauris & Co Ltd
6 Salem Road, London W2 4BU
175 Fifth Avenue, New York NY 10010
www.ibtauris.com

In the United States of America and Canada distributed by
Palgrave Macmillan a division of St. Martin's Press
175 Fifth Avenue, New York NY 10010

International Library of Economics 2

ISBN: 978 1 84511 472 5

A full CIP record for this book is available from the British Library
A full CIP record for this book is available from the Library of Congress

Library of Congress catalog card: available

Printed and bound in India by Replika Press Pvt. Ltd
camera-ready copy edited and supplied by the author

CONTENTS

LIST OF TABLES

LIST OF MAPS

ACKNOWLEDGEMENTS

To Joanne Bujak, Phyllis E. Bujak, Becky Henderson, Professor Richard Hoyle and Professor Michael Turner – we got there in the end.

A special note of thanks is also owed to Lord Cranworth, Lord Henniker, Lord Tollemache, the Earl of Stradbroke, Gordon and Suzanne Kingsley and the committees responsible for awarding the Alumni Research and Scholarly Activity Fellowships and the Arts, Research and Teaching Grants at the University of Evansville, Indiana.

INTRODUCTION

In writing about any of the titled and untitled owners of the great estates in eastern England and the communities on or near them in the Victorian period, one has to start thirty-nine years after Queen Victoria came to the throne. This is because, throughout the early years of her reign, no one actually knew for certain the size and extent of the great estates. The minimum acreage of a great estate, an estate that brought with it membership of what the Victorians called 'landed society', was 1,000 acres, but how many estates fell into this category? The existence of landed society was real enough; it could be seen in the imposing country seats of the aristocracy and the comfortable halls of the gentry and in the deference of the tenantry whose farms belonged to the occupants of these houses. One could thumb through the lists of Dukes, Marquesses, Earls, Viscounts, Lords and Baronets recorded in the *Royal Kalendars* and, having noted where their seats were, cross reference them with local directories such as *Kelly's Directory of Suffolk* or William White's *Gazetteer and Directory of Suffolk*. These local directories contained entries listing the largest landowners in each parish in the county and thus made it possible to piece together the approximate geographical size and extent of an estate from the number of times a particular family was cited. The problem was that no one really knew for sure how many acres the aristocracy actually owned and, as for the landed gentry, one could only guess.

All this uncertainty was finally dispelled in 1876 with the publication of the *Parliamentary Return of Owners of Land, (1872–3) for England and Wales*. With every acre now accounted for in what was, in effect, a new *Domesday Book*, it was at last possible to put together a true picture of English landed society. The landscape of great estates in Victorian Suffolk revealed by the *Return* reveals a blend of old and new money among the aristocracy and gentry in the county. The latter had, for generations, utilised the traditional methods for accumulating land, discussed in the historiography of the 'rise of the great estates' namely, cash from high government office, arranged marriages and holding together their estates with the aid of legally binding family settlements. By contrast, new money had flowed into landed society, in the eighteenth and nineteenth centuries, from trade and industry as a succession of merchants and then industrialists ploughed their money into land. The fact they were able to do so indicates that far from being a 'closed shop', landed society was in fact open for business. What is also evident from this movement of new money into land is that despite arable agriculture's recurrent boom and bust character, in the nineteenth century, the attraction of owning a large landed estate in counties like Suffolk never diminished.

Suffolk was very susceptible to fluctuations in the price of wheat in the nineteenth century due to the widespread adoption of the system of farming 'high' which, in this county, was a system with deep roots. These roots stretched back to the development, in the late eighteenth and early nineteenth centuries, of improved systems of mixed arable and livestock husbandry on the light sandy soils of north-west Suffolk, and the transference of a derivative of these systems to the heavier clay soils of central and eastern Suffolk following the end of the Napoleonic War. Subsequently, these localized developments were subsumed into the wider mid-Victorian obsession with trying to counteract the expected effects of free trade, after 1846, through farming 'high'; unfortunately, the belief shared by landowners and farmers in the efficacy of intensive systems of mixed arable and livestock husbandry, or 'high' farming, was no more than a pipe dream. Arable farmers in England were, however, for over a generation, shielded from the full implications of free trade by war and geography.

As Eric Hobsbawm stated, 'It took a generation of railroad and ship to create a sufficiently large agriculture in the virgin prairies of the temperate world: the American and Canadian Middle West, the pampas of the River Plate lands and the Russian Steppes.'[1] Once this generation had passed and this vast arable acreage came on-line, creating a global glut of wheat, the expensive farming systems in use in Suffolk up to the 1880s buckled and collapsed. As a result, Suffolk, as one of England's premier and longest established 'high' farming counties, suffered terribly in the ensuing agricultural depression of the late nineteenth century. When lower farm rents and the perennial problems of debt and running a country house are combined with the falling number of landowners in the House of Commons after 1884, and the rising popularity of land reform and tenant-right legislation in the Liberal party, the question has to be asked: what was the continuing attraction of owning or buying land?

The Earl of Derby famously listed the following five criteria under-pinning the ownership of landed property:

> one, political influence; two, social importance founded on territorial possession, the most visible and unmistakable form of wealth; three, power exercised over tenantry [and] the pleasure of managing, directing and improving an estate itself; four, residential enjoyment, including what is called sport; and five, the money return, or the rent.[2]

Working from this list, *England's Rural Realms* examines the continuing attractions of owning land up to the Great War. Given that owning and improving a landed estate, when coupled to the upkeep of the requisite great country house, produced a lower return than almost any other form of property, there was clearly more at work here than purely economic considerations. Buying land had not, was not, and would never be purely an economic investment to the Victorian businessman. Acquiring a country house and an attendant country estate signalled an intention to belong to landed society and to enjoy its benefits. There was the personal enjoyment to be had from indulging in country pursuits such as shooting, but there was also the enhanced social standing that came with owning land. In Victorian England no one stood higher than the English country gentleman running a large country estate and, by extension, the affairs of the county and perhaps the country. In a society still milling over industrialization and urbanization, owning a landed estate continued to count for far more than owning a factory, and so the route to the top of Victorian society remained in the countryside among the old landed oligarchy.

By the 1880s however, the old aristocracy began to feel the pinch as the income from their estates began to tumble, and their former disdain for business began to fade as they sought to garner well-paid company directorships. By extension, this also meant that simply having enough money could lead to an entry in *Burke's Peerage*. To the Edwardian plutocrat with a shiny new title, land need only be acquired for form's sake, in a nod to the past. Of course, land still had its pleasures: what could be better than entertaining your new aristocratic friends at a country retreat with plenty of pheasants for them to shoot? By the 1890s and early 1900s, land had become a plaything among the super-rich who wanted to play at being the country squire and for whom shooting was fun. Struggling neighbours within local landed society could now only look on and hope to lease their shooting rights and their ancestral seats for an exorbitant fee. Given this picture, it is then of interest to find that businessmen outside the ranks of the plutocracy, who could easily afford to lease the shooting rights on a sporting estate, should also still want to buy it.

The answer to this conundrum lies in the fact that whilst the landowning aristocracy and gentry, with incomes tied to mixed arable and livestock farming, may have been in retreat economically they still dominated rural society in counties like Suffolk. In continuing to own and administer the English countryside, the great landowners were able to present themselves as the custodians of tradition and property with an old money hauteur and *gravitas* irresistible to new money. As evidence of this, even after 1884, even after the automatic link between landownership and a seat in the House of Commons was finally broken in the countryside, gaining a firm rooting in landed society continued to hold more of an attraction for new money than the pretence of appearing to belong to local landed society as pseudo-gentry, bolstering a beleaguered landowning class by leasing shooting rights and keeping someone else's ancestral seat aired. But by what mechanisms did the old order continue to run the countryside?

The answer to this question has its roots in the wider 'Land Question' and the political influence wielded by the aristocracy and gentry in the Victorian countryside. Whilst the great landowners, representing rural seats in Suffolk and elsewhere, were gradually winnowed out of the House of Commons after 1884, within the localities they were able to put their local influence as cottage builders, allotments providers and farm improvers to good use in bolstering the Conservative party vote. This in turn allowed them to dominate their local party associations and, in swing seats, make or break the Tory candidate. Moreover, the continued social influence that the great landowners could deploy on behalf of the Conservative party, in rural constituencies, explains the continuing animosity of the Liberal party toward the great landowners up to the Great War and their commitment to the land reform campaign outlined by Joseph Chamberlain in Ipswich in 1885. As regards the issues of land reform and tenant-right respectively, the attempt by the Liberal party to woo the labourer and the farmer away from the landlord could of course be thwarted by landlords who could offer tenants better compensation agreements and allotments or cottages with gardens to their labourers.

In other words, the social influence which the aristocracy and gentry continued to enjoy in the English countryside up to the Great War was rooted in the paternalism to be found on the great estates. In the 1820s and 1830s, landowners began to build new cottages and model villages, partly out of a sense of paternal obligation but, also increasingly after about 1837, in an attempt to attract and house hardworking, able-bodied workers to fulfil the new labour requirements of 'high' farming. In a somewhat clumsy attempt at social engineering, the great landowners sought to create industrious, sober and thrifty or model communities on their estates. They did this by building good quality cottages, with gardens or allotments in the so-called 'close' parishes within the estate boundary, and by renting them to the labourer at very reasonable rents on condition the labourers were model citizens. The degree to which labourers conformed willingly or unwillingly to these conditional arrangements is unclear, but what is clear from the 'Lock Out' of 1874 in Suffolk is that the provision of good housing with a little bit of land attached did create a deferential bond between the labourer and the landlord.

In short, by becoming the largest providers of good affordable housing in the countryside prior to the erection of council housing, and providing the physical infrastructure required to farm more highly, the resident aristocracy and gentry progressively built up a reservoir of local goodwill. This goodwill is reflected in the prominence of landowners in local government even after the 1884 Reform Act bundled them out of the House of Commons by giving the vote to labourers in 'open' villages. In 'open' villages dominated by small owner-occupiers and tradesmen and where there was a large element of industrial workers, the social influence of the great rural landlords might indeed be slight as villages of this kind showed a spirit of independence which was often reflected in their politics and their religious nonconformity.[3] By contrast, in the model or 'close' communities on or neighbouring the great estates on which a landed family had expended considerable largesse, voting patterns remained favourable to members of landed society in Parish, District, and County Council elections.

Once in the Council Chamber, nominations for the key posts also tended to go the way of the local landowner. In this regard, the continuing support of the rural middle class and the tenantry was also crucial. The quasi-feudalization of the rural middle class is a topic beyond the remit of this work, but the facts show that in Suffolk enough of the Victorian rural middle class was sufficiently happy to rub shoulders with the grandees of the old order to have a Lord presiding in the County Council Chamber. As regards the tenantry, the position of the tenant farmer in relation to the landlord was complicated by the fact the tenant farmer was responsible for the actual cultivation of the soil. This gave farmers considerably more leeway in dealing with their landlords than the labourers who lived and worked within the great estate system. Alongside this, however, the relationship between landlords and the larger, and thus more influential tenant farmers, had been strengthened by the willingness of landlords to provide the infrastructural investment needed to farm 'high'.

On the other hand, by the late nineteenth century, even with the now almost universal adoption of annual tenancies, the position of the tenant farmer in relation to a now economically weakened class of landowners was becoming ever more blurred especially as the Liberal party looked to loosen the ties binding the tenant to the landlord through legislation. If, as radical Liberal MPs argued, the farmer was the true leader of the agricultural interest, why should farmers continue to defer to landlords to lobby the government on their behalf? Landlords in counties like Suffolk, with big mixed arable and livestock farms to run, would clearly have had to work harder and harder to retain the loyalty of the farmer in the years immediately preceding the Great War, although they were helped by the Liberals' growing flirtation with land nationalization. If it came to a straight choice between the State as landlord or an old aristocratic landlord, a better deal was to be had voting Tory and squeezing concessions from a landlord with a house to keep up, school fees to pay, and burdened with death duties, who had absolutely no desire to take a farm 'in hand'.

What all this demonstrates is that in studying Suffolk, with its classic examples of 'high' farming and improving landlords, we can see both how English landowners sowed the seeds of their own economic decline, whilst at the same time building the social relationships, with the labourer and the farmer, which ensured that the Victorian landlord remained the central figure in the English landscape, for good or ill. This is why the issue of land reform rumbled on within the Liberal party up to the Great War. The aristocracy and gentry still owned the land, and if they chose to stay on their estates and continued to fulfil what they saw as their social obligations by working hard to improve the lot of both the labourer and the farmer and, in so doing, perpetuate their social influence, then they were still the figures who commanded most respect in the English countryside. It is, therefore, too easy to point to the agricultural depression in Victorian Britain's cereal-producing counties and to the subsequent sale of land therein, as indicators of an aristocracy in absolute decline. In Suffolk, as one of the counties to receive the full broadside of the agricultural depression in the late nineteenth century, there was a considerable unloading of land by the local aristocracy and gentry in the early twentieth century. These families were also fearful of holding onto an asset that the Liberals might nationalize and were simply worn out by the high overheads and low returns of owning an arable estate; especially after the introduction of death duties in 1894.

On the other hand, such sales should not be allowed to obscure a subtler picture of retrenchment and renewal. Many of these sales were of outlying portions or secondary estates and, where a member of the landed gentry did dispose of an estate in its entirety, there was a buyer ready to become a country squire. What motivated the buyer before World War One was a combination of the sport to be had *and* the social position that still attached to the actual owners of an estate in the English countryside, which emanated from being a good landlord who built and kept in good repair all the farms and cottages thereon. Businessmen were buying into a landed society still filled by rural grandees and rural squires, imbued with a strong sense of family tradition and social duty. These were the landowners who had managed, by a variety of means, including marriage, sales and leases, to retrench, to try to keep hold of their estates in an age of global competition and who had also, successfully, adapted to the democratization of the English countryside in the years preceding the Great War.

1

THE GREAT VICTORIAN ESTATES
& THEIR OWNERS

By combining the available evidence, namely the definitive parliamentary *Return of Owners of Land* of 1873 for Suffolk, with John Bateman's encyclopaedic 1883 work, *The Great Landowners of Great Britain and Ireland*, 123 great estates of over 1,000 acres, spreading across half the county, can be identified in Suffolk in the 1870s and 1880s (see Appendix). Working from this list, it is readily apparent that these estates included a combination of both large ancestral heartlands and secondary or subsidiary properties. With regard to the latter, these subsidiary estates of between 1,000 and 3,000 acres were also equal in size to the smaller ancestral estates of the resident squirearchy. Fortunately, it is possible to distinguish between these two classes of estate. In total, 62 of the estates surveyed of between 1,000 and 3,000 acres represented total acreages belonging to members of the Suffolk squirearchy. The remaining 51 estates totalling over 1,000 acres belonged to the larger titled and untitled landowners, whose total acreages far exceeded 3,000 acres. Estates in this category included both subsidiary estates and several large ancestral heartlands. Of the remaining 11 largest or magnate estates in the county with acreages in excess of 10,000 acres, their gravitational centres could be either on the poor sandy soils of the Brecklands or on the poorer clays of High Suffolk. [1]

The great estates of Victorian Suffolk were owned by a wide variety of families, ranging from aristocrats proud of their old titles and ancient lineages to equally ancient members of the gentry, as well as lawyers, merchants, brewers and industrialists, all of whom owned over 1,000 acres, consisting of farms, parkland and a rural seat. As the sales particulars of the Icklingham Hall estate boasted in 1898, the lucky purchaser of this property would find himself 'surrounded by the estates of the Duke of Grafton, Earl Cadogan, the Marquess of Bristol, Lord de Saumarez, Lord Iveagh, Sir Robert

Map I: Estates in Excess of 10,000 Acres in Late Victorian Suffolk
(Note: This map provides an approximation of the estate boundaries derived from cross-referencing the names of great landowners in Bateman's *Great Landowners* with the names of principal landowners in the entries for each parish in White's *Directory* [1885] and *Kelly's Directory* [1888].)

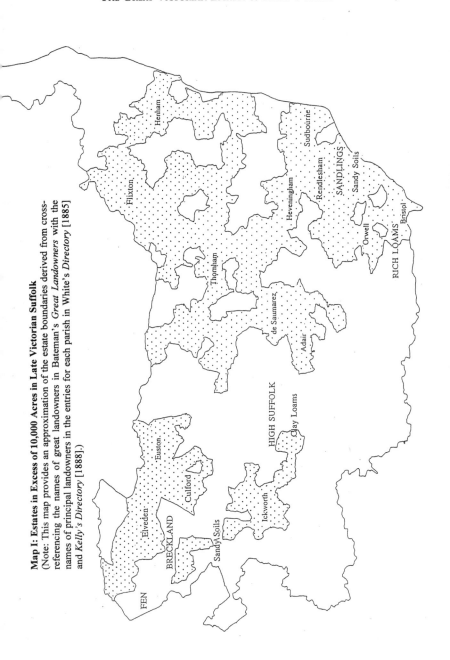

Henham

Sudbourne

Flixton

Rendlesham

SANDLINGS

Heveningham

Sandy Soils

Thornham

Orwell

Bristol

RICH LOAMS

de Saumarez

Adair

HIGH SUFFOLK

Clay Loams

Euston

Culford

Ickworth

Elveden

BRECKLAND

Sandy Soils

FEN

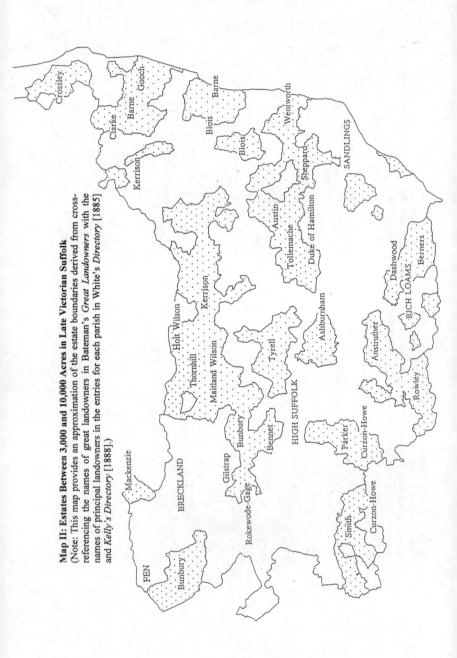

Map II: Estates Between 3,000 and 10,000 Acres in Late Victorian Suffolk
(Note: This map provides an approximation of the estate boundaries derived from cross-referencing the names of great landowners in Bateman's *Great Landowners* with the names of principal landowners in the entries for each parish in White's *Directory* [1885] and *Kelly's Directory* [1888].)

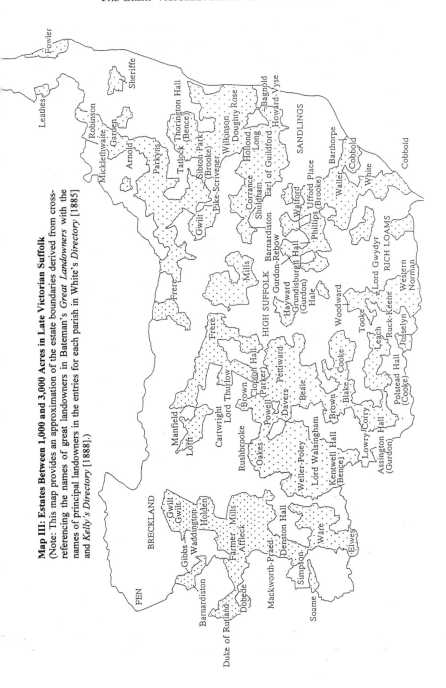

Map III: Estates Between 1,000 and 3,000 Acres in Late Victorian Suffolk
(Note: This map provides an approximation of the estate boundaries derived from cross-referencing the names of great landowners in Bateman's *Great Landowners* with the names of principal landowners in the entries for each parish in White's *Directory* [1885] and *Kelly's Directory* [1888].)

Affleck, Sir Charles Bunbury, Sir William Gilstrap, Prince Victor Duleep Singh, Mr Harry McCalmont, Mr Spencer Waddington, Mr William Angerstein, the Rev J. S. Holden and many others'.[2] Within just this short list, we have three ancient aristocratic landowners, a Sikh prince and two brewers, one with a new baronetcy and another with a shiny new Earl's coronet. Across the county, the largest estates in the 1870s and 1880s, those between 3,000 and 20,000 acres, belonged to either newly landed families who had converted the vast wealth of the commercial and industrial revolutions into land in the eighteenth and nineteenth centuries, or to more ancient titled and untitled families. The latter, having benefited from the Dissolution of the Monasteries in the sixteenth century, spent the seventeenth and eighteenth centuries sidestepping the extinction of their male lines, developing new legal mechanisms to keep their estates together after inheritance and courting and marrying wealthy heiresses. During the same period, this combination of factors, coupled to the financial rewards that came with owning enough land to become an MP and then a Minister of the Crown, gifted to the more durable landed families the wherewithal to continue buying up the small farms and the estates of lesser landed families that bordered their ancestral estates and those acquired through marriage.

Thanks to the redistribution of monastic lands under Henry VIII, the lands owned by the Tollemache family around Helmingham Hall were already substantial by 1700: hence, their elevation to the Baronetage under the early Stuarts. Subsequently, during the Restoration, the Tollemaches successfully courted a series of heiresses. In 1675, Sir Lionel Tollemache married Elizabeth, the heiress of Lord Stanhope, and added an estate in Northamptonshire to the existing possessions of the Tollemache family. Their son further added the magnificent Ham House in Surrey to these by marrying Elizabeth Murray, the heiress of William Murray. During the English Civil War, Charles I had elevated William Murray to the peerage as Earl of Dysart and Lord Huntingtower but, with the King's execution in 1649, these titles were never confirmed. After William's death, the campaign to have them confirmed was pursued by his daughter, the aforementioned Elizabeth Murray, who finally succeeded in securing the necessary Letters Patent from Charles II in 1670. The grandson of Sir Lionel Tollemache now assumed the courtesy title of Lord Huntingtower and with an Earl's coronet to come instead of a Baronetcy, he won the hand of Grace Wilbraham, the heiress of Sir Thomas Wilbraham, and thereby added another large estate, this time in Cheshire, to those in Suffolk, Surrey and Northamptonshire already attached to his future Earldom.[3]

With by now considerable agricultural rents at their disposal, successive Earls of Dysart would have been able to spend the eighteenth century pondering ways to finance the acquisition of neighbouring farms belonging to yeoman freeholders or the estates belonging to the lesser gentry. The latter could include a good-sized house and a paddock with perhaps one or more farms yielding an overall sum of between £250 and £1,000 a year. This process of agglomeration would have been greatly assisted, if we accept H. J. Habakkuk's model, by an extremely buoyant land market in the sixty years between 1680 and 1740. During this period, the 'general drift of property was in favour of the large estate and the great lord'[4] as a burdensome land tax wore down the incomes of the lesser gentry and yeomanry and encouraged them to put their estates and farms up for sale at a time when the greater gentry and aristocracy monopolized the best-paid posts in the government.

This model has, of course, been subjected to critical re-examination on the grounds that the aristocracy also sold land to reduce accumulated debt. In 1791, Sir John Rous, (created Lord Rous in 1796 and Earl of Stradbroke in 1821) who belonged to another of Suffolk's pre-Reformation landed families and owned the Henham estate in east Suffolk, arranged for the sale of land in Norfolk to reduce his debts.[5] Nonetheless, the broad trend was toward the agglomeration of land into great estates, thanks in part to the local purchasing power enjoyed by aristocrats to whom the cost of buying land was counterbalanced by the political benefits that came with ownership of large acreages, namely a seat in the House of Commons and access to highly paid posts in the government that thereby came their way. Landlords could also of course, sell land in one county to enhance their holdings in another. The Rev Sir William Bunbury, for example, who inherited estates in Cheshire and Suffolk in 1746, sold the bulk of the former in the mid-eighteenth century, in order to raise the money needed to purchase more property in the parishes of Great Barton and Mildenhall.

Given the size of the great aristocratic estates by the nineteenth century we have to look on the whole of the eighteenth century as a period of expansion by larger landowners at the expense of their smaller neighbours. During the eighteenth century however, the great landed families were experiencing a demographic crisis caused by high rates of mortality and low fertility, as Linda Colley states:

From the later seventeenth century to the 1770s, the landed establishment of England, Wales, Ireland and Scotland [was] caught up in a major demographic crisis. For reasons that are still unclear, many landowners did not marry, and many who did marry failed to produce male heirs . . . As families died out, because of their inability to produce male heirs, their estates passed to other landowners: through indirect inheritance to distant male cousins, or through the female line or through sale. Altogether, about one third of all landed estates seemed to have changed hands this way in this period.[6]

With regard to indirect inheritance, the inability of large landowners to produce male heirs up to the 1770s and the consequent transfer of landed property to collateral male relatives also meant that, as a secondary result, land continued coming onto the market, facilitating the continued expansion of already large estates. Indirect inheritance of this sort 'was much the most important single factor in bringing land onto the market'.[7] If a landowner had no direct heirs, why bother to reduce the encumbrances charged to his estate for the benefit of a distant nephew or a unknown cousin? Under this scenario, the eventual heir would put any land inherited through an indirect line up for sale because it came encumbered with unpaid debts. Land inherited in this demographic lottery could also be a considerable journey from the heir's own seat and not large enough to justify engaging an agent to run it. In these circumstances, the new owner would again be better advised to put the property up for sale in either a single or in several lots and reinvest the proceeds closer to home by buying some of the neighbouring farms and small estates that were regularly coming onto the market.

By contrast, a large estate could support a considerable weight of debt (although the burden of aristocratic debt would rise considerably after 1770) as well as justify engaging the services of an agent to administer it. The possession of a large estate also conferred considerable social and electoral advantages upon its owner within a particular locality. Under these conditions, larger estates would have been less frequently broken up into lots and sold. To summarise, then, whilst the direct effects of marriage and inheritance are apparent in all groups in landed society, the tendency toward the retention of grander properties suggests that, of the vast quantity of land changing hands as a result of indirect inheritance, a larger proportion of small units than of large came onto the market. In other words, up to the 1770s, sales arising from the working of this factor would have been 'eroding the holdings of the lesser gentry and freeholders faster than those of the greater landlords'.[8]

With regard to marriage and the demographic crisis, if many great aggregations of land were being broken up, despite the development of the strict family settlement, then this also means that whole estates were being transferred between families to make new landed jigsaws. The propensity for landed families to die out in the male line prior to 1770s and the consequent passage of estates from one family to another through the marriage of an heiress explains the prominence of marriage and inheritance in the rise of so many landowning families in England.[9] The Hervey family of Ickworth Park in the west of Suffolk, like the Tollemache family in the east of the county, were likewise beneficiaries of the bloom of heiresses that appeared between 1680 and 1770. Sir John Hervey catapulted his family from among the county gentry into the ranks of the Whig aristocracy through his shrewd support for the Glorious Revolution of 1688 and, subsequently, the Hanoverian Succession. In 1713, Sir John, having made sure he was at Greenwich to welcome George of Hanover to England, was created Earl of Bristol. He was equally busy adding to his estates by marrying firstly Isabella Carr, the heiress of Sir Robert Carr, in 1688 and latterly, in 1695, Elizabeth Felton the daughter of Sir Thomas Felton. These marriages added an estate near Sleaford in Lincolnshire and an estate at Playford in Suffolk to the lands belonging to the Herveys in the west of the county. Subsequently, in 1752, the fourth Earl, by marrying Elizabeth Davers, also obtained the Rushbrooke Hall estate in Suffolk. In the eighteenth century, therefore, successive Earls of Bristol would, in theory, have been able to add to the Ickworth Park estate by buying up neighbouring small properties and by mortgaging farms on these subsidiary estates to increase their local purchasing power. To quote Habakkuk's famous phrase, the aristocracy were able to raise themselves up by their own bootstraps.

Overall, the majority of the greatest concentrations of landed property in existence in 1873 had come together through marriage, especially in the eighteenth century, although further instances can also be found well into the nineteenth century.[10] For example, in 1882, Lord de Saumarez, by marrying Jane Broke, the eldest daughter and heiress of Captain Charles Broke, acquired the 2,700 acre Livermere Park estate. In so doing, he also came into the 9,500 acre Shrubland Park estate and the 1,300 acre Broke Hall estate, which passed to his wife via her uncle Admiral Sir George Nathaniel Broke-Middleton under the will of Sir William Middleton.[11] This is, of course, only a vestige of what was a far more commonplace phenomenon during the late seventeenth and eighteenth centuries. One could examine how, in addition to the string of successful alliances made by the Tollemache and Hervey families, the FitzRoys also established themselves in the county through marriage.

The Euston Hall estate had belonged to the Bennett family but they died out in the male line and, in 1682, Lady Isabella Bennett, the daughter and heiress of Henry Bennett, Earl of Arlington, married (at the instigation of King Charles II) Henry FitzRoy, the first Duke of Grafton and Earl of Euston. The young Duke was the second son of the King by his mistress Barbara Villiers, Duchess of Cleveland. But a Duke needs a country seat with an estate appropriate to his title. Henry's marriage to Isabella completed the jigsaw by transforming what would otherwise have been a paper Dukedom into a territorial reality centred on Euston Hall. A second successful marriage followed in the eighteenth century when George FitzRoy, the second Duke, married Dorothy Boyle, the daughter of the Earl of Cork and the heiress to a £40,000 fortune. Sadly, the marriage was so unhappy that, when Dorothy succumbed to smallpox, she was said to have been 'delivered from misery', leaving Horace Walpole to lament 'do you not pity the poor girl of the softest temper, vast beauty, birth and fortune, to be so sacrificed?'[12] The ambition of the Earl of Cork to buy a Dukedom for a grandson was equalled by that of the Duke of Grafton who recognized that, alongside the agglomerative effects of marriage in bringing together landed property, marriage also provided the means of extending the boundaries of an ancestral estate in the form of generous marriage portions.

Significantly, the great estates in Suffolk 'flourished in areas where the land was relatively cheap', as on the edge of the sandy Breckland.[13] In 1820, the Euston estate was said to have a circumference of forty miles, encompassing six parishes and parts of several others. Significantly, much of this expansion was the work of the abovementioned second Duke, whose coffers had been filled by the Earl of Cork, and by the third Duke, who enjoyed the fruits of a career in government, culminating in his appointment as Prime Minister. Unsurprisingly, the combination of a huge dowry and of posts in the government enabled both Dukes to successively and:

> assiduously acquire land around Euston. In some cases they embarked on a policy of purchasing individual holdings within a manor and finally bought out the Lord himself. When the land was bought under control, it could be re-organized and improved by re-allotting the parson's glebe, extinguishing commons, enclosing open fields and marling.[14]

Of course, the real dynamic in bringing together land, houses, and money remained marriage as it enabled landowners to buy up neighbouring farms, either by mortgaging the farms that had formerly belonged to their wives' families or by utilising the lump sums transferred between families in the form of dowries.

The importance of these cash transfers is evidenced in a letter of 1796 sent by the fourth Earl of Bristol to his son Frederick (created Earl Jermyn of Horningsheath and Marquess of Bristol in 1826). The fourth Earl had himself married a local Suffolk heiress back in 1752 and so pleaded with Frederick to reconsider marrying Elizabeth Upton, the daughter of the impoverished Lord Templeton. This was, in his father's opinion, nothing more than a 'love match' while by contrast, the Countess de la Marche, the illegitimate daughter of the King of Prussia, was 'one of the prettiest, sweetest, most accomplished women' in Europe with '£100,000 down' as a dowry and the reversion of a landed property in Germany. To try and drive home the sheer folly, as he saw it, of choosing Elizabeth Upton over the Countess, the Earl drew up a comparison of Elizabeth and Frederick's respective prospects:

On my side	On his side
£5,000 a year down	No fortune
£5,000 a year in reversion	Wife and children beggars for
An English Dukedom which the	want of settlement
King pledges to obtain	No connexion
Royal connexion: Princess of Wales	A love match
and Duchess of York[15]	

While Frederick went ahead and married Elizabeth in 1798, in general, love matches were thwarted as fathers could bring immense financial pressure to bear on a wayward heir by cutting their allowances. In this way, the marriage of an heir or heiress was carefully regulated to bring greater wealth, land, or influence to a family. Of the 102 marriages arranged in the eighteenth century for the heirs to an English Dukedom, 53 were with the daughters of fellow peers (including 12 with the daughters of other Dukes), while 49 were with commoners of whom only five lacked a gentle background. The question this poses is, given that financial considerations were obviously a key determinant in deciding a family's marital priorities, were marriage portions automatically applied to the purchase of landed property? According to J.V. Beckett:

Heiresses were regarded as particularly good catches for relieving financial troubles . . . [between] 1700–60 . . . twenty per cent of in-marriages among the peerage were to heiresses. But there were never enough heiresses therefore . . . eldest sons marrying outside the [landed elite] compensated for social difference by seeking financial wealth.[16]

Landowners prepared to refill their family's coffers by marrying the daughter of a wealthy merchant could offer the latter the much sought-after *entrée* to polite society in exchange for the substantial dowry such a bride would bring. Conversely, the merchant could augment his social standing and connections without having to divert his capital into purchasing a landed estate and a country seat. In 1788, when Anne, the only daughter of the London merchant Sir John Henniker (created Lord Henniker in 1800), married the Earl of Aldborough, she brought with her a dowry of £50,000.[17] In this case, the marriage was made slightly more acceptable to the Earl's family by the fact that Sir John, having inherited his father-in-law's estates in Suffolk in 1781, was himself a great landowner.

Marriage portions or dowries were transferred from one family to another under a marriage settlement. On the marriage in 1830 of Isabella Manners to William, Earl Jermyn, Isabella's father, the fifth Duke of Rutland, agreed to provide her with a portion of £10,000 'to be raised by way of mortgage in the lifetime of John fifth Duke of Rutland'. The size of the bride's jointure was related to the size of the fortune she brought to the marriage; the usual proportion was ten per cent of the fortune. Thus, a bride with a dowry of £10,000 would, as a widow, receive a jointure of £1,000 a year for as long as she lived but, during her married life, her husband had use of the £10,000. This conforms to the Habakkuk model, which sees the ability of landed families to derive a 'substantial accession of wealth . . . through an heiress or from collateral relatives'[18] as integral to the gradual aggregation of landed property in the hands of the landed elite – but was Habakkuk right?

Any financial gains enjoyed by those landowners who married well were counterbalanced by the fact that they, in turn, had to provide marriage portions for their own daughters. In essence, 'the greater the importance attached to wealth as an object of marriage, the more necessary would it be for a landowner who wished to secure for his daughters good marriages to the eldest sons of landowning families to provide them with large por-tions'.[19] The financial burden that this imposed on families could, however, be ameliorated by taking out a mortgage or by placing an interest bearing charge on the estate, rather than through the sale of land. As a result, in Habbakkuk's opinion, the giving and receiving of marriage portions could frequently lead to the extension of estates by purchase but only rarely to their diminution by sale. Of course, this presupposes that portions were used to purchase land. The role of marriage portions in extending the boundaries of the great estates has perhaps been exaggerated, particularly as 'we cannot positively say to what use portions were put'.[20] The Restoration diarist John Evelyn records that the dowry of £12,000 received by Lord Cornwallis, the owner of the Culford estate, on his marriage to Elizabeth Fox, the daughter of Sir Stephen Fox, restored his financially 'intangled family besides'. Similarly, in 1836, the portion of £5,000 that Theodosia Meade brought with her on marrying Robert Adair of Flixton Hall was 'laid out by the trustees appointed under the settlement and invested in the Funds'.[21]

On the other hand, marriage portions could significantly enhance the local purchasing power of landowners with ambitions to aggrandise an ancestral estate by allowing the purchase of neighbouring freehold properties. It would certainly help to explain how the aristocracy and greater gentry could afford to buy land in such large quantities between the late seventeenth century and the 1770s, even allowing for the purchase of poorer quality and thus relatively cheap arable land. Putting marriage portions into a pot already filled with mortgages, supported by the greater rent rolls obtained by marrying into land, and topped off by generous government sinecures, would explain why the proportion of land in the possession of the greater landlords during this period (especially those with a peerage on which to hook an heiress) was increasing and why the economic gap between them and the gentry was widening.

What should also be recognized is that, as a result of marriage and the inheritance of estates through collateral male lines, many of these landed families were, in fact, creating an illusion of continuous ownership and unbroken accumulation. The determination of landed families to preserve the association of their name with a particular estate at all costs, even if it meant that a remote heir was forced to sacrifice his own surname, ensured that many landed families created the illusion of survival despite the extinction of the patriline. As G. D. Squibb points out, the requirement to take the settlor's name and arms as a pre-condition of receiving an inheritance became increasingly popular from the early eighteenth century onwards. In 1803, George Pretyman (William Pitt's tutor and latterly Bishop of Lincoln and Winchester) whose family were long-established landowners in west Suffolk, assumed the new surname of Tomline in compliance with the testamentary injunction of Marmaduke Tomline as a precondition to inheriting the Riby Grove estate in Lincolnshire.[22]

On the other hand, the descent of lands and titles to distant cousins could cause a patrimony to 'fly apart' as in the case of the Elwes family of Stoke College in Suffolk. The death of Sir Hervey Elwes in 1763 extinguished the male line of the Elwes family. With no direct male heir to succeed him, his Baronetcy devolved on a nephew, whilst the hall and estate went to another nephew. Both cousins, however, assumed the name of Elwes. The nephew who inherited both hall and estate was a notorious miser and bequeathed his huge personal fortune to the two illegitimate children he had by his housekeeper; he left the run-down entailed estates to Sir Hervey's brother-in-law John Timms, who also changed his name to Elwes. Thus, the title, the money, the hall, and the estates were broken up between different people but, crucially, the name of Elwes remained associated with the Stoke College estate up to the 1890s. Overall, the transfer of property to a younger son or sideways to fictive or adoptive kin who adopted the family name, such as patrilineal nephews or paternal uncles, tided the elite over the demographic crisis. In addition, in the ten per cent of cases, between 1840 and 1880, where property transfers took place through women, a change of name or a hyphenation of two family names avoided the public uncoupling of an historic family name from an ancient family seat and estate. In 1837, the Hintlesham Hall estate was devised by the granddaughter of Richard Lloyd to her distant cousin James Hamilton Lloyd-Anstruther.[23]

In 1821, on the death of the sixth Earl of Dysart, the male line of the Tollemache family was extinguished. The patrimony – the houses, the estates and the titles – were now divided between the Earl's two surviving sisters, Lady Louisa Manners and Lady Jane Halliday (d. 1802). Under the terms of his will, Lady Louisa, who became the Countess of Dysart, received Ham House whilst the Tollemache estates in Suffolk and Cheshire went to her nephew, Rear Admiral John Delap Halliday (b. 1772), who assumed the surname and arms of Tollemache. A proviso of the will was that Louisa was left Helmingham during her lifetime. Eventually, following her death aged 95 in 1840, whilst her grandson (b. 1794) succeeded to the Earldom of Dysart, Ham House and the Buckminster Park estate, Helmingham reverted to his cousin, John Tollemache (or Halliday, b. 1805), who had already succeeded his father to the Tollemache estate in Cheshire in 1837. John Tollemache was later elevated to the peerage as Lord Tollemache of Helmingham in 1876.[24] Clearly, this was no more than 'aristocratic window dressing' yet the trend among those families who married well and circumvented demographic extinction from the 1700s onwards was for land to accumulate almost indefinitely.[25] The aristocracy did, of course, occasionally have to sell land to clear their debts, sometimes in considerable quantities, but what was to stop a landowner selling off an ancestral estate in its entirety? The answer lies in the development of the strict family settle-ment. In facilitating the accumulation and preservation of large landhold-ings, it is generally accepted that settlements played a key role in encouraging the drift of landed property towards the greater landowners.

The development in the mid-seventeenth century of the legal device of trustees to preserve the contingent remainders enabled a landowner to settle an estate 'for life' on his eldest son. As a 'life tenant', the heir gained only partial control of the estate and was, in consequence, prevented from dispersing the property through sale, which of course ensured that the estate 'would continue in the family for ever as the basis and hallmark of its greatness'.[26] Throughout the eighteenth and nineteenth centuries, it became commonplace for both established families, and more recent newcomers in Suffolk, to settle their estates in this manner. Habakkuk suggests that the strict settlement was, in fact, employed by all the noble families, by almost all the substantial squires, but only by a minority of lesser squires. It was, therefore, the greater landowners who made the most use of this legal device. This in turn, increased the stability of the large estate relative to the small and enabled the landed elite to expand their estates at the expense of their smaller neighbours over successive generations. Furthermore, as the size of the great estates increased, in addition to attracting wealthy heiresses, the concomitant rise in estate revenues could greatly enhance the local purchasing power of the larger landowners through the application of farm revenues to the purchase of more land or to servicing the interest on a mortgage raised to buy a larger property.

If an estate was to be preserved and passed intact from generation to generation, the estate also had to pass to a single heir and could not be divided. This was achieved through the custom of primogeniture and through the provision for younger children of a lump sum which could be raised by mortgaging another tranche of farms. When Sir Thomas Bunbury of Barton Hall married Lady Sarah Lennox in 1762, their marriage settlement included the following provisions: if there was only one daughter or one younger son, then the portion should be £6,000; if there were a daughter and a younger son then they should each have £5,000, and if there were only daughters and no sons at all, then the said daughters should have £10,000 between them. Similarly, under a settlement dated 31st January 1834, drawn up on the marriage of Frederick Barne, the son of Michael Barne, to Mary Honywood, the daughter of Sir John Honywood, it was laid down that, 'if there shall be two . . . younger children and no more, the sum of £5,000 [was to be raised] . . . for the portions of such two children.' But, 'if there shall be three or more' such younger children 'then the sum of £10,000 was to be paid out', the key proviso being that, 'the said sum of £5,000 or £10,000 as the case may be, [was] to be shared and divided between or amongst such children.' Alternatively, a charge could be placed on the revenue of the estate to provide a large annual allowance or annuity. Under the terms of the settlement arranged in 1830 on the marriage of William, Earl Jermyn, to Lady Katherine Isabella Manners, it was agreed that the Earl, 'shall leave any child or children by the said Lady Katherine Isabella Manners', other than an eldest or only son, an annual sum of £2,000 of 'lawful money'.[27] Nonetheless, what, other than custom, was to prevent a landowner's selling large blocks of land to pay for these portions?

To begin at the beginning, to ensure that an estate always passed to the eldest son, the line of descent had to be defined. This required an estate to be entailed. By creating an estate tail, fee tail, or simply an entail, an entailed estate was inherited according to a defined line. Once the heir to an entailed estate, the tenant in tail, succeeded to the property he could bar the entail and make himself owner in fee simple. As an estate in fee simple was a freehold estate of inheritance 'absolute and unqualified', which granted the owner 'absolute dominion over the land', the heir could proceed to dispose of the property. If, then, an heir was to be so limited in his power over an estate as to be 'incapable of selling it or in any way reducing it',[28] the key was to prevent his coming into the estate in full fee simple. This could be achieved in the first deposition of a deed of settlement. Under this deed, a landowner could impose restrictions on his estate after his death by bequeathing it to his son 'for life'.

As noted earlier, whether called a life tenant or tenant for life, the tenant in tail only held a life interest in the estate, which was less than full fee simple. A life interest was created by 'splitting the fee' through the appointment of trustees to preserve the contingent remainders, that is, trustees representing the interests of any unborn grandchildren. For example, if A, an owner in fee simple, bequeathed land to B for life and, after B's decease, to C and his heirs, trustees had to be appointed to protect C's interests. As a limited owner with only a life interest in the estate, B was entitled to nothing more than the income of the estate and was not allowed, under the strictest interpretation of his position, to sell it, commit waste of it, or mortgage it. By limiting the power of landowners over their estates, the strict settlement reduced the chances of an estate's being broken up. If the settlor could prevent the heir from inheriting the estate in fee simple by creating a life interest, could that life interest be extended to future generations? The rule against perpetuities prevented 'any disposition by which the absolute vesting of property [in fee simple] is or may be postponed beyond the period of the life or lives of any number of person living at the time of the disposition.'[29] In other words, whilst the settlor could reduce his eldest son to the position of a life tenant, he could not reduce an unborn grandson to the same status. Put simply, the settlement ensured that the estate remained intact until the male issue of the heir reached his twenty-first birthday.

To circumvent the rule against perpetuities, landed families had to continually resettle their estates from generation to generation. To do this, the settlor or the life tenant in possession, with the agreement of the heir, the tenant in tail, had to cut off the entail and bring the original settlement to an end. After this was accomplished, both parties would draft a new settlement in which the son (the tenant in tail) would be reduced to a life tenancy after the death of his father; thereafter, the estate would be entailed on his own son 'as yet unborn' who would in turn some day be expected to join in a similar settlement. Thus, despite the rule against perpetuities, generation might follow generation with there never being an absolute owner among them. The glue that kept this legal mechanism stuck together was, of course, money. Heirs were kept notoriously short of money. As a result, very few were in a position to refuse the offer of a generous income in the years preceding their accession. However, this offer of income was conditional; in what was basically a form of familial blackmail, the heir had to agree to join his father in cutting off the entail to bring the original settlement to an end and then draw up a new settlement. By agreeing, on his marriage in 1889, to renew the settlement covering the 7,300 acre Tendring Hall estate and become a tenant for life 'with remainder to his sons in tail male', Colonel Joshua Rowley saw his annuity rise from £500 a year to £2,000.[30]

By continually settling and resettling their property, landowners were able to circumvent the rule against perpetuities and ensure that their estates never came into the hands of an absolute owner. Clearly, the ability of landed families to keep their landed estates together from one generation to the next would have greatly enhanced their opportunities to add to their estates over time, and thereby facilitated the concentration of landed property in the hands of this landed elite. Seen from this point of view, the adoption of the strict settlement successfully preserved many great estates and thereby assisted in the accumulation of both land and great wealth. Although a potential flaw in the proactive role of resettlement in the rise of the great estates does exist, and it relates to the preservative nature of the strict settlement. This preservative aspect could be illusory for if the timing of the resettlement was tied to the marriage of the heir, then the circumstances described by Colley could have seriously hindered the resettlement of land. In which case, whilst, 'the workings of marriage and inheritance brought land into the hands of numerous families, as it did indeed for previous generations . . . it could appear that great estates were preserved by other factors rather than strict settlements.'[31]

The relationship between resettlement and the marriage of the heir is, however, blurred by the fact that whilst resettlement could and did take place on the occasion of the heir's marriage, the coming of age of the heir could also be the date used for the resettlement. But was resettling land on the marriage of the heir necessarily a great stumbling block? In the eighteenth century, the acquisition of land through marriage and inheritance, long considered instrumental in the rise of certain landed families, 'came to operate in part due to the operation of the strict settlement, according to a fixed pattern'.[32] If settlements followed a fixed pattern, then would families who settled their estates on the marriage of the heir in the nineteenth have done anything differently in the eighteenth century? In Suffolk, among the landed gentry who would presumably have copied the practices of their more aristocratic neighbours, the Sotterley Hall estate was successfully resettled in 1834 on the marriage of Frederick Barne, and again in 1871 on the marriage of Frederick St John Barne to Lady Constance Seymour, the daughter of the fifth Marquess of Hertford of Sudbourne Hall in east Suffolk. On the other side of the county, the Ickworth Park estate was successfully resettled on the marriage of Earl Jermyn to Katherine Manners in 1830 and again in 1862 on the marriage of the future third Marquess of Bristol to Geraldine Anson.[33]

The degree to which landowners were hemmed in by their settlements also needs to be treated with some caution. Habakkuk's suggestion that, by the mid-eighteenth century, nearly half the land in England was already held under a settlement, underestimated the tendency of settlers to leave a proportion of their estates un-entailed to give the life-tenant some elbowroom. Thus, whilst most of 32,000 acres owned by the third Marquess of Bristol in 1883 were held in trust, over 6,400 acres in Suffolk, Lincolnshire, and Essex were still held in freehold.[34] In practice, the strict settlement itself was also a remarkably flexible device. Life tenants were allowed to make agricultural leases of up to twenty-one years, to exchange parcels of land, and to take out mortgages on the property to cover the payment of portions to their younger children. By contrast, the elbowroom of landowners whose portfolio of landed holdings was entirely settled was negligible. In Suffolk, the Flixton Hall estate of Sir Robert Adair and the Sotterley Hall estate of Frederick St John Barne were wholly entailed and, by extension, their ability to arrange leases, mortgages, exchanges or sales, unless specified in the settlement, was completely dependent on the agreement of their trustees.[35]

If a landowner wished to sell part of an entailed estate and there were no provisions covering the sale of land included in the settlement, then the property could only be withdrawn from the settlement by an Act of Parliament or when the estate was resettled. The latter could only be accomplished with the agreement of the life tenant, the heir, and the trustees. Sales were often, therefore, the product of a deliberate decision after a protracted family debate that would have kept any disposals to an absolute minimum. Prior to the resettlement, the trustees could block any proposed sales. In the case of Sir George Broke-Middleton, his trustees blocked any disposals on the grounds they would be 'detrimental to the future interests of the daughters of Captain Charles Broke'.[36]

Fortunately, following the passage of an Act to Facilitate Leases and Sales of Settled Estates in 1856, the Court of Chancery was granted the power 'to authorize Leases and Sales of Settled Estates where it shall deem that such Leases or Sales would be proper and consistent with a due regard for the interests of all Parties entitled under the Settlement.' In Suffolk, one of the first landowners to take advantage of the Act was Frederick Barne who, in addition to the Sotterley Hall estate, also owned an estate in Kent. In the case of the latter, Frederick was constrained from selling any land and from granting leases in excess of twenty-one years by the will of Miles Barne. Thus, when the Hon William Napier requested a ninety-nine year lease with a view to re-opening a redundant sawmill, Frederick's trustees were 'unable to do so by reason of the power of granting leases . . . being limited to the term of twenty-one years'.[37] In 1861, Frederick successfully petitioned the Court to allow him to grant a ninety-nine year lease.

By contrast, the Trustees Act of 1850 complicated Frederick's efforts to sell a mere 'slip of land'. This Act was designed to protect the children's interests in matters relating to the conveyance of land held in trust. Under the Act, guardians, appointed by order of the Court of Chancery, were required to give their consent to the sale on the children's behalf. Thus, Frederick had to petition the Court to appoint his sister, Lady Bowater, and her husband, Sir Edward Bowater, to act as the guardians of his two sons, Frederick and Philip Barne, in the matter of the sale of the aforesaid 'slip of land'. Sir Edward and Lady Bowater were eventually appointed by order of the Court in April 1860, at which point they were 'at liberty to consent on behalf of the said infants, to an Order on the petition presented by Frederick Barne for the sale of the piece of land'. The actual sale, however, remained 'subject to the approbation of this Honourable Court'. It appears, though, that the Court was disinclined to allow the sale because, in May 1860, Frederick's solicitors began petitioning Parliament for a 'private Act to effect the sale of [a] . . . parcel of land'.[38] With even the courts ill disposed to the dissipation of landed estates, the emphasis was inevitably toward preservation and thus accumulation.

The Settled Land Act of 1882 finally freed life tenants from the necessity and expense of petitioning the Court of Chancery or Parliament. Under this

Act, all the land held under a life tenancy could be sold except for the mansion, the pleasure grounds, and the park, so long as the proceeds were invested in the hands of trustees to carry out the provisions of the settlement. In other words, the Act moved the restrictions of a settlement away from land onto the equivalent in capital, such as equities or shares. The Act itself was a product of the so-called Land Question. This 'Question' arose out of the belief that the more restrictive elements of family settlements held back agricultural improvement at a time of growing foreign competition and prevented a free market in land, thereby keeping 'fools' in possession of great estates.

In reality, of course, as B. A. Holderness has shown, entailed estates were broken up, divided, or reduced in size, particularly if land had to be withdrawn to pay off debt. In essence, strict settlements were meant to protect family fortunes from spendthrift heirs but they could 'only delay somewhat the ultimate sale of land to meet mounting encumbrances'[39] caused by overindulgent mortgages, overgenerous jointures, and charges placed on the estate. Similarly, many families, by opting to raise a mortgage rather than sell land to clear their most pressing debts, were merely postponing the sale of land as, eventually, servicing these mortgages exceeded the proportion of overall income set aside for the purpose. Thus, as a consequence of larger portions and jointures, mortgages grew in size and the property of landowners as a whole became more heavily burdened by debts. In fact, in the course of three or four generations, the debts could grow so large as to force a breaking of the entail and to bring about sales of land.[40]

Having said this, as settled lands carried payments for the family and could not usually be mortgaged except for specified purposes, the existence of the settlement protected many estates from terminal indebtedness. Nevertheless, the actual renewal of these settlements often owed as much to inertia as to any sense of family tradition for, 'if the character, customs and feelings of landowners inclined so strongly to the conservation of undivided estates, this was in itself enough to attain that object'.[41] In which case, if the strict settlement was used by all the nobility, by almost all the substantial squires, but only by a minority of lesser squires, thereby increasing the stability of the large estate relative to the small, then what we still have in the eighteenth and nineteenth centuries is a legal mechanism favourable to the expansion of the great estates. But, if land was being bundled up in the great estates by a combination of preservation and accumulation, did the land market progressively dry up?

The old position was that the land market did indeed dry up in the late eighteenth century. In this model, mortgages played a major role in enabling landowners to carry a heavy burden of debt without resort to large sales of land. Apparent verification of the model was found in a falling off, in the eighteenth century, in the number of private Acts of Parliament seeking to set aside an existing settlement. This, it was assumed, was *prima facie* evidence that landed families were better able to carry their debts without resorting to the sale of land. When coupled to the settlement of landed estates, the obvious conclusion was that the amount of land coming onto the market in the late eighteenth century *was* being restricted. This conclusion appeared vindicated, when it was found that the value of land rose to 30 years' purchase in the 1770s from 20 years' purchase earlier in the century. Under this model, the late eighteenth century was a period of consolidation in which the aristocracy began to concentrate on the internal restructuring of their by now huge estates, in favour of engrossing formerly small freeholds into large capitalist farms.[42]

F. M. L. Thompson disputed this interpretation on the grounds that sales by auction actually increased in the late eighteenth century – hardly what one would expect to find if the land market was drying up. Secondly, Thompson argued that any rise in the price of land, far from being evidence of a contraction of supply, was in fact attributable to land prices tracking the soaring price of wheat and that 'we must therefore regard very sceptically any idea that the volume of land sales was actually declining because of a withholding of supply'.[43] When there really was a shortage of land on the market, as in the 1860s, land values soared to between 40 and 65 years' purchase. The model favouring a closing of the land market in the second half of the eighteenth century has thus become untenable. There was certainly a continued availability of estates on the market in Suffolk; Sir William Middleton of Crowfield Hall, for example, purchased the Shrubland Hall estate, in 1787.[44] Meanwhile, between 1789 and 1800, the second Earl Cornwallis encountered little or no difficulty in expanding his family's ancestral estate across the poor sandy soils of northwest Suffolk by purchasing small estates neighbouring his seat at Culford.

The Cornwallises were another of the county's pre-Reformation landed families that had become both titled and great landowners by sitting as MPs and tapping into the monetary rewards of being Ministers of the Crown. In 1753, Lord Charles Cornwallis was created Earl Cornwallis. Subsequently, during his period in office as Governor General of India between 1786 and 1793, Charles became the first Marquess Cornwallis and amassed a personal fortune of over £100,000. This was augmented by a pension of £5,000 a year awarded after the conquest of Mysore in India. With such deep pockets, he decided to extend the Culford estate in the belief that 'the first Lord Cornwallis who comes into a cash fortune will spend every last half penny of it. Now parting with land causes a lot more heartache'. In 1789, while still in India, he considered buying the estate of Sir Charles Kent at Fornham St Genevieve. However, his brother James, acting as his agent, advised against this acquisition and instead persuaded Charles to purchase the 1,589 acre manor of Little Saxham from the Croft family for £25,000. In 1795, Charles purchased the 3,000 acre parish of West Stow from the Rushbrooke family in exchange for part of Little Saxham. He later sold the remainder of Little Saxham to Robert Rushbrooke and, in 1800, an estate in the parish of Whepstead, which was purchased by Sir Thomas Hammond for around £12,000. These two properties were sold to raise the £33,000 required to purchase the parish of Wordwell from Lord Bristol, who was in the process of building a huge mansion at Ickworth. Charles also purchased the manor of Cavenham but this property was later sold by the second Marquess in 1809 to Henry Spencer Waddington for £35,000. Robert Rushbrooke, meanwhile, exchanged Little Saxham for the Rushbrooke estate held by Lord Bristol.[45]

In Suffolk, therefore, the period of the late eighteenth century was not one that could be said to be lacking in suitable properties for sale, especially as the aristocracy also sold land, sometimes very considerable amounts of land when necessary, as in 1813, when the Earl of Albemarle sold the Elveden Hall estate for £30,000 to William Newton, a wealthy West India merchant. The existence of this active land market in the late eighteenth century also brings into question the old idea, predicated on the belief that the land market *had* dried up, that the 'openness' of the landed elite to new blood was in fact a myth, and that the degree of upward social mobility in England was 'surprisingly small and not of great social significance'.[46] But the fall of many older gentry families operated in favour of the aristocracy only up to 1740s. Thereafter, when an old gentry family was obliged to sell its estate, it was more often than not purchased by wealthy lawyers, merchants, or naval captains with prize money in their pockets, rather than being absorbed into the estates of neighbouring aristocratic landowners along with the farms and smaller estates of the yeomanry and lesser squires.

Beginning in 1702 with the purchase of the Redgrave Hall estate by Sir John Holt, a former Lord Chief Justice of England and in Defoe's opinion one of the most eminent lawyers of his day, a number of estates across the county were bought in the eighteenth century by first-time buyers, all of whom, like Sir John, succeeded in fixing their families in the county; in 1883, the Redgrave Hall estate belonged to one George Holt-Wilson, a descendant of Sir John's. Similarly, when the Sotterley Hall estate was put up for sale in 1744, it was bought by the ancestor of Frederick Barne, one

Miles Barne, a London merchant and the MP for Dunwich. Two years later, in 1746, the neighbouring Benacre Hall estate was snapped up by the Gooch family. In addition, the nearby Flixton Hall estate (about 2,000 acres) was bought from the Wybarne family about 1752 by the Irish landowners, the Adairs, who added considerably to the estate between 1760 and 1850. Subsequently, in 1773, Charles Berners acquired the Woolverstone Hall estate for £14,000. On the other side of the county, the Dalham Hall estate was snapped up by Gilbert Affleck about 1782, Sir William Rowley bought the Tendring Hall estate about 1784 and, in 1786, Sir Henry Parker purchased the Melford Hall estate.[47]

Among all these new faces there is a clearly discernible group: the merchants. As Adam Smith noted in the 1770s, 'merchants are commonly ambitious of becoming country gentlemen'. In March 1752, Sir Joshua Vanneck, a London merchant, purchased the Heveningham Hall estate near Halesworth from the Earl of Leicester and Lord Coke, presumably the life tenant and tenant in tail, respectively. Subsequently, the family was elevated to the peerage with Sir Joshua's son being created Baron Huntingfield of Heveningham Hall in 1796. Similarly, Peter Thellusson, another London merchant and a Director of the Bank of England, was created Baron Rendlesham of Rendlesham in 1806, having inherited the Rendlesham Hall estate which his father had purchased from Sir George Wombwell in 1787 for £51,400. Sir John Henniker, a wealthy London timber merchant and shipbuilder, was also ennobled in 1800, having inherited the Thornham Hall and Worlingworth Hall estates on the death of his father-in-law, Sir John Major, in 1781. Sir John Major, who had also built up his fortune as a London merchant, had acquired these estates in 1756. As J. H. Round observed, 'apart from fortunate marriages, the leading English families . . . owed their rise to three great sources: successful trade; the law; and [for the older families] the spoils of the monastic houses'.[48]

In the early nineteenth century, the depressed price of wheat following the end of the Napoleonic Wars, coupled to mounting rent arrears, meant that by the 1820s, many landowners with high fixed charges based on wartime wheat values were forced to place their estates on the market. As a result, a further tranche of new families were able to enter the ranks of the landed elite. In 1823, the second Marquess Cornwallis, with five daughters and no son to succeed him, sold the Culford Hall estate for £195,000 to the London property speculator Richard Benyon de Beauvoir. The millionaire businessman Mathias Kerrison purchased the remainder of the Cornwallis estates in the parishes of Oakley and Brome. Having earlier purchased the Bungay Navigation company and levying charges for shipping timber, coal, and corn throughout the Napoleonic Wars, Kerrison could also afford to buy the Hoxne estate from Lord Maynard and put it together with the Oakley and Brome estates, thereby giving the Kerrison family control of the Eye constituency. Meanwhile, in 1829 the Rev Edmund Holland bought the Benhall estate from the trustees of his cousin Edward Holland (d. 1829) for £81,900 – Edward having earlier bought the estate from the devisees under the will of Admiral Sir Hyde Parker in 1810.[49]

By the 1830s, the movements of rents and taxation in relation to the gentry's living costs were such that the conditions of survival for these families became easier, slowing down the rate at which they sold their estates. There were, in consequence, far fewer ready-made estates of over 1,000 acres on the market than had been usual in the eighteenth century. This would have further intensified the competition between established landowners and their new neighbours for the seemingly endless supply of smaller freehold properties comprising between one and one thousand acres. The apparent disappearance of the small landowner – the small squire, the yeoman and the 'peasant' – from the English countryside is one of the questions that continue to dog rural historians. What is agreed is that smaller properties remained particularly abundant on the land market between the mid-eighteenth and mid-nineteenth centuries, which is why Charles Austin was able to build up the Brandeston Hall estate in the mid-nineteenth century in an entirely piecemeal fashion.[50]

Reputed to be the most eminent advocate of his day, Austin was 'unrivalled for lucidity of expression, for promptitude and powers of persuasion'.[51] In 1848, he retired with a large fortune to the 650 acre Brandeston Hall estate he had purchased back in 1842. Subsequently, in the 1850s, he extended the estate through the purchase of numerous small freehold farms and the estates of the lesser squirearchy – the smallest he considered being just 58 acres – until the estate covered over 3,000 acres.[52] There were, of course, ready-made estates, over 1,000 acres, still coming up for sale in the nineteenth century. In 1838, Captain E. R. S. Bence acquired the Kentwell Hall estate for £85,000 while the papers of Charles Austin reveal that, alongside smaller estates belonging to the lesser squirearchy such as Brandeston and the Shadingfield Hall estate, there were still ready-made gentry estates available in the 1850s, such as the 1,700 acre Brettenham Park estate. The problem was that the declining number of tailor-made gentry estates, as compared to the previous century, coupled to the dwindling number of small freehold properties after 1850, coincided with an upsurge in demand for large landed estates by Victorian industrialists during the 1850s, 1860s and 1870s.[53]

Of course, established Victorian landowners were still buying land. George Tomline for instance, the wealthy grandson of George Pretyman-Tomline, purchased the Orwell Park estate in 1848, eventually expanding the estate to cover an area of 18,473 acres. His neighbours, however, were now concentrating on 'rounding-off' their great estates. In 1853, the second Earl of Stradbroke exchanged land in the parishes of Brundish, Bedfield, and Tannington with Lord Henniker. Subsequently, in 1859, the Earl sought to add to the land he already owned in the parish of Westhall by buying the 400 acre Westhall Hall estate. Meanwhile, between 1861 and 1862, the third Marquess of Bristol spent £3,000 on the purchase of farms in the parishes of Chevington and Rushmere. Subsequently, in 1864, Sir Edward Kerrison purchased the Yaxley Hall estate from Lord Huntingtower; meanwhile freehold estates in the parishes of Heveningham and Ubbeston were sold, in 1875, by the trustees of Sir Robert Adair to Lord Huntingfield: whilst Lord Waveney set about rounding-off the Flixton estate. The only other exception, alongside Tomline, to the mid-nineteenth fashion for rounding off an estate, was Lord Rendlesham. In 1857, the Rendlesham Hall estate covered an area of 14,965 acres however, by 1883, according to Bateman, the estate covered an area of 19,869 acres, an increase of 4,904 acres.[54]

If Rendlesham was an exception and most landowners were contenting themselves with rounding-off their estates, then clearly the high land prices associated with the land market boom of the late 1860s and 1870s can only be attributable to the rise of competition between industrialists for a rapidly declining number of suitable properties. As Thompson concludes, it was the competition between businessmen 'probably more than that from established landowners which pushed land prices up'.[55] But how many industrialists were involved in this land grab? Surely, as land prices escalated the number of industrialists competing for land would drop, leaving the price of land to be determined by a decreasing number of richer and richer businessmen? On the contrary, W. D. Rubinstein has shown that the majority of very wealthy businessmen in nineteenth century Britain were in fact landless or owners of estates too small to be recorded by Bateman. This was because those businessmen who did buy estates in the nineteenth century were disinclined to purchase immense amounts of land and so often restricted their purchases to estates of under 2,000 acres.[56] In general, 'the number of very wealthy entrepreneurs of the post-1780 period who purchased land on a large scale was very small indeed, either in terms of the total number of men of wealth or of the total landed acreage of Britain; fewer still transformed the bulk of their property into land'.[57] Of the 700 or so largest estates in the United Kingdom recorded by Bateman in 1883, only 7 per cent were constructed from business fortunes and less than 10 per cent were the product of business and professional wealth created since 1780.

Evidently, families whose wealth was tied to the burgeoning industrial wealth of the nation failed to buy land in sufficient quantities to make a real dent in what Rubinstein, quite rightly, described as the overwhelming domination of the pre-industrial landowners. Thus, of the 'enormous and unprecedented potential investment which might have been directed into land purchase by the vast new business class created by the commercial and industrial revolutions . . . little actually went to that end' and so this potential was never realized.[58] Of course, the focus here is on the very richest of the new industrialists who had the potential to buy land on a scale large enough to challenge the very greatest of the established aristocratic magnates, whose estates had been built up over centuries and who were also still intent on buying neighbouring farms and estates. But it was here, among the market for farms and gentry-size estates, that competition would have been at its fiercest, hence the rising price of land, given the complementary pressures of dwindling supply and rising demand. And so it is here, among estates broadly between 1,000 and 5,000 acres, that we need to look for those Victorian businessmen looking to fulfil their dreams of becoming English country gentlemen.[59]

The situation in Suffolk conforms to the bigger picture of 'a burgeoning interest'[60] among Victorian businessmen in buying land. The maltster, Sir William Gilstrap, used the wealth he derived from the boom in beer sales in the 1860s to purchase the 1,600 acre Fornham Park estate in 1862 from Lord Manners (who had bought the estate in 1843 for £75,500 from the Duke of Norfolk) for £85,000 and subsequently to purchase farms in the adjoining parish of Fornham All Saints. In the following year, Francis Crossley, the Halifax carpet manufacturer, purchased the 3,000 acre Somerleyton Hall estate from the civil engineer Sir Samuel Morton Peto who had earlier acquired that estate in 1843. In the same year that the Crossley family moved into their new home at Somerleyton Hall, the Rev James Holden purchased the Lackford estate. Meanwhile, another northern industrial weaver who came south was John Brooke who, having made his money in the manufacture of broad woollen cloth in his factory in Huddersfield, purchased the 1,500 acre Sibton Park estate in the parishes of Sibton and Yoxford. Alongside these industrialists, W. H. Smith used the income from his bookstalls to purchase 5,200 acres in Suffolk in the parishes of Hundon, Great Thurlow and Great Wratting, although the largest buyer of land was Edward Mackenzie, the civil engineer, who acquired an 8,800 acre sporting estate in the county. As Thompson states, like it or not, wealthy Victorians did purchase land.[61]

The key point is that due to the escalating cost of land, Victorian businessmen were unlikely to repeat the feats of the Hanoverian merchants who arrived in the county intent on building up estates in east Suffolk to rival the Henham estate on the heavier clays and the Sudbourne estate of the Marquess of Hertford on the Suffolk Sandlings. In so doing, these new arrivals built up a clump of estates rivalling the clump of older estates on the poorer sands in the west of the county, whose ownership had traditionally been monopolized by the grander families who resided there. In the case of these west Suffolk families, the variables differed but some common threads can be identified. By becoming MPs and entering government service, they enjoyed the monetary and titular rewards of public office such as knighthoods, baronetcies and peerages. And, from the monies obtained from the heiresses hooked on these titles and the monies obtained from the public purse, they were able to fund the expansion of their ancestral estates at the expense of their smaller neighbours and then ring-fence their acquisitions with settlements. But by the 1870s, the biggest estates in the west, put together with all the advantages of time, marriage, money, settlements and public office, were rivalled in the east by the estates of London merchants.

During the eighteenth and nineteenth centuries, lawyers, industrialists, and merchants such as the Barne family bought land in Suffolk thereby fixing their families in county society as if 'to the manor born' alongside such families as the Blois of Cockfield Hall, a family described by *Debrett's* as of great antiquity in Suffolk. However, only the Vannecks, Thellussons, and Henniker-Majors, whose estate around Thornham had covered between 2,000 and 5,000 acres in the eighteenth century, went on to amass acreages in excess of 10,000 acres. It was only these eighteenth century arrivals who were able to match the older estates of, for example, the Rous family around Henham which, between 1544 when the family arrived in the neighbourhood and 1874, grew to cover an area of over 12,000 acres, or of the Herveys who owned the manor of Ickworth in the 1480s and nearly 17,000 acres by the 1880s.

In nineteenth century Suffolk, businessmen continued to buy land but, due to the escalating cost of agricultural land, they were disinclined to buy it on the same scale as their eighteenth century predecessors. They did not challenge the hegemony of the oldest families in the same way as the merchants had done, but their appearance in the countryside reminds us that the sign 'open for business' remained on the door of landed society and whilst 'by no means all successful businessmen sought to set themselves up as landed gentlemen . . . that a good many of the most able and forceful could do so was a great strength to the landed interest.'[62] Whether in time these Victorian businessmen would have gone on to build far larger estates is a moot point, given that the price of agricultural land slumped after 1874. The problem is that the slump after 1874 was so catastrophic that it effectively called into question the whole great estate system. The root of the catastrophe was, ironically, the agricultural success enjoyed by landowners after 1837. This created a false sense of security, delaying retrenchment after 1874 by at least a decade, until eventually agricultural rents tumbled so far that the margin between income and outgoings, often associated with servicing accumulated debt, was effectively wiped out. Once this point was reached, land had to be sold to reduce debt. In these circumstances, buying vast additional acreages would have been foolish, as the families one would seek to rival were possibly about to disappear. The irony, then, is that late Victorian and Edwardian businessmen continued to want an estate in the country but, before looking at this issue, and the survival of English landed society, we need to examine the collapse of mixed arable and livestock farming, as exemplified by Suffolk, during the reign of Queen Victoria.

2

AGRICULTURE &
THE GREAT ESTATES
1837–1901

In the mid-nineteenth century, the fashion for agricultural estates to be farmed more intensively or 'high' increased in popularity among those landlords willing and able to cover the cost of the expensive agricultural improvements required. As James Caird observed in 1848, the landlord was the party chiefly interested in the question of improvements and with him 'any improvement ought to originate'.[1] The important point is that after about 1837 the fashion for agricultural improvement began to take on a momentum of its own that progressively paid less and less attention to economic gain. Thus, money continued to be spent on improvements to farm buildings and field drainage well into the 1870s even though, by then, experience would surely have shown landowners that the actual return on these investments was, in fact, extremely low. The success of high farming in boosting the output of arable land during the 1850s and 1860s was such that the viability, in an era of unfettered foreign competition, of a high intensity system of mixed arable and livestock farming biased toward cereals rather than milk or meat, and based on expensive farm improvements, was never seriously questioned. When it was, as in the 1880s, did this reappraisal come too late?

The *raison d'être* of high farming was to boost wheat yields through the investment of large amounts of both fixed and working capital. With regard to the latter, tenants were given compensatory inducements by their landlords to supplement the animal feed produced on their farms by purchasing concentrated animal feedstuffs such as linseed or oilcake. These additional supplements enabled tenants to keep more cattle over the winter in yards and thereby increase the quantity of manure produced on their farms; more manure improved the fertility of the soil. The intensification of livestock husbandry in the 1840s on arable farms, or 'high' farming, which evolved out of the system of 'high feeding' was, therefore, in the opinion of Philip Pusey, undertaken 'more for the purpose of making the straw into manure than anything else'.[2] When tenants purchased store-cattle in the autumn for sale between the following February and June, and fattened them in yards over the winter on a diet of turnips, swedes, beet, corn and purchased cake or pudding, they did so not so much to profit from the production of meat as to produce dung to improve wheat yields. On the Helmingham Hall estate, for example, the scale of the compensation paid to an outgoing tenant by Lord Tollemache was linked to the quantity and quality of the manure he left on the farm. On estates on the lighter Breckland soils of north-west Suffolk, the greater quantities of manure produced by increasing the number of cattle fed loose in open yards greatly enhanced the 'expanding circle' of light land agriculture.[3]

Ever since the turn of the century the light lands of north-west Suffolk had reaped the benefits attendant upon the introduction of the Norfolk four-course rotation, whereby sheep were folded alternately over fodder crops of turnips and clover planted in between sowings of barley and wheat. This rotation system enabled tenants to keep more sheep and cattle on their farms. The purchase of artificial feedstuffs and the consequent rise in the quantity and quality of the manure already being produced was thus merely an extension of this existing light land system. On the Euston Hall estate, by the 1840s, tenants were giving their sheep an additional supplement of between a quarter and half pound of oilcake per day, whilst the bullocks fattened over the winter in yards received a daily intake of seven pounds of cake, three quarters of a 'peck' of meal and one bushel of cut mangold-wurzel and sainfoin hay.

Moreover, the dung produced by the intensification of livestock husbandry on arable farms in the district was being applied to land that had, in many cases, already been greatly improved by the application of huge quantities of artificial fertilizers such as crushed bone, guano and, eventually, super-phosphates. To take the case of the Euston estate again, prior to the autumn sowing of turnips, tenants dressed their fields with over six and a half hundredweight of rape dust, or two hundredweight of guano or 16 bushels of bones per acre, the dung from the bullocks being reserved for the wheat crop. Once again, the landlord was instrumental in all this as tenants looked for and received assurances from the Duke of Grafton that, should they have to leave their farm, any compensation would take into consideration the money spent on fertilizers.

By contrast, arable farming on the heavier soils had traditionally been looked down upon as the poor relation of light land farming because of the

historical bias toward dairying on farms on heavy land. Between the end of
the French Wars and about 1850, however, arable farming on the heavier
soils was transformed by the drainage schemes that accompanied the decision
of landlords and tenants to abandon dairying and plough up their pastures.
The decision to move toward mixed arable and livestock farming, to boost
arable output under a four-course shift (with local variations) of roots, barley,
clover and wheat, was taken in an attempt to counter the depressed price of
wheat in the aftermath of the Napoleonic War. The ensuing transformation
was given additional momentum by the introduction of improved pipe and
tile drainage in the 1820s and 1830s alongside the more traditional forms
of bush drainage. In 1847, the agent for the Tollemache estates in Suffolk
reported that the owners of several estates were undertaking tile drainage,
and then charging their tenants interest on the capital invested.

Elsewhere, tenants were carrying out tile drainage on their own initiative,
especially as on the Flixton and Helmingham estates, where tenant right
agreements included compensation for the remaining value of any
improvement to the soil, so-called unexhausted improvements. Pipe and tile
drains were far superior to the more traditional methods of bush drainage,
making the heavier clays far easier to work. Given the growing fashion after
about 1837 for agricultural improvement among landlords, laying such
drains, when coupled with the introduction of improved seed drills, left
William and Hugh Raynbird in little doubt that by 1849 improved field
drainage and drill husbandry had transformed this region into 'one of the
finest corn districts in England'.[4] Essentially, pipe and tile drainage, in
conjunction with the application of greater quantities of animal and artificial
fertilizers, made the heavier soils friable enough to allow turnips to be grown
on the bare fallows and reduced the need for a clear fallow every four years
in which farm land had been repeatedly ploughed and pulverized to reduce
the stiffness of the soil. Large crops of turnips, in turn, increased the
livestock carrying capacity of heavy land farms, and thus assisted other crops
in rotation through the augmentation of supplies of animal manure
produced by this livestock.

Put simply, improved field drainage meant the expansion of mixed
farming and the heavier stocking of land. At the very least, improved field
drainage, coupled with the application of large quantities of artificial
fertilizer and manure from stall-fed cattle, allowed tenants to reduce the
number of fallows that had traditionally hindered attempts to raise the
productivity of heavy land farms in Suffolk. Thus by 1849, best practice on
the heavy land estates of central Suffolk involved a four-course rotation, with
a clear fallow once every eight years as opposed to every four. Consequently,

when James Caird visited Suffolk in 1850, he heaped praise on the farming of the heavier lands, stating 'the chief characteristic of Suffolk agriculture is the success with which heavy land farming is carried on'.[5] The driving force behind this transformation was of course the improving landlords who sought to ensure that their estates were rendered sufficiently dry to allow the 'union' upon them of livestock husbandry with tillage by either undertaking drainage programmes themselves or encouraging their tenants to do so through the offer of generous compensation packages. Against this has to be set this question: why bother to go to all this trouble?

Experimentation by landlords can perhaps explain the early examples of agricultural improvement and fashion can perhaps explain later improvements but why was there a sudden surge of farm improvements, coincidentally, following the accession of Queen Victoria? With the formation of the Anti-Corn Law League in 1838, the momentum toward free trade began to grow. In these circumstances, the looming prospect of 'low prices and universal competition compel agricultural improvement'.[6] To the Earl of Stradbroke, the President of the Suffolk Agricultural Association from 1831 to 1865, and the 'diehard Tory Protectionist' John Tollemache, the Corn Laws represented a bulwark protecting 'the agriculturalists of this country against foreign competition'.[7] With the Corn Laws' likely repeal, farming high based on agricultural improvements to boost the productivity, efficiency, and overall competitiveness of the pre-existing system of 'high' feeding was thought to be the only way for arable farming to move forward. The great fear was that, with the removal of tariffs, the value of wheat, measured in quarters (a measure equivalent to eight bushels of wheat or one-fourth of a hundredweight) would collapse which would inevitably 'fall most heavily on the least wealthy portion of the landed proprietors . . . and press immediately and severely on the tenant farmers, and through them, with ruinous consequences on the agricultural labourers'.[8] It was this anxiety which acted as a spur to investment once landlords, such as the Earl of Stradbroke and John Tollemache, grudgingly agreed that protectionism was a lost cause.

After 1846, the price of wheat did indeed fall. Between 1848 and 1852, the increased volume of imports in conjunction with good domestic harvests in 1848 and 1849 pushed wheat prices down to 40 shillings a quarter in 1850 and 38 shillings in 1851, forcing landlords in Suffolk to assist their hard-pressed tenants by reducing their rents. On the Chediston Hall estate of Eugene de Lacroix, temporary rent reductions of 12.5 per cent in 1851 and 1852 were followed by a further 10 per cent reduction in 1853, although the agent had actually recommended a reduction of around 15 per cent:

it becomes necessary again to refer to the reduction of the Chediston
rents which it will be necessary to make . . . in order to keep things
together. Prices are about the same as last year . . . I have no hesitation
[therefore] in recommending that the 12.5 per cent we reduced last
year should be made 15 per cent this year . . . This was the reduction
Lord Huntingfield is making on his farms in the neighbourhood.[9]

These reductions were, however, made against a backdrop of gradually rising
investment. The rise in fixed capital investment in Suffolk was clearly
observable to Caird, who records that 'until within the last two or three years
landlords gave themselves very little concern about the welfare of tenants,
or the management of their estates; . . . expenditure on drainage or farm
buildings was hardly ever made by the proprietor';[10] although the evidence
of William and Hugh Raynbird suggests that this negative assessment was
something of a generalization. The new mood of improvement evident
before 1849 was understandable, for 'if the farmers of England are to be
exposed to universal competition, the landlords must give them a fair chance
[and if] they refuse to part with the control of their property for the
endurance of a lease' thanks to the growing popularity of tenancy-at-will
then 'they must themselves make such permanent improvements as a tenant-
at-will is not justified in undertaking',[11] such as better accommodation for
stock.

To the immense relief and perhaps surprise of both landlords and tenants,
the price of wheat climbed back above 50 shillings a quarter after 1853,
suggesting that greater investment in greater efficiency and greater productivity was indeed the way forward for arable farmers in the absence of
protection. In reality, farmers continued to be indirectly 'protected' by war
and geography. The outbreak of the Crimean War (1853–1856) blocked off
imports of wheat from Russia and delayed the construction of the railways
required to access the fertile Russian steppe. Similarly, following the end of
the Crimean War, farmers and landlords in Suffolk again benefited from the
outbreak of the American Civil War (1861–1865). Once again, the war
delayed the building of railways into the fertile interior of the Mid-Western
United States. It was this sequence of events, blocking off the productive
capacity of the prairie and the steppe, that kept the price of wheat relatively
stable and gifted arable farmers, on their costly but more efficient and
productive farms, a so-called Golden Age.

Taking an average of prices between 1853 and 1874, the price of wheat
in the United Kingdom stabilized at an average of 53 shillings a quarter,
which was only five shillings less than the average price of wheat during the

last twenty-six years of protection. When we look at the price of barley and oats, which were more responsive to the growth of Britain's industrial population and a rise in real incomes, they rose in value by around 20 per cent between 1848–57 and 1867–77, whilst the price of meat and dairy produce rose 30 to 45 per cent. In this context, the stable price of wheat indicates that regardless of higher investment and rising productivity, imports had in fact already managed to completely offset the growth of home demand and had already begun to adversely affect prices.[12] What these prices also indicate is that the owners and tenants of improved, mixed arable and livestock enterprises should have listened more closely to Caird who had urged them to farm high to capitalize on the greatly increased consumption of butter and meat in the manufacturing districts or, in the case of the large clayland estates in Suffolk, to shift the bias *back* to milk and meat and *away* from wheat![13]

Farming was clearly at a crossroads but, with wheat at 53 shillings a quarter, both landlords and farmers remained fixated on King Corn and on improving wheat yields on the back of expensive farm improvements. Landlords such as John Tollemache and the Earl of Stradbroke, therefore, looked to encourage their tenants to improve the fertility of the soil on the Helmingham Hall and Henham Hall estates by providing them with improved field drainage, better cattle sheds and feeding yards, and new farmhouses. In this sense, the prime exemplars of high farming were the large landowners with sufficient amounts of capital to afford the sometimes lavish expenditure on their estates this type of farming required.[14] Nonetheless, whilst ever-increasing sums of money were invested by landlords in their estates between 1850 and 1875, prompted by the thought of higher rents based on the upward surge in the aggregate price index of agricultural products after 1853, the underlying assumption (already evident in the earlier 'arabilization' of the heavy clays in the 1820s and 1830s) that greater efficiency could counterbalance a lower price per quarter for wheat was never subjected to any empirical test.

Despite this glaring omission, in the 1850s and 1860s, on the Oakley Park estate, Sir Edward Kerrison purchased drainage pipes at his own expense, and then sold them to his tenants as cheaply as possible at about 10 shillings to 15 shillings per thousand. The Crowfield and Baylham estates were similarly improved by the Trustees of the late Sir W. F. F. Middleton at a cost of £1,500 in 1875. Williamson and Wade-Martins also suggest that tile drainage on large clayland estates increased in popularity in the 1850s and 1860s, as landlords took on more fixed capital expenditure, buoyed by rising rents and the increasing investment of working capital by the tenantry. In addition, whilst the intensification of livestock husbandry through the use of artificial feedstuffs and improved field drainage on heavier land was one of the basic tenets of the drive to boost arable output, it was the landlord who frequently provided the better, more suitable buildings also needed to achieve this. In Suffolk, completing the transition from dairying to arable farming on heavier land in the 1820s and 1830s was accomplished with little thought to the arrangement of new buildings among older barns. Between 1850 and 1880, therefore, improvements to farm buildings often consisted of integrating new buildings with older established buildings to create a more ordered arrangement calculated to improve the production of manure, a point recognized by John Tollemache who argued that better cattle sheds and feeding yards were 'essential to the improved modes of agriculture'.[15] Indeed, how could tenants be expected to farm high if they lacked the feeding yards required to do so?

Working from this principle, Lord Tollemache initiated a successful building programme on the Helmingham estate by offering to provide the materials required if the tenant agreed to pay for the labour. Under this arrangement, a considerable number of new farm buildings were erected on the Helmingham estate throughout the mid-nineteenth century. As an additional inducement, Lord Tollemache also offered to repay a proportion of the labour bill in compensation to any tenants who decided to leave their farms within four years of erecting new farm buildings. Significantly, the absence of the Tollemache family from Helmingham in the 1850s did not prevent the estate being the first in the Woodland High Suffolk region on which farm yards were replanned and improved under a system of tenant-right. The improvements underwritten by Lord Tollemache were also aimed at putting right years of neglect that had accumulated during the lifetime of his aunt, Lady Louisa Tollemache, who only spent enough to keep her farms in tenantable repair. As the *Report of the Select Committee of the House of Lords on the Improvement of Land* (1873) notes, farm improvement also included clearing any arrears in maintenance that might have been allowed to build up. But, while a question mark looms over the whole business of high farming, did landlords at least recoup some of their outlay, given that their improvements raised the capital value of their farms and the rent payable upon them? As Robert Rodwell wrote to Sir Thomas Gage in 1863, regarding a farm on the Hengrave estate, the buildings, 'being excellent, added considerably to its value'. In Caird's opinion, any increase in rent represented no more than a 'fair interest' for the capital expended by the landlord on improvements.[16]

As on the Helmingham Hall estate, a backlog of repairs from the agriculturally depressed 1820s and 1830s meant that not all Sir Thomas' farms were so well appointed. On one, the house and farm buildings required a considerable outlay in repairs and alterations. A report compiled by William Biddell on another farm on the estate described the premises as being 'in so bad a state that it is inadvisable to repair them . . . but consider how much more it might be worth if the premises were good'. This expenditure would have been in addition to the money already laid out by Sir Thomas in 1855 to complete 'the cattle shed so as to range with the present new buildings' on a neighbouring farm and the improvements made to the arable land on another of his farms.[17] Sir Thomas' overall investment in the Hengrave estate during the 1850s and 1860s was 40 shillings or £2 an acre. The Earl of Stradbroke and Sir Shafto Adair spent around half this amount or 20 shillings an acre per annum on improving their estates in the 1850s and 1860s. Meanwhile, Sir George Broke Middleton and the Marquess of Bristol were improving their farms through the erection of bullock and cowsheds with yards, piggeries and barns. But did all this building activity represent a historically high level of investment?[18]

B. A. Holderness suggests that the peak of investment by landlords in their estates actually occurred between 1770 and 1830 rather than between 1820 and 1880, when landlords like the third Duke of Grafton and the Earl of Albemarle were enclosing and fertilizing their fields with marl against a backdrop of almost continuous warfare and the consequent rocketing price of wheat. There is, of course, no denying that landlords in Suffolk spent a considerable amount of money on improvements during the late eighteenth century. The remaining open-fields and wastes of the Brecklands were enclosed by hedges during this period by 49 Parliamentary awards encompassing an area of over 100,000 acres. The majority of these awards were made during the height of the Napoleonic War, between 1800 and 1815, when the improvement of even marginal land was at a premium. These awards were pushed through Parliament by landlords eager to enclose their farms and dispense with older and less efficient open-field farming systems: namely, the infield-outfield-breck system, with its reliance on foldcourses and the winter shackage of sheep between Michaelmas (29th September) and the Feast of the Annunciation (25th March). By enclosing their farms and subsequently improving the soil by adding clay or marl, landlords were able to introduce the more productive Norfolk system of husbandry (livestock with arable), traditionally associated with the estates of north-west Norfolk.

On the Euston estate, the open-fields which, up to 1786, had been farmed under a three-course or shift system of husbandry and the sheep-walks in the parishes of Euston, Pakenham, Bardwell and Sapiston were all enclosed by the third Duke of Grafton to form a rectilinear landscape of arable fields bordered by whitethorn hedges. These fields were then heavily marled. On the neighbouring Elveden estate, the Earl of Albemarle is known to have applied at least 70 cubic yards of marl to the acre and thereby 'throw them . . . into a regular course of crops and gain immensely by the improvement'.[19] Nonetheless, whilst the suggestion that landlords invested more money in their estates before about 1837 may indeed be accurate, it remains that, after Victoria ascended the throne, landlords still 'retained much of the initiative and bore much of the costs . . . particularly on run-down estates'.[20] Moreover, the millions available to landlords from the British government in the form of farm improvement loans must also be factored into the equation.

After 1846, the Government, in partial compensation for the loss of protection, granted life tenants the right to borrow both public and private money to pay for agricultural improvements, the loan being repayable through a rent charge placed on the lands so improved. Under the Public Money Draining Acts of 1846 and 1850, the Treasury made four million pounds available at 3.5 per cent interest repayable over 22 years to landowners wishing to improve field drainage on their estates. After 1849, life tenants could also borrow money for drainage improvements from private investors under the Private Money Draining Act, these loans being repayable over 22 years at 4.5 per cent. The Private Money Draining Act was subsequently repealed in 1864 and replaced by the Improvement of Land Act, which expanded the range of improvements for which private funds could be borrowed and extended the period of repayment to 25 years. A total of five Lands Improvement Companies were established between 1847 and 1860. These Companies were backed by the insurance industry and were empowered to lend money to landowners for both drainage and improvements to farm buildings, redeemable through a rent charge amortizing both the principal and the interest.

It appears however, that by 1876 only a very limited number of landowners in Suffolk had borrowed to pay for their drainage schemes. This was because the more traditional system of bush drainage was still considered by many farmers to be more than sufficient to do the job, especially when we consider Glyde's 1856 estimate that wheat yields had risen from 24 to 32 bushels an acre between 1770 and 1850 on the Suffolk clays as a result of this style of drainage. Moreover, where tile drains were being laid, during the 1850s and 1860s, this was usually as part of a drainage scheme undertaken by the tenant under the terms of an allowance, granted by their landlord, for the unexhausted value of their improvement. Mr R. B. Harvey, land agent and tenant of the Flixton estate, stated that such allowances had been part of the agreements between landlord and tenants on the estate since 1840. [21]

On the other hand, the Marquess of Bristol did borrow £2,400 from the General Land Drainage and Improvement Company in 1875 to pay for improvements to farm buildings on the Ickworth estate, the principal and interest to be repaid by means of an annual rent charge to be paid over 31 years. Lord Waveney, having inherited the Flixton Hall estate from his father in 1869, also borrowed £5,500 from the Lands Improvement Company in 1874 to improve the quality of the farm buildings on his estate. This followed a valuer's report which pointed out that, over the whole estate, with a very few exceptions, many of the farm buildings were now in need of repair. The report also highlighted the lack of good feeding yards and sheds on the estate. But in what was in effect a Victorian rural building boom, many contractors were quick to take advantage by overcharging. In 1873, Thomas Cadge presented the Marquess of Bristol with an estimate for £1,500 to build a new farmhouse at Chevington. This was considered to be excessive by the surveyor, R. Phipson, who believed Cadge was clearly looking to make 'a very exorbitant profit'. The final bill was £2,100, a figure which Phipson believed arose from the fact that 'Minton tile hearths and many other luxuries not known generally in farmhouses seem to have been indulged in – at whose order I don't know'.[22]

Overall, by 1878, landowners in England and Wales had borrowed millions of pounds to pay for drainage improvements, new farm buildings and cottages. What, then, was the return on all this investment? Well, between 1852 and 1882, rents rose by around 25 per cent in Suffolk. Indicative of this trend was the 'very considerable advance made in the rentals'[23] by the Earl of Ashburnham on the Barking Hall estate near Needham Market in 1872. Viewed from this angle the improvements made to farm buildings and drainage by landlords in Suffolk were successful in that they enabled tenants to increase the productivity and thus the profitability of their farms, enabling them to pay higher rents following the upward revaluation of their farms. When measured against the capital actually expended by landlords however, on building farmhouses, feeding yards and bullock and cowsheds and yards, barns, cottages and on improving drainage, the return was in fact quite low.

The usual return on drainage improvements was only about 3 per cent on an outlay of £5 an acre. By contrast, acts of enclosure had yielded a return of 15 to 20 per cent on a similar outlay, making it one of the best investments of its day. The returns on improvements to farm buildings and feeding yards were equally derisory and were well below the dividends yielded by railway stocks or, for that matter, by mortgages. The decision by the Duke of Northumberland to spend half a million pounds on improving his estates in the north of England provides a perfect illustration of this point. These improvements produced a return of 2.5 per cent, which was considerably less than the return of nearly 4 per cent which the Duke received on a £5,470 mortgage charged to the Flixton Hall estate. In purely commercial terms, the decision of landlords to invest in improvements simply did not pay.[24]

Despite this, during the 1850s and 1860s, the momentum built up behind agricultural improvement was such that it became fashionable for landowners to indulge in 'conspicuous investment'.[25] Sir Edward Kerrison spent over £120,000, or nearly £12 an acre, between 1853 and 1882 on improvements to his Oakley Park and Brome Hall estates. This huge sum was expended entirely out of his income, Sir Edward having proudly boasted he had borrowed nothing. What makes this level of expenditure all the more remarkable is the fact that Sir Edward did not seek to revalue his estates accordingly, stating 'my property has never been revalued in sixty years: consequently, there has been no rise in rents except in cases of fresh tenancies';[26] Sir Edward was, therefore, the quintessential improving landlord in mid-Victorian Suffolk.

Of course, the success of high farming, upon which these hugely expensive investments depended, was in turn reliant upon the relatively stable price of wheat in the two decades after 1853 and this rested on the, crucially, unrecognized impediments that war had thrown up to delay the fertile interiors of Imperial Russia and the United States coming under the plough. The Crimean War and the American Civil War had effectively given English farmers a twenty-year remittance. Now, with their conclusion, the fertile plains of the Mid-West came under the plough, increasing the total acreage of farmland under wheat in the United States from approximately 15 million acres in the mid-1860s to almost 45 million acres by 1898. Alongside this expansion of the total wheat acreage in the United States, the freighting costs of carrying a quarter of wheat from Chicago to Liverpool fell from an average of 11 shillings between 1868 and 1879, to a mere 4 shillings a quarter by 1892, thanks to the construction of more and more railways and bigger and faster steamships. As a result, the volume of wheat imported into Britain from America rose sharply during the late nineteenth century from around 40 million hundredweight in the 1870s to around 70 million by the 1890s.[27] Would the Cairdian system employed on the great estates, of large outlays of cash by tenant-farmers on feed and fertilizers and landlords on farm buildings and drainage, be able to cope as the price of wheat began to tumble? Or would landlords, when push really came to shove, discover, to their cost, that they had harnessed their estates to a system that was economically unviable?

Looking back over the period, Lord Ernle was to observe that 'since 1862 the tide of agricultural prosperity had ceased to flow; after 1874 it turned, and rapidly ebbed. A period of depression then began which, with some fluctuations in severity, continued throughout the rest of the reign of Queen Victoria, and beyond'.[28] During the late 1870s, however, having experienced nearly twenty years of prosperity based on the intensification of mixed arable and livestock husbandry, both landlords and farmers attributed the depreciation in the price of wheat after 1874 to the succession of inclement seasons which characterized the latter half of the decade. As a consequence it was assumed that given time and the reappearance of fine seasons, things would eventually put themselves right. Neither the landlord nor the tenant thought at the outset that the fall in prices would last, although it is perhaps putting the bar a bit high to expect that their assumptions would adjust overnight after decades of relative price buoyancy.[29] It was also believed that the price of wheat was being artificially depressed by the appreciation of gold relative to silver following the abandonment of the bimetallic system in 1873–4.

Of course in reality, lower prices were caused by neither the currency nor the weather but by the growing glut of American, Russian, Canadian and Argentinian wheat now coming to market. In these circumstances, there was no straightforward means of circumventing low prices through high levels of investment designed to raise productivity, but this fundamental truth was ignored in the late 1870s as attention focused on the 'bad seasons' referred to by Sir Edward Kerrison in 1882, in evidence to the Royal Commission on the Depressed State of the Landed Interest.[30] A letter from James Beaumont to Captain Cartwright, agent to the Flixton Hall estate in 1879, illustrates the difficulties faced by tenants, particularly on the heavy clays, during these wet cold years:

> I beg to acknowledge receipt of your note this morning and to express my thanks for the reduction Lord Waveney has made in my rent . . . [as] my loss this year will be a very heavy one the prospect was bad enough when I wrote to you on the matter but it has turned out worse than I could have expected in consequence of the excessive floods, which have in addition to the injury to the corn made my low pasture land of scarcely any value at all this year, [as] I have not been able to get the hay off them yet. I fear the prospect for roots is a very bad one,

which makes the thing look very gloomy . . . [But] our landlord
meeting us in the difficulty will be our incentive to use our best
endeavours to keep our farms in a good state of cultivation.[31]

Writing to his son, Frederick Barne also complained of the fact that:

We now have a Spring till June, and Summer not till towards August.
We have eternal rain, the whole county will [soon] be flooded. . .what
the heavy lands now want is drought.[32]

When faced with such an unparalleled deterioration in the weather, it is
perhaps unsurprising that both landlords and tenants in the county
confidently assumed that the reappearance of fine seasons would produce a
modest recovery. Landlords therefore adopted a policy of wait and see,
preferring to make phased rather than wholesale reductions in rent.

While spending the summer in Southampton, the Marquess of Bristol
was somewhat surprised to receive a letter from his agent suggesting that he
offer one of his tenants an abatement of rent given that 'the weather is now
finer . . . I think it may be the same at Ickworth', in fact, 'the crops do not
look badly about here – though late'. The final decision was referred back to
the agent 'if you think [it is] necessary you can offer . . . an abatement of rent
for two years of £30'.[33] The Marquess of Bristol was not alone in being
sceptical of the need for wholesale reductions in rent. Sir Edward Kerrison
was equally cautious and did not think it 'right to reduce upon the whole in
the first instance', preferring instead to take 'special cases: and all those cases
where either fresh property had been brought in or a fresh tenancy had been
created', reducing 'each of those as I saw fit'.[34] Of the 58 tenants on the
neighbouring Flixton Hall estate, (recorded in the mortgage held by the
Hand in Hand Insurance Society), 41 were still paying the same rents in
1885 as they had paid in 1882. Of the remaining 17, six were paying
between 10 and 20 per cent less in 1885 than in 1883, whilst only 11 were
granted reductions in excess of 25 per cent. As a result, Lord Waveney's
overall rental income in the years preceding 1885 fell by around 9 per cent.
Similarly, by the early 1880s, out of 47 farms on the neighbouring Henham
Hall estate, rents had been reduced on only 30. Of these, the Earl of
Stradbroke granted reductions in excess of 30 per cent to only four tenants.
Seven received reductions of between 20 and 30 per cent, 12 of between 10
and 20 per cent, whilst seven more had had their rents reduced by 10 per
cent or under. These adjustments meant that, by 1882, the Earl's overall
rental income had also only fallen by around 10 per cent.[35]

The selectivity with which rents were reduced during the first decade of the depression was ameliorated by the liberal attitude of landlords when it came to the question of arrears. Generally speaking, landlords erred towards leniency when dealing with tenants who fell behind in their rent as it would have been deeply unpopular in the current economic conditions to initiate proceedings for the non-payment of rent. Besides, it was assumed that any arrears would be quickly recovered once prices began to pick up although, by the early 1880s, these arrears were beginning to mount up alarmingly. When Sir Edward Kerrison was called to give evidence before the Commissioners appointed to inquire into the Depressed State of the Agricultural Interest in 1882, he informed the committee that his rents were in arrears by around £10,000, stating 'of course one had a few arrears before the depression, but £9,000 out of the £10,000 have been accumulating since the depression began in 1875'.[36] In addition, by 1883, the combined arrears of 33 of the 58 tenants referred to above on the Flixton Hall estate totalled over £2,800.[37]

Regardless of these figures, the general mood among landowners into the early 1880s continued to remain one of quiet optimism. Recovery, it was felt, was just around the corner; how could it be otherwise given that the heavy investment made during the 1850s and 1860s, coupled with the scientific application of the principles of good husbandry, had apparently given their tenants a more than sufficient 'cushion' against foreign competition for the previous twenty years? Subsequently, a more pessimistic mood began to take hold due to the failure of prices to pick up once the seasons began to improve after 1882. In fact, contrary to expectations, prices continued to fall. As the depression deepened, Lord Waveney borrowed an additional £18,500 in 1885 from the Lands Improvement Company to cover the cost of additional farm buildings. The Marquess of Bristol, meanwhile, spent nearly £12,000 on new farm buildings and cottages between 1882 and 1892, having borrowed a further £350 from the General Land Drainage and Improvement Company in 1892 to improve the drainage on three more of his farms. When set against a backdrop of falling rentals, these loans cannot be seen as anything more than a desperate attempt by these landlords to keep their farms let. As the schedule detailing the improvements made to Westley Hall farm in 1882 reveals:

> the farmhouse and outbuildings . . . were in a dilapidated condition and past repair. They were therefore pulled down and entirely rebuilt at a total cost to the Tenant for Life of £1,800 . . . if the rebuildings had not been carried out there would have been an annual loss to the

Estate [as] . . . the land would have been thrown on the hands of the Tenant for Life.[38]

In other words, by the mid-1880s, landlords had realized that agricultural improvement was an increasingly ineffectual substitute for protection but they still needed to keep their farms tenanted by continuing to improve them and keep them in good repair even though, in the present conditions, continuing to farm high would have been considered foolhardy. According to figures provided by Henry Rew, heavy inputs of manure put the cost of growing an acre of wheat at between £5 and £6 an acre. When prices were high, as in the 1860s when the return on wheat grown on heavy land was around £10 an acre, profits were between £4 and £5 per acre. As the price of wheat began to fall, profit margins fell accordingly. By the mid-1880s, the return on an acre of wheat had fallen to around £7 and reduced the margin of profit to just over £1 per acre. In these circumstances, foolish, stubborn and indebted farmers quit their farms in ever-increasing numbers. It is worth remembering, however, that new tenants were still forthcoming, being attracted by the opportunity to get good farms at knock down prices as a result of the continued improvements shouldered by their landlords. Such was the growing concern felt by landlords caught between the rock of lower rents and the hard place of making repairs and improvements to avoid taking farms in-hand, that 31 landowners in Suffolk joined with the by now deeply troubled Marquess of Bristol, in 1886, to petition the Prime Minister, the Marquess of Salisbury, for assistance (see Table 1) on the grounds that:

> for the last seven years, since the disastrous harvest of 1879, very great distress has prevailed in Agriculture in many Counties in the United Kingdom; and that although a Royal Commission was appointed to inquire into the depression, which suggested measures of relief, yet the general condition of all classes connected with the land has not improved. The low range of prices of corn for the last three years has greatly reduced the margin of profit, where existent at all, and nothing but the fact of favourable seasons [after 1882], coupled with the timely forbearance of landlords, has enabled the cultivators of the soil to remain on their holdings. The condition of many of them has now become serious in the extreme, and unless some immediate relief is afforded, many farmers will be ruined, more labourers thrown out of employment, and the poorer soils cease to be cultivated. The attention of Her Majesty's Government is earnestly invited to these

facts, in the confident hope that steps will at once be taken by them to introduce into Parliament measures of necessary relief.[39]

If proof were needed of the declining political influence of the Landed Interest over the Conservative party we need look no further than the Government's response to the petition – they ignored it. No direct assistance was forthcoming; indeed, the slight recovery during the years 1890–91 led the Liberal Prime Minister, William Gladstone, to conclude that it was 'wholly out of the question to suppose that British agriculture would not always continue to be the great pursuit it had always been in former times'.[40] In the event, the first half of the 1890s was characterized by an unprecedented slump in the price of wheat, leading many landlords to the conclusion that the ruin of her farmers was the price Britain was prepared to pay for the benefits her industry obtained as the great free trading nation of the world.[41]

By the early 1890s, the return on an acre of wheat grown on the Euston estate on the light Breckland soils, or on the Rendlesham Hall estate on Suffolk's sandy coastal strip, or on the large clayland estates, had fallen to between £3 and £4 an acre – the era of high farming was over. A slump in profits of these proportions would have produced significant out-of-pocket losses under a system of high farming. Fortunately, the more pragmatic farmers had by now, reluctantly, abandoned farming high and had, with the consent of their landlords, reduced their costs by laying-off labourers, cutting back on weeding, hoeing, hedging and all but the most pressing repairs. As a result of this reversion to 'low' farming, arable land in Suffolk was said by Mr B. Cooper, formerly agent to the Duke of Grafton, to have fallen back '50 per cent in condition since the depression began'.[42]

On the lighter soils of Breckland and the Suffolk coast, where a four-course rotation of roots, barley, seeds and wheat had been common, farmers responded to the lower prices of the 1880s and 1890s by reverting to older rotations, lengthening the seed break and reducing input levels: a return to low farming. Fields which once grew good crops of wheat and barley were put down to rye-grass worth 1 shilling or 2 shillings and devoted to the rearing of game because 'when prices of corn were high and labour cheap it paid to fertilize these [light] lands with clay . . . spreading 100 loads to the acre. At present [prices] this is . . . out of the question'.[43] Evidence of the move toward farming low on the lighter lands also comes from conversations between Rider Haggard and the Rev John Holden, who owned and farmed 2,000 acres in the parish of Lackford. Haggard records that 'in speaking of his system of farming . . . [Holden] told me that this light land was not

Table 1. Signatories to the Petition of 1886 sent to the Marquess of Salisbury

Bristol	Ickworth	Owner
Henniker	Thornham Hall	Owner
Rendlesham	Rendlesham Hall	Owner
Hamilton	Easton Park	Owner
Huntingfield	Heveningham Hall	Owner
Tollemache	Helmingham Hall	Owner
Agnes Bateman	Brome Hall	Owner
Rutland	Newmarket	Owner
Robert Affleck	Dalham Hall	Owner
G.N. Broke Middleton	Shrubland Park	Owner
Alfred Sherlock Gooch	Benacre Hall	Owner
William Parker	Melford Hall	Owner
Thomas Thornhill	Pakenham Lodge	Owner
R H Lloyd-Anstruther	Hintlesham Hall	Owner
St John Barne	Sotterley Park	Owner
Windsor Parker	Clopton Hall	Owner
William Biddell	Lavenham Hall	Owner and Occupier
W.R. Bevan	Plumpton House	Owner
E.R. Starkie Bence	Kentwell Hall	Owner
Wm. N. King	Great Barton	Owner and Occupier
Herbert Praed	Ousden Hall	Owner
N. Barnardiston	The Ryes, Sudbury	Owner
Arthur M. Wilson	Stowlangtoft Hall	Owner
H.S. Waddington	Cavenham Hall	Owner
John S. Holden	Lackford Rectory	Owner
Arthur Heywood	Sudbourne Hall	Owner
Wm. Lowther, MP	Campsea Ashe	Owner
Hugh Adair	Flixton Hall	Owner
Hugh Berners	Woolverstone Hall	Owner
J. R. Blois	Cockfield Hall	Owner
J. Hayward	Stowmarket	Owner

(Source: SRO [Bury] HA 507/6/20)

cropped on a four-course shift but was worked as cheaply as possible, the common plan being to lay down a field for three years or so, then break it up and take a root crop'.[44]

For their part, landlords assisted the farmer in these adjustments by relaxing the covenants governing the cultivation of their farms. This relaxation of the rules of farming, allied to the continued willingness of landlords to keep their farms in good repair, all stemmed from the need to keep farms let. If the farm fell in-hand, the landlord would then have to find the working capital needed to run the holding whilst a new tenant was found. Sir Hugh Adair, who inherited the Flixton Hall estate from his brother in 1886, had to find £18,000 to cover the running costs and the losses generated by the farms taken in-hand on the estate between 1893 and 1898. Far more seriously, between 1884 and 1892, the Marquess of Bristol had fifteen farms in-hand. On average, he was farming 4,500 acres (rising at one time to 6,000 acres). Overall, the loss entailed in farming this land amounted to £50,000. Having farms fall into hand was therefore best avoided.[45]

In recognition of this fact and of the collapse of high farming, landlords were also forced to abandon their former policy of making selective and often quite limited reductions in rent in preference for wholesale and often quite drastic reductions. By 1895, the Marquess of Bristol's rents from the Ickworth estate had fallen by 54 per cent. Whilst this inevitably placed the Marquess's finances under considerable strain, he was at least able to stem his losses by attracting new tenants to the estate through the offer of very low rents; in 1895, Fox reported that the Marquess had no land in-hand. Across Suffolk, landlords had, by the mid-1890s, been forced to make similar reductions. The estates of Lords de Saumarez and Henniker, the Hon William Lowther, Colonel Barnardiston, Hugh Berners, Colonel Pretyman and W. H. Smith, were all bringing in half the rent money they had yielded in the 1870s. By the early 1900s, Colonel Barnardiston calculated that the loss upon his rentals since the 'good times' amounted to nearly 70 per cent and that around 60 per cent was the general figure. Rent reductions of this magnitude were way above the national average. According to R. J. Thompson, the average rent of agricultural land in England and Wales in 1900 was 30 per cent below the figure for 1872. That, on average, rents in Suffolk were between 50 and 60 per cent lower reflects the severity of the agricultural depression in Suffolk. The rent received by the third Earl of Stradbroke (succeeded 1886) from the Henham Hall estate in the early 1890s, for example, was 64 per cent lower than that received by his father in the mid-1870s. Given the scale of this reduction, it is somewhat surprising to find that rents on the neighbouring Helmingham Hall estate only fell by 40 per cent. Why did the deflationary pressures of the 1890s fail to push down rents on the Helmingham estate to the same extent as at Henham? The answer would appear to lie in what is known as the 'Fletcher Effect'. [46]

In the 1960s, T. W. Fletcher questioned the view that agriculture in the 1890s was universally depressed across the country. His research revealed that meat, milk and dairy products retained their competitive edge throughout the latter half of the nineteenth century. Milk, being perishable, could not be imported, whilst the demand for top quality British beef held up remarkably well in the face of burgeoning competition from refrigerated beef from the United States and Argentina. The owners of estates in the pastoral districts of the north and west of England were particularly fortunate as every fall in the price of cereals, so damaging to corn growers in the south and east, was to them clear gain because it meant a reduction in the price of their most important input – feed.[47] In relative terms, livestock husbandry had in fact been more profitable than the cultivation of cereals since at least the 1850s, a fact noticed in 1868 by Caird who wrote 'since 1850 the price of bread on the average has remained the same' while by contrast meat, dairy produce and wool 'has risen 50 per cent'.[48]

The growth of demand for meat and dairy products provided an invaluable boost to the overall success of high farming. As a consequence, the mixed agriculture of the early 1870s was quite different in character from that of thirty or forty years earlier:

> Then the livestock side had been considered supportive of the arable enterprises – that is, the fatstock had been overwintered not for their direct returns but for the dung which they supplied to the crop land. Now, despite an incomplete acceptance of the turn-about [in prices] which was to prove disastrous in the 'Great Depression' receipts from . . . stock were . . . much valued.[49]

In recognition of this trend, in 1873, H. W. Keary had urged Lord Waveney to erect new cattle sheds and feeding yards for 'without stock in these days no farmer can pay his rent'.[50] Unfortunately, whilst receipts from stock were now more valued, the fact remains that the livestock side of mixed arable and livestock husbandry was still considered supportive of the arable. A 50 per cent rise in meat prices was still considered a boost to farming high but this was a system of farming where the emphasis remained on growing wheat. For example, when H. W. Keary presented his *Report and Valuation of the*

Flixton Hall Estate to Lord Waveney in 1873, he made no reference to the measures undertaken, since the 1860s, by landlords in other heavy land districts across the country, or the encouragement given to tenants to expand their livestock enterprises by laying arable land down to pasture, leaving only enough in tillage to provide the necessary straw and fodder. Rather, it was suggested that Lord Waveney ought to 'inaugurate a better system of drainage, whereby the land might be permanently improved and the foundation laid for a *higher* system of farming than at presently prevails'.[51] The fact that grass would pay, and pay much better for all the manure applied than corn, went unrecognized. Throughout the 1870s, therefore, both landlords and tenants continued to view the business of fattening livestock over the winter in terms of its contribution to the overall success of high farming, rather than as a successful business in itself. This point is underlined by H. W. Keary, who argued tenants on the Flixton estate needed new buildings in order to 'keep more stock and . . . farm *more highly*'.[52]

The transition to a predominantly livestock based system of husbandry was further delayed by the disastrous epidemics that afflicted both cattle and sheep during the early years of the depression. These acted as major disincentives to anyone thinking of investing in the heavier stocking of land. According to Sir Edward Kerrison, the outbreaks of foot and mouth disease in the early 1880s left tenants on the Oakley Park and Brome Hall estates badly bruised, having 'bought stock dear' the previous December only to find that by the spring, their stock had fallen in value by around 2 shillings per stone 'so that in fact they hardly recouped themselves for the fattening process'.[53] A similar pattern emerges on the neighbouring Flixton Hall estate. In 1878, James Block, of Heath Farm Flixton, wrote to the agent, 'I shall be obliged to give up my farm next Michaelmas. I hoped to have pulled through but the adverse seasons of the last four years combined with heavy losses in stock compel me to come to this decision . . . I have lost £1,000 here in the last eight years.'[54]

As the depression deepened, landlords came to recognize that allowing covenants governing ploughing to lapse, and deliberately allowing varying proportions of arable land on their farms to revert to rough grazing land, were about the only things that would make farms with heavier soils pay. In so doing, tenants would be able to derive some benefit from the continuing profitability of beef and mutton whilst also reducing their costs. By cutting the area under roots and leaving some land unploughed and thereby 'summering' more livestock on grass and so feeding fewer in winter, tenants were able to reduce the cost of folding sheep, in temporary enclosures, over the residues of the root crop and hauling roots to cattle yards and hauling farmyard manure back to the fields. Evidence for this change can be found in the *Agricultural Returns*. Interestingly, the *Returns* also show that, whilst between 1880 and 1895 the arable acreage under wheat in Suffolk did indeed fall by 33,000 acres, the total still remained over 100,000 acres by the mid-1890s. The simplest explanation for this is that farmers in Suffolk were a conservative lot and having been brought up to grow wheat they were reluctant to abandon mixed arable and livestock farming, besides they still needed straw for a variety of farmyard tasks. Nonetheless, the acreage 'laid away' as grazing land in Suffolk expanded by 13 per cent over the same period to cover an area of 185,000 acres; as a corollary, the area under root crops contracted by 5 per cent.[55] Converting arable land to permanent pasture, as opposed to simply allowing arable land to revert to rough grazing land, was, however, quite expensive. Rew estimated that to convert an acre of arable land to permanent pasture cost 24 shillings. Unsurprisingly, the tenantry looked to their landlord to provide the money required to convert arable land to permanent pasture. In so doing, landlords were, ironically, often restoring the pastures for which the clayland region of High Suffolk had been rightly famous in the eighteenth century and which had been ploughed up at their great grandfather's instigation during and after the Napoleonic Wars. In addition, the heavier stocking of farms with either bullocks or dairy cows inevitably required from the landowner a certain level of expenditure, both on land *and* on farm buildings:[56] which brings us to Helmingham.

Having spent £8,000 on new farm buildings and repairs during the early 1870s, Lord Tollemache, like Lords Waveney and Bristol, spent heavily on new farm buildings and repairs during the late 1870s and early 1880s. Between 1877 and 1884, Lord Tollemache spent nearly £15,000, double that expended during the dying days of high farming. Of particular significance is the fact that, between 1878 and 1884, a further £3,400 was spent on grass, seeds and other improvements, all of which points towards the laying down of arable land to pasture and increasing the amount of livestock on the estate.[57] Confirmation of this comes from the *Royal Commission Inquiring into the Housing of the Working Classes*, in which the Helmingham estate was described in 1884–5 as being 'almost entirely a dairying estate'.[58] By shifting the emphasis on his farms over to livestock and dairying during the early 1880s, Lord Tollemache enabled his tenants to offset their declining wheat revenue through a greater emphasis on meat, milk and dairy products. Of equal importance, by reducing his rents by nearly 37 per cent during the early 1880s, rather than the 9–10 per cent reduction made by his neighbours, Lord Tollemache reduced the pressure on his tenants to draw on their capital reserves and thereby lessened the need to make further rent reductions as the depression deepened. This meant that, between 1885 and 1892, the rent received by Lord Tollemache from the Helmingham estate fell by only a further 3 per cent. The contrasting fortunes of landlords such as the Earl of Stradbroke were summed up by one Suffolk landowner in his evidence to Fox:

> My tenants all round are throwing up their farms. I have done all in my power to let my land, advertising it all over the county, but no one will have anything to do with clay land at any price, no matter how much other land of superior quality may be included. A tenant on 300 acres will give up his farm at Michaelmas unless he can get 3 shillings to 4 shillings an acre reduction. Another tenant, an auctioneer on a farm of the same size, will give up two years hence, and will refuse to take it at any price. He has, I believe, never made a penny profit out of the farm. At my next audit in January 1893, one of my oldest tenants who only a year ago rehired his farm on practically his own terms, informed us that he would carry it on no longer. This is no case of rent. If he had the farm free at present [wheat] prices he could not make it pay.[59]

For landlords unable to afford the cost of laying arable land down to pasture, salvation of a sort was at hand, with the arrival of Scottish and West Country dairy and stockmen lured to Suffolk by the absurdly low rents now on offer in the county. Moreover, Scottish farmers circumvented Rider Haggard's observation that pasture, paid for by the landlord, 'required as good treatment as arable', by simply letting arable land revert to rough grazing land for two or three years at a time, much to the disgust of their more conservative contemporaries who believed that such practices amounted to the ruination of good arable farming: a somewhat ironic criticism given the current state of arable husbandry on the heavier clays. As Mr Trotter, agent to the third Earl of Stradbroke commented, the Scotchmen recently arrived on the estate 'don't understand the management of heavy land. They leave it worse than when they take it, but they save themselves with cows. They are thoroughly up on dairying'.[60] Their overheads were also lower as they employed their families rather than labourers and preferred to keep their dairy cows under cover in sheds rather than in yards, feeding them on spent grains purchased from local breweries and beans, linseed and roots grown on the land which they had left in tillage. Keeping dairy cows under cover, however, required more shed accommodation than was generally available on most farms in Suffolk at the time. The landlord had to rectify this situation in the context of the 1890s, and thus, these sheds were more likely to have been cheap corrugated iron structures rather than brick. What, then, was the level of fixed capital investment on estates in Suffolk during the 1890s?

On the Orwell Park estate, the 1890s saw a significant increase in the level of fixed capital expenditure. This sudden rise in activity is attributable to the arrival of Colonel George Pretyman, who inherited the estate from his uncle George Tomline in 1889. Under Pretyman's direction, there was a sharp increase in the amount of money expended out of estate revenue on repairs between 1891 and 1893. Unsurprisingly, this had a knock-on effect on the overall level of revenue he received from the estate, which in 1893 was a mere £1,400. This expenditure was accompanied by a further outlay of around £9,200 on new farm buildings, the bulk of which, some £6,000, was laid out in 1892. As all this money came out of agricultural revenue, Pretyman's net income from the 15,400 acre Orwell Park estate in 1892 was only £1,200, whilst the accounts for 1893 actually posted a net loss of £80. W. H. Smith, having spent nearly £22,000 on new buildings, close to £4,000 on 'seeds' and nearly £7,000 on repairs between 1878 and 1884, also made no effort to curtail his expenditure. Moreover, despite his rental income being halved, a further £4,000 was spent on new buildings between 1885 and 1893, nearly £3,000 on 'seeds' and £10,000 on repairs. In 1892, his balance after expenditure was only £900. But Smith was fortunate to have an alternative revenue stream from of his book retailing empire. Similarly, the fortunes of the Pretyman and Tollemache families were linked, respectively, to the port of Felixstowe and to brewing, not to farming. Not all families were so well-placed to weather the storm. As Thompson states, after 1879, 'the economic distinction was certainly becoming more marked year by year between landowners who were purely agricultural and landowners who were guaranteed a share in the wealth generated by industry and commerce.'[61]

There is, of course, no denying the fact that many owners of large agricultural estates in the county found themselves in a sticky situation by the time of Queen Victoria's Golden Jubilee in 1887, as evidenced by the petition of the previous year, and a parlous one by the time of her Diamond Jubilee in 1897. Indeed, by now, to use H. L. Beales' well-worn quote, 'people thought they were depressed whether in fact they were or not!' There is no denying that many landowners in Suffolk sold up once the price of agricultural land recovered slightly after 1901 – but they were able to do so because of the successful adaptation of farmers to the changed times, who were now farming as low as possible, fattening livestock or, when they could afford to do so, shifting back to the dairy farming abandoned in the early nineteenth century.[62]

An analysis of the accounts of a Suffolk farm undertaken by S. H. Carson reveals what may well have been a typical experience on better-managed farms in the old arable districts, namely a recovery beginning in 1897–8 with more rapid acceleration from 1907–8 onwards.[63] This, of course, raises a question: was this re-adjustment delayed because of lower levels of investment by landlords? This issue formed the basis of a very closely argued debate between Perren and Cormac O'Grada in the late 1970s, the former suggesting that, while the relative reluctance of landowners in arable districts to spend money before 1879 on adapting their farms may have been because they thought it unnecessary to do so while cereal prices were being maintained, their failure to do so afterwards may have been because they found the costs of transformation, especially for heavy land, coming with the precipitate fall in rents, too much for them to meet.[64] Corroboration comes from Fox in his 1894 report on Suffolk compiled for the *Royal Commission on Agriculture*, who reported landlords 'without incomes except from land . . . had to considerably curtail [levels of] expenditure on their property'.[65]

Under this model, families without large non-agricultural sources of income had to balance the need to keep their farms in reasonable repair, in order to keep them let, against the cost of trying to maintain and run a country seat, pay for their children's education, meet the payment of mortgage interest and cover the repayment of improvement loans. As Fox again states, 'it is undoubtedly the case that . . . especially on the smaller properties . . . expenditure on buildings has not been maintained [at anywhere near their former levels] . . . this is also true on some of the larger ones, *particularly where the owner's income derived almost entirely from the land*.'[66] Feinstein and Pollard suggest that the sharp fall in rents received combined with a contraction in the proportion of rent devoted to new works and improvements to reduce capital expenditure by about 40 per cent, from its peak in the 1850s and 1860s. Thompson, on the other hand, argues that, 'on most estates, it appears that the *proportion* of gross rents spent on repairs and improvements was only very slightly, if at all, lower in the twenty years before 1914, than it had been in the 1870s.'[67] Given that Thompson's point tallies with the idea that most landlords were determined to keep their farms in reasonable shape in order to keep them let, it would appear that Fox may have been over-egging the pudding a little when he concluded that landowners in Suffolk:

see their incomes steadily diminishing, and they know not one year what their income will be the next, they see their land deteriorating and their buildings falling into disrepair, they are unable to borrow [due to the depreciation in the value of agricultural land] money, and those free to sell can't find a purchaser for agricultural land. And out of this diminished and diminishing income the same family charges and the same interest have to be paid.[68]

Still, the picture is blurred. Holderness concluded that those who surveyed the English landscape after 1900 would have seen that the agriculturalists' duty to manage their environment 'seemed to have fallen into abeyance'; on the other hand, was this deceptive?[69] Collins suggests that agriculturalists were achieving the 'no mean feat' of keeping output at pre-depression levels.[70] Landlords could of course retrench, by letting their homes, letting their shooting, but they also made sure they avoided the onerous costs of taking their farms in-hand by keeping them in repair with loans from one of the lands improvement companies. With regard to the last point, landlords also oversaw the abandonment of the time-honoured assumptions of what constituted best practice namely, bumper harvests and tidy hedgerows, by allowing farmers to farm low, by providing them with greater accommodation for livestock and allowing them to let arable land revert to rough grazing. Writing in the early 1900s, Herman Biddell, one of Suffolk's more renowned farmers, reported:

> The covered yard is steadily gaining ground; but the reduced rents prevent the landlord from spending more money on farm building than is absolutely necessary to secure a suitable tenant. Unfortunately, for the needy owner, as the demand for farms becomes less, the tenant is apt to make his condition of hire include the outlay of monies on the premises.

Of course, this outlay could be ameliorated by the use of cheap alternatives such as corrugated iron, a material:

> far inferior to the best pantiles for cattle sheds, being hot in summer and cold in winter; but the Suffolk farmer has of late years become alive to the value of straw and declines to keep up large quantities of thatched roof.[71]

The adoption of a bastardized version of mixed arable and livestock farming ensured that farmers could at least continue to fatten livestock and continue to keep some arable land in tillage. Of course, the rents farmers could afford to pay their landlords were far less, with inevitable consequences for the landlord who was still expected to do the requisite repairs and the odd improvement to these farms, at a time when the State, despite the lamentations of Fox and later Rider Haggard regarding the collapse of best practice, remained steadfastly uninterested in a return to protectionism. Yet, despite these adjustments, Thomas J. Grierson agent to the Flixton estate 'could see no hope unless Protection was revived'.[72] Whilst this perception was based upon the end of the heady days of high farming and a disparaging attitude toward the real benefits of low farming, this pessimistic outlook was nonetheless the prevailing view of things at the time, even after signs of recovery began to be seen in the late 1890s, which begs the question why buy an estate in Suffolk? Was it just for the sport?

3

THE LANDED INTEREST
&
THE LAND QUESTION

Prior to the 1832 Reform Act, it can be said the Landed Interest, that great collection of Whig and Tory magnates who colonized the House of Commons on behalf of the landed aristocracy sitting in the House of Lords, effectively monopolized both Parliament and the Government. The basis of this monopoly was, of course, the control exerted by the Landed Interest over the rural borough and county constituencies that, before the redistribution of seats to Britain's centres of manufacturing industry, constituted the bulk of the seats in the House of Commons. Among these constituencies, the smaller boroughs were effectively in the gift of a great territorial magnate 'whose right of nomination was no more doubted than his right of presentation to a living'.[1] Consequently, in 1832, of the 658 Members of Parliament sitting in the unreformed House of Commons, 137 were the nominees of 84 landed families who controlled a small borough whilst a further 150 were returned by virtue of the territorial influence exercised by the 70 landed families who held sway over a particular county or district. This was 'real power, of which gilt coaches and Blue Ribbons, outriders and running footmen were only the outward and visible emblems'.[2]

But, as Earl Grey recognized, the Industrial Revolution and the subsequent emergence of industrial middle class property owners in the north of England required some modifications in the pro-aristocratic character of the constitution. Under the Reform Act of 1832 therefore, in addition to a widening of both the borough and county franchises to encompass new middle class voters, parliamentary seats were redistributed to provide the new manufacturing districts with parliamentary representation at the expense of 'rotten' or 'pocket' boroughs in agricultural counties such as

Suffolk. This meant that, in the aftermath of the 1832 Reform Act and further changes in 1844, the number of MPs travelling up to London from seats in Suffolk fell from 16 to 9. This reduction resulted from the abolition of the small, two member parliamentary boroughs of Aldeburgh, Dunwich and Orford. These particular boroughs had previously returned six MPs nominated, respectively, by their patrons the Marquess of Hertford, Lord Huntingfield and the Barne family of Sotterley Hall. In addition, one of the two MPs formerly sitting for the borough of Eye, a seat controlled by the Kerrison family, was abolished. Subsequently, in 1844, the two member borough of Sudbury was also abolished but, as a *quid pro quo* for the loss of so many small borough seats, Earl Grey increased the number of MPs representing the county from two to four; Grey was, after all, reforming Parliament to preserve and to legitimate the continuing influence of the aristocracy.

Given the need to find seats in the House of Commons to accommodate the new middle class industrialist MPs from the north of the kingdom, the 1832 Reform Act was seen by even deeply conservative landowners such as John Tollemache as a 'necessary evil'.[3] On the other hand, once all was said and done, it was pretty obvious that the owners of landed property, as opposed to the owners of cotton mills, iron foundries and engineering work-shops, continued to carry far greater weight in the Palace of Westminster. They would continue to do so up to the Third Reform Act in 1884, due to the proportion of seats that were still situated in the countryside. In the counties, where the vote was still largely held by the tenant farmers, who (prior to the 1872 Secret Ballot Act) voted in the open, it was their landlords who continued to determine who should stand and who should win, as a letter from Sir Charles Bunbury in London to his father back at Barton Hall makes plain. Having heard 'much talk about politics in Suffolk', Sir Charles was concerned that, 'my election for Bury is not so sure as [events] had led me to fancy . . . it would make some difference [if] . . . you were in the country or not'; if, in fact, his father stood for the seat of West Suffolk. Local Whigs were 'very anxious that you should stand again for the Western Division, for . . . there is no other Whig gentleman there who would have a chance'.[4]

Moreover, in the countryside itself, the influence exerted by the great landowners through their property and through their social position remained truly enormous. This was because a large landed estate in excess of 1,000 acres formed a 'functioning centre of political and social influence across the territory which it comprised, often extending into the surround-ing area and sometimes across a whole county . . . in short, over the entire locality and its inhabitants'.[5] For example, Sir Edward Kerrison represented the borough of Eye from 1832 to 1866, but, when his attention shifted to the seat of East Suffolk, his Eye seat was kept warm with his blessing by Viscount Barrington. Unsurprisingly, the character of the House of Commons, and with it the British constitution, continued to be overtly aristocratic as the number of MPs belonging to the aristocracy showed little sign of decline between 1831 and 1865. In mid-Victorian Suffolk:

> the landed [aristocracy and] gentry . . . still held great influence in social and political life. The man on horseback still dominated the countryside and many of the small towns where the new class of society had yet to come into existence and the old society of patronage and deference to the squire and parson still held sway. In spite of the Great Reform Act of 1832 he still dominated Parliament, for the House of Lords remained a powerful body and since a majority of the seats in the Commons still belonged to the counties and the smaller towns landowners [still] formed a majority of the MPs.[6]

A report in the *Suffolk Mercury* of the re-election in 1859 of the Attorney General Sir FitzRoy Kelly, as one of the two Conservative Members of Parliament who sat for East Suffolk, provides ample testimony to the continued prominence of local landed families in party politics in the county. Sir FitzRoy had sat for East Suffolk since 1852. Prior to this, the seat had been represented by Lord Henniker (1832–1846), Lord Rendlesham (1843–1852) and Sir Edward Gooch (1846–1856). With Sir Edward's death, Lord Henniker returned to the Commons in 1856 and stayed there till 1865, alongside Sir FitzRoy who took the berth left vacant by the decease of Lord Rendlesham. The evident dominance of the Conservative party in the East Suffolk constituency was, however, according to the *Suffolk Mercury*, sorely tested by the Liberal party in 1859:

> when Sir FitzRoy Kelly . . . came down for re-election [the Suffolk landowner] . . . Colonel Adair came forth to defeat him, [with] . . . the support – or at least the neutrality – of the late Sir William Middleton Bt, Sir FitzRoy knew whom to go to. In a few hours Sir Edward Kerrison [whose estates were adjacent to those of Lt Colonel Robert Shafto Adair] had repaired the weak places in the Conservative line; he [then] came down to Ipswich . . . and from the platform of the Old Assembly Room – he gave the lie to every rumour of defection. Three weeks later the Attorney General was returned with ease, [but it was]

to [the influence of] Sir Edward . . . that the gallant Colonel owned that defeat.[7]

Such was the aristocracy's continuing influence in the House of Commons that, by 1865, there were 180 baronets or sons of peers sitting in the Chamber. This was only marginally less than the figure of 217 returned in 1832, although this number fails to convey the true extent of the Landed Interest's overwhelming presence. Overall, the House of Commons in 1865 still boasted one Marquess, five Earls, 18 Viscounts, 34 Lords, 72 Baronets, 58 Honourables and around 100 other MPs 'palpably belonging to the historic names of the land'[8] interspersed among both the new Conservative and Liberal Parties that had superseded the old pre-1832 Tory and Whig parties. As a consequence, even the official 'Old Whig' wing of the Liberal party, that had engineered what they considered to be the final settlement of the constitutional question back in 1832, now conceded that further moves toward an even more democratic constitution were necessary given the continuing growth of Britain's new manufacturing towns. Indeed, wherever one went 'whether in town or country . . . no man was satisfied with the present House of Commons'.[9] On the Radical wing of the Liberal party, the MPs John Bright and Richard Cobden predicted the downfall of an aristocracy which failed to concede universal household suffrage by granting the vote to the ordinary ratepayer.

Bright's comments expose the fault line that existed in a Liberal party that comprised on the one hand, aristocratic landowning 'Old Whigs', and, on the other, Radical MPs calling for land reform as a prelude to democratic constitutional reform. Cobden and Bright had already set out their stall as founder members of the Anti-Corn Law League by attacking the Corn Laws as a visible legislative symbol of the predominance of the Landed Interest, arguing their Repeal would 'be welcomed by all who resented the privileges and entrenched influence of the aristocracy in national life'.[10] They now called for the abolition of the legal and customary means through which the aristocracy kept their estates intact: namely, settlements and primogeniture. They also called for the simplification of the endless formalities and intricacies of English land law that hampered the conveyance of land held in freehold. They hoped this 'free trade' in land would lead to the gradual erosion or even break up of the great estates.[11]

Their grand vision was that the great estates would, through the removal of monopolistic practices in the land market, be supplanted by a property owning citizen-democracy. By making land easier to dispose of and easier to buy, land would be transferred from the aristocracy to the agricultural labourer and thus bring about the re-emergence of an English peasantry and yeomanry who would then enjoy the liberty and happiness that Radicals attached to the ownership of landed property. And if landownership meant happiness and liberty then 'the possession of one large estate or . . . three or four such estates by one Duke must produce a less amount of individual enjoyment than the division of his lands among thousands of landowners'. Moreover, 'the abolition of the land monopoly would also strike a crushing blow at the feudal system on which rested the whole fabric of an aristocratic constitution'.[12] Hence, Cobden's rueful comment in 1864: 'If I were five-and-twenty or thirty instead of, unhappily, twice that number of years, I would take Adam Smith in hand . . . and I would have a League for Free Trade in Land, just as we had a League for Free Trade in Corn.'[13]

Unfortunately, Cobden and Bright were unable to make any headway toward the abolition of either primogeniture or entails owing to public opinion being largely indifferent to the issue. If proof were needed, concluded Cobden, 'see how every successful trader buys an estate and tries to perpetuate his name'.[14] Interestingly, for all his antipathy toward Britain's still overtly aristocratic constitution and House of Commons and the land monopoly on which it was predicated, Bright remained a friend of John (later Lord) Tollemache. Despite Tollemache being as conservative as they come, he and Bright were regularly seen walking arm-in-arm in the West End of London. This was because John Tollemache was considered to be one of the best landlords in the country. On his estate at Helmingham labourers could hire three acres of grass land and keep a cow.[15] By contrast, there was an evident divergence of opinion within the Liberal party. On the one hand, there was the Radical vision of a democracy of ordinary landowning Britons, each with a home with an allotment or garden attached. On the other, were the aristocratic Whigs who were prepared to give the vote to the 'respectable', skilled industrial working class in the sprawling artisan suburbs of the great industrial towns, but were not prepared to endorse a Radical land reform programme to extend the ownership of land at the expense of the great estates. William Gladstone regarded it as 'a very high duty to labour for the conservation of estates, and the permanence of the families in possession of them as principal source of our social strength, and as a large part of true conservatism'.[16] This is why, when Hugh Adair (the brother of Lord Waveney) sat as the MP for Ipswich 'at the feet of Lord Palmerston', between 1847 and 1868, the *Suffolk Mercury* reported he was for ever having to try and satisfy the 'somewhat complicated wants of the various sections of the Liberal party in this old borough' namely, the 'extreme Liberals' on one side and the 'Old Whigs' on the other.[17]

Of course, in 1867, Tory grandees had effectively put their party above their order by endorsing the Second Reform Act which so increased the number of voters in borough seats that these constituencies simply became too large for landowners to influence. After 1867, the aristocracy 'had to woo the votes of the other classes instead of taking them for granted or, perhaps, for purchase'.[18] Of course, Disraeli had sweetened the pill somewhat by adjusting the boundaries of county constituencies to shave off potentially problematic overlaps with the new borough electorates and had increased the number of county seats to preserve the Conservative party's position in its aristocratic strongholds in the English countryside. Given that the Act also limited the new ratepayer franchise to the borough constituencies, what then was the effect of the Act upon the position of the landed aristocracy and gentry in arable counties such as Suffolk? In rural constituencies such as the Eastern and Western Divisions of Suffolk, where the bulk of the electorate continued to be composed of a tenantry voting in the open air, landowners continued to dominate the political scene. In East Suffolk, the general election of 1868 was once again fought on behalf of the Liberal Party by Colonel Robert Adair. On this occasion, Adair, standing with Mr T. S. Western, was defeated by the Conservative candidates Frederic Corrance, who owned 1,800 acres in and around the parish of Parham, and the Hon. John Henniker Major, the twenty-six year old son and heir of the Irish peer Lord Henniker (but now elevated to the House of Lords as Lord Hartismere).

During the campaign, however, many tenant farmers in the Division, whilst obliged to follow their landlords' lead in political matters were, according to a report in the *Suffolk Mercury*, 'a little sulky' at the putting forward of a mere 'schoolboy' even if he was the son of the much respected Lord Henniker. This was because, in 1866, John had entered the House of Commons under the wing of his uncle, Sir Edward Kerrison, who had swapped his Eye seat to sit for East Suffolk. But now, in 1868, John was trying to fill his uncle's boots. Clearly, a little wooing was required to bolster John's standing. When news broke that the Lord Lieutenant the Earl of Stradbroke, had stirred himself to meet with the Biddells, who were among the leading farmers in the county and 'half-a-dozen or so of other good men and true at the White Horse' and had 'made things as pleasant as might be for the candidature of the son of that fine old English nobleman Baron Hartismere' this, combined with the deference and respect commanded by those who possessed both land and a title, dispelled any doubts. For whilst:

Nobody then formed the opinion of him that he would set the Thames on fire . . . in his evident goodwill and kindly disposition they saw something of the qualities which had rendered his father's name so well-favoured throughout the Division . . . they [also] saw some slight hint of the cleverness and vigour of his uncle, Sir Edward Kerrison, [particularly when] Radicals waylaid him in the market place.[19]

Significantly, the influence in the English counties of the landed aristocracy persisted even after 1872, when tenant farmers could at last cast their votes in a voting booth. After 1872, and especially as the agricultural depression began to bite, the aristocracy had to work harder at keeping 'on-side' with the farmer. Election results up to 1884 suggest that in this they were successful as both the Eastern and Western Divisions of Suffolk continued to be represented by great landowners on behalf of the Conservative party. This continuing presence of the Landed Interest in the House of Commons after 1867 saw Radicals again raise the banner of land reform as a way to end the monopolization of land ownership by the aristocracy and thereby undermine their rural power-base. Central to this renewed Radical campaign to reform the land laws was the *Census* of 1861. According to this document, out of a total population of nearly 19 million, only 30,000 were landowners; this figure was, unsurprisingly, condemned as wholly inaccurate by Lord Derby:

> There was from time to time a great outcry raised about what is called the monopoly of land, and, in support of this cry, the wildest and most reckless exaggerations and mis-statements of fact are uttered as to the number of persons who were the actual owners of the soil. It had been said again and again that, according to the Census of 1861, there were in the United Kingdom not more than 30,000 landowners . . . [but] this estimate arose from a misreading of the figures contained in the Census returns.[20]

In view of the supposedly ill-informed basis of the attacks they were enduring from their Radical critics regarding the Land Question, the Duke of Richmond proposed that it was time to knock these ill-informed opinions on the head once and for all by compiling a *Parliamentary Return* listing all the owners of land in the United Kingdom. Unfortunately, the *Return*, when it was finally published in 1874, far from dispelled the supposed ignorance and misinformation of the Radicals, as the aristocracy had hoped, but actually confirmed the Radicals' case.

In fairness, the *Return*, compiled by the Local Government Board, and nicknamed the *New Domesday Book*, did confirm that there were after all nearly a million landowners in England and Wales, excepting London, who owned a freehold in land whether it be only a house or a garden. On the other hand, the *Return* also exposed the existence of 710 individuals who each owned around 5,000 acres in any one county and who collectively owned 'within a fraction of a fourth of the entire geographical area of the country'.[21] At a broader level, it was also revealed that four-fifths of the soil was in the possession of a mere 7,000 proprietors, a monopoly that Radicals blamed on primogeniture and entails enabling the aristocracy to amass and preserve their ancestral estates. Through these legal and customary devices, the Landed Interest had acquired 'not only what may pay so much per cent' but also social position and power over their tenants and neighbours and it was 'precisely this', complained George Broderick in 1881, 'which renders the undue concentration of landed property so detrimental to the public interest'.[22]

So long as these legal and customary safeguards remained in place, the free play of economic forces would, in Broderick's view, continue to be subject to an unfair distortion in favour of the great landowners who, it was alleged, were for ever swallowing up smaller estates that, once brought within the park palings or the ring fence, rarely reappeared on the market. Indeed:

> To say that a land system founded on the law of Primogeniture and guarded by strict family settlements has a direct tendency to prevent the dispersion of land, is only to say that it fulfils the purpose for which it was instituted. It is hardly less evident that it must have the further effect of promoting the aggregation of land in a small and constantly decreasing number of hands. The periodical renewal of entails is intended to secure, and does secure, ancestral properties against the risk of being broken up; and, practically, they very seldom come onto the market, except as a consequence of scandalous waste or gambling on the part of successive life-owners.[23]

Under Broderick's model, scarcely a day went past without some yeoman farmer of ancient lineage being erased from the roll of landowners by the cumulative augmentation of ancestral properties by new purchasers. Such views were part of a wider campaign against the perceived bias in favour of large landownership inherent within the laws of primogeniture and entail. These devices were also particularly blamed for producing a competition between landowners whose political and social influence were dependent to a great degree on the extent of their landed possessions. When the workings of the land market were assessed from this vantage point, the conclusion was clear: 'If a small freehold of a few acres comes onto the market, it is almost certain to be bought up by an adjoining owner, either for the purpose of rounding off a corner of his estate, or for extending political influence.'[24]

In Suffolk, F. B. Zincke cited the creation of the Wherstead Park estate near Ipswich, owned by the Dashwood family, as a prime example of the gradual erosion of small landowners caused by the expansion of the great estates under the system of primogeniture and entails. By the late nineteenth century, the estate encompassed the whole parish; however, according to Zincke, there had been at least ten distinct properties in the parish in the eighteenth century. These were then gradually acquired by the Dashwood family and were now protected by entails and settlements and so passed 'from generation to generation inaccessible as property to those who laboured on them, and to all others' when, if things had been allowed to take their 'natural turn, instead of at this day having only one proprietor in Wherstead . . . we should [still] have farms of all sizes . . . suitable to the means and aims of all kinds of people . . . little people beginning with gardens of a quarter-of-an-acre . . . rising up to enough for the keep of two or three cows'. All that was wanted, concluded Zincke, for these 'little people' to reappear was 'that conveyance should be cheapened and facilitated, and that every acre in the country should be everywhere and at all times saleable at the will of an absolute owner. This involves the prohibition of charging and settling land'.[25]

On the other hand, could the abolition of all laws allegedly restricting the sale of land and of all customs favouring the aggregation of landed property in the hands of a few necessarily lead to the multiplication of small freeholds and the re-colonization of the countryside with independent yeoman farmers and small-holders at the expense of the great estates? James Froude castigated those who complained about the law of entail as if it interfered with the sub-division of landed property by suggesting that it protected what small estates still remained. If we follow Habakkuk's thinking in Chapter One however, it is open to debate as to how far down the social ladder the practice of settling estates actually permeated. If all the nobility and almost all the gentry practised the settlement of land but only a minority of the lesser gentry did so, it is unlikely to have preserved the farms and freeholds of the yeomanry and peasantry. There is also the issue of who would buy all this land if it were released onto the market? For, even if land were freely sold, it would still be 'monopolized by millionaires who alone could afford to hold property returning such a poor interest'.[26] Freeing the soil of its fetters and leaving its redistribution to the workings of a reformed land market was thus unlikely to lead to a sharp rise in the number of smaller landowners at the expense of larger landowners given the general tendency, as Gladstone recognized, among rich Englishmen to look upon land 'as a luxury rather than an instrument of production, and to covet its possession as a source of social influence'.[27]

On the other hand, in Suffolk, an agricultural county dominated by great estates geared to high intensity, large-scale farming, there was still a considerable number of small landowners in the late nineteenth century. *The Return of Owners of Land for the County of Suffolk* compiled in 1873 reveals that there were, in fact, over 12,500 small freeholders in the county owning under one acre each, amounting to over 3,500 acres in total, and a further 5,000 proprietors owning property of between one and a hundred acres, totalling nearly 103,000 acres, or an area equivalent to 12 per cent of the county. Clearly, the disappearance of the small landowner, here defined as the owners of under a hundred acres, needs to be reconsidered. For, while there is no doubt that the aristocracy and gentry were by far the largest players in the unreformed land market and were, as we saw in Chapter One, still intent on buying up smaller properties, the survival of over 100,000 acres in parcels of under a hundred acres suggests that disappearance of the peasantry as a class is still a moot point. This is especially so as many of these so-called peasants were in fact *rentiers* enjoying a second income. Howkins has also argued that 'peasant proprietors' who worked their own small plots of land, whilst earning a weekly wage working on a neighbouring farm, represented a far larger proportion of the agricultural workforce in the late nineteenth century than has been previously thought. To the Victorian Radical, however, an English peasantry, enjoying the liberty that came with owning and working a plot of land was being forced into servitude by an aristocracy hell-bent on buying up more and more land and keeping hold of it by entailing it. With the aristocracy monopolizing the ownership of land, the peasant was reduced to the level of a landless agricultural labourer derisorily known to Radical-Liberals as 'Hodge'.[28]

To the Radical land reformer, the question was how to liberate 'Hodge'? So long as land was considered a luxury item that appealed only to the rich, the flaw inherent in merely cheapening and facilitating the transfer of land by abolishing settlements and entails was obvious. Equally obvious was the general lack of momentum behind the rather dull issue of land law reform within the Gladstonian Liberal party and the country. So, rather than reform the land laws, Gladstone gave the agricultural labourer the vote in 1884. But was this enough to satisfy the Radical wing of the Liberal party? The Third Reform Act in 1884 was followed, in 1885, by the Redistribution of Seats

Act which abolished two-member constituencies and redrew the boundaries of parliamentary seats across rural England and, at first glance, it would appear that the fortunes of the landed aristocracy were badly shaken by these two measures. By 1897, only 98 out of a total of 670 MPs were the sons of either a Peer or a Baronet.[29]

The winnowing out of the aristocracy and gentry from the House of Commons can clearly be seen in rural counties such as Suffolk (see Table 2), where the former two-member constituency of West Suffolk was split to form the new one-member constituencies of North-West Suffolk (or Stowmarket Division) and South Suffolk (or Sudbury Division). Between 1832 and 1885, the surnames of

Table 2: General Election Results in Rural Suffolk, 1885–1910

General Elections	North Suffolk	N.E. Suffolk	N.W. Suffolk	South Suffolk	S.E. Suffolk	Bury St Edmunds
1885	L*	L	L	L*	L	C*
1886	LU*	L	C	LU*	C*	C*
1892	C	L	L	LU*	L	C*
1895	C	L	C	LU*	C*	C*
1900	C	L	C	LU*	C*	C*
1906	L	L	L	L	L	C*
1910	U	L	U	U*	U	C*

(Key: L: Liberal Party. LU: Liberal Unionist Party. C: Conservative Party. U: Conservative and Unionist Party. An asterisk – * – indicates a landowner. Source: J. Vincent and M.Stenton (eds), *McCalmont's Parliamentary Poll Book of all Elections, 1832–1918* [Brighton, 1971]).

the MPs who had sat for the seat of West Suffolk amounted to a roll-call of landed families in the west of the county – Waddington, Bennet, Parker, Hervey, Wilson, Thornhill, Rushbrooke and Tyrell. After 1885, whilst the Stowmarket Division alternated between the Liberal and Conservative parties, whenever one of the surrounding Tory landowners stood as a Conservative candidate, they were defeated. This suggests that among the agricultural voters in this constituency landowners were something of a local liability to the Conservative party, which puts an entirely different spin on one Conservative commentator's quip that '"Hodge" knew nothing and desired little' and was given the vote 'much to his own surprise and his masters'.[30] Clearly, it was the Conservative landowners, standing for seats like Stowmarket, (Sir Thomas Thornhill, Sir Edward Greene, Viscount Chelsea and the Hon. W. E. Guinness, who stood in 1885, 1891, 1892 and 1906, respectively) who got the bigger surprise! By contrast, in the Sudbury Division, the emerging local influence and popularity of Sir Cuthbert Quilter ensured that from 1885–1906 the seat was held by the Liberal Unionists.[31]

On the other side of the county, the former constituency of East Suffolk, which between 1867 and 1885 had been represented by Lords Henniker and Rendlesham, Sir Edward Gooch, Frederic Corrance, Frederick St John Barne and Viscount Mahon (Lord Henniker's brother-in-law), was split into three. The new seats were North Suffolk (or the Lowestoft Division), North-East Suffolk (or the Eye Division) and South-East Suffolk (or the Woodbridge Division). The Liberal Unionist MP Sir Savile Crossley did win in 1885 and 1886 in North Suffolk but thereafter no local landowners contested the seat. Meanwhile, in the Eye Division, formerly a borough constituency dominated by the Kerrison/Henniker interest, the agricultural voters returned the Liberal candidate, Francis Stevenson, in 1885; thereafter the seat became a Liberal stronghold. True, agricultural labourers were not an absolute majority in the Eye Division, however here as elsewhere it was now their votes that could swing a rural seat from Conservative to Liberal or *vice versa*. For example, in villages in the old borough of Eye household suffrage had existed since 1867, giving labourers the vote, and they had voted Conservative, which suggests that this vote had been overwhelmed by labourers in the 'open' villages which were now part of the new Eye Division where the Kerrison interest had less social pull.[32] The key to electoral success, post 1885, as Thompson has suggested, was the ability of landowners to 'manage the agricultural labourer'[33] and here they patently could not do so.

The demise of Sir Edward and the financial difficulties of the Hennikers may also have contributed to a sense of disillusionment with politics in Thornham Hall. In this regard the Hennikers would not have been unique as the agricultural depression rolled on. But alongside the financial considerations of standing for Parliament, landowners also had to be willing to canvass for votes in the more 'open' villages, and the absence of a strong showing by the Hennikers in these villages may well account for the dip in the fortunes of the Conservative party in the Division. By contrast, voters in the Woodbridge area continued to elect Conservative or Liberal Unionist landowners. In 1886 the seat was held by Colonel R. C. Anstruther on behalf of the Tory Party. Subsequently, after the Colonel's defeat in 1892, the seat was held by the Conservative MP and leading Suffolk landowner, Colonel E. G. Pretyman, who remained its MP from 1895 up to 1906.[34]

Both Crossley and Pretyman were insulated against the effects of the agricultural depression by large non-agricultural incomes. This lends weight to the point that in the absence of such funds, many more financially pressed landowners, such as the Henniker-Majors, who effectively inherited the leadership of the Kerrison interest in and around Eye after Sir Edward's death, decided against standing as candidates. Similarly, in a democratic countryside, the aristocracy could no longer merely doff their hats to the tenantry and expect to be elected. The days when landowners such as Lord Hartismere and the Earl of Stradbroke could win an election by swaying the votes of a 'few good men' were over. For example, whilst agricultural labourers in the Woodbridge Division of Suffolk swung back to the Tories in 1886 by electing Colonel R. C. Anstruther, Lord Rendlesham, who had sat for the old seat of East Suffolk from 1874 to 1884, was defeated in 1885 by the Liberal candidate R. L. Everett. Similarly, in 1906 and 1910, the Liberal candidate for North-East Suffolk, W. H. M. Pearson defeated the Conservative Marquess of Graham.[35]

It was now a bit of a gamble as to whether or not a local landowner would be elected, especially in the Stowmarket Division where landowners appear to have acted as lightning rods for anti-landlord feeling. Of course, landowners did still stand and did, on occasion, get elected to Parliament; however, there were more misses than hits, simply because actually winning now meant canvassing for votes among the agricultural labourers in the more 'open' villages who lived at the margins of the more direct influence that could be exerted by landlords over the 'close' villages. This point is highlighted by Flora Thompson's insight that women thought it 'a pity the men had taken up with these Liberal notions. If they've got to vote why not vote Tory and keep in with the gentry? You never hear of Liberals giving the poor a bit of coal or a blanket at Christmas'.[36] In other words, even where paternalism still held sway it would have been a mistake to expect that the 'unspoken assumptions of deference would work'[37] automatically. By giving the vote to the agricultural labourer the Liberals had given 'Hodge' the key to the door of the countryside and in 1885 'Hodge' had let the Liberals in, but were the Liberals able to make themselves at home?

In 1886, the Liberal party had been ruptured by Gladstone's decision to support Home Rule for Ireland, as, in protest, the bulk of the old Whig aristocracy had moved *en masse* into the Conservative or Liberal Unionist camp. This would, as we shall see, have major implications for how the

Conservative party dealt with the Land Question as, irony of ironies, the Liberal Unionists included Joseph Chamberlain, the arch-critic of the landed aristocracy. Chamberlain (the Liberal MP for Birmingham, 1876–1885) had, in 1885, been the champion of Radical-Liberal reform and in particular land reform. Chamberlain believed that reforming the land laws was a dead letter. Such a measure would only serve to leave the land in the hands of the same class of people who 'toil not, neither do they spin' for 'the rich will always win in competition with the poor'.[38] What was needed was an issue that would really engage the country, something that attacks on the dull, Byzantine system of conveyancing had signally failed to do.

Chamberlain found the issue he was looking for in a Bill proposed by Jesse Collings, the Radical-Liberal MP for Ipswich. Under this Bill local authorities were to be given the power to transfer land from private into public ownership, regardless of the views of the local landowners, to provide every labourer with 'three acres and a cow'. Believing this to be a major vote winner among the agricultural labourers enfranchised under the 1884 Reform Act, Chamberlain launched his 'Unauthorized Campaign'. In a speech delivered in Ipswich in January 1885, Chamberlain explained that, while the Liberal party was willing to complete the programme of Cobden and Bright and introduce free trade in land by doing away with settlements and primogeniture and thereby cheapen the transfer of land, surely the most:

> urgent and pressing need of all [was] ... as far as maybe ... to re-establish the peasants and yeomen who were one of the most prosperous ... most independent, and ... most comfortable of all classes in the community.[39]

In one fell swoop, the great aristocratic estates in counties such as Suffolk would begin to crumble allowing the farm workers to buy the land, liberating them from their pitiable existence on the great estates. Chamberlain therefore wholeheartedly endorsed the legislation 'which is honourably connected with the name of my friend Mr Collings' for attempting 'to gratify the land hunger which exists in the breast of every labourer'.[40] This was of course a Radical stereotype and took no account of George Sturt's view that, on the whole, the labourers on the great estates harboured no real animosity against their landlords especially if they had been providing them with cottages with allotments or gardens attached. On estates such as Helmingham, where labourers could actually hire three acres and a cow, as opposed to listen to Liberal promises, labourers were said to 'value their position accordingly'.[41] By 1886, however, Chamberlain found himself nestled among the 'Old Whigs' and the Tory aristocracy in opposition to Home Rule for Ireland – politics does indeed make for strange bedfellows!

The Conservative party was, however, evolving as Bagehot commented in 1872:

> The Reform Act of 1867 . . . unmistakenly completed the effect which the Act of 1832 began but left unfinished. The middle class element has gained greatly by the second charge, the aristocratic element has lost greatly . . . most [of our] prominent statesmen are [now] not men of ancient or of great hereditary estate; they are men mostly of substantial means, but they are mostly, too, connected more or less closely with the new trading wealth [of the nation].[42]

This assessment is exemplified by the career of the book retailer W. H. Smith, as a leader in *The Times* in 1891 noted:

> It is a characteristic of modern Conservatism that a man like Mr Smith should have held his high position [as the Conservative Leader of the Commons] in the party. Conservatism in England was wont to be aristocratic, and bound up with the fortunes of the great landed class. The Tories of fifty years ago disliked PEEL; their successors hated DISRAELI though they were obligated to follow him; and in both cases the origin of the feeling was that the Leader was a man who did not belong to the old aristocratic English caste. The modern spirit of the Act of 1867 has changed all that; and our age has seen the Conservative party in the House, and the House itself following . . . with positive affection, a simple man of business, without any pretensions to 'family' [whose] first entry into the House of Commons should rather symbolically have occurred in 1868 in the very year after the 'leap in the dark'.[43]

When a businessman *did* decide to buy an estate as in the case of Smith, while it was, on the one hand, an expression of the desire of the newly-rich to play the country squire, it was certainly no longer an automatic route into the House of Commons, nor did it make any economic sense. On the other hand, the ownership of a large landed estate, with farms and cottages, continued to imbue its owners with considerable influence in English society and the Conservative party was canny enough to realize that it needed to retain its rural roots and patina. Aristocratic or landed candidates were not always guaranteed winners but the great landowners themselves were still a powerful pro-Tory lobby in rural seats. Despite the fact that by 1914 they were a minority in the Commons, within their localities members of even impoverished aristocratic families 'remained and in some respects still remain, important, influential and powerful people'.[44]

The enfranchisement of the agricultural labourer had of course ended the ability of landowners to run their local constituencies as their own personal fiefs, paying lip-service to their parties. In 1804, Lord Cornwallis, who through his estates (later purchased by the Kerrison family) controlled the borough of Eye, had told his brother to act 'entirely for yourself and consider yourself as you really are, as independent as any member of the House of Commons'.[45] Eighty years later, the extension of the vote to the agricultural labourer and the Conservative Central Office's establishment of local party Associations and appointment of local party agents ensured that the interests of the party, rather than those of the local landowners now predominated – hence, there was no return to protection despite the petitions and appeals of the great landowners. But the social influence enjoyed by landowners, as the largest landowners and landlords in the English countryside, still 'survived with little diminution through the nineteenth century, and is still far from dying'.[46] This point was recognized by contemporaries such as Arthur Ponsonby who wrote, in 1912, 'Apart from their actual political power, which after all is a mere ghost of what they formerly enjoyed, in the social world they reign supreme, and their supremacy would be maintained here even if they were divorced absolutely from all political power.'[47] And, as their endorsement still carried considerable weight in 1905, the local party agent G. H. Tippet was keen to add the name of the future fourth Marquess of Bristol, Captain Frederick Hervey, to a 'representative list of landowners . . . prepared to support the candidature of Sir Cuthbert Quilter at the coming election in South Suffolk'. [48]

Many landlords also played a prominent role within their local party Associations. Colonel Pretyman was President of the Woodbridge Division of the Conservative and Unionist Association, whilst Lord Rendlesham and C. H. Berners were its Vice-Presidents. The third Earl of Stradbroke was President of the North Suffolk Conservative and Unionist Association whilst its Chairman was Major Miles Barne of Sotterley Hall. In Eye, the Marquess of Graham was the President of the Eye Conservative and Unionist Association, G. Stuart Ogilvie was Chairman while Lord Huntingfield, Sir Ralph Blois, Colonel Bence-Lambert, Captain Venon-Wentworth, Major Miles Barne, Charles Austin and W. E. Long were Vice Presidents of the Association. Similarly, despite having to move to the local rectory as a result of the continuing agricultural depression, Rowland Holt-Wilson, as heir to the 5,500 acre Redgrave Hall estate, was made Chairman of the Hawstead Conservative and Unionist Association. The extent of the on-going influence enjoyed by the great landowners and its deployment in lobbying voters on behalf of the Conservative party is revealed by the fact that in the few remaining small, rural boroughs, heirs to titles and younger sons of the nobility *did* remain 'attractive candidates for many rural and some urban constituencies in which the traditions or memories of family connections and property [were] strong.'[49]

Voters in Bury St Edmunds, for instance, returned a succession of Tory candidates drawn from the ranks of the neighbouring landed aristocracy. These included Lord Francis Hervey (1885–1892), the brother of the third Marquess of Bristol, Viscount Chelsea (1892–1900), the son and heir of the Earl of Cadogan; Sir E. W. Greene (1900–1906), the son of the Bury brewer and landowner Edward Greene; Captain Frederick Hervey (1906–7), the nephew of the third Marquess of Bristol; and the Hon Walter Guinness (1907–1914),[50] the second son of the first Earl of Iveagh. In the case of Captain Frederick Hervey, Conservative Central Office had actively canvassed for him to stand for Bury given the 'connection your family had with the seat'.[51] When it became clear that Sir Walter Greene intended to stand for re-election, Captain Wells, the Principal Agent at Central Office, offered Captain Hervey Sir John Colomb's seat in Great Yarmouth. In rejecting this offer, Hervey replied, 'I would if I were offered it at any time consent to stand for Bury St Edmunds . . . but as things stand, I am not prepared to retire [from the Navy] . . . so as to work up influence in a constituency where I am not at present known.'[52]

Thus, when Sir Walter suddenly announced his decision to retire at the forthcoming general election, Captain Wells immediately wrote to Captain Hervey asking if he could put his name forward as a prospective candidate as 'There is really no time to be lost, as we shall have other people after the seat, but I am sure the Committee will be only too glad to get you.'[53] One of the members of the Committee was the Marquess of Bristol, who wrote to his nephew, 'I have this morning received a notice to attend a meeting of the Bury Constitutional Club on Friday . . . to decide a course of action' in the wake of Sir Walter's announcement. Significantly, the Marquess concluded that 'if Bury must be represented . . . a member of the family should be the individual [rather] than a stranger.'[54] With the backing of both his uncle and Conservative Central Office, Captain Hervey was, unsurprisingly, unanimously elected at the meeting as the Conservative candidate for Bury St Edmunds and was duly elected as the Member of Parliament for the seat in 1906.

The evidence from Bury is merely the tip of a far larger iceberg for, wherever a large landowner continued to live a greater part of the year on his estates 'and took pains to associate himself with local life, his social influence might be enormous'.[55] Of course, this could no longer guarantee that the local landowners would win in the larger rural seats. This was certainly the case in 1885, in new constituencies, with many new agricultural voters living in villages on the margins of the great estates where the pull of the revived National Agricultural Labourers' Union (see Chapter Four), under Joseph Arch, was considerable. Arch and the N.A.L.U. were practically an 'adjunct to the Liberal party' in the countryside as battle was joined in Westminster, in 1884, between Gladstone, fighting for the agricultural labourer, and a territorial House of Lords determined only to compromise on a redistribution of parliamentary seats to eject 'alien town elements from some rural seats'.[56]

With the Gladstonian Liberal party championing the agricultural vote, Chamberlain unofficially campaigning on 'three acres and a cow' and Arch also advocating compulsory cultivation of the land, the signs were propitious for the Liberal party in the countryside. Unfortunately, it is doubtful 'whether the union or the Liberals . . . had a real remedy [to the Land Question] . . . and subsequent disillusion must be part of the explanation for the fact that the Liberal triumph in the counties was shortly to be reversed and never to be repeated'.[57] To Radical-Liberals, there could be only be one explanation for the implosion of support for their party in county constituencies in the 1886 General Election, after having enjoyed so much support in 1885 (see Table 2): Tory landlords had 'so bullied the labourer for voting Liberal that . . . he may choose the broad and easy path of remaining indifferent or voting with those who control his wages and his charities.'[58] The alternative explanation is set out by Thompson who suggests that what we really see in 1886 is a return to deferential or common-interest voting among rural workers on and around the great estates after an initial flurry of defiantly independent Liberal-Radical voting in the 1885 election[59] – perhaps thereby putting a shot over the Conservative party's bows over the issue of labourers' allotments? If this was the case, then the Conservative party had one great advantage over their Liberal opponents – the great landowners – who could supply allotments by voluntary arrangement with their labourers. It is worth pausing here to note that there was a substantial increase in the availability of small-holdings and allotments on the great estates in the late 1880s 'in a largely successful attempt to pre-empt the need for publicly owned land'.[60]

In other words, the aristocracy's continued influence as landowners could be deployed in those parts of a constituency where their estates were situated to the benefit of the Conservative party. This combination of disillusionment with the Liberals and the offer of allotments by Conservatives could prove decisive, given the willingness, after 1885, for labourers on or near the great estates to return to voting *with* their landlords *for* the Conservative party candidate. In these circumstances, a seat could swing the way of the Conservative party. In the final analysis, 'the influence of the landed elite, increasingly battered as it was, still yielded appreciable electoral results as late as 1910' and in English counties 'a high degree of deference and major swings in party allegiance were all prominent.'[61] This in turn explains why a Radical-Liberal party, denuded of the old aristocratic Whigs in 1886, targeted the landed elite in the countryside after that date.

In rural seats, therefore, the Conservatives under the Marquess of Salisbury could still win because the Tory aristocracy could shore up their party's core vote behind Conservative (and occasionally landed) candidates who appreciated that Hodge 'now expected to be flattered and cajoled at election times, not told to tug his forelock'[62] and this meant bringing more land within accessible reach. For example, good Liberal results in the English county constituencies in 1885 appeared to confirm the popularity of the Liberals' proposed allotments scheme among rural voters. So in September 1887, Salisbury, having won the subsequent 1886 general election, brought forward a Bill to Facilitate the Provision of Allotments for the Labouring Classes (50 and 51 Vict.c.48). The political pragmatism inherent within this approach to the whole question of wider landownership echoed the views of Suffolk landowners such as Frederick Barne who wrote to his son prior to the 1884 Reform Act:

> Gladstone is bound greatly to enlarge the constituency. This will admit a great number of agricultural labourers. Under these circumstances . . . if you stand again, I would advise you to state that you are ready to support measures likely to benefit the agricultural classes [though] without binding yourself [as] . . . the labourers will follow those who promise them a share of the land.[63]

The passage of the Allotments Act, by a party traditionally associated with upholding the rights and privileges of the landed aristocracy and gentry, illustrates the degree to which patricians such as Lord Salisbury were now, habitually, prepared to concede ground on behalf of his class if it could be shown to be advantageous to the Conservative party. More importantly, Salisbury's administration was also heavily dependent on the support it received from the large body of anti-Home Rule Liberals or Liberal Unionist

MPs led by Joseph Chamberlain. Essentially, the dependence of the Conservative party on the Liberal Unionists compelled Salisbury to take a broader view of domestic questions than perhaps he would otherwise have done.[64] In August 1887, for example, an Act to Provide Compensation to the Occupiers of Allotments and Cottage Gardens for Crops Left in the Ground at the end of Their Tenancies (50 and 51 Vict. c.26) also passed through Parliament with the support of the landowner and Liberal Unionist MP for Lowestoft, Sir Savile Crossley, who subsequently became Chairman of the Liberal Unionist Council.

Whilst Salisbury's willingness to allow the Labourers' Allotment Bill to pass through Parliament owed a great deal to the support his government received from the Liberal Unionists, Offer suggests that Salisbury had already begun to see the broadening of the ownership of landed property as a way to bring to an end the gentry's social isolation.[65] In so doing, Salisbury envisioned a broad rampart of property-owning voters defending the holders of large estates against the attacks of radical Liberals and Socialists who were leaning more and more towards either Henry George's punitive landowners' tax or Alfred Russell Wallace's land nationalization schemes as mechanisms to finally smash the power of the aristocracy in their rural heartlands. The Liberals' 1907 and 1908 Small Holdings and Allotments Acts, for example, were both closely modelled on Wallace's vision of a small-holding State tenantry in that they gave County Councils the power to compulsory purchase landed property to meet the anticipated demand for small holdings. Inevitably, as the Marquess of Salisbury observed in 1883, 'the members of the classes who are in any sense or degree holders of property are becoming uneasy at the prospect which lies before them. The uneasiness is greatest among those whose property consists in land, because they have been the most attacked.'[66]

But how to square the circle, how to create a bulwark of small landowners whilst also being unwilling to countenance legislation embodying the compulsory transference of landed property from the aristocracy who owned most of the land, to the labourers who did not? As to immediate need, Salisbury calculated that there was more than enough surplus land in the hands of various local charities and corporations which could be released onto the market to meet the aspirations of those who wished to purchase a small parcel of land. As a result, the Labourers' Allotment Act (50 and 51 Vict., c.48) was passed to placate his Liberal Unionist colleagues, but was actually drafted in such a way as to be largely unworkable. Under the provisions of the Act, local Boards of Guardians were granted the power to compulsorily acquire any land deemed suitable for allotments and to let these allotments to any labourers resident in the district or parish who wanted them. There was only one proviso: the Board was only required to act in cases where allotments could not be obtained at a reasonable rent and on reasonable conditions by voluntary arrangement between the owners of the land and the applicant. In addition, local Boards of Guardians, many of whose members were in fact either landlords or tenants of a local landowner and who were elected on a weighted property franchise, were only allowed to initiate proceedings against an uncooperative landowner if six parliamentary electors requested them to do so. Once such a request was received the Board had to refer the matter to the Quarter Sessions. If the local magistracy then agreed that there was a case to answer, which was unlikely given the preponderance of local landowners on the Bench as well as on the Board of Guardians, the Board was then obliged to approach the Local Government Board instructing them to bring a private act of parliament against the said landowner! [67]

Needless to say, the sheer expense and delay inherent within what was an extremely convoluted and demonstrably biased procedure was frequently more than enough to deter labourers from tackling a recalcitrant landlord who had refused to sell or let them a plot of land near to their cottages. In other words, whilst broadening the ownership of landed property became a growing theme within the Conservative party, from the 1880s onwards, Tory landowners remained wary of introducing the compulsory measures required to bring this transformation about. In 1892, for example, during the last parliamentary session before the General Election, a Small Holdings Act (55 and 56 Vict., c.31) successfully negotiated the House of Commons, but not before Lord Francis Hervey, the then MP for Bury St Edmunds and brother of the third Marquess of Bristol, tried to force an amendment to the Bill.

Hervey, alarmed at the implications of the Bill, sought to amend its wording by inserting the words lease and hire to modify what he saw as the main aim of the Bill, namely to facilitate the acquisition of small holdings. As Lord Francis told the House of Commons:

The real question before us is whether it is to be made a necessary condition that any person applying for the benefit of this Act should come forward with an already-formed desire to purchase the land. I know something of the agricultural labourers in Suffolk. They are very reserved, and they do not form their conclusions in a hurry. I am perfectly certain that if this condition which, the Right Hon Gentleman [Mr Jesse Collings] seems determined to insist upon is imposed, the agricultural labourers of Suffolk will have no advantage out of this Bill [as] there are many of them who would be willing and desirous to hire land in order to see if they can make it pay; and if so, they will afterwards have a desire to purchase the land. Is it not within the knowledge of the Right Hon. Gentleman that what we are asking people to do is a thing which the late Sir James Caird declared that nobody but a fool would do? Sir James Caird's view was that a man could make a profit of 10 per cent on his capital as a cultivating occupier, but only 2 per cent as an agricultural owner. Why, then, deny agricultural labourers the opportunity of hiring small portions of land which they would be able to cultivate with some advantage and insist that they should come to the County Council with a formed desire to buy the land before they know whether they can make it pay?[68]

In reply, Jesse Collings reiterated the principles upon which such legislation was based:

This Bill is for the creation of peasant proprietors in all the independence and freedom which cultivating ownership alone can give, and the object, as I take it of those who support this Amendment, is to curtail that principle as much as possible . . . Therefore, it is not an issue of supplying land to the labourer who cannot afford to buy, for that is amply provided for further in the Bill. The principle upon which we are going to divide is whether we shall maintain the primary object of the Bill to create an independent class of peasant proprietors through the country.[69]

In the end, Hervey's amendment was defeated by a resounding 152 votes to 72. Nevertheless, Salisbury, aware of the concerns felt by many landlords, remained wary of introducing a system of unfettered compulsory purchase. Thus, the Bill, when passed, was found to be permissive. As Part I, Section 1 (I) of the Act makes clear:

If the council of any county are of opinion that there is . . . a demand for small holdings in their county . . . the council *may* . . . acquire any suitable land for the purpose of providing small holdings for persons who desire to buy and will themselves cultivate the holdings.[70]

Thus, on the one hand, Chamberlain, making the best of a bad job, could claim with a Small Holdings Act embodying the principle of compulsory purchase on the Statute Book that the 'inspiration and support of Liberal Unionism had secured from the Tory party the acceptance and broad

realization of his unauthorized programme'.[71] On the other hand, Salisbury
was content to have squared the circle of Liberal Unionism's flirtation with
land reform whilst keeping faith with his own party by keeping the
provision of allotments and small holdings on a voluntary basis, as called for
by Lord Tollemache during the debate on the Allotments Bill in 1887:

> With regard to the Bill now before the House, upon the face of it . . .
> it was perfectly right and just; [by calling for compulsory purchase of
> allotments] but . . . practically it could have the effect of deterring
> many landlords from granting allotments. If allotments were granted
> . . . the voluntary principle answered a great deal the best.[72]

Interestingly, Lord Tollemache had also argued that in certain cases compulsory measures were perhaps needed, on the grounds that if:

> Compulsory powers . . . were contained in Acts of Parliament they
> would very seldom have to be exercised because, if landlords knew
> that if they did not give allotments they could be compelled to do so,
> there would be very few estates without an abundance of allotments.[73]

But given that Salisbury had engineered the small holdings and allotments
legislation in such a way as to satisfy the demands of Liberal Unionist
colleagues such as Sir Savile Crossley without completely alienating
Conservatives such as Lords Tollemache and Hervey, how was Salisbury to
create his broad rampart of small landowners to protect the larger
landowners against the Liberals and nationalization? In Salisbury's opinion,
the only way the Conservatives could create a bulwark of pro-Tory small
property owners was to introduce legislation enabling every landowner to
register the title deeds to their land in their own name in full fee simple. By
replacing the exorbitant fees commanded by lawyers for expensive searches
of the title deeds with a straightforward registration of title, the legal costs
and long delays encountered by those seeking to buy even a small parcel of
land would be removed, allowing for the re-emergence of the small
landowner, who as the owner of a freehold would be inherently opposed to
the nationalization of landed property. In summary:

> It is [in] the interests of the country that the transference of land
> should be as easy as that of personal property, because it is important
> there should be a larger number of proprietors of land who should
> have a deeper interest in the stability and institutions of the country.[74]

More controversially, Salisbury also proposed to abolish the law of entail, which he considered an arcane and ineffectual means of defending the interests of the great landowners. Essentially, whilst the law of entail was seen by many, on both sides of the so-called Land Question, as pivotal to the preservation of the great estates, in Salisbury's view, entails served merely to further highlight the aristocracy's social isolation.

In reality, entails were, as noted earlier, often no more than an expression of the strength of family tradition in that they could be easily broken or altered. Similarly, the Radical accusation that they kept estates in the hands of fools to the detriment of agricultural improvement has also been shown to be somewhat spurious. Furthermore, under the provisions of Lord Cairn's 1881 Settled Land Act, life tenants were, as we have seen, granted the right to sell, lease or even, under certain circumstances, mortgage their settled estates, so long as they safeguarded 'the material interests of their successors by causing all capital money arising from a sale or a mortgage to be paid either to the trustees or into Court'.[75] Yet, in spite of the fact that the Act largely nullified the restrictions placed on life tenants, tradition ensured that aristocratic families continued to settle their estates, thereby presenting Radical politicians with the ammunition they needed to mount their attacks.

It was with these considerations in mind that a comprehensive Land Transfer Bill covering the compulsory registration of title was brought before the House in 1886. But, despite repeated attempts between 1886 and 1889, the Bill failed to get passed the concerted opposition of the more conservative landowners in the House of Lords, many of whom were fearful that the abolition of entails and primogeniture, so long 'the pet project of the extreme Radical Party' would inevitably 'lead to the destruction of the landed gentry and eventually of this House'.[76] If the law was altered and the law of primogeniture was abolished, would not the whole principle of arranging settlements, the foundation, as they saw it, on which the order of estates was fixed, effectively collapse leaving nothing more than estates being divided indefinitely? In reply, Salisbury pointed out that the great aristocratic estates were just as likely to stay together in freehold as under an entail and that, by easing the transfer of land their Lordships would also be bringing happiness to many thousands who would otherwise not have considered buying a small parcel of land. Despite this intervention, he could not save the Bill from defeat.[77]

In reality, however, many landowners had already made significant strides towards satisfying the perceived craving of their labourers for a small parcel of land. The craving for land was always a moot point. Lord Francis Hervey, in his attack on the 1892 Small Holdings Act, had highlighted the economic question marks that hung over the whole idea of the labourer trying his hand at farming at a time when well-heeled farmers were having trouble. Moreover, landowners were building and had built hundreds of cottages, usually with a garden or an allotment attached, during the course of the nineteenth century. For example, of the 281 cottages on the Oakley Park estate built or renovated by Sir Edward Kerrison during the latter half of the nineteenth century, 233 had allotments. A further 400 allotments on the estate, averaging a quarter of an acre each, were also made available to men of 'good character'. Elsewhere, there were around 110 allotments on the Ickworth estate, 597 allotments on the Rendlesham estate and a further 65 allotments on the Henham estate. These were concentrated in the parish of Wangford and comprised rectangular blocks of 20 rods each. By 1884, the total number of allotments and gardens on the Henham estate had risen to 88, with a further 10 allotments being created in 1895. As Frederick Clifford observed, 'there exists no better means of attaching the labourer to his employer, of sweetening his toil and making him contented with his position, than by giving him a comfortable cottage and satisfying his craving for a bit of land.'[78] Which perhaps explains why, when a survey was taken of the number of instances that County Councils had acquired land for allotments, applicants in Suffolk were found to have usually been 'supplied by voluntary arrangements'.[79]

In other words, the aristocracy and gentry, in counties such as Suffolk, were required to perform a careful balancing act between satisfying the interests of the tenant-farmer, after 1872, and those of the agricultural labourer after 1884. That they were able to do so is reflected in the continuing presence of landowners in local government, on elected local bodies and in the Liberals' repeated attempts up to 1914 to break the aristocratic lobby by trying to woo (sometimes successfully, sometimes unsuccessfully) both the labourer and the farmer away from their landlords, the former with land reform and the latter with tenant right legislation. Clearly, whilst the aristocracy no longer dominated the House of Commons, the strength of the Landed Interest as a powerful lobby in the countryside, among rural voters, in favour of a Conservative party committed to the preservation of private property, explains why land reform continued to excite the Liberal party. Put simply, 'even in the Edwardian period much work had still to be done in dismantling the "aristocratic state" and the Radical-Liberals cannot be accused of living in the past when they reminded the country of its necessity.'[80]

In the English countryside, as the evidence of the swings in seats across Suffolk in the general elections up to 1914 demonstrate (see Table 2),

and admired, even by Radical politicians, as being one of the best English landlords, having spent vast sums of money on improving his estates and rebuilding or repairing his farm houses and cottages. As a result, cottage building represented the third major area of expenditure undertaken by the landed aristocracy and gentry during the latter half of the nineteenth century. But what were the forces that prompted landowners in Suffolk to build cottages? Secondly, how extensive was the cottage building pro- gramme, and finally, what were its implications on the fabric of rural society in Suffolk?

Under the Poor Removal Act of 1846, landlords whose estates frequently encompassed an entire parish were in effect encouraged to let their cottages fall into decay, or even to pull them down to compress the Poor Rate in their parishes. The Poor Law Guardians in the Mildenhall Union criticized the Act for affording an inducement to the owners of what were termed 'close' parishes to 'prohibit the residence of the labouring classes upon their estates, compelling them to resort to the already overcrowded suburbs of the adjacent towns'.[3] Of course, this was a long standing phenomenon in closed parishes as landlords sought to limit the number of labouring families gaining settlement and thus eligibility for poor relief in 'their' parishes. As a result, when G. A. à Beckett visited Suffolk in 1850, he was 'greatly struck' by the contrast which existed between the habitations of those labourers fortunate enough to live on the Barton Hall estate of Sir Henry Bunbury and the 'miserable hovels into which many of the rural poor [were] packed' in market towns such as Bury St Edmunds.[4] The latter were then forced to walk every morning to work on the farms in the neighbouring close parishes. In consequence, there began to develop a separate community of labourers in the more populous 'open' villages where the ownership of land was more widely diffused.[5] Labourers living in these communities would, after 1884, be susceptible to Liberal ideas but were also still open to the inducements of the local landlords on whose estates they worked, namely the offer of an allotment or cottage with a garden which, paradoxically, began to become available after 1846 to men of 'good character'; this was because change was already afoot in the close parishes.

By 1846, it was becoming increasingly clear that, to improve the produc- tivity of their farms, landlords needed to ensure a better economic distribution of labour between their estates and the neighbouring open parishes. In 1849, the Duke of Bedford wrote, 'the improved methods of cultivation, extensive draining, and general improvement of husbandry [requiring additional hands] . . . have caused . . . an increased want of cottage accommodation' so he rebuilt the worst of his cottages and added 'to their number in those parts of my estate in which it appeared necessary to do so'.[6] In Suffolk, landowners were also well aware of the lack of suitable cottage accommodation on their estates. The Duke of Grafton, for one, was concerned that his labourers had to walk a long way to their work because of the scarcity of cottages on his larger farms. Similarly, a report examining the provision of cottages on the Ickworth estate, compiled in 1870, advised that as there were 'cases where from the various farms being large, and being long distances away from the villages, additional cottages might be built with great advantage, as the distances traversed by the men in going to and from their work entails extra expenditure on the part of the farmer, without compensating advantages.'[7] But estate villages were not just 'economic entities'. They had distinctive social structures, and many were also the subject of social experiments, but one thing was common to all estate villages or 'close' parishes: 'the particularly close relationship between the big house, the estate and the workforce created special kinds of social relationships.'[8]

Aside from an understandable desire to house the best labourers to attract the best farmers, there was also a philanthropic aspect to the erection of cottages. Buoyed by rising rent rolls, it was felt that 'one of the truest pleasures of every landlord' ought to be to improve the dwellings of the labouring class to raise their social and moral habits 'as a social service'.[9] The cottages built by the Rev E. R. Benyon on succeeding to the Culford estate in 1852 were intended to 'benefit exclusively the labouring class'; indeed, 'good roomy cottages' were seen as an essential precondition to the continued health and morals of labourers and their families.[10] When the Rev James Fraser toured southern England in 1867, he was gratified to find that 'in the districts over which I have travelled, amid many instances to the contrary, it was pleasant . . . to find not a few of the largest landowners setting a noble example of their consciousness of responsibility in respect of the dwellings of the labourers who cultivate their land.'[11] Fraser was particularly impressed by the cottages built by Sir Edward Kerrison on the Oakley Park estate and those built by the Duke of Grafton on the Euston Hall estate. According to the Duke's agent Kersey Cooper:

> Much depends upon the style in which [the cottages] are built and the quality of the materials used – The cottages in this district [around Euston] are mostly of ancient date being built of clay or plastered walls, with Thatched roofs – One Building usually comprising two Tenements, such being more economical than building separate houses, as one Chimney serves for both – and fewer walls required – I myself prefer the modern plan now adopted, in using brick and stone for walls – it being more durable, sightly and warm, with slated or

tiled roofs, I give preference to the slate; being a lighter covering, and less timber used in the roofs.[12]

Yet, despite the highly commendable efforts made by landlords such as the Duke of Grafton, the Rev Fraser concluded that:

I do not mean to say that the estates of these noblemen and gentlemen are everywhere adequately supplied with labourers' homes . . . but all are working onward in the right spirit to the right end, and their example tells upon the other landowners with an effect proportionate to its conspicuousness. There are grounds for hoping that, twenty-five years hence, the villages of England will present a different and more pleasing picture to the eye of the traveller than they present now.[13]

This was certainly the case in the parish of Helmingham, where an entirely new model village was built during the mid-nineteenth century by John Tollemache. When he inherited the estate in 1840, most of the cottages in the village were found to be in a 'ruinous and tumble-down condition'.[14] During the next four decades, Tollemache built over 300 new labourers' cottages in Helmingham and elsewhere on the estate, usually in pairs, at a cost of around £340 per pair. Overall, therefore, approximately £51,000 was invested in improving the standard of cottage accommodation on the estate during the mid-nineteenth century. For those families whose finances were encumbered or who simply did not wish to spend out of income the £150–£300 required to build a cottage, loans were also available from the Lands Improvement Companies. In 1869, for example, the Marquess of Bristol being 'desirous to avail of the assistance of the General Land Drainage and Improvement Company' applied for a loan of £280 to build two labourers' cottages in the parish of Playford, and a further loan of £320 to build two cottages in the parish of Horringer. This application was subsequently increased to £620.[15] These loans were, it appears, part of a far wider programme of improvements. In the report compiled by G. H. W. Hervey into the condition of cottages on the Ickworth estate in 1870, he noted that 'generally speaking I have found the cottages in fair repair, much indeed appears to have been done of late years in improving them.'[16] Lord Waveney, meanwhile, borrowed £2,100 from the Lands Improvement Company to build six new cottages on the Flixton estate. Thus, by the 1870s, estates across Suffolk had had their stock of housing considerably improved. What, though, was the return which landowners could expect on the capital invested in the erection of cottages?

The actual financial return on this form of investment was notoriously low. Thomas Wing, in evidence given to Her Majesty's Commissioners of Inquiry into the Housing of the Working Classes in 1885, declared, 'Cottages are absolutely a poor investment; there is no income in the shape of rent from a cottage that is at all [proportionate] to the cost of its erection.'[17] But then, as Fox points out, landowners frequently built cottages without expecting a direct return for their money; this was because cottages were seen as an investment in the improvement of their farms and also in the improvement of the morals and thus reliability and industry of the labourers. Rents were therefore often set well below the true market value of their cottages with the usual return averaging around a mere 2 per cent. Of the 125 cottages on the Henham Hall estate, none exceeded a rent of £4 per annum. These cottages included two storey, four-room double dwellers and two storey, six-room double dwellers comprising two bedrooms upstairs and a bakeroom, living room, pantry and back bedroom downstairs.

Similarly, the 286 cottages on the Rendlesham Hall estate, of which 249 had gardens, were let by Lord Rendlesham for between £2 12s. and £4 10s. per annum. Lord Tollemache, on the other hand, let his cottages on a more commercial basis with, symbolically, three acres of land on the grounds that, while letting a cottage on its own for a mere £3 10s. constituted an act of benevolent paternalism, letting the same cottage with three acres of land valued at £2 an acre obtained a small but fair return on his building investment. Nevertheless, the fact remains that the cottages themselves were still being let at far below their true market value. On the Ickworth estate, excellent cottages with gardens worth at least £5 or £6 per annum were let by the Marquess of Bristol for as little as one shilling a week. The occupiers of those cottages were, therefore, around two shillings a week better off in real terms 'than labourers who live in an open village and pay £5 a year for a house which is not worth half the money, and which has no garden'.[18]

The issue of what rent landlords ought to charge their labourers was one which, inevitably, aroused considerable debate. Significantly, it would appear that economic considerations were far outweighed by the aristocracy's determination to influence or control the moral habits of their labourers. When the Duke of Grafton wrote to his agent asking for his opinion on the matter, he replied that if His Grace was thinking of offering his labourers a low rent, much depended on the character of the intended occupiers:

> If they were frugal and industriously disposed, they richly appreciate
> so benign and liberal a landlord but . . . if [they were] of an opposite
> disposition . . . [and] find that no effort on their part is required to

provide for an almost nominal rent, that part of their savings which ought to be appropriated for such purpose is too often squandered away in drinking . . . thereby entailing upon themselves and families much . . . distress . . . which if their energies had been called into action to provide [for] a reasonable rent for a comfortable house, might and would, in all probability, have been avoided.[19]

High rents were equally objectionable in that 'when a cottager of hitherto industrious habits feels himself burdened with what he . . . considers a high rent . . . instead of increased exercises on his part to meet such demands' the labourer was more likely to 'neglect his endeavours [when] . . . every shilling which he might earn [went] in the shape of rent'. On balance, therefore, he advised the Duke to set a fair and reasonable rent in order to cultivate 'habits of industry and morality on the part of the labourer' which would in turn 'greatly add to their domestic comforts, and . . . create an inward satisfaction to the proprietor'.[20]

By contrast, in the open parishes, cottages were owned predominantly by a *petit bourgeoisie* of tradesmen, shopkeepers and artisans many of whom, along with the out-and-out building speculator, were looking to squeeze every last penny out of their properties by levying high rents and holding-off on any repairs. As a consequence, the living conditions of the agricultural labourers' resident in these parishes remained overcrowded and insanitary. When, in 1893, Wilson Fox visited Ixworth, an open parish in the Thingoe Poor Law Union in West Suffolk, he condemned the deplorable standard of housing in the parish. The majority of agricultural labourers in Suffolk were, however, forced to accept these sub-standard conditions because of the comparatively limited number of estate or tied-cottages and because of the aristocracy's insistence on making good character references a pre-condition of any letting agreement. Fox captures the mood of the aristocracy perfectly in his summation: 'Blame can scarcely be laid on [the] owners of property for taking steps to secure the best class of cottage tenants, and if character [was] made a qualification to obtain a good cottage cheap, it would seem that the most deserving are calculated to obtain some advantage.'[21]

Unfortunately, it was these same restrictions which ensured that the demand for rented accommodation in 'open' parishes remained high enough for building speculators, lacking the means to carry out improvements or repairs, to make a handsome profit on the dilapidated properties which they preferred to purchase rather than build. Essentially, the return on building cottages costing between £150 and £300 was so unremunerative, even at £5 or £6 per annum, that it made more sense financially to purchase what were, in effect, already sub-standard properties. These were frequently built of lath, plaster and thatch with inadequate sanitation and no gardens and could be bought-up for a minimal outlay. As Fox observed:

> The fact that speculative builders do not build cottages in the open villages would seem to be a proof that such a speculation would be unsuccessful at the rents which labourers can afford to pay, but they are never likely to make the attempt so long as they can buy up old houses cheap and make a good profit by letting them without having to diminish it by spending money on repairs.[22]

More importantly, many of these cottages were mortgaged and thus had no margin available for outlay even if the owner had wanted to undertake improvements. In summary, the condition of the cottages owned by the aristocracy tended to be better than those of the lesser gentry which in turn were still considerably better than those belonging to the village tradesmen or speculator.[23]

The detrimental effects of such property speculation were revealed by an Inquiry held in 1891 into the housing of agricultural labourers in the parish of Ixworth conducted by Lord Francis Hervey, under the Housing of the Working Classes Act (1890). In his report, Lord Francis concluded:

> In some instances there was proof of serious overcrowding. In others decrepitude and decay have gone so far as to make it more than doubtful whether the time for patching and mending has not passed. In others glaring structural defects and faults of arrangement seem to make half measures futile; in some the ground itself seems to be overcrowded with hovels . . . [which] are themselves overcrowded with inhabitants . . . upon the whole I am driven to the conclusion that further accommodation is necessary for the housing of the working classes in Ixworth . . . [and] that in several cases demolition will be found imperatively requisite.[24]

The concern and indignation expressed by Lord Francis eventually led the Thingoe Poor Law Union to erect six new houses on quarter-of-an-acre plots in the parish. But, whilst the actions of Lord Francis are illustrative of the gentry's concern at the housing of the working classes, the poor standard of housing in the open parishes also serves to emphasize the attractiveness of a cottage on the great estates. Nor was the significance of this point lost on the hundreds of labourers fortunate enough to reside on one of these estates or perhaps on those aspiring to do so. In other words, the cottage building programme of the mid-nineteenth century had an immense impact on the fabric of rural society in that it gave landlords in the county either direct or indirect influence over the lifestyle of the agricultural labourer, depending upon whether the labourer lived on or at the margins of the great estates. If the labourer lived on the estate, his relationship with his landlord was particularly close, as the Report of the Select Committee on the Housing of the Working Classes Acts Amendment Bill (1906) states:

> On certain large, well-managed estates the cottages are kept in hand by the landlord, who can afford to pay an agent or a clerk to collect the rents from the occupiers direct, [rather than let the] farmers [who] as a rule prefer to have cottages with the farm . . . sub-let to their hands, so as to have more control over them.[25]

In other words, the power conveyed by the threat of eviction remained firmly in the landlord's hands and his influence 'where wisely exercised' was, therefore, felt in both the 'farm-house and the cottage'.[26]

During the late Victorian heyday of the great estates in Suffolk, of the 215 cottages on the Culford estate, 209 were let directly from the Earl of Cadogan, who acquired the estate in 1889 from Richard Benyon Berens. On the neighbouring Euston Hall estate, only 55 of the 235 newly erected and renovated cottages owned by the Duke of Grafton were actually let with a particular farm. Finally, of the 250 cottages on the Ickworth estate, over half were let directly from the third Marquess of Bristol. As Clifford noted, in an age where Radical politicians were looking to sweep away the gentry, there existed no better way of ensuring that the agricultural labourer remembered where his loyalties ought to lie than by providing him with a comfortable well-maintained cottage and an attached allotment. Once built, these cottages also had to be properly maintained: 'It is frequently the practice for owners of estates to keep the management of their cottages in their own hands, and thus the internal and external repairs are properly attended to.'[27] Most cottages were, in fact, found to have been kept in an excellent state of repair by their respective landlords.[28] Yet, by the 1890s, it was clear to contemporaries such as Rider Haggard that, at the rents currently paid in Norfolk and Suffolk, it was practically impossible for the large landowners to continue to build, repair and keep their cottages in such a condition as to meet modern requirements.

Given that the return had always been a trifling 2 to 2.5 per cent, what Haggard should have said was that many landowners could no longer afford to continue subsidizing the building and repair of the cottages on their estates out of agricultural incomes alone. Despite this, many landowners were compelled by the commercial exigencies in dealing with their tenants to continue building cottages to secure good labourers in order to tempt incumbent or prospective tenants to stay on their farms. Thus, in 1881, the Marquess of Bristol, having already borrowed a total of £1,380 from the General Land Drainage and Improvement Company to build several cottages on the Ickworth estate, borrowed an additional £923 in 1884 and a further £1,923 in 1885. In 1891, however, the 24 cottages belonging to him in the parish of Little Saxham and representing an investment of £3,600 (if each were valued at £150), generated only £58. 12s. in rent, or a return of only 2 per cent.[29]

Of course, for landowners with substantial non-agricultural resources at their disposal, such as the Earl of Cadogan, the onset of the agricultural depression was no more than a mild inconvenience. As a result, during the early 1890s, Cadogan was able to continue the tradition of building cottages established by his predecessors at Culford during the prosperous years of 'high' farming. Similarly, during the late 1890s, Lord Iveagh was also able to rebuild the village of Elveden in red brick. On the other hand, those landlords who were wholly dependent on their dwindling agricultural incomes were finding it increasingly difficult merely to keep their cottages in good repair, let alone build new ones. Indeed, as many of their cottagers were falling into arrears even with their minimal rents, Sir Edward Kerrison, for instance, reported arrears of over £1,000 in 1882.[30] As a result, the overall number of cottages erected in Suffolk after 1880 fell dramatically as landed families sought to retrench. Nevertheless, as a result of the cottages already built, landlords had instilled a sense of residual deference that continued to persist despite attempts at the unionization of the agricultural labourer and the democratization of local government.

With regard to the former point, the key moment occurred in 1874 with the so-called 'Lock Out' by farmers of unionized agricultural labourers. The origins of this dispute can be traced to the decision of the Exning and Alderton Branch of the N. A. L. U. to vote for strike action in February 1874, in support of their demand for an extra one shilling a week in pay, to take their weekly income to 14 shillings. In response, the membership of the Newmarket Agricultural Association, which included farmers in both Suffolk and North Essex, voted to lock-out all union men with one week's notice, the notice period beginning on the next pay-day of each of the members respectively, and that said lock-out was to continue so long as the men continued to strike. Two weeks later, a further resolution was passed declaring that 'taking into consideration the inflammatory . . . language used by delegates of the N. A. L. U. at their meetings in the neighbourhood . . . the members of this Association shall not in future employ [or re-employ] any men to work for them who are members of the union'.[31] Events now began to take on a momentum of their own in Suffolk and elsewhere, as more and more Associations across the Eastern Counties began to follow the Newmarket farmers' lead by locking-out unionized labour. As a result, by May 1874 nearly 10,000 men stood idle across southern England. The West Suffolk Farmers' Defence Association (Colonel A. M. Wilson, Chairman), meeting at Bury St Edmunds in April, captured the new mood of confrontation when it declared its aim was 'to resist, by the united action of employers, any unfair demands [that arose from] . . . the united action of the men' so that farmers might never hear of the union again.[32]

Landlords were convinced that the dispute was the result of Radicals wantonly stirring up trouble in the countryside. In reply to a letter sent to *The Times* by the Bishop of Manchester dated 16th April, 1874, the redoubtable Countess of Stradbroke placed the blame for the dispute squarely on the actions of delegates 'sent down from [industrial] districts like your own, where class has been fighting against class for a quarter of a century'.[33] These delegates had, in her opinion, stirred up her labourers who, until the appearance of these Radical elements, had been a most 'contented, peaceable, honest and industrious set of men', due in no small measure to the charity and paternalism bestowed upon them by members of the landed elite such as herself. A view endorsed by fellow landowners such as Thomas Thornhill and Sir Edward Kerrison. The former wrote 'in countering that . . . Priest . . . you have done a great public good'.[34] Of course, as J. H. Bettey notes, the aristocracy's attitude toward their labourers could range from a 'genuine concern for the plight of the needy and unfortunate to harsh indifference and a demand for total subordination'.[35]

Nonetheless, the facts, as the Countess saw them, and now explained, were that labourers on the Henham estate were able to rent good homes with three bedrooms, a kitchen, a parlour and a quarter of an acre of land for a garden for as little as 1s 9d a week. As a result, in her 'personal experience', the labourer, 'marries, settles in a cottage near his work and whilst he has three or four children is very comfortable'.[36] The Rous family, like other landed families across Suffolk, also supported numerous clothing, coal and shoe clubs on the estate, gave their labourers dinners and treats at Christmas and harvest-time, and kept up the local school entirely at their own expense. Meanwhile, on the Helmingham estate, the Dowager Lady Tollemache gave three shillings each October to every child in the villages of Helmingham and Framsden who belonged to the village clothing club, as well as 6d to those in the boot club and 1s 6d to those in the coal club. She also provided the poorer families in Helmingham with venison soup during the winter months and plum pudding at Christmas. Subsequently, in 1899, Lord and Lady Tollemache gave away 61 stones of beef and 508 lbs of plum pudding at the village school (built by John Tollemache in 1853 at a cost of £1,200) to the cottage tenants on the estate. A further 75 lbs of plum pudding was also sent to the allotment holders. In the Countess of Stradbroke's opinion, therefore, there was no reason for labourers to become involved in taking action against their employers, hence her and others' firm conviction that the dispute was the result of outside agitation.[37] The emphasis on highlighting the goodwill shown by the aristocracy toward the labourer is perhaps indicative of how edgy the former were regarding the dispute. There was a real sense that this was the thin end of a Radical wedge being driven into the countryside to prise apart a rural society glued together by deference. Hence this unusual story in the *The Times* regarding egg-stealing: apparently, a gentleman confronted 40 to 50 men taking eggs from one of Lord Rendlesham's coverts. When it was pointed out that these belonged to His Lordship, they replied that they had as much right to them as anybody else. This was described as an act of 'open defiance' and was blamed on the antagonism which had arisen as a result of the 'Lock-Out' – conveniently ignoring the problems associated with game preservation.[38]

The question that confronted landowners was how best to counter the unrest being stirred up by these 'Radical agitators'. Sir Edward Kerrison was particularly fearful that, unless such agitation was countered, landowners risked allowing a ferment to take hold that could ultimately 'humble both the occupier and the landlord'.[39] In his view, landlords had to strive to remind their labourers of the benefits they derived from deferring to the leadership of the larger farmers, the parson and the squire. In so doing, landlords would be capitalizing on the ties of paternalistic affinity which clearly existed between landlords and their labourers in Suffolk and which had led many labourers to turn to their landlords for support during the strike. But, whilst Sir Edward Kerrison felt a moral duty 'to protect the labourer who occupies my house' from being abused by the farmer, he also had a duty to protect the interests of 'the tenant farmer who puts his capital on my land'. Consequently, Sir Edward was keen to find a settlement which was acceptable to both sides: 'What I want is justice to both parties, and not justice to one alone.'[40]

Sir Edward first sought to convince his tenants of the inexpediency of locking-out labourers where no advance in wages had been demanded.

Rather than joining in actions which were clearly designed to crush the
N. A. L. U., Sir Edward managed to persuade his tenants to recognize the
Union and to campaign instead for a modification of its strike rules, in
particular the rule vesting the power of ordering strikes at a week's notice in
the hands of the union's executive. This rule was regarded as intolerable, as
it left farmers not knowing from one week to the next whether they would
be subject to arbitrary strike action. As this was deemed unjust, Sir Edward
suggested that at least one month's notice ought to be given prior to any
action and that this power should be vested in district associations drawn
from no more than five parishes. Turning to his labourers, Sir Edward
appealed to them not to provoke the tenantry by going on strike for, while
there were bad farmers just as there were bad landlords, there were many
farmers who had the 'kindest feelings towards their labourers' yet were being
driven to distraction by arbitrary strikes.

Having set out his stall, Sir Edward attended a meeting in the village of
Hoxne at which delegates from the N. A. L. U. were present. However,
beforehand, he preceded the meeting with a dinner at which one of his
tenants carved the joints of beef that had been laid on. After this dinner, Sir
Edward then called the meeting to order and addressed his labourers:

> It would be odd indeed if a meeting should be held in the village close
> to my house, and I [should not attend] . . . I, who am constantly
> among you, who am to be seen in this village and the surrounding
> villages almost every day among the labouring people, who speak to
> them, and who live among them, and who know more about them
> than I do about any other class around me . . . [and who can see] that,
> although the farmer may suffer, the labourers will suffer [as a result of
> any strike action] ten times more.[41]

Sir Edward now began to outline what the labourers would be placing at risk
if they decided to join in the actions of the N. A. L. U.: 'Since you have lived
in the parish of Hoxne, have you ever known the poor people of this parish
so contented and so well off as at the present moment? . . . You want the
landlords to build you better cottages and to give you a bit of land . . . [this]
I have endeavoured to do.' Yet, no landlord could be expected to provide
such amenities if the countryside was in a state of upheaval and so 'if terrible
suffering and privation was to be avoided, there had to be a recognition of
the need for peace.'[42] In apparent confirmation of the affinity referred to by
Thompson, Clifford records that, throughout, Sir Edward's speech was
received by the men in an excellent spirit and was followed by three hearty

cheers for Sir Edward and Lady Caroline Kerrison. This led Clifford to conclude:

> I cannot but think that had the example thus set in Hoxne been followed elsewhere, and that if farmers as well as landlords had mixed more with the men, and had tried to understand these Agricultural Unions in their earlier history, objectionable rules might have been modified, employers and employed would have shown greater sympathy and respect for each other, and much of the bitterness of this quarrel might have been avoided.[43]

In highlighting the benefits that his labourers derived from their adherence to the squirearchy and tenantry, Sir Edward was able to quell any enthusiasm for going on strike and to ensure that around Hoxne, at least, the worst effects of the dispute were not felt. Writing to *The Times* in April 1874, Sir Edward declared, 'In a desert of strikes and lock-outs my property forms a sort of oasis.'[44] In other words, the ties of paternalistic affinity, which undoubtedly existed on many other estates across Suffolk, could give landlords considerable leverage over the choices made by the labourers who worked on their estates. It was, therefore, against this backdrop of lock-outs that the Earl of Stradbroke established the Suffolk Provident Society. The aim of the Society was, according to William Long (who owned 2,800 acres near Saxmundham), to let labourers see that the squirearchy and the tenantry rather than the N. A. L. U. were 'his best friends, and ready at all times to promote his welfare'. They would, according to the Earl, 'save the industrious labourers from . . . [ending] his . . . days in the workhouse' by creating what Lord Rendlesham termed a society to assist labourers 'to provide for themselves a comfortable maintenance in sickness and . . . [old] age'.[45] In addition to the above, the idea also received backing from Lord Gwydyr, F. S. Corrance, Sir George Broke-Middleton, Lord Henniker, Lord Mahon, Lord Waveney, Sir William Rose and the Rev Edmund Holland.

The Society was clearly an attempt to build bridges with the labourer given the fact that, beyond the oasis of Sir Edward Kerrison's estates, labourers were prepared to combine against the farmer. But by involving themselves with an organization which *both* farmers and the landlords (to whom the farmer appealed for support) perceived as harbouring a Radical agenda, most of these labourers quickly found themselves subject to far more punitive measures. Hence, the Countess of Stradbroke's appeal to the Bishop of Manchester to 'earnestly . . . reconsider this subject and to give good advice to those poor deluded men who are going to throw away [their] homes, happiness and contentment' by setting themselves against their masters.[46]

The move by some landlords toward more overtly coercive action, tempered by the olive branch of a Provident Society, again stemmed from the belief that the speed with which unionism spread through Suffolk was due to the work of outside agitators stirring up labourers with their Radical propaganda. This view of things completely ignored the fact that support for the N. A. L. U. fluctuated from village to village and was, in fact, frequently no more than a response to often quite localized differences between masters and men. Yet even a liberal-minded landlord like Lord Walsingham was concerned at the involvement of Radical Liberal MPs in the movement. Their interference in the dispute was, in his opinion, 'as ridiculous . . . as it would be if . . . farmers . . . interposed [themselves] between the Manchester cotton-spinners and their hands'.[47] It was, however, Joseph Arch's claim that the aristocracy had, through the use of enclosures, stolen 7,000,000 acres from the people which, more than anything else, appeared to confirm what many landlords already believed. Namely, agricultural trade unions were no more than a vehicle for Radical elements determined to bring about their overthrow through the eventual 'confiscation of property'.[48]

Many landowners were therefore extremely hostile toward the N. A. L. U. and sided with their tenants against their labourers. The Marquess of Bristol was so incensed by Joseph Arch's remarks that he felt obliged to point out that these enclosures had been based upon Acts of Parliament and that, as such, 'The title to such land was as sacred as though it had been bought in the market.'[49] He also joined with the Rev E. R. Benyon, Colonel A. M. Wilson, and Captain E. R. S. Bence, and many other large landowners in the West of the County in offering his 'hearty concurrence' with the resolution passed by the West Suffolk Farmers' Defence Association to:

> have nothing whatever to do with delegates, and [to] . . . decline the overtures of independent supporters of the union, till the striking power was expunged from the union rules; till the voice of Mr. Arch . . . was no more heard to influence the men; and till the *Labourers' Chronicle* was suppressed.[50]

Thus, we see the two sides of English landlordism. On the one hand, Sir Edward Kerrison, by pulling on the deferential ties which clearly existed between himself and his labourers, was able to quell the dispute around Hoxne before matters got out of hand. But where strikes did occur, where the labourers did show themselves ready to opt out of their deferential arrangements with the aristocracy, landowners were prepared to withdraw their benevolence and side with their tenants against their labourers in seeking to crush the N. A. L. U. The Marquess of Bristol explained his decision to support the actions taken by his tenants as follows:

> I have spoken to several large occupiers in the county who are all much interested in the lock-out, and they all say it is the only way of counteracting the work of the Union. I am glad to say that in every instance in this district in which the men have struck by order of the Union, the farmers, by working themselves, by help received from neighbours, and by means of the few men who stuck to them, have had most of the men back on the master's terms.[51]

In the end, the bulk of those who went on strike were forced to come back to work on their master's terms or leave the district, as the finances of the N. A. L. U. buckled under the strain of having to support the large numbers of men thrown out of work by their employers.

With defeat, and the collapse, for now, of combination as a form of collective protection, the agricultural labourer had to return to the older, deferential model on offer from their landlords. Clearly, the investment of tens of thousands of pounds by Sir Edward Kerrison in new cottages, schools and churches in and around the village of Hoxne gave him immense leverage over his labourers. It could, of course, be used to exert varying degrees of pressure. At one level, paternalism was intended as a palliative to keep the labouring population quiescent and content. It was also designed to propagate a sense of affinity between labourers and their landlords, which landlords could manipulate to dampen down any unrest – as at Hoxne. At another level, it could also be deeply coercive, in the sense that landlords could threaten to withdraw their benevolence from those who chose to defy their landlords and employers. Such overt coercion, accompanied no doubt by actual evictions, was what Dunbabin termed the unacceptable face of English landlordism. But there was still much to be gained out of the deferential model.

From the aristocracy's position, cottage building and the provision of allotments was discussed in terms of proto-social engineering, especially after the 1865 Union Chargeability Act finally abolished any lingering need for a close parish where cottages were allowed to decay or were pulled down. The offer of a good cottage with an allotment was viewed as an ideal mechanism to imbue labourers with the virtues of industry, sobriety and thrift. Successful examples of this, as at Helmingham, were therefore lauded.

Frederic Impey in his Report to the Royal Commission inquiring into the Housing of the Working Classes records a conversation he had with Lord Tollemache who 'told me that when he first succeeded to the administration of the estate the condition of the labourers was excessively bad: that the cottages were in a ruinous and tumbledown condition, that the men were of notoriously bad character and that the whole district was in a sad state', hence the cottage rebuilding programme and the three acres of land for cultivation and to keep a cow and some pigs. Impey's concluding paragraph is even more illuminating: 'It was most interesting to find on private inquiry from the employers of these men, that though objecting at first to their becoming small farmers on their own account, they have found by the experience that the added responsibility had been the means of improving the men in every way. They were stated to be more trustworthy and more easily managed'[52] – hardly surprising, the labourer now had something to lose! A similar pattern can be seen on the Oakley Park estate. As all the cottages that had been allowed to fall into a 'bad state of repair' in the early nineteenth century were repaired by Sir Edward Kerrison, there was a 'very remarkable' improvement in the habits of Sir Edward's people.[53]

Of course, cottage building and the provision of allotments did not produce robots, as the popularity of the N. A. L. U. reveals. Nor does the popularity of the Union expose a deep antipathy toward the landlord but rather to the farmer. It was the farmer after all who opposed labourers having allotments for fear it would make them work-shy. But labourer antipathy, particularly when unionized, towards the farmer, forced the landlord to protect the farmer whilst at the same time trying to take the edge off any counter-measures through a gesture such as the establishment of a Provident Society. Similarly, if we take the issue of allotments as another example, Burchardt indicates, given that the social equilibrium of rural parishes was delicate, 'The implicit bargain on which landowner benevolence rested was precisely that requests for assistance made within the language and framework of deference would be received sympathetically.'[54]

Further, as many estates spilled over into the more open parishes, the result was an aristocracy in a position to meet the applications for an allotment from labourers in these parishes as well as in the close parishes within the borders of the great estates. That they were prepared to do so appears in evidence in a report published, in 1892, into the use made by the Boards of Guardians for the Hartismere, Hoxne, Plomesgate, Samford, Sudbury and Woodbridge Unions of the 1887 Allotments Act. In each case, the Board reported that the Act had proved unnecessary as the applications received by them had been successfully met through 'voluntary arrangements'. In the case of the Woodbridge Union an application under the Act from the parish of Charsfield was turned down on the grounds the Board 'saw no cause to interfere, as it was shown that allotments could be had by voluntary arrangement'[55] – as Lord Tollemache had predicted. The Wangford and Thingoe Boards also reported that the Act was 'not required'. In 1908, W. Hasbach concluded that the Poor Law Boards had proved much less suited to carrying out the provisions of the Allotments legislation 'than private persons who . . . provided allotments of their own free will'[56] which was precisely the way the landowners who controlled the more rural Boards wanted to keep things. Again, the comparative failure of the Liberal land reform legislation of 1907–8 was due to the unattractive terms under which it was offered to labourers by Tory County Councils.[57] On the other hand, the Blything Board of Guardians, again as Lord Tollemache had predicted, were prepared to use the allotments legislation to spur the more recalcitrant landlords into action. Overall, however, voluntary arrangements were enough to meet the level of demand, although as W. L. B. Freuer, agent to Sir Edward Kerrison, observed, there was always 'great competition' when one of his allotments fell vacant.[58]

The value of a cottage with a small garden was encapsulated by an allotment holder on the Barton Hall estate who stated, in the 1840s, that a piece of land 'helps us in so many ways: a bit here, a bit there. It helps the children and feeds the pigs and fowls. It is the best thing done for a poor man'.[59] The landlord's generosity brought with it expectations of the labourer. If the cultivation of an allotment was neglected or if the allotment holder was convicted of poaching, a quit notice was immediately issued. According to the oral testimony recorded by George Ewart Evans concerning life on the Helmingham Hall estate prior to the First World War, 'the owd Lord' regularly went round the estate inspecting his allotments. All the rows of vegetables had therefore to be 'pointed inwards from the road so the Lord could see the rows were straight and properly weeded'; they had to be 'or else you had to go'.[60]

Similarly, children were expected to learn 'industrious habits' by working alongside their parents on an allotment. Kersey Cooper believed that the 'united industry' of parents and children trained boys to 'industrious habits which are not forgotten in manhood', a point echoed by Sir Henry Bunbury who observed that, instead of idling about the parish being a nuisance, boys on his estate were 'brought up in industry and learnt its advantages in early days'.[61] This was the bargain: the labourers had to follow a strict code of behaviour, work hard and doff their forelocks when addressed by their so-called 'betters', but in exchange landowners gave their labourers an allotment and a cottage (with rents low enough to indirectly compensate for the low wages paid by the farmer) topped-off with a pudding at Christmas. That many labourers preferred to live in a more open village is hardly surprising, nor should it be surprising that many others on the great estates and many of those in the more open parishes in the border country between the great estates were prepared to stick with the gentry. Besides, after 1884, they had an outlet to express their dissatisfaction – they had the vote. The fact that labourers on the great estates continued to vote with their Tory landlords for the Conservative party's preferred candidate and the fact that, on occasion, labourers in the more open villages could be lobbied by the great landowners into voting Conservative is indicative of the electoral pull of benevolent despotism in the Victorian countryside. Of course, there were simply not enough votes in this to propel the landowner into Parliament – unlike the old days of courting the tenantry – but there were enough here, by working with fellow landowners, to potentially sway a seat the way of the Conservative party, especially as cottage building continued up to the Great War.

Whilst the number of new cottages being erected was below the levels achieved in the era of 'high' farming, when cottages were springing up across the county, on those estates where the landlord was insulated against the effects of the agricultural depression cottages continued to be built, often in considerable numbers. On the Elveden estate, Lord Iveagh rebuilt Elveden village. Similarly, on the Orwell Park estate Colonel Pretyman 'spent great sums on cottages, of which he had built about a hundred during the twelve years that he had held the estate' because 'given good houses and gardens [good] men could be found'.[62] When coupled to the success of the voluntary system of allotment provision, the construction of cottages with gardens would appear to explain why both the land reform campaigns of the Land Restoration League and the Land Nationalization Society misfired. Like the League, with their distinctive red vans, who began their campaign in Suffolk in 1890, the Society, which painted its vans yellow and began its campaign in 1891, encountered grass roots indifference among farm workers.[63] On the other hand, land reform continued to be a powerful generator of Liberal energy, if only they could agree on what land reform actually meant. While all agreed on the removal of the fiscal privileges enjoyed by landowners, hence Harcourt's 1894 Budget introducing death duties, there was the real problem of what to do with the land itself: ought it be nationalized or should local authorities have the power to compulsorily purchase land and lease it to labourers as allotments or small holdings? Should landownership be abolished or more widely diffused?[64]

However, the extension of the franchise in 1884 made it almost inevitable that local government would also be reformed along democratic lines. This involved the transference, in 1888, by the Conservatives, of administrative power from Quarter Sessions to new democratically elected County Councils. This was followed in 1894, by the creation, by the Liberals, of Parish and District Councils and the abolition of 'plural' voting in elections to the Board of Guardians. The Liberals also looked to legislation (in 1892 and 1895) to give these local bodies the power to push forward that part of the land reform programme advocating that local authorities have the power to provide labourers with allotments and small holdings, but in this they were thwarted by the continuing prominence of local landowners in local government. The continuing willingness of the labourer to defer to the leadership of the aristocracy in local government and to vote for them remained based on the aristocracy's willingness to voluntarily provide labourers in their Counties, Districts or Parishes with allotments, cottages and gardens. In the next chapter, we need to look at the implications of deferential voting patterns in local government. If the great landlords were unable to guarantee themselves a seat in Parliament but could still expect a seat in the County Council chamber, does this not reveal the lobbying power they deployed on behalf of the Conservative Central Offices' preferred candidate at a general election?

5

LANDOWNERS AND LOCAL GOVERNMENT

According to G. D. Phillips, the Acts of 1884 and 1888 had a profound effect on families who had formerly governed 'as of right'. As Lady Winterbourne remarked to Lord Maxwell, 'We have lost our sense of right in our place and position – at least I find I have.'[1] This suggests unwillingness on the part of local landowners to remain actively involved in local government but, on the other hand, it should not be forgotten that most were still Justices of the Peace. These judicial responsibilities remained in place long after JPs' administrative functions had been removed. In addition, up to 1911, JPs were still nominated by the Lord Lieutenant, who in turn was selected by the Prime Minister from among the leading landed families in each county. But was the gentry's fall from power quite as dramatic as some contemporaries had feared it would be following the passage of the County Councils Bill under, ironically, the Conservative Prime Minister, the Marquess of Salisbury? Surely landowners were bound to be in the minority on these new councils, especially as the majority of farm workers lived in 'open' villages where the gentry were more remote figures, who had traditionally taken 'little or no interest in either the housing or [indeed] welfare of the inhabitants'.[2] In these villages, contact with the gentry had always proceeded in a far more official, and far less informal, manner.

Up to the 1880s, the landed gentry, being the local factotums on whom the government depended for ensuring the good order of their districts, were also expected to involve themselves in the administration of local government. This was because, prior to the reforms of the late 1880s, local government was in the hands of the magistracy, who held both a judicial and an administrative function. Since JPs were in effect held responsible for running the country, they were expected to be men of some standing in their localities. As a result, the local squire and his fellow gentry tended to predominate on the magistrates' Bench. Having said this, the gentry who sat on the Suffolk Bench did not possess a straightforward numerical advantage over their fellow JPs. The Return of Justices of the Peace for England and Wales records there were 263 individuals, who having been nominated, had taken their oath of Commission and sat as JPs for Suffolk in 1887. Of these, 54 or only 21 per cent of the total were large landowners. In addition, not all landlords on the Commission of the Peace chose to attend Sessions. In 1887, out of the 54 landed JPs, 37 per cent had failed to attend Quarter Sessions during the previous twelve months. On the other hand, JPs were nominated by the Lord Lieutenant, who, as Sir Arthur Arnold noted, was as a matter of course almost always a peer. In other words, non-landed JPs were nominated by a landowner usually in consultation with his fellow landowners.[3]

In these circumstances, the gentry remained the 'paramount figures in the English countryside',[4] as it was largely on their recommendation that nominees were approved. Prior to the reforms of the late 1880s, therefore, it was the aristocracy and gentry influencing the classes who habitually followed them such as the clergy, (of whom 36 sat on the Bench in 1887), the lesser gentry (those with estates under 1,000 acres) and the retired military (there were 22 individuals who held a commission sitting as JPs in 1887) who dispensed justice and 'good' government in the county. Landlords were also perfectly placed to bolster their position locally, by either being lauded for their leniency or feared for their harshness. Frederick Barne chose to act leniently. In a letter sent to his son, he wrote, 'I have summoned William Pearce to appear at the Petty Sessions. He is quite in my power, but he shall escape with a small fine.'[5]

By contrast, a report in the *Suffolk Mercury* described most of the landlords sitting on the judicial Bench as exhibiting all the worst prejudices appertaining to 'the condition of [a] . . . country gentleman'. These prejudices were based on the conviction that the ownership of broad acres had granted them the 'divine right' to administer justice and to 'act in the place of Her Majesty absolutely in that portion of Her Majesty's dominions which lies around his own domain' with a view to keeping 'the common people in order'.[6] This was especially true in cases where the offence touched upon their almost feudal rights and privileges as landowners, the classic example being that of poaching. Having spent considerable sums of money rearing thousands of game-birds for their annual shoots landlords were determined to prevent their investment ending up on the kitchen tables of the labourers living in villages bordering their estates. Queen Victoria, on the other hand, was less enthusiastic. In 1878, she wrote to Duleep Singh chiding him for his excessive preservation of game on the Elveden estate: 'I have for some time wished to mention to you, as it is unpopular in the country . . . the great extent to which you preserve game – it is very expensive and much disliked for many reasons in the country.'[7]

It was under these conditions that labourers in the more 'open' villages often came into contact with the great landowners. In cases involving poaching, the usual course of action was for the labourer to be summoned before Petty Sessions (which in Suffolk were held weekly, fortnightly or monthly) and fined or imprisoned according to the provisions laid down by the various Game Laws. Under the 1862 Prevention of Poaching Act, the 'poor man on foot with bulging pockets' could be stopped and searched by police officers if they suspected an offence had been committed. As Section Two of the Act states, 'It shall be lawful for any Constable or Police Officer . . . to search any person whom he may have good cause to suspect of coming from any land where he shall have been unlawfully in search or pursuit of Game.'[8] Faced by a landlord on the Bench, the labourer was now exposed to the additional penalties that would be imposed by his own landlord. On the Culford estate, those convicted of poaching were also denied employment by the Rev E. R. Benyon and served with a notice to quit their cottages. By contrast, the view of many ordinary countrymen was that game-birds such as pheasants and partridges, together with other game defined by the Act such as woodcocks, snipes, hares and rabbits, had no legal owner, any more than 'thrushes or blackbirds do'.[9]

This was the correct interpretation of the law, as the offence in poaching was in the act of trespassing on private property in pursuit of game and not in the taking of wild animals that could have no legal owner. Consequently, the Game Laws were held in contempt by countrymen, who failed to see anything morally reprehensible about poaching. In the eyes of the rural magistracy, however, the 'crime' remained the theft of their furred and feathered property which they had spent considerable time and money rearing. They utilized the full powers of the Bench to prosecute without mercy those indicted for poaching. Of the 319 individuals who came before the Bench in Suffolk, in 1869, 318 were eventually prosecuted, giving the county a prosecution rate of 99 per cent; this compares with the situation elsewhere in East Anglia (see Table 3). As R. M. Garnier states, 'When a landed proprietor goes to considerable expense to confine, breed, rear and preserve naturally wild animals, it would be decidedly unjust to refuse him rights of property over them.'[10] In other words, control of the Bench gave the landed gentry an unparalleled level of control over the lives of those living in the Suffolk countryside. As Tsar Alexander once remarked, the next best thing to being Tsar of Russia was to be an English country gentleman.[11]

Table 3: Convictions under the Game Acts for the Year 1869 in the Eastern Counties

County	Total	Summary Convictions			Total Convictions	Overall Prosecution Rate	On Indictment	
		Trespassing in Day-Time Pursuit of Game	Night Poaching & Destroying Game	Illegally Selling or Buying Game			Poaching Act (1862)	Being Out Armed, Taking Game & Assaulting Game Keepers
Suffk	319	298	13	4	315	99%	3	1
Essex	310	298	3	–	301	97%	9	–
Herts	302	259	23	–	282	93%	15	5
Norfk	258	233	–	–	233	90%	22	3
Cambs	110	92	11	–	103	94%	6	1
Total	1,299	1,180	50	4	1234	–	55	10

(Source: 'Returns of the number of convictions under the Game Laws in separate counties in England and Wales for the year 1869', *British Parliamentary Papers* LVII [1870], p. 105).

The magistracy also had a heavy administrative burden as the volume of business coming before the Bench rose alarmingly during the latter half of the nineteenth century. Over time, Quarter Sessions were made responsible for supervising the mass of overlapping jurisdictions created by the establishment of Poor Law Unions and Boards of Guardians, Highway Boards, School Boards and Sanitary Districts. As a result, Quarter Sessions, meeting at Ipswich and Bury St Edmunds, came to resemble nominated county Parliaments under the supervisory control of the gentry. When, in 1869, the Court of Quarter Sessions in East Suffolk appointed a Select Committee to consider the duties and salary of a new County Bridge Surveyor, the 12 man Committee included Colonel Sir R. A. S. Adair (Chairman of Sessions), Charles Austin, J. G. Sheppard, the Hon. John Henniker-Major MP, Frederick Doughty, H. A. S. Bence, Charles Berners and William Beeston Long. [12]

Beyond the Committee rooms, in the actual Courtroom, the Chairmanship of the Bench in both East and West Suffolk was also monopolized by members of the landed aristocracy and gentry. In East Suffolk, the period during which Charles Austin QC was Chairman of Quarter Sessions was regarded by the author of an article that appeared in the *Suffolk Mercury* in 1875 as:

> a golden time [for] public business in this part of the county . . . He looked straight before him at the business to be done, and was down without mercy on the slightest sign of wandering or irrelevancy. And he got through business with a rare expedition and with a singular absence of mistakes [and with] . . . none of that prejudice of property . . . which so often strikes the impartial spectator of the proceedings of [the] Courts of Justice in the county.[13]

Austin was succeeded as Chairman by Lord Gwydyr, who owned the 2,000 acre Stoke Park estate near Ipswich. However, he quickly gained a reputation in the *Suffolk Mercury* for a scrupulous attention to detail which meant proceedings became so protracted that 'magistrates who wanted to go home to dinner . . . would sigh for half-an-hour of the Chairmanship of the Squire of Brandeston'.[14] Subsequently, in 1904, the post was held by Lord Rendlesham. In the same year, the Chairmen of Sessions for the Western Division of the County were Colonel Nathaniel Barnardiston and the Hon H. W. Lowry-Corry – the youngest son of the third Earl of Belmore and owner of the 2,000 acre Edwardestone Hall estate. Lord Henniker, meanwhile, was also one of the Chairmen of East Suffolk Sessions for 'many years', there often being more than one Chairman of Sessions at any given time.[15]

Of course, unlike the situation at Westminster, the extension of the franchise in 1884 failed to give the mass of the labouring population living in Suffolk any say in the choice of those attending these nominated Quarter Sessional Parliaments. Given this anomaly, it was perhaps inevitable that a system based on the nomination of JPs by the Lord Lieutenant, in consultation with the gentry, would have to be reformed. As the Marquess of Salisbury observed, 'Representative bodies are the fashion of the day, and against a fashion it is almost impossible to argue'.[16] Thus it was that, in 1888, Salisbury brought forward a Local Government Bill, setting up elected County Councils in each administrative county in England and Wales. Under the County Councils Act, County Councillors, elected for a term of three years, assumed responsibility for all administrative and financial business formerly handled by the magistracy in Quarter Sessions. In so doing, Salisbury hoped to pre-empt the introduction of more radical proposals by the Liberal party. But how did the Act apply in Suffolk, which for centuries had been divided into the administrative divisions of Eastern and Western Suffolk? Secondly, how successful were the resident aristocracy and gentry in adjusting to the new representative nature of local government?

Following their party's lead, the new County Councils were readily agreed to by the Conservative Members of Parliament sitting for Suffolk. There was, however, heated debate in the county and in the Commons on the issue of whether there should be one unitary authority for the whole county. This issue was first raised on July 13th 1888, when Lord Francis Hervey (the member for Bury St Edmunds) moved an amendment to the Local Government Bill, calling for the insertion of the words 'and the eastern and western divisions of Suffolk'. In so doing, he hoped to secure for the Western Division of Suffolk 'that position as a separate county, and that power of administrative independence, which, time out of mind, it had enjoyed'.[17] Supporting his proposal were many former members of the House of Commons, including Mr Hardcastle, Mr Biddell, Mr Rodwell and Sir Thomas Thornhill.

On the other side of the debate was the Tory landowner Colonel Robert Lloyd-Anstruther of Hintlesham Hall, described in the *Suffolk Mercury* as 'a gentleman of unstinted honour – of undoubted Conservative principles – [and] of excellent blood'.[18] Together with his fellow MPs from East Suffolk, Anstruther opposed the amendment on the grounds that one unitary authority would create a far more economical system of local administration:

It was [he observed] only thirty years ago that there used to be four Quarter Sessions in Suffolk, and four separate rating authorities; but now they had succeeded by Act of Parliament in altering this, which alteration had turned out to the great advantage of the county both in respect of efficiency and economy. They had now one Chief Constable, one gaol, one lunatic asylum, and the magistrates were in the Commission of the Peace for the whole of the county, while the Quarter Sessions were held at Ipswich and Bury St Edmunds, but were adjourned to the latter place.[19]

Keeping Suffolk divided, as envisaged by Lord Francis' amendment, would, in his opinion, 'entail the most unnecessary burden on the ratepayers of the county of Suffolk'.[20] This was a point of particular concern for landowners who were understandably alarmed at the thought of having to pay higher local rates out of what were, by the late 1880s, greatly reduced agricultural incomes. Sir Savile Crossley (the member for Lowestoft) was similarly concerned at what he felt would be the inevitable inefficiencies that would arise from having two County Councils. Speaking in support of the amendment, Edward Greene (the member for Stowmarket) countered that 'if a poll were taken in the Western Division of Suffolk . . . few of the inhabitants would be in favour of the county being one.'[21] Whilst Greene's intervention came too late to sway the debate – the amendment being defeated by 157 votes to 130 – this was far from being the final act in the drama.

Three weeks later, the Marquess of Bristol sought to amend the Act as it passed through the House of Lords. This time the amendment was opposed by Lord Henniker, who had been actively involved in the business of local government as Chairman of Quarter Sessions in East Suffolk for more than eighteen years. Lord Henniker believed that the Marquess of Bristol's intervention was purely a matter of sentiment. Moreover, in his experience, opinion in East Suffolk was unanimously in favour of one County Council for the whole of the county. Lord Gwydyr was similarly convinced that the inhabitants of North, East and South Suffolk were practically unanimous in their desire for one unitary authority. Then there were the financial aspects to consider. Rateable values in East Suffolk were rising as a result of the construction of the east coastline of the Great Eastern Railway. East Suffolk was, in consequence and in Henniker's opinion, the 'improving part of the county' while West Suffolk, being 'purely agricultural', was as everyone knew, 'decreasing . . . in value'. Amalgamation would, therefore, allow West Suffolk to profit from the increased rateable value of Eastern Suffolk, whilst sharing in the enormous savings which Colonel Barnardiston (as Chairman of West Suffolk Quarter Sessions) also believed would ensue from joint action.[22]

But while sentiment may well have played a part in the Marquess of Bristol's decision to press ahead with the amendment, he was also reflecting the views of the magistrates and ratepayers in the west of the county. They looked to him as the leading Conservative magnate in the Western Division and as Lord Lieutenant of the County to exercise his influence in the House of Lords on their behalf on the issue of 'Home Rule' for West Suffolk. Far from seeing the potential benefits and savings envisaged by Lord Henniker, the Marquess of Bristol and his supporters were fearful that much higher rates might be imposed on the whole county by their more prosperous neighbours in the East. Crucially, the Marquess of Salisbury, having received a deputation from West Suffolk, was inclined towards the position of 'his Friend', the Marquess of Bristol, whom he believed had successfully made out his case.[23] With Salisbury's backing, the amendment was passed by 59 votes to 20.

Two points are of great significance here. Firstly, the leading players in this debate are all landowners who have an opinion on an issue that pertains to what they considered to be their field of expertise, namely, local government. Secondly, at no time do they question the far more fundamental change inherent in this piece of legislation: the significant diminution in the overall level of influence previously wielded by the landed gentry over a formerly nominated system of local government. This, of course, is in keeping with the junior partner role adopted by relatively impoverished landlords in a democratic era *vis à vis* the Conservative party. As Lord Henniker makes plain, whilst the Bill 'did away to a great extent with the powers of Quarter Sessions' and, by implication, with the aristocratic structure of local government, 'No one of their Lordships would . . . for a moment [wish to oppose the policies of a Conservative Government, and risk alienating ordinary voters in the countryside by bringing] . . . such an argument forward as an argument against the actual passing of the measure.'[24] Having said that, was the Act as damaging to the interests of the landed elite as many contemporaries feared? In other words, were the resident aristocracy and gentry, given their obvious sense of expertise in the arena of local government, able to adapt and gain election to the new County Councils?

Ostensibly, the transfer of administrative power away from Quarter Sessions to the newly elected County Councils marked a decisive weakening of the landed elite's power to influence the conduct of affairs in their localities. Diehard supporters of the old system were convinced that these changes heralded the disappearance of the larger landowners from local affairs and the direct transfer of power into the hands of the middle classes. Salisbury was similarly convinced that many squires would feel a sense of 'unutterable wrong' suffered at the hands of a government supposedly sympathetic to patrician concerns. On the other hand, he firmly believed that having made local government 'more acceptable to the people', the gentry's circumstances and ability would still secure them sufficient representation on these new bodies.[25]

Salisbury's prediction was soon vindicated. In the aftermath of the first county council elections, in 1889, nearly half of the newly-elected councillors were magistrates. Furthermore, around two-thirds of counties elected the Chairman of Quarter Sessions or the Lord Lieutenant as Chairman, thereby confirming Liberal suspicions that the change would be more one of form than substance. In East Suffolk, the *Suffolk Chronicle* reported that:

> With courtesy and despatch, Lord Rendlesham proposed Lord Henniker to fill that position [as Chairman of East Suffolk County Council] – a proposition which, in view of the long services which his Lordship has rendered as senior Chairman of Quarter Sessions, could not fail to command unanimous support. In acknowledgement of the compliment, Lord Henniker spoke as became a leading member of the old body addressing the new.[26]

Indeed, in 1904, whilst only 32 of the 107 councillors elected to sit on East and West Suffolk County Councils were JPs and only 10 of these JPs were large landowners (see Table 4), landowners continued to be selected by their predominantly middle class colleagues to sit as the Chairmen of both East and West Suffolk County Council. In 1904, Colonel Nathaniel Barnardiston was the Chairman of West Suffolk County Council, whilst Lord Rendlesham had succeeded Lord Henniker as Chairman of East Suffolk County Council. Lord Rendlesham was, in turn, eventually succeeded by the third Earl of Stradbroke, who held the post in 1912, whilst the Chairmanship of West Suffolk County Council was held by the fourth Marquess of Bristol from about 1916 up to 1929. As Cannadine states:

> In the relative calm of the county council chamber, grandees . . . could still [act in] a patrician style no longer acceptable in the . . . Commons, or at the hustings. They were no longer [in many cases]

Table 4: Landowners in Local Government in Suffolk in the Early 1900s

East Suffolk County Council	West Suffolk County Council
Aldermen	Aldermen
Captain E.G. Pretyman, JP	Colonel Nathaniel Barnardiston
The Earl of Stradbroke	The Marquess of Bristol
The Rev J.F. Hervey	The Earl of Cadogan JP
	The Hon Henry Lowry-Corry
	Sir Edward Walter Greene Bt JP
	Lord Francis Hervey
	Sir William Hyde Parker Bt JP
	Sir William Cuthbert Quilter Bt JP
Councillors	Councillors
John Kendall Brooke JP	Sir William Brampton Gurdon
William Evelyn Long JP	Colonel Edward Mackenzie JP
Captain Charles Shuldham Schreiber JP	Duncan Parker JP
Commander EB Levett-Scrivener JP	Sir Joshua Thellusson Rowley Bt JP
George Rowland Holt-Wilson JP	Lord Charles Edward FitzRoy

(Source: *Kelly's Directory of the Counties of Cambridge, Norfolk and Suffolk* [London, 1904] pp. 15–17)

> powerful figures . . . but presented themselves instead as loyal countrymen, and masters of county business, who successfully justified their inherited broad acres by disinterested, non-contentious public service. Aloof, Olympian and detached, totally decent and totally incorruptible, they lent a tone of aristocratic grandeur to the proceedings, and elevated the whole level of county council business.[27]

Even more significantly, landowners were frequently among those recommended to sit on the key committees. In East Suffolk, in 1889, a Special Committee appointed Lord Henniker, Colonel Robert Anstruther, Lord Gwydyr, W. P. T. Phillips, R. J. Pettiward, Colonel George Tomline and the Rev Thomas Holt Wilson, to the General Purposes Committee. Lord Henniker, together with Colonel William Beeston Long and the Earl of Stradbroke, was also asked to consider sitting on the Finance Committee. The Rev Thomas Holt-Wilson, together with Lord Henniker, Lord Rendlesham, J. K. Brooke, Sir Alfred Sherlock Gooch and the Rev J. F. A. Hervey, were also recommended to sit on the Roads and Bridges Committee.[28]

More importantly, the fact that landowners continued to be elected at all is evidence of the residual attachment which continued to exist between landowners and the labourers living in certain wards, a phenomenon Beckett termed the strength of residual deference. It is also evidence of the fact that in rural districts the administration of local affairs had traditionally been associated with the landowning classes and, as a result, 'When a man of sufficient local prominence offered himself to serve on the county council . . . he was frequently elected without effort or opposition' [29] by labourers who were themselves in no position to actively participate in local government and were prepared to defer to the experience of their landlords in local administration. Besides, as George Ewart Evans recognized, 'Only very rarely is a wage earner able to serve on either a county or a rural district council . . . By the nature of their jobs, farm workers or small farmers are debarred . . . only moneyed or leisured people can afford to spend up to two days a week in local government work.'[30] The common belief, therefore, that the necessity of competing in elections would drive the landed classes from local government proved in many cases to be illusory as their labourers still voted for them. Once in the Council Chamber, whilst they found themselves outnumbered by the farmer, the shopkeeper and the tradesmen, residual deference continued to persist as, in Suffolk at least, they did not 'elbow aside' the gentry. As Evans again points out:

It is true that the old landowner class has, by and large ceased to have the great power it had at the beginning of the century, they would not be able to act . . . as they once did. Their real power has been diminished and public opinion is able to act as a brake on the misuse of power that still remains to them. Yet, a great deal of their former influence remains . . . out of a kind of social inertia, long after much of its reality has disappeared. This tendency is assisted by . . . the regard for status shown by the new men . . . moving out into the country . . . businessmen, professional men and old retired military men who are attracted to the old social hierarchy and hope there will be a place for them in it.[31]

Subsequently, in 1894, the Liberal party passed legislation establishing Parish and District Councils throughout England and Wales. The first Parish and District Council elections in 1894 were, however, also marked by the continuity of aristocratic influence. In 1898, the District Councillors sitting on Blything District Council included Commander E. B. Levett-Scrivener, Colonel G. L. Bence Lambert and J. K. Brooke. The influence of the 'old order' could still be felt even without the actual physical presence of local landowners around the Council table. This was because there were plenty of potential councillors among the groups who habitually followed the aristocracy and gentry for whom the labourer was prepared to vote in conjunction with their landlords. Thus, while Liberals lamented the fact that both Parish and District Councils were too weak and 'dominated by farmers and men of the rural middle classes' rather than by labourers (which explains why the Liberals 1895 allotments legislation misfired), most Conservative landowners, according to Phillips, 'professed pleasure with the elections and believed they could work very well with the new councillors'.[32] Interestingly, of the thirteen Chairmen of District Councils and five Mayors of Municipal Boroughs in East Suffolk in 1895, nine Chairmen and four Mayors were made JPs by the Lord Lieutenant, as were five of the eleven Chairmen of District Councils and one of the two Mayors of Municipal Boroughs in West Suffolk. This is interesting because it suggests a 'cosying up' of the new District Councillors with the 'old order' given that the magistracy was still in the hands of the great landowners.[33] In 1898, for instance, the members of Blything District Council sent the Earl of Stradbroke a letter congratulating him on his impending marriage.[34]

Despite the reforms of local government, the Petty and Quarter Sessional Benches in Criminal Jurisdiction continued to be staffed by JPs nominated by members of the aristocracy through their position as Lord Lieutenants. Whilst the nomination of magistrates by the Lord Lieutenant was a process apparently bereft of any overt political patronage, Liberals were concerned at the opportunities for such patronage to occur given the large number of Conservative Lieutenants. Ironically, in the early 1880s, most Lord Lieutenants had in fact been Liberals and more likely to be sympathetic to non-landed magistrates. Following the Liberals split over Irish Home Rule, however, most of these Whig magnates went over to the Unionists. This in turn enabled Conservative Prime Ministers to appoint a succession of Conservative or Unionist peers to 36 of the 42 English Lord Lieutenancies that became vacant between 1885 and 1905.[35] One of the first appointments was made in Suffolk, in 1886, following the death of the second Earl of Stradbroke, who had held the office of Lord Lieutenant since 1844.

Salisbury's preferred choice to replace him was the third Marquess of Bristol. Assailed as he was by his creditors, Lord Bristol was reluctant to take on the heavy responsibilities and expenses which being Lord Lieutenant entailed. Nevertheless, Salisbury went directly to the Queen, who agreed to his choice. Salisbury then presented Lord Bristol with what was in effect a *fait accompli*, to which he was forced to consent, as a letter dated 4th February 1886 makes clear:

> February 4th 1886.
>
> My Dear Lord Bristol,
> It becomes, on the death, or rather after the funeral, of Lord Stradbroke my duty to recommend to the Queen a successor to the Lord Lieutenancy of Suffolk.
> [Having been twice denied] I. . .took the liberty, without consulting you, of laying your name before Her Majesty, as that of the fittest person to succeed to the vacant office.
> She has been sincerely pleased to approve of the submission – and I hope I shall be fortunate in obtaining your approval also.
>
> Salisbury[36]

Having accepted Salisbury's offer, Bristol retained the Lieutenancy until his death in 1907. The previous year, in recognition of the 'valuable services . . . rendered to the County in this capacity', Bristol was presented 'in the presence of a brilliant gathering of the county families' with a portrait of himself by the Earl of Cadogan, who described Bristol as someone who had shown 'how duty can be performed with . . . self-denial', which echoes Cannadine's comments regarding the shift within the aristocracy toward public service at the local level after 1884.[37] The Liberal party viewed things somewhat differently and, when they returned to power in 1906, they were keen to bring to an end the 'power of socially exclusive selection' as well as the 'privilege and patronage' wielded by the predominantly pro-Conservative body of Lord Lieutenants.[38]

To begin with, the Liberals abolished the property qualification for those wishing to be JPs. Subsequently, in 1911, the power of Lord Lieutenants to appoint magistrates was also abolished. In his evidence to the Royal Commission to consider the whole question of appointments to the Bench, which he had set up, the Lord Chancellor Lord Loreburn, stated:

> Social life in most counties among those who are well-to-do is mainly Conservative . . . and it is natural that men should regard more

favourably those who are of the same opinions as themselves. I think
this largely accounts for the . . . constant disposition to prefer
Conservatives [rather than Liberals] in the recommendations made to
Lords Lieutenant.[39]

The Commission hoped that in future Lieutenants would 'attach no heed' to
the political or religious opinions of those whose names were put forward
and to ensure this the Commission recommended that Justices' Committees
be appointed by the Lord Chancellor to 'advise' the Lord Lieutenant. More
tellingly, it was also envisaged that the Lord Chancellor would 'consult' these
Committees regarding the 'fitness' of those candidates nominated by the
Lieutenant, thereby effectively bypassing him. But despite the tendency of
Liberal Lord Chancellors to bypass the body of predominantly pro-
Conservative Lord Lieutenants through the use of these advisory committees,
these committees were slow to be set up. Even as late as 1913, not all the
members of every committee had been appointed. In consequence, a
considerable degree of discretionary power remained in the hands of the Lord
Lieutenant.[40]

Consequently, the pre-1914 magisterial crop continued to reflect a bias
toward the 'old order'. On the other hand, since the 1880s, as in the County
Council Chamber or the Parish and District Council, there was an
increasingly diverse mix of backgrounds appearing on the Bench. In Suffolk,
the Return of Justices of the Peace for 1892, like its counterpart for 1887,
only refers to members of the clergy, members of the armed forces and
'Esquires'. The Return of Magistrates Appointed in Suffolk Between 1892
and 1894 reveals a similar pattern. If, however, the names that appear in this
Return are cross-referenced with the 20 whose names also appear in the
Return showing the magistrates appointed in Suffolk since May 1893 (see
Table 5), a far more diverse picture emerges.

This was because the latter Return, unlike those for 1887, 1892 and
1892–4, described their backgrounds. Thus, among those who described
themselves as gentlemen, there were in fact a provision merchant, a manure
manufacturer, a clothier, a timber merchant, a brewer and several large
owner-occupier farmers. Yet, snobbery being what it was and still is, they
chose to obscure their backgrounds by describing themselves elsewhere as
'Esquires'; clearly, the code of behaviour governing what was considered
'suitable for a gentleman' disguised a variety of social changes.[41]

Between 1892 and 1894, only four of the county's new magistrates were
large landowners: Captain Frederick Adair (who succeeded his father Sir
Hugh Adair in 1902), William Long of Hurts Hall, Sir William Hyde

Table 5: Return of Justices of the Peace Appointed in Suffolk 1893–1894

Name	Description
Adam Adams	Provision Merchant
Robert Hyatt Cook	Landowner/Farmer
James Oliver Fison	Manufacturer
William Nathaniel Whitmore	Manufacturer
Robert Mattingley	Clothier/Outfitter
Thomas Nunn Scarfe	Landowner/Farmer
John Amis Hempson	Landowner/Farmer
John Wm Read	Landowner/Farmer
Wm Evelyn Long	Landowner
Samuel Base	Retired Postmaster
William Palgrave Brown	Timber Merchant
Nathaniel Catchpole	Brewer
Charles Cooper	Retired Surgeon
Gerard Ferrand	Landowner
Samuel Thomas Harwood	Landowner/Farmer
George Edwards Jeaffreson	Surgeon
Sir Wm Hyde Parker Bt	Landowner
John Slater	Farmer
Clifford Smith	Merchant
George Rowland Holt-Wilson	Landowner

(Source: 'Return showing county Magistrates appointed since May 1893', *British Parliamentary Papers* LXXI [1894], p. 150).

Parker of Melford Hall and George Holt-Wilson of Redgrave Hall.[42] But, as Loreburn recognized, the aristocracy did not need to enjoy a straightforward numerical advantage to dominate the local Bench, especially as, after 1886, the Liberal party's growing obsession with reforming the ownership of private property in land tended to strengthen ties between landed society and the landowning rural middle class.[43] Thus it was that on the eve of the First World War, in 1913, when new Chairmen of East Suffolk Quarter Sessions had to be appointed following the death of Lord Gorrell and the decision of the Hon John de Grey (who succeeded his half brother to become the seventh Lord Walsingham in 1919) to stand down, those driving the selection process forward were all great landowners. De Grey's preferred candidates, to replace both himself and Lord Gorrell, were Charles Lomax and Robert White of Boulge Hall. In a letter sent to de Grey in May 1913, he states:

> To carry the matter through comfortably . . . I suggest you should instruct [Townshend] Cobbold [the Clerk of the Peace] on your behalf to circulate to the [Petty Sessional] Benches of the County asking them to send a representative to an informal meeting to consider the question of nominations at the [forthcoming Quarter] Session. This would give the general local opinion an opportunity of expressing itself and also [avoid] the appearance of having the appointment settled behind the back of the body of magistrates.[44]

Two points are worthy of note here. Firstly, the incumbent Chairmen were both landowners, as was one of the suggested replacements. Secondly, and of even greater significance, is the fact that three of the seven representatives chosen to attend the meeting, by the predominantly middle class membership of the petty sessional divisions in East Suffolk, were also landowners. The Samford Bench, for instance, sent Charles Berners of Woolverstone Hall, Blything sent J. K. Brooke of Sibton Park, whilst Stow sent Charles Pettiward of Finborough Hall. F. M. Youngman, meanwhile, who was sent by the Framlingham Bench, did so at the request of Captain Schreiber of Marlesford Hall, who was unable to attend. In other words, half of those who attended the meeting, which was chaired by Charles Berners, were in fact either members or representatives of the 'old order'. Unsurprisingly, both Charles Lomax and R. E. White were recommended for appointment. As Phillips states, 'Despite the gradual changes which had taken place in Quarter Sessions, appointment to the Bench and selection of the Chairmen of Quarter Sessions remained firmly in the hands of the traditional ruling classes throughout the period 1880–1914.'[45]

The continuing influence enjoyed by the aristocracy on the Bench, dispensing mercy or punishment, complemented the standing they continued to enjoy as munificent cottage builders and allotment providers. Moreover, in addition to their judicial duties, JPs also retained a prominent role in the administration of poor relief. This was because all JPs were *ex-officio* Poor Law Guardians; indeed, their meetings were generally held on the same day and in the same place as the Petty Sessions. Thus, 'In one capacity or another, the landed interest retained its supremacy.'[46] But how was the provision of poor relief organized in Suffolk and what role did *ex-officio* Guardians play in its administration?

Under the Poor Law Amendment Act of 1834, all hamlets, tythings, liberties or any other sub-divisions pertaining to the administration of the Old Poor Law were brought together to form unions. Each union was administered by an elected Board of Guardians. These Boards introduced tight fiscal controls on the level of poor relief and imposed order through the erection of workhouses in each union. Within this framework, magistrates were included as *ex-officio* Guardians. Under the Old Poor Law, individual JPs could only act on the appeal of an applicant who had been denied relief by his parish. After 1834, as *ex-officio* members of the Board of Guardians, landlords became more directly involved in the administration of poor relief:

> As the magistrates will necessarily be members, and the most influential members of the Board of Guardians, the bill does not take away their power, but enables them to exercise it . . . it converts the magistrates from a functionary without jurisdiction till an appeal has been made to him, into an . . . [administrator] it enables him to form and carry into execution his own plans . . . instead of being a spectator.[47]

As the Report from the Select Committee on Poor Law Guardians concluded, the purpose of admitting Justices of the Peace as *ex-officio* Guardians was to give the resident gentry, the people with social influence and position in the neighbourhood, an opportunity to actually assist in carrying out the new law. Their duties as guardians were firstly, to decide upon all applications for relief and to take the necessary measures required to carry out such decisions and, secondly, to exercise a constant supervision with regard to the administration of relief and the establishments in which paupers were maintained.[48]

Despite such direct involvement, Dunkley suggests that the establishment of Boards of Guardians, far from strengthening the position of landlords, actually diminished their former executive influence. Firstly, by widening the membership of these Boards to elected guardians, Dunkley argues that the Act effectively forced landed JPs to share their executive powers with guardians drawn from among the ranks of the wealthier farmers and the middle classes in each union. Secondly, Dunkley suggests that having now lost their indirect but effectual control over the level of poor relief set by the old parish Overseers, landlords ceased to be the ultimate arbiters in local relief matters.[49] On the other hand, given that roughly half the county was owned by members of the landed gentry, elected guardians possessing the requisite property qualifications, those 'who shall be rated to the poor-rate in respect of hereditaments of the annual value or rental of Forty Pounds'[50] were more often than not tenants of the *ex-officio* members of the Board.

The influence wielded by the landed elite over the administration of poor relief was further enhanced by the system of open voting (which was replaced by secret ballot under the Secret Ballot Act of 1872). This required ratepayers to cast their vote in public. This system practically guaranteed the election of the landlord's preferred candidate. Moreover, under the plural voting system (introduced by the 40th clause of the Act), in elections in those parishes where the ownership of landed property was more widely diffused, the larger landowners could still be reasonably confident of getting their preferred candidates elected to the post of guardian. Under the plural voting system, landowners could cast one vote for the first £50 of annual land value and a further vote for each additional £25, up to a maximum of six votes. In addition, under the new ratepayer franchise, one vote was allocated for land values up to £200. For land valued at between £200 and £400, two votes could be cast while for land valued at over £400, the number of votes that could be cast rose to three. In consequence, the balance of electoral advantage was tilted firmly in favour of the great landowners who as both owners and ratepayers could cast up to nine votes each.[51] Although, as Beckett has pointed out, much depended upon whether or not local landlords actually chose to exercise their plural voting rights. Which begs the question, how diligent were the landed elite in shoring-up their position on the Board of Guardians?

According to Dunkley, it was far from certain that magistrates in other parts of England devoted the same energy to conducting humdrum board business as did their counterparts in Brundage's preferred example of Northamptonshire. This would suggest farmers were likely to be in the ascendant in the Guardians' boardroom as they had been before 1834 in the parish vestry thereby 'weakening the hold of the large landowners'.[52] But is it likely that landlords would have been as lackadaisical in exercising their voting rights as they were in attending Board meetings? Is it likely that landowners would have allowed to lie dormant a rigged electoral system that would produce Boards unwilling to do anything 'inconsistent with their interests'?[53] Under these conditions there would, of course, be no need to attend a meeting of the Board.

In Suffolk, only the Earl of Stradbroke actually held the Chairmanship of a Board of Guardians; this is compared to six peers in Northamptonshire. On the other hand, of the 17 Boards of Guardians in Suffolk, excluding those Boards in the municipal unions of Bury St Edmunds and Ipswich, nearly a third were chaired by a non-titled large landowner. The Blything, Hartismere, Mildenhall, Plomesgate, Stow and Woodbridge Unions were chaired respectively by the Earl of Stradbroke, the Rev Robert Gwilt, Colonel William Long, Robert Pettiward and William Phillips, who between them owned around 20,000 acres in the county. In addition, what about the *ex-officio* Board members who were landowners? The *ex-officio* guardians in the Blything Union, for example, included Lord Huntingfield, Sir Alfred Sherlock Gooch, Sir William Rose and J. K. Brooke who, together with their fellow guardians, presented the Earl of Stradbroke with a bound testimonial in 1884 congratulating him upon his 'fiftieth unanimous election as Chairman of the Board'.[54]

The gentry were, therefore, closely involved in the administration of the New Poor Law in Suffolk and could, if they so chose, manipulate the provision of poor relief accordingly. As Brundage states, 'It is evident that many of the great magnates looked upon the new machinery as giving them a greatly increased [level of] control over their workers.'[55] When John Glyde described the operation of the New Poor Law in Suffolk, he noted in particular the:

> spirit of domination strongly manifested by some of our country gentlemen . . . The independence of their positions places them beyond the pale of contradiction in their own sphere, and they will not brook the violation of authority . . . why should not these rascals of paupers be placed in solitary confinement and be shortened of their diet for disobedience, [to] . . . bring their tempers as well as their stomachs into subjection, and make them feel the power of the village squire.[56]

With Gladstone's re-election in 1894, the reform of the Poor Law Electoral System under the 1894 Local Government Act (56 and 57 Vict., c.73) swept away much of the landlords' recognized power. Under this Act, all *ex-officio* members of the Board, together with their plural voting rights and all property qualifications and proxies, were replaced by the ballot box. But, in spite of these changes in the first elections conducted under the new one ratepayer one vote system:

> The majority of the old elected guardians were re-elected – often without contest. *Ex-officio* guardians, as such, of course disappeared. But almost all those who had taken an active part in poor law work were either returned as elected guardians, or were chosen as 'additional guardians' by the new boards.[57]

In other words, whilst the Act ended the landed aristocracy's formal control of the Boards of Guardians, it by no means deprived them of all influence. Of course, as with the abolition of the old nominated Quarter Sessional 'Parliaments', the gentry could no longer oversee local government 'like the feudal Lords . . . whom they succeeded, virtually by right of their acres'.[58] But the fact that, in these new circumstances, landowners who stayed put in the county and kept up their local ties continued to be elected to public bodies is further evidence of the deep-rooted affinity which persisted between themselves and the labourers in the wards on or near their estates. The resident aristocracy and gentry, for their part, sought to re-invent themselves as impartial, uncontroversial exponents of public service. It was in this role that they continued to monopolize both the Chairmanships of the new County Councils, the Chairmanships of the Quarter and Petty Sessional Benches in Criminal Jurisdiction and the Chairmanships of several Poor Law Unions in the county up to 1914, with their tacit support of the Conservative wing of the rural middle class. Thus, for all the changes and reforms of the late nineteenth century, the landed aristocracy and gentry, though subservient to the will of the Conservative party and financially troubled, were able to maintain a foothold in the key public institutions of their localities thanks to their continuing social influence. As Roy Perrot states:

> Even after the 1880s, when county and rural district councils came into being, an approving nod from the man at the Big House [or increasingly, the Home Farm] was necessary in most areas of local decision.[59]

For example, Lord Henniker, in addition to being the Chairman of both Quarter Sessions and East Suffolk County Council, also sat on the County Council's Roads and Bridges Committee, just as he had done under the Quarter Sessional system.[60]

This discussion has, however, concentrated on the continued deference of their labourers and the Conservative-voting rural middle class. But what of the tenantry? Having been involved in local government on the various elective Boards supervised by the old Quarter Sessions, tenant-farmers were inevitably among those elected to sit on the new District Councils which replaced them. While this is why most Conservative landowners felt able to work with the new district councillors, does this necessarily imply that the tenantry were still under the gentry's thumb? The primary basis of their relationship was their mutual economic inter-dependency. As Chapter Two

6

THE LANDOWNER AND
THE TENANT- FARMER

Given the near monopoly of landownership enjoyed by the landed aristocracy, the majority of farmers in Suffolk, and across the country, were tenants of the great landowners. The business of the tenant-farmer was the cultivation of the soil with a capital independent of the landowners. In other words, it was the tenant's capital which ensured that the landlords' farms were kept in cultivation. Unsurprisingly, the economic importance of the farmer to the landowner helped to create a remarkably close working relationship between the tenantry and the aristocracy. Estimates vary on the level of working capital required by a tenant. In the mid-nineteenth century, it was agreed that the most valuable tenants were those with a working capital of £7 to £10 per acre. In this chapter we shall be focusing on these deep-pocketed farmers, yet the bond which existed between them and their landlords, given the closeness of their day-to-day working relationship, inevitably extended far beyond purely monetary concerns.

On many estates in Suffolk, as elsewhere, there was a considerable degree of social interplay between the two parties, often built up over several generations as it was not unusual for a farm-tenancy to pass from father to son. This social interplay formed the foundation of the so-called 'Landed Interest' and was at its most visible in the various festivities, lunches and dinners laid on by the landlord during the course of the year or in the key events affecting the lives of the family living in the great hall. Witness the address of congratulations sent to the Earl of Stradbroke by his tenants on the birth of his son in 1862. Similarly, when Edward Gooch came of age in 1864, the seven hundred guests invited to Benacre Hall were attended by Sir Edward and his wife, as well as his principal tenants, who together served the food and drink. Each tenant also wore a blue ribbon in his buttonhole as an emblem of the political party to which Sir Edward and his family belonged.[1]

The reason for this is quite straightforward. Under the Reform Act of 1832 farmers became the largest single group in most English county electorates. Despite this numerical advantage over their landlords, as we saw in Chapter Three, except when required to cast their votes, the great majority played no part in rural politics and preferred to follow their landlord's lead. As Anthony Trollope observed in *The Vicar of Bullhampton* (1870), 'The Marquis's people were all expected to vote for the Marquis's candidates, and would soon have ceased to be the Marquis's people if they had failed to do so.'[2] On estates where the landlord was actively engaged in politics the pedigree, politics and character of a prospective tenant often received as much attention in the landlord's deliberations as the depth of his pockets. The Earl of Yarborough stipulated that none of his farms was to be let to a 'too political party man, or one that would make himself too busy in parochial matters, or a dissenter'.[3]

But whilst they might be a deferential group, farmers, especially those with deep enough pockets, were not dependants of their landlords to the same degree as the labourer. However, deferring to their landlords in local affairs and in politics had its rewards. Long-established or favoured tenants could hold their farms at rents well below the true value of their land. Similarly, during depressed periods, it was not uncommon for landlords to grant their tenants remissions of up to half-a-year's rent all round. It was this liberal behaviour which gave landlords much of their influence as it engendered a belief among farmers that their 'personal interests [were] in the main . . . the same as the interests of their landlords'.[4] Besides, up to the 1880s 'landlord representation offered more substantial Parliamentary representation (at minimal direct cost) than farmers acting alone could ever hope to achieve.'[5] As *The Economist* noted in 1853:

> The relation of the tenant to his landlord consists primarily in a compact or agreement, by which the farmer binds himself to pay a certain sum of money, in consideration of being permitted to occupy and cultivate for his own emolument the land of the latter . . . but . . . the landlord is [also] connected with the tenant by ties of a moral and social character . . . The British proprietor is engaged in connections either of mutual interest or of kindly feeling with those who cultivate his lands. It is a happy circumstance for our country that while to those whom the possession of landed property has placed in exalted status is secured the undisturbed enjoyment of, as well as the dignity and influence legitimately due to their wealth, there is also accorded to them the inestimable privilege of being on terms of friendly

intercourse with their [tenants] . . . ; it is this circumstance which . . .
conduces more than anything else to the solidity and compactness of
our social system.[6]

Thus, when a landlord offered one of his farms to a prospective tenant, he did so
in the expectation that the new tenant would conduct his affairs in accordance
with the wishes of his landlord when sitting on the Board of Guardians or voting
in a parliamentary election. In return, the tenant looked to his landlord to abate
or to reduce his rents during times of agricultural depression and not to turn him
out of his farm before receiving a suitable return on his investment. But was this
gentleman's agreement adequate protection for the capital invested by tenants
in their landlord's farms? Was this a potential time-bomb that could undermine
the traditional relationship between the landowner and farmer given the
growing capital requirements of 'high' farming? To answer this question, we
need to look at the actual arrangements covering compensation for acts of
improvement and the terms under which farms were offered to tenants in Suffolk
during the era of 'high' farming.

Throughout the wartime boom of the late eighteenth and early
nineteenth centuries, tenants usually farmed their holdings under a 21-year
lease. Under this arrangement, tenants who accepted such a lease in the
1790s enjoyed nearly a quarter of a century of high wartime prices and
exceptionally high returns. By contrast, tenants who accepted a lease towards
the end of the Napoleonic Wars soon found themselves exposed to the
agricultural depression of the post-war years and were unable to pay rents
which had been pegged to the previously high wartime price of wheat.
Despite offering their tenants abatements in their rent, many landlords saw
a large number of tenants quit their farms during the agriculturally depressed 1820s and 1830s. Having had their farms fall into hand, a growing
number of landlords came to the conclusion that a far more flexible system
of tenure was required if they were to continue enjoying a relatively low, but
also relatively secure, return of 3–4 per cent per annum, without running the
risk of incurring the direct costs of farm management. Out of this desire
there arose annual tenancies or tenancies-at-will. Unlike a lease for a certain
number of years, tenancies-at-will were yearly agreements based on a verbal
understanding between the landlord and the tenant. These could be
terminated at any time by either side with six months' notice. Landlords
were, in consequence, able to adjust their rents according to the price per
quarter of wheat in any given year. Such agreements also gave landlords
greater control over the political opinions of their tenants who were now
subject to a six month notice to quit.[7]

But by the 1840s, was the growing popularity of annual agreements potentially dangerous to agriculture's future? Remember the belief had now taken hold that boosting output by improving productivity through agricultural improvement was the only way to beat free trade. But if a farmer could not look to the future with security, 'little can be hazarded by him beyond the expenses which the returns of the year will defray'. Indeed, 'If we shall deny to the farmer that security of possession which is essential to the safe and profitable application of his funds, we may rest assured that his capital will be sparingly expended on another man's property.'[8] William and Hugh Raynbird were equally dismissive of annual agreements given that:

> The continuance of the tenant-at-will in his occupation, and the safe investment of the tenant's capital . . . hang upon a thread – a difference of opinion, a trifling dispute, the dislike of the steward, a change of ownership, the death of his landlord, the demands of creditors upon the estate, and even his own . . . farming may cause that thread to be broken at a moment's notice: is it to be wondered . . . that tenants-at-will . . . are prepared for a notice to quit? Therefore, they do not add sufficient value to the land.[9]

To the landlord this argument was as broad as it was long given that tenants on long leases 'systematically . . . exhaust [their] land' towards the end of their leases.[10]

The inherent vulnerability of tenants-at-will was highlighted at a stormy meeting of the Leominster Agricultural Society in Herefordshire in 1854. During the meeting, the President, Lord Bateman (Sir Edward Kerrison's brother-in-law) was subjected to a great deal of criticism for raising his rents by 50 per cent. What made these increases so galling was that Lord Bateman had allegedly assured his tenants that, although their agricultural improvements had raised the capital value of his farms, this would not be used as a pretext for raising their rent. In response, Lord Bateman denied any breach of good faith. On the contrary, having reduced his rents in 1851 and spent £26,000 on improvements over the previous ten years, he felt justified in raising his rents. Particularly as the price of wheat was now beginning to recover. *The Economist*, on the other hand, concluded that such cases demonstrated that a yearly tenancy which allowed for the raising and lowering of rents according to the varying prices of each year was one 'wholly unfitted for promoting agricultural enterprise'.[11] This august journal took the view that 'The longer the period during which the occupier is sure that . . . he will occupy his farm, the more safely may he organize plans of cultivation as profitable operations.'[12] But did this editorial position reflect the realities on the ground?

Interestingly, during the mid-nineteenth century, more and more tenants opted to accept annual agreements from their landlords in preference to a lease. This was because tenancies-at-will gave occupiers the freedom to assess the future prospects of their farms at regular intervals. As Robert Raynbird noted in a letter sent to his landlord Sir Thomas Gage in 1853:

> Under the present great fluctuations in the price of produce it will be best both for you as Landlord and myself as Tenant that it should be as a yearly Tenant as you will then have the opportunity if the Farm is not properly managed of giving me notice, whereas if I take it on a Lease and the price of corn and meat should alter very much it would be quite impossible for me to pay the Rent except by expiring the farm and the labourers employ'd upon it.[13]

The mid-nineteenth century was, therefore, a period of considerable upheaval and change across Suffolk as landlords gradually moved their estates over to yearly agreements once their existing leases began to expire. By 1849, annual agreements had already become the predominant form of tenure around Framlingham. Similarly, around Hoxne, on estates such as Oakley Park and Brome Hall, most tenants were also from year to year, although several tenants are known to have still been on leases of eight to fourteen years. Leases of between eight to twelve years were also still in existence in the Hundred of Thingoe. However, in Stow Hundred, 'a great quantity' of land was being farmed on a yearly hire.[14]

The trend was clearly in favour of annual agreements. By 1841, of the ten tenants on the Bramford estate which formed part of the estates of Sir George Broke, seven were already on yearly agreements. On the Helmingham estate, farms could also be held either on a lease or a yearly agreement. Significantly, according to Henry Kersey, Lord Tollemache's agent, when given the choice new tenants opted for annual agreements. A derivative of the yearly tenancy known as the 'lease note' was also employed on the Helmingham estate. A 'lease note' bound the landlord to allow a tenant undisturbed possession without any increase in rent for 21 years, upon condition that the tenant kept the land clean and in good condition, and executed certain specified improvements. Thus, while the tenant enjoyed the freedom of an annual agreement and remained free to give up his farm whenever he chose, so long as he did not breach any of the conditions laid down by the landlord, he could stay on the farm long enough to ensure an adequate return on his improvements. Leases were still obtainable, as on the Henham estate where, while one of the Earl of Stradbroke's farms in the parish of Sotherton was let to William Golding 'from year to year' another farm in the same parish was let at Michaelmas 1874 on an eight-year lease. Overall, however, by the late nineteenth century, tenancy-at-will was the dominant form of tenurial agreement operating in Suffolk. In the early 1900s, of the 72 farms on the Ickworth Park estate, five were held under leases of between five and 20 years, whilst 67 were on yearly agreements. Similarly, on the Shotley Park estate in East Suffolk, out of 15 tenants, 12 were on yearly agreements. Meanwhile, on the Flixton Hall estate, 82 out of a total of 88 tenants were, by 1913, on yearly agreements.[15]

More importantly, tenants on yearly agreements were prepared to invest the considerable sums of money required in 'high' feeding. Robert Raynbird, for one, was quite prepared to buy the supplements of linseed cake and the artificial fertilizers needed to farm 'high' under a yearly tenancy. This was because most tenants were willing to trust in the liberal character of their landlords, but they also expected their tenancies to be renewed given that landlords were keen to have their newly improved farms occupied by enterprising tenants. As Biddell points out, 'Formerly the farmer took the tenancy as the last occupier left it, and so it went on in this county until the premises in Suffolk were probably some of the worst in England.'[16] Having invested heavily in improving the quality of their farms, landlords were obviously keen to attract and keep the very best farmers to run them.

As farmers with pockets deep enough to farm 'high' were always at a premium, their scarcity value represented a form of security. There also existed a customary system of compensation known as tenant-right, which compensated an outgoing tenant with a cash sum based on a valuer's estimate of the remaining benefits to be derived from his acts of husbandry. Taken together, these elements add up to Caird's assessment of the 'confidence which subsists between [landlords and tenants] in England generally' especially as the landlords, given their unwillingness to grant their tenants long leases 'for reasons of maintaining political control, it was often suggested' were providing 'the permanent improvements that tenants-at-will could not be expected to make'.[17] Indeed, the confidence that these elements generated was such that tenants-at-will even began to undertake so-called permanent improvements, such as field drainage, or even the erection of new buildings, under yearly tenancies, but it is to this issue of permanent improvements that we now turn.

During the 1840s and 1850s, the leading agriculturalist Philip Pusey became increasingly concerned that the existing systems of customary tenant-right, by only providing compensation for acts of husbandry rather than acts of improvement, were in fact discouraging tenants from making further improvements to their farms. These concerns were echoed in Suffolk in 1856 by John Glyde, who wrote:

> The high system of farming . . . [in Suffolk required further] improvements to be made . . . a larger amount of capital [needs] to be expended in cultivating the soil; and a strong feeling has for some time existed amongst the most intelligent farmers of the county in favour of a more general system of 'tenant-right'. A tenant may feel himself secure under his present landlord, but the uncertainty of life, and the prospect, in consequence, of being compelled to relinquish his farm before he had received the additional profit for his outlay, and no chance of remuneration for unexhausted improvements, deter him from adopting that good arrangement that could be most profitable to himself, and most advantageous to the proprietor.[18]

Pusey therefore began to campaign for legislation to provide tenants-at-will with a legal right to claim compensation for the unexhausted value of any permanent improvements, *in addition* to any compensation for acts of husbandry undertaken prior to the expiration of their tenancies. In the absence of such legislation, however, what could outgoing tenants actually claim for under the traditional system of tenant-right as it existed in Suffolk? Under the customary agreements in Suffolk, the incoming tenant reimbursed the outgoing tenant according to a valuer's estimate of the cost of the latter's husbandry in the last year of his tenancy. This was known as the custom of the country or customary tenant-right. Where farms were taken in hand, the responsibility for compensating the outgoing tenant fell to the landlord. In Suffolk, the date at which farms were vacated was usually Michaelmas. In consideration of the time of year, the custom was for the outgoing tenant to prepare the fallows. He would then, following a valuation, be paid by the landlord or the incoming tenant for the seeds he had planted and for the manure and straw left on the farm. On the Shotley estate in East Suffolk, the Marquess of Bristol allowed outgoing tenants the 'Rent, Rates and Taxes on the Fallows on leaving and . . . the usual Tenants Fixtures, and the Muck, Hay and Clover . . . of the last year'. Similarly, on the Henham estate, tenants were paid 'for tillage of fallow and for the muck'.[19]

As a side point, many incoming tenants in Suffolk disliked the Michaelmas custom of paying for the tillages undertaken by the outgoing tenant. As an alternative, they would have much preferred the Norfolk custom of paying only for the crop as it was considered 'hard to have to pay for tillages which may result in no crop'.[20] The Norfolk custom was allowed to operate on the Euston Hall estate by the Duke of Grafton. Still, in general terms the custom of the county for valuation under Suffolk covenants only entitled the tenant to claim for:

> hay, manure, tillages, seed, and rent and rates of roots, and of fallows. Cost of small seeds and sowing them, farmhouse fixtures [stoves and coppers etc.]. The incoming tenant pays cost of the threshing, dressing, and delivering to market of the last year's crop of corn, receiving the straw, chaff and 'colder' arising there from as equivalent.[21]

Of course, what has to be remembered here, as was pointed out in a letter to the Earl of Stradbroke, is that this was still only a custom. Under common law where there was 'no writing whatever – no lease – no agreement, the rule [was that] . . . everything [was] forfeited to the landlord'.[22] On the other hand, how many tenants would come knocking at the door of a landlord who broke with this custom? Nonetheless, it is a sobering thought that all this expenditure was undertaken on the basis of custom and trust. This is amplified when we factor in the cost of permanent improvements undertaken by the tenant as tenants in Suffolk were not entitled to claim compensation for improving their farms through either draining or claying their fields under the existing customary code. Nor could they claim for the guano or oilcake they had purchased.

Referring to the situation as it pertained in the late 1840s, J. G. Cooper complained of the limitation of compensation under the current customary systems to acts of husbandry on the grounds that:

> for the want of being paid at the expiration of their terms for unexhausted improvements, there are a great number of labourers discharged two or three years before the tenant quits his occupation, to lessen expenses, had he a [right to] claim for . . . improvements he would continue to employ his full number of men up to the expiration of his term.[23]

The conservative attitude displayed by landlords 'despite the tenants as a body' desiring such an arrangement was due, in Cooper's opinion, to the fact that many landlords in East Suffolk 'cannot be considered men of business; they do not understand the practical bearings of the case, they are exceedingly tenacious of coming to any system different from that they have followed many years . . . [nor do they] . . . make themselves practically acquainted with farming matters'.[24] Of course, Cooper was commenting on the cusp of a change in attitude. It was, after all, at this juncture that a growing number of landowners shrewdly began to recognize the inducement that agreeing to provide compensation for the unexhausted value of permanent improvements would give to their more enterprising tenants. In Lincolnshire, for example, the leading landlords had already realized that as leases were not the fashion of the County, they had to give their tenants some other form of security: namely, compensation for the unexhausted value of their improvements if they were to induce their tenants to invest in such schemes.[25]

Under the Lincolnshire custom, compensation was paid according to the age and character of an improvement. It was, for instance, calculated that chalking benefited the soil for a period of seven years. If the tenant left his holding three years after he had undertaken this improvement, the incoming tenant would, therefore, receive four years' benefit from an investment he himself had not made. Thus the incoming tenant or his landlord was required to compensate the outgoing tenant to the extent of four-sevenths of the original outlay. The first recorded instances of this system being used were between 1815 and 1825; by the 1840s, however, the custom was well established in Lincolnshire, leading Thirsk to conclude that the custom developed out of the growing popularity of the yearly tenancy in Lincolnshire. More importantly, if compensation was considered to be an acceptable substitute for security of tenure on the grounds that it did not hang the weight of a long lease about the neck of the tenant, then the spread of this custom was clearly an 'essential concomitant of agricultural advance'.[26]

Significantly, in Suffolk, the progress of 'high' farming, coupled as it was with the increased popularity of annual agreements, *was* paralleled by the introduction of private agreements compensating tenants for the unexhausted value of the permanent improvements they made to their farms. This conjunction of factors disproved the predictions of J. G. Cooper who, in evidence to the Select Committee on Agricultural Customs in 1848, believed a more formalized system of compensation was an inevitable step. When asked 'Are you of opinion that it would be better to leave things to private agreement between landlord and tenant?' he replied that, in his experience, 'If it is left to private agreement between landlord and tenant, we shall remain in the same state we are now in.'[27] On the Helmingham Hall estate, for example, the introduction of these agreements was thoroughly approved of by the agent Henry Kersey who noted the improved condition of the land which resulted from the willingness of the landlord to allow tenants such compensation. In his opinion, 'If a person had no compensation under an agreement, it would be but little use his spending an extra quantity of property upon that estate in way of improvements, because at the expiration of the time he would be obliged to go out and leave it.'[28]

On the neighbouring Henham estate, meanwhile, tenants were allowed 'the unexhausted value of all clay, loam, or marsh earth carted and spread on the said . . . premises in the last two years . . . and for the unexhausted value of all under-draining done on the said . . . premises in the last three years'.[29] This all indicates the growing importance attached to raising the overall level of tenant's capital employed in the progress of agricultural improvement.[30] But while enlightened landlords such as John Tollemache and the Earl of Stradbroke were prepared to offer their tenants compensation for the unexhausted value of their improvements, they were still under no legal obligation to honour their informal agreements. Given the sums that were now being invested by tenants on annual tenancies in drainage and other permanent improvements, the absence of such legal protection was considered by agriculturalists to be potentially damaging to the longer term interests of agriculture and to the continuing flow of tenant's capital into such improvements. In essence, therefore, the progress of legislation establishing a legally-based system of English tenant-right was a response to 'the increased importance of tenant investment relative to that of the owner'.[31]

For example, some landlords keen to improve their farms were equally keen to keep their own investment to a minimum. They sought to encourage richer tenants to undertake fixed capital improvements by offering to take into account their expenditure when setting their rent. As a valuer's report of 1855 for Stanchels' farm on the Hengrave Hall estate reveals, 'The tenant has expended a considerable sum in improving the property through draining, planting, road making and general good management . . . I have taken [this] into consideration in estimating the annual value, and made a fair allowance for the same.' On another farm on the same estate, whilst the landlord, Sir Thomas Rokewode-Gage, agreed to repair the house and the surrounding premises, the tenant was 'allowed £40 per annum for the first four years . . . towards the outlay required for draining and improving' the soil. In other words, if the tenant agreed to pay for these improvements Sir Thomas was willing to allow him 5 per cent of his annual £740 rent 'for so doing'.[32]

Tenant-right became the cause of the farmer who had the financial resources to venture further use of technological methods in pursuit of abundant yields. As a letter sent to the Earl of Stradbroke by Charles Lane reveals, 'The most active of the tenant class would feel better disposed toward their landlords, [if] . . . they found their landlords in Parliament sanctioning as a principle, compensation.' As for the landowners, given that at present all the tenants' improvements were technically forfeit under common law to the landlord, they risked turning their tenants into 'Red Republicans'.[33] But by keeping matters on an informal basis the bulk of the tenantry remained under the landlord's tutelage.[34] As for the more enterprising farmers, they too had to play by the landlord's rules, although their reliance on the character of the landlord was tempered by the knowledge that their willingness to invest in improving the productivity of a farm would act as a form of security. Thus in the opinion of Herman Biddell the tenantry in Suffolk 'lived on the best of terms with both agent and landlord'.[35] On the other hand, in the context of the post-Repeal era, the issue of granting the more active and enterprising farmers legal safeguards to both protect their existing investments and to encourage further expenditure was clearly an issue that was not about to go away.

In 1847 and again in 1848, Philip Pusey introduced a Tenant Right Bill into Parliament but on both occasions the Bill failed to pass through the House of Lords. This was largely due to the fact that landlords were disinclined to see their discretionary authority replaced by a legalized framework. It was on precisely this point that Lane took issue with the Earl of Stradbroke:

> I agree in nine tenths of your letter, but still adhere to my wish to institute a law of compensation for permanent improvements for a law of Protection . . . why should not the universal rule be compensation if the landlord does not make his own agreement in writing . . . [such a] rule . . . will not . . . prevent you or any other landlord making his own agreement with his own tenants. The plan I propose would produce no effect whatever in the cases of the best landlords because in all these cases there exists a written agreement [on the question of compensation] . . . [which] excludes the operation of the common law.[36]

Pusey did, however, obtain the appointment of a Select Committee in 1848, referred to above, to inquire into the law and custom between outgoing and incoming tenants and also between landlord and tenant regarding the issue of unexhausted improvements. The Committee recommended that landlords adopt a policy of compensating their tenants for the unexhausted value of their improvements, which, of course, they were already beginning to do.

The Committee also recommended the amendment of the law relating to items affixed to the freehold by calling for the tenant to be allowed to remove any temporary structures he had put up. An Act was subsequently passed in 1851 granting tenants the right to remove temporary structures but it failed to give the tenant any legal right to claim compensation for the unexhausted value of any improvements to the soil.

Regardless of this, the reality was that the great landowners owned a disproportionately large quantity of land and, if one wanted to farm, one had to apply for a tenancy subject to the terms offered by the landlord. Against this, farmers with the cash required to operate the larger more valuable mixed arable and livestock enterprises were always at a premium and as such they were in a strong negotiating position. In 1873, a prospective tenant looking to rent one of the farms on Lord Waveney's Flixton Hall estate assured the agent he had the £10 an acre necessary to properly stock the 300 acre farm he was hoping to hire. In the place of a bankers' guarantee for the money, however, he produced a letter from his mother indicating her readiness to advance him £3,000. Given that he was prepared to invest such a sum in the farm *he* wanted, 'a house or shed built for horse gear', somewhere on the farm for cutting chaff or grinding oil-cake, and a henhouse, he further hoped for a clear understanding about the rights of shooting 'which I am rather fond of'![37] Granted, Lord Waveney was about to embark upon an extensive programme of improvements to his farms and here was £3,000 to actually run one of them as a profitable enterprise – the farmer was clearly in a position to negotiate.

Hence, to emphasize the point made above, tenant-right legislation was an issue bound to exercise the large farmer who had committed considerable sums of his own money in boosting the productivity of his landlord's farm. Whilst this had given the larger farmers more leverage, the issue of compensation for any permanent improvements remained a legally grey area. And as more cash was committed, larger farmers became more sensitive to the issue until eventually the camel's back of landlord intransigence over the issue of legislation was broken by the straw of a controversial eviction, that of George Hope, a deep-pocketed improving tenant. In 1864, Hope had stood as a Liberal candidate against a friend of his Conservative landlord. As a result, when his lease expired in 1872, he was told to leave. The pettiness of his landlord's action exposed the slim thread by which a tenant occupied a farm. In response, in 1873, Clare Sewell Read (a Norfolk farmer elected to Parliament as a tenant-farmer representative in the face of opposition from both Liberal and Conservative landlords) and James Howard (a farm machinery manufacturer and farmer) confronted the landlord's preference of keeping compensation on an informal basis by drafting a Landlord and Tenant Bill. The Bill stalled but with the tenantry, regardless (or perhaps because) of their notoriously Conservative sympathies, up in arms. In 1874, Disraeli, in an address to the electors at Newport Pagnell stated, 'I am asked if I will vote for the Landlord and Tenant Bill, or for a measure securing to the occupiers compensation for the unexhausted value of their improvements . . . I recommended my friends to support the principle of that measure.'[38] Subsequently, in 1875, during Disraeli's second term of office as Prime Minister, the first Agricultural Holdings Act was passed.

Under the terms of the Act, landlords found themselves subject to their tenants' claims for compensation for the unexhausted value of their improvements. The Act also introduced a disputes procedure and gave the tenant the right of appeal to the County Court. The Act had one fundamental flaw: the legislation was permissive, which meant that the landlord could contract out of its provisions. This was a key concession and was largely a response to the disquiet felt by many Conservative landlords alarmed at the prospect of the State intervening in areas currently covered by private agreements. Lord Henniker, for example, argued in 1875 that:

> One of the principal reasons for the cry for legislation, and for legislation of a compulsory character, was that tenant farmers very often rushed into the farming business without due consideration and without sufficient capital. It was said that persons in this position required protection; but [such]. . .legislative interference was [unlikely] . . . to be a benefit to either landlord or tenant.[39]

Lord Henniker, like his father, was, according to the *Suffolk Mercury*, a 'Liberal-minded Conservative-agricultural member' of Parliament; he was therefore 'not a mere landlord's legislator. He is not one of those who is in a constant state of alarm about the territorial interest'. Rather, in the Commons and in his election business, he 'threw himself into questions involving the tenant's interests'.[40] Thus, when it came to the question of the compulsory payment of compensation, his views carried considerable weight. In his opinion, compulsion was an unnecessary interference given that:

> The most energetic advocates of a compulsory measure [have themselves] . . . acknowledged that legislation was only required for exceptional cases. The fact was that landowners, as a rule, gave more liberal agreements than any of the Bills that had been proposed; and where no agreement existed, there would be, nine times out of ten,

such a liberal custom of the locality, or of the particular estate
concerned, that the tenant had ample security.[41]

In particular, 'It was as much to the interest of the landlord as the tenant to
give liberal agreements.' Indeed, when it came to the question of compulsion,
he believed that 'If the whole tenantry of England were canvassed, a majority
would be found to be opposed to it.'[42] This was because, if the landlord were
stripped of his discretionary powers to determine the level of compensation
paid out on his estate, he would, in Lord Henniker's view, be reduced to the
status of a mere rent-charger. He would, therefore, be no different from
landlords in Ireland who were 'afraid to spend money on estates' and preferred
instead, 'to obtain as much rent as possible, leaving the rest, as it were, to take
care of itself'. And that would never do, would it![43]

   This is not to say that Lord Henniker was entirely opposed to all forms of
legislation. He was keenly aware of the need to codify and clarify the various
customary systems of tenant-right particularly as customs were, in many
cases, no longer applicable to the places where they existed. It would thus
be something of a boon if 'a good sound rule or custom' were laid down in
legislative form upon broad lines that could 'be pretty generally followed'.
After all, whilst 'his own agreements were nearly according to custom; he
saw where he could alter those agreements beneficially in many respects. He
was also of opinion that the customs of his own county might be amended.
It was everything to a tenant to have a fair valuation, and if a too high
valuation were given by any Bill it would be injurious.'[44] Hence the need for
the guidelines to be both permissive and broad enough to leave sufficient
scope for individual interpretations of the law. By digging their heels in on
this, landlords did not, however, turn their tenants into 'Red Republicans'.
They avoided this because they were putting generous compensation
schedules on the table and continuing to honour their side of the bargain by
continuing to build cottages, barns, feeding yards and drain fields. Also,
consider the timing: in 1874, landlords had sided with the farmer against
the labourer during the 'Lock Out' re-emphasizing the commonality of
interest that existed between them. The Countess of Stradbroke had been
commended for her 'noble energetic, bold and fearless' defence of the farmers
in her neighbourhood. As a consequence, the Agricultural Holdings Act,
though flawed, was accepted as it at last put the issue of tenant-right onto a
statutory footing. But could this compromise withstand the agricultural
depression?

   In 1865, John Bright wrote that farmers 'are not asked who shall
represent them, but the Lords and squires of the county name the

candidate, and as a rule the tenant farmers vote for him' but the time was coming:

> when tenants will dare to believe and act for themselves in the performance of their political duties. They can combine with great ease . . . farmers meet almost every week at their market towns [and] in every county they should select a 'farmers candidate' . . . a good tenant farmer or a landowner who is willing to be just to the tenant farmers both in his private conduct and in respect of the legislation that affects them. [45]

Significantly, both John Henniker, a 'farmers man', and Frederic Corrance presented themselves in 1868 as 'farmers candidates' or the 'farmers nominees'. But a decade later, it looked as if farmers were about to act for themselves with the establishment of the Farmers' Alliance in 1879 by James Howard and William Bear. The Farmers' Alliance was an expression of the growing dissatisfaction of those farmers who believed their landlords had failed in their political function to protect them from foreign competition and could offer nothing 'by way of redress for their woes'.[46] In 1880, the leading Suffolk farmer William Biddell representing the Alliance was elected as an Independent MP for the county; the non-conformist farmer R. L. Everett, having stood unsuccessfully as an Alliance candidate, was later to represent Eye as a Liberal. But the Alliance emerged at a time when, as we saw in Chapter Two, landlords had yet to come to terms with the depression. The Marquess of Bristol, remember, was still of the opinion in 1879 that an improvement in the weather would set everything to rights. Once landlords set about reducing rents and offering redress to their tenants' woes, the level of tension dissipated taking the Alliance with it. In its wake, large English farmers remained in a political alliance with the landed interest.[47] But there were now two issues with which Gladstone's Liberal party could tempt the traditionally Conservative-voting big farmers in the county seats: compulsory tenant-right legislation and game.

The damage caused by ground game had, in fact, been a major bone of contention between landlords and tenants in Suffolk throughout the nineteenth century. Writing in 1852, Robert Raynbird complained to Sir Thomas Gage of the damage done to his crops by hares and rabbits. Many farmers also deeply resented having game keepers wandering over their farms. As one Suffolk farmer recalled, 'The Rendlesham Hall estate was [always] highly preserved for game.' In consequence, 'There was a small army of keepers all dressed in a livery of blue velvet with buttons bearing their master's coat of arms, parading about the countryside.'[48] On the other hand, it was in the best interests of both parties to find some form of compromise. Frederic Corrance, who owned the Parham Hall estate and was reputedly one of the most distinguished sportsmen in Suffolk, as well as being a friend to the farmer believed that 'Upon the whole [during the era of "high" farming] the relations between the owner and the cultivator were friendly, and the farmers doing pretty well in other respects, with wheat at 65 shillings could afford to take some interest in the sport.'[49] The involvement of the tenant farmer in shooting is significant, as it illustrates the growing influence of the large farmer because as a rule in the early Victorian era 'no tenant-farmer shot', although on the Barking Hall estate, in 1841, the Earl of Ashburnham divided his shooting-rights between his tenants in return for £100 per annum, each tenant paying a 'fair proportion of the same [for] the privilege'.[50] But for those farmers who did not shoot and who were not prepared to tolerate game despoiling their crops, compensation was available. On estates which were highly preserved, 'Tenant farmers are liberally compensated for any damage done to crops; and they are given many days sport amongst themselves.'[51] Given this arrangement existed in one of the most highly preserved counties in England, we can perhaps begin to see why the Gladstonian Ground Game Act of 1880, with its allowances for tenants to shoot game without the written permission of the landlord, failed to bring the farmer into the Liberal camp despite the farmer's now not doing quite so well. But how did landowners get round the even more controversial issue of compulsory tenant-right?

By the 1880s, the imperfections of the 1875 Agricultural Holdings Act, coupled to the deepening agricultural depression, gave fresh impetus to the campaign to compel landlords to provide compensation for the unexhausted value of their tenants' improvements. The motivation behind compulsion was again the mistaken belief that the provision of effective protection for tenants' capital would stimulate greater investment and thereby, 'greater productivity, which, hopefully, would provide the sure reply to the the unrelenting tide of low priced cereals from North America'. This echoed the position of forty years earlier when Lane had argued that compensating tenants for their improvements would 'enable us to struggle against this infernal nonsense of free trade'.[52] In William Bear's opinion, given that at present only a 'bastard security pertains – that is a security depending upon personal goodwill, which is at the best but an uncertain safeguard', it was hardly surprising that 'Tenants have been less tempted to liberal expenditure, and have for the most part farmed as Scotch tenants farm at the fag-end of their leases.'[53] Nonetheless, considerable sums of money were still tied up in the mixed arable and livestock enterprises of counties like Suffolk which led, with the election of the Liberal party in 1880, to a second Agricultural Holdings Act appearing on the statute book in 1883.

Unlike its predecessor, the Act abolished the right of landlords to contract out and gave tenants the right to claim for a series of improvements for which the landlord was now legally bound to provide compensation. Significantly, opposition to the Act was surprisingly muted. This was due in large measure to the fact that landlords in Suffolk, as elsewhere, were increasingly desperate to keep or attract new tenants. In these circumstances, being seen to have actively opposed an Act intended to give greater protection to tenants' working capital would have been extremely counter-productive. But what effect did this piece of legislation have in practice? Essentially, the provisions of the Act left landlords feeling compelled to offer their tenants far more generous terms regarding the level of compensation payable at the termination of a tenancy, as an agreement drawn up by the third Marquess of Bristol in the 1890s, reveals:

> If upon the determination of this tenancy the tenant continues to farm [on a renewed agreement] the improvements, with the exception of the last two items of the First Schedule [of the 1883 Agricultural Holdings Act] for which [had he quitted the occupation] he would have been entitled to compensation under the . . . Act [of] 1883, may be valued in the manner by that Act, or as by this agreement provided, and the tenant shall thereafter during his resumed tenancy receive interest upon the sum awarded at the rate of 4 per cent per annum. Such interest to be deducted at the time he pays his half year's rent. But if the landlord at any time during the resumed tenancy pays the amount awarded, or any part thereof, in such case the said interest . . . shall cease to be paid.[54]

Sir George Broke-Middleton was also quick to codify his compensatory arrangements with his tenants. As a result, all new tenants received a printed form outlining precisely what Sir George was prepared to pay them in compensation. For example, in cases where no crop had been taken on a field recently drained, Sir George allowed the tenant the whole cost of the labour. Where one crop had been taken, three-fourths of the said cost was allowed; where it was two crops, the sum allowed was half of the said cost; where three crops had been taken it was only a quarter, and nothing after four crops. This followed the pattern already established in the aftermath of the

1875 Act. On the Flixton Hall estate, a draft lease for Battisford Hall farm drawn up in 1880 stipulated the 'agricultural holdings act to apply'. Similarly, Sir Edward Kerrison leased his farms 'on yearly agreements according to the exact lines of the Agricultural Holdings Act'. [55]

Essentially, landlords were concerned that unless they made a clear and unequivocal statement as to what they were prepared to offer their tenants, they risked having tenants make an exaggerated claim. This would then force the landlord into the expense of making a counter-claim. Most tenants were not prepared to find out exactly what was their landlord's idea of an exaggerated claim. This was based on the widely-held belief that any judge was more likely to 'split the difference', awarding so little to either party that any compensation was 'swallowed up in costs'.[56] Given these concerns, many farmers 'won't touch the Agricultural Holdings Act, because it is only calculated to benefit solicitors'.[57] Across Suffolk, it would appear that neither side willingly resorted to either the 1875 Act or its successor, the 1883 Agricultural Holdings Act. Generally, tenants appear to have chosen compromise over contest, preferring to continue to receive compensation based on private agreements. Farmers around Bury St Edmunds claimed 'the custom of the country gives us all we could get from the Act without the bother'. As Mr Cheney, agent to Lord Henniker, explained, 'My impression is that tenants do not put the Act into operation because they fear the counter-claims that would be made by the landlords.'[58]

On the other hand, by the 1890s, despite being on yearly agreements and the inevitable complaints that the landlord still had the whip hand and that there was no equality of bargaining, the sitting tenant now had a much better chance to secure a satisfactory agreement. According to farmers in the county, 'Twelve years ago . . . there [were] twelve or fourteen men after a farm before a man's body was cold, now there is no competition . . . a farmer can now drive his own bargain. Formerly a man's pedigree, politics and character had to be right. The apron string farmers have gone.'[59] By the 1890s, new farmers were haggling over the terms of a tenancy on a strictly commercial basis: 'It is now a free bargain, and the landlord has no more advantage in dealing with the tenant.' This led Fox to conclude there were:

Practically no complaints . . . as to insecurity of tenure [in Suffolk] . . . I do not think it can be said anything of the sort exists; [this was because] a great deal of land is unlet, [while] a very great deal is let at almost nominal rents, [and] . . . owners cannot afford to cultivate it themselves; landowners find great difficulty in retaining their tenants, and still greater difficulty in getting new ones; in short, tenants in the greater part of the County can dictate their own terms, and landlords are prepared to make any sacrifice to retain or acquire them.[60]

Further confirmation of the tenantry flexing their muscles comes from the pen of Herman Biddell who wrote:

> Years ago . . . the tenant seldom made stringent terms for his own protection. He was content to submit to any condition with regard to game, hedgerow timber, sale of produce, which even the most careful agent of the present day would think of asking a tenant to adopt . . . [but now] occupations which were keenly sought after some years ago are now gladly disposed of to any tenant with capital sufficient to take a farm.[61]

But surely this was the inevitable culmination of a trend that began to be observable during the era of 'high' farming? Wasn't this the greater bargaining power of the farmer with deep pockets? But what of the farmer struggling to make do and mend? As Caird had observed back during the heady days of 'high' farming, there had always been tenants whose farms were well-drained and well-fertilized, where the soil was tilled by modern equipment, while on the other side of the hedge there persisted waterlogged, infertile clays, antiquated implements and crops harvested by the sickle.[62] It was these more commonplace farmers who complained 'There is not sufficient security for a good man . . . what we want are long leases', but across the eastern counties, leases had almost entirely disappeared by the late nineteenth century. This group really were occupying their farms 'subject to the custom of the country' and, once again, it was this insecurity of tenure which was blamed by one Suffolk farmer and JP for preventing 'farmers from cultivating the land to the best advantage'.[63] This, of course, brings us back to the issue raised by Collins of whether 'low' farming really was a regressive step.[64] Moreover, the fact that landlords were desperate to avoid running their own farms does much to nullify the complaint of insecurity of tenure. Taking even the most badly run-down farm 'in hand' would have been a burden on the landlord's purse.

Nonetheless, the presumed link between insecurity of tenure and the absence of investment to counter overseas competition led the Liberal party in 1906 to give the tenantry further legislative protection. Landlords now found themselves liable for causing tenants 'unreasonable disturbance'. Thus, if a landlord, without good cause and for reasons inconsistent with good estate management, terminated a tenancy with a notice to quit, or if the landlord refused to renew a tenancy if so requested at least one year before its expiration, or if the landlord raised his rents forcing a tenant from a farm which that tenant had capitally improved, the tenant was now entitled to claim compensation. This was contrary to the recommendations of the *Final Report of the Royal Commission on Agricultural Depression*, published in 1897, in which the Commissioners stated 'We are unable to see on what grounds a quitting tenant who has received the compensation fairly due to him for his unexhausted improvements could justly maintain a claim for compensation for disturbance . . . we are of opinion that no countenance should be given to any such demand.'[65] Whilst one can argue that the *Final Report* would reflect the views of assistant commissioners like Wilson Fox and was in consequence biased towards the already hard-pressed large agricultural landowners, the fact that the Liberals chose to ignore the *Report* is indicative of their continuing attempt to split off the farmer from the landlord lobby in rural constituencies. For example, the act of 1906 also gave the tenant compensation for the damage caused by game; this further enhanced the position of the tenant who already had the right to shoot hares and rabbits under the Ground Game Act of 1880. The subsequent 1914 Agricultural Holdings Act also enforced the payment of costs of disturbance whenever a tenancy was terminated on the sale of the estate. In other words, by 1914, the relationship between the landowner and the farmer had been modified very substantially in favour of the tenant.[66]

Whichever way one looks at this legislation, the legal entitlements granted to tenants by the Liberal party had undermined the arbitrary power of the squire. The arbitrariness of this power is, however, a moot point. Landlords had always needed to curry favour among farmers with deep enough pockets to farm 'high' and now, in the 1890s, they were desperate to avoid taking farms 'in hand'. But by giving tenants a degree of security in the occupation of their farms by making it impossible for the landlord to turn them out except through payment of heavy compensation for any unnecessary disturbance, the Liberals confirmed that the balance had tilted away from the landlord. The landlord was left to ponder on the value of retaining property over which he had less and less control. Moreover, evidence of the clear blue water beginning to open up between the landlord and the farmer can be seen in the creation of the Lincolnshire Farmers Union, which was to evolve into the National Farmers Union in 1908 and its counterpart the Country Landowners Association (est. 1907). This represented the beginning of a parting of the ways, as the N. F. U. was founded by farmers to represent farmers and *only* farmers. There was no attempt at an accord with landlords, as there had been when large farmers had established the Central Chambers of Agriculture to give farmers a voice, since the Chamber was now the preserve of their landlords. Consequently, the N. F. U. threatened the local hierarchical authority of landlords by replacing the vertical links between landlord and farmer with horizontal links between farmers, especially as landlords were no longer in any position to provide either the political leadership of the agricultural interest, as evidenced by the failure of their great petition, or to offer genuine solutions based on their largesse.[67]

On the other hand, it would perhaps be too much to say that the 'identity of sentiment' which existed between tenants and their landlords was entirely destroyed by the agricultural depression. Similarly, whilst the formation of the N. F. U. can be seen as an attempt by larger farmers to become the political leaders of their class rather than junior partners of their landlords, the N. F. U. did not make 'a great deal of difference . . . in landlord-and-tenant relationships'[68] before the First World War. After all, as Lord Hartington was forced to concede, farmers were still a predominantly Conservative body and they had a long-standing alliance with the 'farmers' friends' namely their predominantly Tory landlords who were also bending over backwards with rent reductions and repairs. Indeed, the farmer never really challenged the existing social and political structure of rural England before World War One, because the local unity of interest between the landowner and the tenant-farmer always managed to overcome any temporary problems.[69] In addition, while the Liberals tried to woo the farmer, they also sought to woo the labourer with allotments, having calculated that the agricultural labourers had replaced farmers as the most important 'interest' in the county seats after 1885. But playing second-fiddle to the labourer was not likely to enamour the farmer to the Liberal party. Finally, just as we saw in Chapter Two's discussion of the reluctance of farmers to move away from growing wheat before World War One, we can also see that, whilst the future lay with the farmer (despite his grumbles and worries about insecurity of tenure) this was not apparent on the County, District or Parish Council or the Board of Guardians, as they were loath to seize the baton from the landowner.[70]

DEBT, COUNTRY SEATS AND COUNTRY PURSUITS

Whilst the aristocracy, still resident in the countryside, retained the control of the reins of local government, the fact remains that they were in serious financial difficulty. This was due to their farm rentals having been halved as a result of the agricultural depression (see Chapter Two). But what really made this bite was that this decline in income made their debts harder to carry. Landed families were habitually burdened by debt in the form of charges made against their annual estate income. The bulk of these charges dated from the mid-nineteenth century, when many landlords had borrowed money to improve their estates in the expectation that their rents would continue to rise on the back of increased productivity. This was merely one of many potential source of debt as, for example, debt was also incurred by families who, on deciding to rebuild their ancestral seats, raised the necessary capital by mortgaging their estates.

Of course, in the 1850s and 1860s, when rents maintained an upward curve, servicing a mortgage presented families with little or no difficulty. Once rents started to fall, however, meeting these charges inevitably began to produce problems. These were compounded by the fact that in addition to the various improvement loans and mortgages raised for building purposes, many landowners were also burdened by the payment of portions and jointures to their younger brothers and sisters. As mentioned in Chapter One, one of the basic tenets of the strict family settlement was providing for younger children through a fixed sum of money rather than a parcel of land, thereby keeping the estate intact from generation to generation. These portions could take the form of a lump sum or an annuity. In both instances, it fell to the heir to honour them. In consequence, a sizeable proportion of the revenue received by a landowner from his estate was often already spoken for before it was even collected.

The heir, on the other hand, received his income directly from his father. The latter would often keep an allowance deliberately small to ensure that the heir agreed to renew the settlement. The classic example was Joshua Rowley, who saw his allowance rise from £500 a year to £2,000 a year. Among the aristocracy, who had far more at stake when it came to securing the heir's signature, allowances could be even smaller. The fourth Earl of Dysart gave his son an allowance of only £400 a year. But small allowances could sow the seeds of later disaster because it could encourage an heir to borrow against his expectations. Thus some families preferred to treat heirs to the carrot rather than the stick by giving them one of the family's secondary seats as a home, complete with the income from the surrounding estate. Wakefield Lodge, the Northamptonshire property of the Dukes of Grafton, seated at Euston Hall, was, for instance, occasionally occupied by the Earl of Euston.[1]

Given that debt, avoiding it and clearing it, was a problem endemic to the landed aristocracy and gentry, this chapter will examine three issues: firstly, identifying the causes of indebtedness in Suffolk; secondly, determining whether landed families had, as suggested by David Spring, managed to recover by the 1850s from the debts incurred during the lavish extravagance of the Regency period; and thirdly, discovering the burden of debt being carried by landed families during the agricultural depression of the late nineteenth century. Further, the effectiveness of the measures taken by landowners to save money and the effect that this had upon their lifestyles, particularly in relation to sport, need to be considered. As the Earl of Derby noted, in 1881, alongside the political influence, the social importance, the power over the tenantry, the pleasure of improving an estate and the rent, one also has to take into account the residential enjoyment or sport to be had living in the countryside.[2]

But as rents fell, any fixed annual charges, resulting from mortgage interest repayments or settlements, which had hitherto been kept within manageable proportions, inevitably began to take an ever increasing proportional share of what were declining agricultural incomes. The burden of this debt has, however, been the subject of much debate among historians, most notably between F. M. L. Thompson and David Spring in the 1950s and, more recently, Spring and David Cannadine in the 1970s. Spring maintains that, by the early 1830s, heavy indebtedness had become rife among those landed families where heirs had failed to marry heiresses or had failed to plug into the Industrial Revolution. Their debts had arisen out of a conspicuous love for the lavish, that included the erection of magnificent country houses, the provision of over generous settlements and a predilection for gambling, mistresses and other expensive vices. As a result, whilst the pattern of aristocratic expenditure 'was probably much the same as in the eighteenth century' aristocratic overspending in the early nineteenth century assumed 'larger proportions than before'.[3]

Settlements were a particularly worrying form of debt, because there was no way of knowing for certain how many children would eventually have to be provided for financially. Under the settlement arranged on the marriage of the second Duke of Grafton to Lady Henrietta Somerset, various permutations were taken into consideration. If there was only one younger child, its portion was to be £20,000. If, however, there were two or more younger children, £30,000 was to be divided equally between them. In the event of there being no male issue, an only daughter was to receive £30,000, while two or more daughters were to receive an equal share of £40,000. Fortunately, as most marriage settlements stipulated that portions were to be vested in sons at the age of twenty-one, and in daughters on their marriage, it was often quite some time before such a portion needed to be raised. Eventually the money would have to be found and since most families chose to meet these payments through mortgaging part of their estate rather than out of savings, the financial provisions inherent within the strict family settlement frequently increased the burden of debt carried by a particular family.[4]

On the other hand, by the early nineteenth century, the strict family settlement may have been far less likely to be the cause of serious indebtedness. This was due to the increasing popularity of providing for dependants through annual annuities rather than through portions vested in a family trust. By opting to give younger children an annual annuity, paid for out of income, landed families obviated the need to raise a mortgage. Under the deed of settlement, arranged on the marriage of the second Marquess of Bristol to Lady Katherine Manners in 1830, Lord Augustus Hervey (1837–1875), Lord John Hervey (1841–1902) and Lord Francis Hervey (1846–1931), each received an annual annuity of £400 a year. In total, these annuities worked out at £6,800 for Lord Augustus, assuming the annuity dated from his twenty-first birthday, £16,000 for Lord John, £25,600 for Lord Francis and £18,000 for Lady Adeliza who died in 1911, assuming her annuity was paid from the date of her marriage.[5] As a result, the third Marquess of Bristol, who succeeded his father in 1864 and who in consequence came into an income of over £12,000 per annum from the Ickworth estate, had to pay out £2,000 each year in annuities charged to the estate, to his younger brothers and sisters. In addition, a further £400 was owed to each of his two great aunts.[6] Thus, by opting to place an annual charge on the revenues received from the estate rather than by borrowing the money, the second Marquess of Bristol had seen to it that his younger children were adequately provided for without encumbering his son and heir with a series of burdensome mortgages. Clearly, 'this method of provision diminished the income at the disposal of the head of the family, but did not involve him in the creation of capital debt.'[7]

In reply, while Spring concedes that indebtedness may well have been less than overwhelming, it may yet have pressed harder than Thompson seems to suggest. Consider the huge sums of money, raised by way of a mortgage, which were lavished on building a country seat: to replace an original destroyed by fire, to be able to host one's neighbours and become their MP, or simply to rebuild in the latest style. Whatever the motivation, 'debt was the inevitable consequence.'[8] In Suffolk, one of the premier house-building projects was Ickworth Park, begun around 1796 by Frederick Hervey, Bishop of Derry and fourth Earl of Bristol. Between 1796 and 1810, Frederick spent nearly £15,000 on the house; however, the funds for this project came out of his Irish see. Frederick intended Ickworth to be 'quite classical' and to 'unite magnificence with convenience, and simplicity with dignity'.[9] But it was precisely because he intended the house to be magnificent that he had to bequeath the task of actually completing the project to his son – along with the costs of doing so. The central rotunda and the east wing were completed by the fifth Earl during the 1820s at a cost of nearly £40,000. Given that he did not have access to a fat bishopric in Ireland, the project was not finally finished until 1829, work having been frequently brought to halt by escalating costs and lack of money.[10]

When completed, Ickworth was rivalled only by Heveningham Hall, the seat of the Vanneck family. In the absence of an Irish bishopric, Heveningham was paid for by mortgaging the surrounding estate. This suggests that, at Ickworth too, mortgages would also have had to have been raised by the fifth Earl, but that this was done in a piecemeal fashion. Hence, the stop-start approach to building Ickworth, in contrast to Heveningham where the project had enough money behind it to allow the builders to get on with things. Heveningham Hall, which dates from 1778, was designed and built for Sir Gerard Vanneck by the architects Sir Robert Taylor and James Wyatt. The Hall itself was described by the Duc de la Rochefoucauld as 'extremely dignified and magnificent' and whilst no figures exist regarding the cost of building it, the fact that in 1839 the estate was burdened by a mortgage for £110,000 is perhaps significant.[11]

Subsequently in 1793, Wyatt was also commissioned by Sir John Rous (created Earl of Stradbroke in 1821) to rebuild Henham Hall, the original Elizabethan mansion having burnt down in 1773. The twenty year delay in rebuilding Henham was probably because up to 1788, Sir John, whose annual income was under £5,000, had to contend with debts of around £20,000. Following his marriage to the heiress Frances Wilson of Bilboa in County Limerick in 1788, however, Sir John's finances improved markedly, as she brought with her both the rents of an estate in Ireland and a substantial dowry. In 1791 Sir John also arranged the sale of property held by his mother in Norfolk. This sale left Sir John with £40,000 in hand. He was therefore, at last, in a position to begin rebuilding Henham. As Alan Mackley states, rebuilding the Hall 'was only made possible by the acquisition of capital from a marriage settlement and the sale of land'.[12]

But once an architect was commissioned and building work commenced on a new country seat, the landowner could suddenly find himself in the lap of the gods when it came to controlling costs. The architect, James Wyatt, who in addition to Sir Gerard Vanneck and Sir John Rous, received commissions from Philip Broke and Sir Charles Kent, drew his commission on the original estimate rather than the final cost, for 'when business is done the other way it is a great temptation to architects to increase expense for the sake of percentage.'[13] Even in those instances where the architect was on a lower commission, cost overruns were all but inevitable. Thus, the final cost for rebuilding Henham was nearly double Wyatt's original estimate, finally coming in at over £20,000, or £8,000 above the initial costings. By comparison, Redgrave Hall was remodelled in about 1770 at a cost of nearly £30,000. Across Suffolk therefore, the established families of Rous and Hervey were being matched, both in the grandeur of their homes and in their ability to foot the bill, by the new families of Vanneck, Wilson, Berners (who rebuilt Woolverstone Hall after he bought the estate in about 1773) and the Keppels at Elveden. Even remodelling a house had its attendant risks as, for example, when Philip Broke decided to remodel Broke Hall. Not only was the final bill nearly £8,000, £5,000 above the original estimate, even more gallingly the work was so poor that the house was all but rebuilt by James Wyatt in 1791–2!

By the early nineteenth century, the risks of a family falling into debt through house-building were greatly reduced by the development of quantity surveying, which is fortunate given that both Oakley Park and Thornham Hall were remodelled in the 1830s.[14] Debts could, of course, still be incurred through gambling, and one of the most notorious scandals of the period revolved around the gambling debts of Lord Charles FitzRoy, the son of the fourth Duke of Grafton. In 1827, the Duke, in conjunction with Charles' father-in-law, Lord George Cavendish (created Earl of Burlington in 1831, third son of the fourth Duke of Devonshire), was forced to intervene to rescue Charles 'from the disgrace which awaited [him]'.[15] Their intervention was, however, conditional on Charles assigning over to them the whole of his life income (or portion) of £20,000. Having done so, he would then be unable to make use of it 'for other purposes' and would be dependent upon them for his annual allowance. The Duke of Grafton hoped, thereby, to avoid a repetition of the 'disagreeable business in which we have been engaged'.[16] In the meantime, the Duke turned to Messrs Drummond & Co for a loan of nearly £10,000 to settle his son's affairs with his more 'patient creditors' and instructed his solicitors to sell all his Consols to raise another £10,000 which was owed to a Mr Singleton. Once this was done, the Duke wrote to Cavendish that 'difficult as it has been for me to take the share which I have on this occasion' it gives 'one pleasure to think the sacrifice I have made of my own money as well as of those who are to come after one, was likely to be to . . . good purpose'.[17]

After the scandal had abated, the Duke was appalled when informed by his wayward son of a new scandal in 1836. Charles wrote to his father asking for further financial assistance 'in order that I may rid myself of my embarrassments'. Given the 'desperate state' of his affairs, Charles proposed to borrow the money needed to pay off his new gambling debts, 'the principal of which will be secured by my insuring my life. Therefore, it will not cost you a farthing.' But, for this plan to work, he needed to use his father's name as security for the interest. Anticipating his father's reaction he appealed to him to 'pause and grant me [this] request . . . Remember . . . you are now the only person that can do this for me. How can you refuse this request?'[18]

The reaction of his father was one of growing disillusionment with his son's inability to reform. Nevertheless, 'My son's case is one out of which he must be extricated, or be left, not only in a state of great difficulty, but of such disgrace as might . . . affect [his] office' as Vice Chamberlain of the Royal Household.[19] The Duke therefore agreed to pay the interest due on his son's life insurance policy, as Charles would 'at once be relieved from his embarrassments'. As to the future, the Duke believed that Charles should 'be left to settle his gambling debts as he can, with his creditors' out of his income 'which would leave him with his hands so tied-up with regard to gambling as to make it very difficult [for] him for some time at least to relapse into such habits'.[20] Indeed, given his son's fear of the 'disgrace, to which he has exposed himself' by his gambling debts and that such disgrace was 'perhaps, the only security against him indulging the same propensities' the Duke concluded, 'It strikes me . . . that, if his Gambling debts were settled there would no longer be any restraint upon him, again resuming his old habits.' In which case, it might be for the best if 'the present inconvenience and disgrace which he is undergoing, be left in its full force'.[21]

With regard to the £2,500 his son owed to Messrs Drummond & Co the Duke wavered slightly from this new stance on the grounds that 'if we were to relieve him of this part of the charge on his income' it might induce him 'to buckle to, with more spirit, in the application of a portion of his income to the liquidation of his debts'. Such an act of kindness, it was hoped, would finally end his 'great principle of not paying any Gambling debts' and thus aid his 'future salvation from misery and ruin'.[22] The Duke also advised his son to put his affairs in the hands of a solicitor, 'in whom you can confide'.[23] Unfortunately, on examining the state of Charles' finances, the solicitor recommended by the Duke steadfastly refused to have anything to do with the affair. As usual, though, Charles had his own ideas on how best to solve his financial difficulties. Writing in August 1836, he determined that, 'having heavy debts to pay I feel myself under the necessity of giving up and selling the House and the furniture'[24] – thereby compounding the losses endured by the family.

By the mid-nineteenth century, Spring suggests that such a scandal was less and less likely to occur as landed families were less inclined to hazard their wealth by spending beyond their means. This was because extravagance tended to fall out of fashion among landed families 'with the unfolding of Victoria's and Albert's respectable domesticity'. Thus, the spendthrifts of one era were gradually replaced by a 'generation more careful about how its money was spent' although it was to be many years before the abstinence and thrift of this new generation cancelled out 'the backsliding of the old' as the 'legacy of encumbrances was far from small'.[25] For example, following the death of the second Lord Huntingfield in 1844, whilst his Trustees were able to use £29,000 of the £33,239 which was yielded by his life policy to repay part of the aforementioned mortgage for £110,000, the family still remained deeply in debt.[26] It was this recovery that David Cannadine sought to re-examine. Having done so, he concluded that the distinction between an early Victorian crisis and a mid-Victorian recovery had been overdrawn. In his opinion, a relatively high, though far from ruinous, level of debt may well have been a more persistent feature of life for many landed families between the 1800s and the early 1870s.[27]

The clearest evidence of persistent aristocratic indebtedness in mid-nineteenth century Suffolk comes from the accounts of the Hervey family. Between 1861 and 1862, the second Marquess of Bristol, far from reducing the mortgages that had been charged to the settled portion of the Ickworth estate by his father, actually opted to borrow an additional £17,700 (see Table 6), and thereby raised the total burden of debt carried by the estate to £30,790. This of course, was not an excessive burden of debt for the estate to bear, as the interest needed to service these loans only absorbed 9 per cent of the £15,137 that Bristol received in rents from the settled portion of the Ickworth estate each year.[28] Similarly, a mortgage for £10,000, charged at 4 per cent interest to the family's Sleaford estate in Lincolnshire, only absorbed £400 of the £21,267 that the Hervey family received in rents each year from this estate.[29]

Table 6: Mortgages Charged to the Settled Portions of the
Third Marquess of Bristol's Estates in Suffolk in 1865

Year	Mortgage with	Amount	Charged to	Interest
1806	George Holford	£1,090	–	4% (£43)
1827	Frederic Corrance	£7,000	Barrow Hall	4.5% (£315)
1854	George Law, Rev James Barnes, James Lyon	£5,000	Lands in Eyke and Bromeswell	4.5% (£225)
1861	Messrs Jackson and Sparke	£4,000	Hereditament in Tuddenham	4% (£160)
1861	Lord Charles Hervey Lord Alfred Hervey	£11,000	Estates in Rushmere and Playford	4% (£440)
1862	Arthur Hervey	£2,700	Property in Playford	4% (£108)
	Total	£30,790		£1,291

(Source: SRO [Bury] HA507/4/39)

A more detailed examination of the finances of the third Marquess of Bristol

reveals that, during the 1860s, he was in receipt of an overall income of
£36,404 gross, £31,564 net, after the payment of tax, rates, insurance and
repairs, from his 16,981 acre estate in Suffolk and his 13,745 acre estate in
Lincolnshire. In proportional terms, therefore, the £2,800 owed in annuities,
together with the £1,691 owed in mortgage interest, represented only 14
per cent of his overall net annual income.[30] As a result, even after the money
owing had been paid, he was still in receipt of an overall income of
£27,073.[31] When set against the debts still carried by Lord Huntingfield,
this level of debt was clearly an acceptable part of aristocratic life in mid-
nineteenth century Suffolk, particularly as the level of overall income
absorbed in servicing these charges was being reduced in proportional terms
anyway by the steady rise in agricultural rents. As Cannadine states,
'Provided indebtedness could be sustained without discomfort, why should
the tenant for life bother to reduce it?'[32]

Moreover, for many families the perennial problem of providing for
younger children continued to see mortgages charged to estates. Whilst the
Hervey family opted under their marriage settlements to pay out annuities,
others continued to opt for portions. Under the will of Sir William Middleton,
drawn up in 1857, a portion of £30,000 was to be paid to his niece Frederica
Broke on her twenty-first birthday or on the date of her marriage, whichever
occurred first. The payment of such a sum could, of course, have only been
met by mortgaging part of the estate. Similarly, under the proposals relating
to the marriage settlement of Colonel Joshua Rowley, he was granted the
power of raising £20,000, the whole to be paid out as portions to his younger
children.[33]

In addition, new sources of debt in the form of improvement loans also
emerged in the mid-nineteenth century. Lord Waveney borrowed close to
double the gross annual value of the Flixton Hall estate from the Lands
Improvement Company during the 1870s and the 1880s to fund estate-wide
improvements (see Chapter Two). By contrast, between 1875 and 1892, the
third Marquess of Bristol borrowed a total of £7,645 from the General Land
Drainage and Improvement Company to pay for improvements to his farms
in order to keep them tenanted to avoid the greater catastrophe of taking
them in hand. These loans resulted in a series of rent charges amounting to
£452 per annum being placed on farms on the Ickworth estate. The
Marquess borrowed a further £1,073 in 1892 under the 1864 Improvement
of Land Act. This, and subsequent loans, meant that by 1897, the overall
level of improvement charges levied on the Ickworth estate amounted to
£703 per annum (see Table 9).[34] A further £548 was owed in interest for
improvements made to the Sleaford estate. Taken as a whole, these loans,

together with mortgage interest totalling £820 (see Table 9), meant that, far from recovering, the Marquess of Bristol (exclusive of annuities) actually owed more in interest in 1897 than in 1865, and this on a far lower level of income. But looking back on the mid-nineteenth century, up to the 1870s, it is also clear that, though families remained in debt, their debts, though high, were far from being totally unmanageable.

The heady optimism of the mid-nineteenth century also encouraged landowners to borrow money to build or rebuild their family homes. Working from a sample of 500 country houses which were either built or remodelled between 1835 and 1889, Mark Girouard has shown that house-building remained a constant feature of aristocratic society throughout the period 1835 to 1880, and did not, as David Spring and M. W. Flinn believed, peak somewhere between 1815 and 1830. On the other hand, as Wilson and Mackley point out, whilst the chronology of country house building, viewed nationally, shows peaks and troughs, at county level the actual decision to build was a complex equation calculated around the variables of marriage, money, taste and ambition. But if out of all these variables a trend does emerge, then Girouard's interpretation is backed by Lawrence and Jeanne Stone, who have uncovered evidence of continued building activity in mid-nineteenth century Hertfordshire lasting up to the 1870s. They base this on the additions which families were making to their homes in the shape of stables, offices and servants' accommodation. In Suffolk, the Marquess of Bristol spent £2,947 on repairs to the exterior of Ickworth between 1859 and 1865. A further £920 was spent on various modifications to the interior of the Hall, including alterations to both the north-east and south-west bedrooms of the east wing. In addition, Bristol also commissioned designs for a new coach-house and harness room.[35]

On a grander scale, the Rous, Adair, Thellusson and Tomline families all decided to either remodel or completely rebuild their homes in the mid-nineteenth century: Lord Tollemache, meanwhile, was engaged in building the magnificent Peckforton Castle in Cheshire. In Suffolk, Sir Charles Barry was commissioned by the Earl of Stradbroke to redesign the eighteenth century exterior of Henham Hall. Under Barry's direction, this plain house of three storeys was 'encased in a restrained Italianate disguise' composed of a cornice and balustraded parapet, a loggia along the whole length of the ground floor with a small portico above in place of the Wyatt window, and architrave surrounds to all the upper windows.[36] By contrast, after a fire had completely destroyed the interior of Flixton, Sir Robert Adair commissioned Anthony Salvin (who also designed High House, Campsea Ashe, for John Sheppard) to completely rebuild the Hall in the new Jacobean style. As a result, when it was completed in 1850 it 'bristled with a forest of chimney's and polygonal angle buttresses with circular decorated pinnacles'.[37] Rendlesham Hall, which was designed and built by William Burn between 1868 and 1871 for Lord Rendlesham, was also built in the Jacobean style. By comparison with Flixton, it was a singularly 'uninspired building' and it was certainly a poor imitation of the original seventeenth century hall, which had been described as a 'princely residence . . . surpassed by few in the Kingdom'[38] before it burnt down in 1830.

By the 1860s, all that remained of the original Rendlesham hall were the ruins of the front doorway. The loss was therefore a considerable one and was compounded by the loss of most of the furnishings. The overall damage was estimated at around £100,000, but, as no part of the property was insured, the cost of rebuilding and refurnishing the Hall in the 1870s fell on Lord Rendlesham. Fortunately, his building programme could be funded out of his share of the fortune of Peter Thellusson (see Chapter Eight). Similarly, George Tomline could cover the cost of William Burn's redesign of Orwell Park (completed between 1851 and 1853) out of his grandfather's clerical fortune and income from his estate in Lincolnshire. But for those without such a fortune, the large, short-term expenditure associated with country house-building could not have been borne 'without resort to external assistance'[39] in the form of a mortgage. Indeed, Sir Robert Adair raised a mortgage for £51,000 at around the same time as work commenced on rebuilding Flixton Hall in 1844. Clearly such a large sum could have had only one purpose, to pay for the rebuilding of the hall. Borrowing heavily on rebuilding the hall would also explain the somewhat run-down character of the estate by the 1870s. This huge sum was, however, subsequently cleared by Lord Waveney in 1873, through the sale of 2,800 acres in Suffolk. This, on the one hand, does accord with Spring's model of a concerted effort on the part of landowners to reduce debt in the mid-nineteenth century. On the other hand, a second glance suggests this more likely to have been a case of clearing the decks to allow Lord Waveney to borrow large sums from the Lands Improvement Company.[40]

Whilst still on the subject of country house building, it should also not be forgotten that, as in the eighteenth century, many new nineteenth-century landowners were keen to build themselves a country seat. Between 1844 and 1851, the Victorian railway and building contractor Sir Morton Peto built Somerleyton Hall near Lowestoft. In 1861, however, it was sold to Francis Crossley, a Halifax carpet manufacturer, together with the surrounding 3,000 acre estate. Meanwhile, in 1859, Henry Wilson, having bought the Stowlangtoft estate in 1825, began rebuilding Stowlangtoft

Hall. Then in the 1860s, Charles Austin also decided to rebuild Brandeston Hall according to a design of the Ipswich architect R. Phipson – the same individual who'd spotted the Minton tiles in one of the Marquess of Bristol's farmhouses – the original Elizabethan Brandeston Hall having burnt down. The new Brandeston Hall was built in the 'Jacobethan' style which, like the prodigy houses of late Elizabethan and Jacobean England, 'reflected the self confidence of a new race of self-made men – manufacturers, merchant princes and nouveaux riches who had got where they were by hard work and a good head for business in an increasingly commercial world, and wanted everyone to know it'.[41] In particular, they wished to announce their arrival to the resident gentry in the surrounding district, and in the county generally. As Girouard notes, 'A grand new mansion, with generous entertainments for the neighbours held within it, was a useful means of accelerating acceptance by the county.'[42] These new boys also threw themselves wholeheartedly into the sporting lifestyle of the more established families of Victorian Suffolk.

The latter, though frequently in debt, were, thanks to rising agricultural incomes, able to carry their debts without undue bother and so could afford to indulge in their leisure pursuits, particularly shooting. During the mid-nineteenth century the rearing and preservation of game became the most widespread and most rapidly growing country pursuit of the Victorian aristocracy and gentry, and the one recreational pastime 'which more than any other made country life and the ownership of estates gratifying'.[43] As Archdeacon Grantly observed in Anthony Trollope's *The Last Chronicle of Barset*, published in 1867, 'Land gives so much more than the rent. It gives position and influence and political power, to say nothing about the game'[44] which is why the brewer, Sir William Gilstrap, having already purchased the Fornham Park estate in 1862, decided in the following year to buy an additional 2,400 acres of light land in and around the parish of Herringswell, purely for sport. This was because with the development of the systematic rearing and preservation of game the sporting potential of agricultural estates began to be realized.

Improving the quality of sport was at the forefront of landowners' minds and on a par with improving their homes and their farms, and throughout the period we can see evidence of this in the size of the bags being taken, and in the refinements being made to the double-barrelled shotgun. Frederic Corrance, reputedly one of the most distinguished sportsmen in Suffolk, recalled that:

With the increase of game a change in guns took place. First, a powerful loading rod superseded the ramrod and materially increased the speed of loading [but this was very dangerous and] Lord Rendlesham and . . . Admiral Rous each lost a finger. It is probable the second barrel had been left on cock . . . very shortly after . . . sportsmen gave up loading for themselves and employed a servant to carry a second gun. When well served the user of the old weapon could shoot nearly as rapidly as with the breechloader at a hot corner or at driven birds; and when walking up partridges there was no halt after a shot.[45]

The practice of 'walking up partridges' was described by T. W. Turner, a former head-keeper on the Elveden estate, who recalled that on one occasion the Maharajah Duleep Singh was 'out partridge shooting. These were the days of muzzle-loaders . . . the Maharajah [who] had three double-barrelled guns, and two loaders . . . with . . . blue and green coats and waistcoats, powder flasks and leather shotbags . . . [would walk] in seed clover, which was ideal for partridges to settle in.'[46] But whilst partridges were shot on the move, pheasants were driven toward the guns. According to Corrance:

Pheasant shooting became more of an art as more trouble was taken in the flushing of the birds. It soon became the custom to put them up . . . so that they rose over high trees before coming to the gun. But the bouquet of birds in a grand rush seldom gave the chance of getting four cocks with four barrels . . . [by contrast, partridges were shot on the walk, over] white turnips [where] . . . even the red-leg would consent to remain long enough for a shot. The lines were kept with mathematical precision, and when a halt was made to load, even if a bird was winged neither dog nor man dared to forestall the advance, [so] there was a second halt . . . to pick up . . . No doubt there was a certain degree of monotony in the solemn and noiseless tramp, but there was always something in front, and it was at least better than the long wait for the driven bird.[47]

However, the two quite different styles of shooting described by Corrance shared one thing in common – the growing quantity of game being shot thanks to the introduction of game rearing. The evidence from Elveden is illustrative of the increase in game being reared on estates in the county, especially pheasants, whose numbers increased greatly thanks to the introduction of a new system of rearing under coops.[48] In 1834, the total for the year was 674 pheasants, 392 partridges, 710 hares, 248; rabbits and 34 woodcock. By 1857, the number of pheasants and partridges shot had risen considerably: pheasants, 1,823; partridges, 3,258; hares, 821; rabbits, 368; woodcock, 33.

It was the growing reputation enjoyed by Elveden as a sporting estate that probably attracted the Maharajah Duleep Singh. In 1863, the trustees of the Maharajah purchased Elveden for £105,000, raised through a loan at 4 per cent interest from the India Office, from the executors of the will of the late William Newton. Subsequently, in 1869 the Maharajah's trustees also decided to purchase the neighbouring Eriswell estate for £120,000 from the New England Company for Propagating the Gospel in Foreign Parts. By 1883 the Elveden Hall estate comprised 17,210 acres of Breckland. Surprisingly, the rental value of this huge property was under £5,000 per annum. This was because only just over 5,000 acres were under cultivation. The rest was left as uncultivated heathland and rabbit warrens and was entirely devoted to the rearing and preservation of game. Duleep Singh was, in consequence, able to indulge his passion for shooting to the fullest. As a result, the number of birds reared on this estate soared, so much so in fact, that during four days' shooting in December 1877, he and his fellow guests shot a total of 6,539 winged and ground game (see Table 7). These figures underline the growing fashion for the *grand battue* in which dozens of beaters were employed to drive hundreds of birds toward the waiting guns and their loaders as well as the continuance of walking up partridges – hence the higher figures enjoyed on 5th December.[49]

Table 7: Game Shot on the Elveden Estate
From 4th December to 7th December 1877

1877	Pheasant	Partridge	Hares	Rabbits	Woodcocks	Gild Duck	Total
Dec 4	2017	62	207	170	1	55	2512
Dec 5	6	165	43	2	1	–	217
Dec 6	916	3	219	337	4	–	1479
Dec 7	1820	44	201	262	4	–	2331
Total	4759	274	670	771	10	55	6539

(Source: Game Card, SRO [Bury] HA513/16/16)

But this card refers to just four days. The total for the season September 1876 to February 1877 was 55,086 winged and ground game, whilst for the season 1885–1886 the figure was 81,577 (see Table 8).

Table 8: Game Shot on the Elveden Estate, September 1876 to February 1877
& September 1885 to February 1886

Year	Pheasant	Partridge	Hare	Woodcock	Duck	Snipe	Various	Rabbits	Total
1876–7	9,803	11,823	1,724	26	–	31	70	31,609	55,086
1885–6	11,921	9,491	1,815	77	8	1	124	58,140	81,577

(Source: Nicholas Everitt, 'Shooting', in William Page [ed], *The Victoria County History of the County of Suffolk, Volume II* [London, 1907], p. 365)

Elveden was now in a class of its own with bags of between 6,000 to 8,000 partridges being considered a good season. But whilst the estate produced bags significantly higher than those taken on any of the other estates in the county, such as Euston, (see Table 9), it was merely an extreme example of the growing popularity for rearing and preserving game.

Table 9: Game Shot on the Euston Estate Between 29th October
and 1st November 1878

1878	Pheasant	Partridge	Hares	Woodcock	Rabbits	Total
Oct 29	555	51	165	1	10	782
Oct 30	45	361	74	–	2	482
Oct 31	3	407	13	–	6	429
Nov 1	311	100	29	1	12	543
Total	914	919	281	2	30	2146

(Source: Game Card, SRO [Bury] HA513/16/1)

The reason, of course, the bags taken at Elveden were higher than those at Euston or Thornham, Rendlesham or Heveningham was because the owners of these estates were also making a substantial commitment towards improving the productivity of their farms as well as their shooting. Duleep Singh on the other hand, preferred to concentrate all his efforts on improving his shooting. As far as the Maharajah was concerned, a large area of cultivated farmland was merely the means by which one encouraged the game reared on the estate to stay on the property. Elveden therefore remained agriculturally underdeveloped, as a letter sent by the Indian Government to the Secretary of State for India, dated 7th July 1879, reveals:

> The question is not whether His Highness the Maharajah shall be maintained at . . . [the] expense [of the Indian Treasury] in a manner befitting his historical position and his proper dignity, but whether he shall be enabled to go on enjoying the luxury of preserving game, and rendering a great estate totally unprofitable.[50]

Nevertheless, four days shooting at Euston, Heveningham and Rendlesham still produced bags of between 2,000 and 3,000 head of game. The widespread pursuit of sport by the gentry in mid-nineteenth century Suffolk was thus a clear expression of the widening margin which was developing between their rising agricultural incomes and their encumbrances. These encumbrances, as in the case of the Herveys in west Suffolk and the Adairs in east Suffolk, were still very much a part of aristocratic life: the Adairs, exclusive of loans from the Lands Improvement Company, owed £10,000 to Messrs Tyrell and Thurlow, £5,500 to the Duke of Northumberland, £1,500 to Messrs Leeke and Horsfall and £5,300 to the Trustees of the Will of Sir R. S. Adair. Similarly, the Tendring Hall estate owned by Colonel Joshua Rowley was charged with two mortgages totalling £23,000.[51] What, then, was the impact upon these families, and their lifestyles, once rents began to fall after 1874?

Given that the lifestyle enjoyed by many landowners in mid-nineteenth century Suffolk rested on a foundation of debt, as a result of the improvements made to their estates, rebuilding their homes and the charges and portions they owed to younger brothers and sisters, their concomitant spending on country pursuits indicates that carrying these debts clearly presented little or no difficulty, so long as rents were rising. Inevitably, once rents began to fall, the fixed nature of these encumbrances began to absorb an ever increasing proportional share of fast diminishing incomes. As Cannadine states, the decline in rentals associated with the agricultural depression clearly assumed ominous proportions for those families whose estates were bearing jointures or fixed interest charges incurred during the 1850s, '60s and '70s on the assumption that rentals would continue to rise.[52] The difficult position in which this placed many landowners in Suffolk, especially those without a large non-agricultural source of income, is again best illustrated by the predicament of the third Marquess of Bristol.

By 1883, the Marquess' gross annual income had risen to £41,270 of which £20,011 was derived from his estates in Suffolk and £19,429 from his estate in Lincolnshire. Fourteen years later they were yielding £12,600, and £12,626 gross, respectively (see Table 10): a fall of 39 per cent. Out of this sum, there still had to be paid the usual expenses incurred by the owners of an estate, such as repairs, rates, taxes, subscriptions and, increasingly by the 1890s, the tithe formerly paid by his tenants. These, together with the costs of running a household and bad debts, brought the Marquess' overall level of expenditure (exclusive of his London and Brighton properties) up to £16,603. This still left him with a relatively healthy balance of £8,623 per annum. But this ignores the increasingly heavy burden now posed by the fixed nature of his encumbrances. These comprised family charges, mortgage interest, improvement charges and insurances amounting to £5,479. Their payment left the Marquess with a margin of only £3,144 between net income and expenditure on rents derived from 32,000 acres. As Cannadine states, there can be little doubt that an important element in the widespread aristocratic anguish felt at the end of the nineteenth century arose out of the continued burden of encumbrances. This anguish should be seen both in terms of the difficulty of providing adequate security when the capital value of land had to be written down and also of bearing the greater burden of interest charges when current income was reduced.[53]

The Marquess of Bristol's underlying financial position was, in fact, far worse than these figures suggest. A letter sent from Francis Pixley reveals that in June 1894, 'His Lordship was indebted to Bankers, Tradesmen and others . . . to the extent of £14,429.'[54] Furthermore, whilst there was £8,403 available in private funds, the 'amount that could confidently be realized was £5,048 [leaving] a deficiency to be provided by Your Lordship of about £9,000'.[55] If the Marquess used the £5,048 to repay part of his unpaid bills, this still left him about £9,000 in debt. Thus, by the mid-1890s, the Marquess, in addition to having to find the money owing to his brothers and sisters and the General Land Drainage and Improvement Company, was also being pursued by his creditors. Embarrassingly, in 1888, he had been taken to court by Messrs Davey & Son and Mr A. H. Monk for the non-payment of bills totalling a mere £63. 9s. 1d.[56] The conclusion would seem clear: for those families encumbered by debt and dependent on their agricultural rents, the 1880s and 1890s were an increasingly bleak period. This is why an indebted aristocracy, tied to their agricultural incomes, petitioned the government for assistance in 1888.

In the absence of any government assistance for agriculture, the Marquess, having tried to maintain an aristocratic lifestyle out of greatly reduced income, had no option other than to retrench. During the 1890s, he began selling timber from the park surrounding the Hall, thereby raising £300 per annum.

Table 10: Statement of Income and Expenditure of the most
Hon The Third Marquess of Bristol 15th May 1897

Suffolk Income	£	Suffolk Expenditure	£
Estate Rental	12,600	Family charges	2,000
		Lady Bristol's Jointure	500
Total	12,600	Lady Katherine Hammond's Allowance	300
		Lady Alice Jolliffe's Allowance	300
		Shotley Mortgage Interest on £18,000	680
		Tithes	2,516
		Glebe and other rents	230
		St John's Church, Bury St Edmunds	100
		Gt Chesterfield Church	150
		Improvement Charges	703
		Insurances	308
		Property, Land and Other Rates	
		And Taxes	800
		Estate Repairs	3,000
		Estate (Miscellaneous)	500
		Total	12,087
Lincolnshire Income		*Lincolnshire Expenditure*	
Estate Rental	12,626	Land and Income Taxes	343
		Parochial Rates	80
		Tithes	1,052
		Drainage Charges	166
		Fee Farm Rents	52
		Improvement Charges	382
		Estate Repairs	1,500
		Miscellaneous Payments	350
		Estate Management	500
		Sleaford Hospital	130
		Mortgage interest to Henry Hervey	100
		Mortgage interest to Bouverie Pusey	40
Total	12,626	Total	4,695
		'Establishment' Payments:	4,000
		Gamekeepers, gardeners,	
		Staff, stables, food etc	
		Bad debts	1,300
		Overall Total	22,082
		To Balance	3,144
Overall Total	25,226	Total	25,226

(Source: Income and Expenditure of the Marquess of Bristol, 15th May 1897, SRO
[Bury] 941/71/4)

In 1890 alone, he cut down and sold 239 ash trees, 24 large elms and two poplars.[57] The following year, he also sold the contents of his conservatories and glass houses. More symbolically, in 1897, he also let the shooting rights of the Ickworth estate for £910 per annum. Four years later, he leased his London mansion, No 6 St James' Square, to Lord Avebury for £2,350 per annum so saving a further £500 in running costs. In so doing, the Marquess was effectively withdrawing from both London society and the county's sporting scene as Charles Adeane and Edwin Savill observed: 'Owing to . . . the late agricultural depression . . . landowners [were] often compelled through stress of circumstances to forgo their pleasures for the sake of income.'[58]

A landowner such as Lord Henniker, meanwhile, who was encumbered by what the present Lord Henniker has described as 'astronomical debts', had to make an even greater effort to retrench. He broke up his household which, in 1851, had included two governesses, a nurse, a nursemaid, a still-room maid, a needlewoman, a ladies' maid, a housemaid, a butler, two footmen, a cook and four kitchen-maids. He then let both Worlingworth Hall and Thornham Hall and applied to Queen Victoria for paid employment, becoming governor of the Isle of Man.[59] Similar arrangements began to made across the county, as Wilson Fox reported:

> I venture to assert that the majority of estates in Suffolk, either large or small, cannot be maintained in a state of efficiency out of the present rentals, and at the same time leave a sufficient margin for the landowners to live in any comfort on their property, particularly if they have a family to educate . . . [in fact] *some cannot {even} afford to live in their residences* . . . I am not referring to men who have squandered money, but to those who have always done their best . . . [however] small owners are usually in the worst plight.[60]

It had, of course, always been the practice among landed families to let a secondary residence. Sir William Middleton, of Shrubland Park, also owned Bramford Hall, Bosmere Hall and Livermere Park, and he would also have owned Crowfield Hall if it had not been pulled down when the Middletons moved into Shrubland Park. As a result, he looked to let Livermere Park because the net annual loss to the estate when it was left un-let in 1856–7 was £600. Similarly, when Sir George Broke Middleton of Broke Hall moved into Shrubland Park on the death of his uncle Sir William Middleton, in 1860, he too was keen to let his other homes. Thus, Bramford Hall, having been let on an eight-year lease in 1858, was re-let in 1866 and again in 1874; Broke Hall was let in 1875 and again in 1878; whilst Bosmere Hall was let in 1861 and again in 1877. Whilst this evidence is somewhat patchy it is clear that a consistent policy of letting subsidiary properties was in place. Broke Hall meanwhile went to Sir George's younger brother Charles Broke.[61]

The difference between the 1880s and 1890s was that families now began to let their principal residences. For example, Lord Henniker let Thornham and John Lloyd-Anstruther let Hintlesham Hall to the stockbroker William Quilter; Marlesford Hall, the seat of Miss Shuldham, which passed on her marriage to the Schreiber family, was let to Edwin Darvall. Robert Sheriffe let Henstead Hall to Heneage Bagot-Chester, Colonel H. M. Leathes let Herringfleet Hall to Colonel Edward Butler and George Holt-Wilson, having successfully managed to let Redgrave Hall, removed his family to the nearby rectory. Essentially, the great agricultural estates could no longer provide enough funds to run a comfortable country seat. Overall, Pamela Horn has calculated that two out of every three country seats in Suffolk were let, primarily to so-called 'sporting' or 'shooting' tenants.[62] In so doing, of course, many families found themselves far better off, as had their predecessors in the eighteenth century when letting the big house was the key to re-balancing the books, as in the case of Sir John Blois who, like Charles FitzRoy, had a predilection for the gaming tables. As one landowner revealed in 1882, 'We have five farms on our hands . . . we have [therefore] hired for a trifling rent the Rectory in our parish, which chanced to be vacant. We have [in consequence] broken up our establishment, and shut up our house [and as a result] we have a better balance at our bankers than we have ever had in our lives before.'[63] Even better than shutting up the house was finding a tenant – but why would a tenant wish to hire a Hall in the midst of the agricultural depression? The answer lies in the evidence provided by Pamela Horn – country pursuits.

Tenants were found for these properties for two reasons. Firstly, as we have seen, it was that trade-mark combination of the English country gentleman, the country house and country pursuits, that continued to attract new buyers who 'were in love with the idea of being a country gentleman, strolling with gun under arm round their own acres'.[64] It was this same combination of factors that drew hirers as well as buyers into the English countryside now that more and more Halls were being let with sporting rights attached. In 1882, Sir George Broke Middleton let Broke Hall with its attendant shooting-rights to William Quilter for £530 per annum. The following year, the Hall and the shooting was let to Edward Bunbury on a five year lease at £650 per annum.[65] Across Suffolk, therefore, to those families who formed the bulk of landed society, below the level of the super-rich, with incomes tied to their farms, the appearance of the sporting tenant was a God-send akin to the arrival of those Scottish and West Country dairy and stockmen who were happy to take good mixed arable and livestock farms at knockdown rents. In the opinion of Nicholas Everitt, writing in 1907:

> The economic value of shooting is well known . . . at the present day nearly all of [north-west Suffolk] has been purchased or leased by men of wealth who cultivate the 'Brecks' for game in order to improve their shooting; game thriving best where cultivation is carried on . . . Now-a-days . . . landowner[s] . . . in Suffolk profit by the system of letting the land to a shooting tenant instead of allowing it to lie waste.[66]

Everitt's analysis is corroborated by a Suffolk landowner who declared 'I would not let the shooting if I could possibly avoid it, but I could not hang on here if I did not.'[67] Similarly, the Rev John Holden who owned the Lackford Manor estate declared, shooting rents were landowners' only hope and 'alone enabled him to keep his light land under the plough; indeed it was necessary to do this, as in places where the land was uncultivated partridges would not stay'. In other words, light land was kept in cultivation by landowners, by keeping their farms let or by taking land in-hand, to attract sporting tenants and sporting rents or buyers. The land was then kept in cultivation by the new occupiers of the Hall, by arrangement with the tenantry or *at the hirer's expense*, so it could be used for 'pleasure purposes by its owners or hirers' who as both owners and lessees also now took on the business of rearing and preserving the game, expending 'enormous sums of money' on their pleasure.[68]

Secondly, new buyers and new hirers still considered brushing up against the residual gravitas of the old order to be the simplest way to rub the shine off their new money. Landowners were still influential figures in English society and the simplest way to get close enough was to associate with them in their bailiwick – the English countryside – where they continued to dominate local government and the rural constituencies. This is why, as Wilson and Mackley have shown, when it would have made more sense for landowners to pull their houses down and plough up the park, they did not do so. Preferring to let their homes 'indicates a strong reluctance to sweep away a potent symbol of landed status, and where owners had gone elsewhere to restore their fortunes, faith that the move was just a temporary one'.[69] The sporting tenantry, meanwhile, aired the homes of the odd aristocrat and the gentry whilst the latter rebalanced their books with the former's cash – but was more at work here?

The majority of country seats, the most potent symbols of landed authority in the English countryside, were now occupied by pseudo-gentry. This represents a major reconfiguration of landed society and perhaps explains why, when we first see William Quilter in the county hiring Hintlesham Hall and then Broke Hall as a sporting tenant, we also see him on the Magistrates Bench. This is highly significant, as it suggests that the sporting tenantry, despite being pseudo-gentry, were being accepted into the ranks of landed society as an additional *quid pro quo* by hard-up aristocratic landowners keen to bolster landed society and avoid finding themselves socially isolated, surrounded by empty Halls. Subsequently, we later see Sir William Quilter contesting and winning the seat of South Suffolk, as the squire of Bawdsey Manor. What this suggests is that the hirers of sporting estates also represented a ready-made pool of buyers who wanted to stroll with gun under arm across their own acres. The *Estates Gazette* advertised many of the estates coming up for sale in Suffolk as purely sporting estates. Similarly, when Rider Haggard toured the county in 1901, his interview with the Rev Holden exposed the total relegation of agriculture to sport: 'During the last fifteen years every property within a radius of six miles had changed hands, for the most part fetching good prices, not on account of their agricultural value, but because that was splendid game country.'[70] Indeed, Holden considered 'local agriculture to be dead and that the land was kept in cultivation merely as a home for game, to bring in sporting rents and generally used for pleasure purposes by its owners or hirers'.[71]

On the other hand, agriculture would show signs of recovery after 1901 (see Chapter Two). It was this that prompted the recovery in the value of agricultural land and thus precipitated the appearance of more and more estates on the market. The buyers of these estates were, however, attracted by the sport, social influence and general one-up man ship that accompanied the ownership of land rather than by any desire to farm, which explains why the Edwardian aristocracy and new plutocracy challenged one another to pull out all the stops when it came to enjoying their sport. On the Euston estate, for example, while the farming side of the estate began to stumble, a new system was being developed for rearing more partridges. This was the so-called Euston System and it was widely adopted across the county.

Starting in mid-May, the gamekeepers began collecting the eggs from every grey partridge nest they could find on their beat. The position of the nest would be marked on a map whilst the wild eggs would be substituted with dummy eggs. The eggs would then be placed under broody hens to incubate for about ten days. As soon as the eggs were about to hatch, they were returned to the nests whence they were taken. So what had been gained

8

THE GREAT ESTATES BEFORE
THE GREAT WAR

The early 1900s were marked by two events which many contemporaries believed precipitated the break-up of the great estates, namely the taxes which the Chancellor of the Exchequer, David Lloyd George, proposed to levy on land and the subsequent attack on the rights and privileges enjoyed by the landed aristocracy as members of the House of Lords. The antecedents to this confrontation between the aristocracy and the Liberal party can be traced back to Gladstone's attempt in 1886 to introduce Irish Home Rule. By pursuing Home Rule for Ireland, which was deeply opposed by most of the great Whig magnates, Gladstone effectively forced the 'great mass of Liberal peers into the arms of the Conservative majority in the House of Lords'.[1] This was termed the 'flight of the Whigs' although the majority of disaffected Liberal peers actually joined the Liberal Unionists, led by the Marquess of Hartington. Thus, between 1886 and 1893, the remaining 84 Liberal peers in the Lords were opposed by 356 Conservatives and 115 Liberal Unionists. Given that Gladstone had in effect created a 'Conservative predominance in the House of Lords of a degree never approached before, not even after the creations of the younger Pitt'[2], it was perhaps inevitable that a future Liberal government would seek to curb the powers of the House of Lords and would look again at the aristocracy's lingering hegemony over the countryside as Searle states:

> Liberalism's weakness in the Upper House . . . gave the party an incentive to curb the powers of that Chamber . . . This in turn made the Liberal party seem a more dangerously radical organization than it really was. The loss of so many great magnates meant that after 1886 the overwhelming majority of Lord Lieutenants were Unionists – which led to a grave imbalance on the county benches.[3]

Gladstone had, of course, expressed the view that the great estates and their owners were a source of social strength, but with the gap left by the old Whigs being filled by advanced Radicals, Gladstone had to go along, albeit reluctantly, with the Radical programme passed by a caucus of the National Liberal Federation in Newcastle in 1891; the so-called 'Newcastle Programme'. Back in 1889, the Council of the N. L. F., meeting in Manchester, had passed a resolution embodying: 'freeing the land' from obsolete legal encumbrances; the application of 'tenant right' to compensation for improvements; leasehold enfranchisement; compulsory powers for local authorities to acquire land for allotments and small holdings; and – most radical of all – the doctrine of land value taxation.[4] The 'Newcastle Programme' of 1891 repeated these five goals. This Programme would, the Radicals hoped, appeal to the labouring voters in the agricultural constituencies who had swept Liberal candidates into power in the general election of 1885, only to desert them a year later. Meanwhile, beginning in Suffolk, in 1890–1, the English Land Restoration League sought to stir up enthusiasm among English farm workers for the doctrines of Henry George by travelling from village to village in their famous red vans. In 1891, the Land Nationalization Society followed suit by travelling around in yellow vans.

All of which led Joseph Chamberlain to declare, 'I neither look for nor desire reunion with the Liberal party.'[5] Chamberlain, who had campaigned to give three acres and cow to every agricultural labourer and who had split from the Liberal party on the issue of Irish Home Rule, described the advanced Radicals as those who would 'merge the individual in the State' and 'reduce all to one dead level of uniformity, in which the inefficient, the thriftless and the idle are to be confounded and treated alike with the honest and the industrious and the capable'.[6] In Lord Salisbury's opinion, Liberals now stood on an inclined plane leading from the position of Lord Hartington, the leader of the Liberal Unionist peers, to that of Mr Chamberlain, the leader of the Liberal Unionists in the Commons (having succeeded Hartington in 1891), and on into the depths over which Mr Henry George ruled supreme: 'at various points on this slippery slope most of the landowners and an increasing number of businessmen chose to jump off.'[7]

Thus, when the Liberal party returned to office in 1906, the Unionist majority in the Lords awoke after slumbering for twenty-odd years under the Tories to be confronted by a Liberal Government ready to embark on a radical programme of land reform. As Lord Rosebery (the former Liberal leader) observed in a letter to Queen Victoria in April 1894, 'When the Conservative Party is in power there is practically no House of Lords: it takes whatever the Conservative Government brings it from the House of

Commons, without question or dispute; but the moment a Liberal Government is formed this harmless body assumes an active life, and its activity is entirely exercised in opposition to the Government.'[8] This can be seen in the reaction of the Lords to Lloyd George's Budget of 1909, and in the Commons, by the reaction of the leading Suffolk landowner Ernest Pretyman. But did the Budget trigger the wholesale disposal and break-up of the great estates?

To answer this question, consider the impact that the massive boom in land sales between 1909 and 1922 had upon landownership in Suffolk. First, how and why did sales of agricultural land occur prior to 1909? If estates *were* being sold prior to 1909 due to the collapse of farm rents, were the sales subsequently made after 1909 due entirely to the Budget? Were they, in fact, part of an already well established pattern of families seeking to rescue their finances? Was the Budget, coinciding as it did with a noticeable improvement in the price of land, merely a convenient excuse used by landowners to break with family tradition and sell, having managed to wait until prices began to pick up? This also raises the question of what was actually being sold. How many families, for example, were selling their outlying estates rather than their ancestral heartlands? Moreover, if many of the larger families were selling outlying properties to rebalance their books whilst retaining the heart of their estates, did they adopt the same policy when it came to the payment of death duties?

In his 'People's Budget' of 1909 Lloyd George proposed seven new taxes, including a Super Tax of 6d on incomes of £5,000 and over, a tax on motor vehicles ranging from £2. 2s. to £40 depending on the car's horsepower, and a duty of 3d on a gallon of petrol. More importantly, he also introduced four new land taxes: a tax of 20 per cent on any unearned increment which might have accrued on the value of a parcel of land; a similar duty (later changed in committee to 5 per cent) on landlords' mineral rights; an annual duty of $^1/_2$d in the pound levied on the capital value of undeveloped land; and a 10 per cent reversion duty on any benefit that accrued to the lessor at the termination of a lease. He also increased the level of death duties.

The new land taxes were viewed by many Liberals as a welcome attack on the House of Lords. One Liberal declared that talking about land taxes to the House of Lords 'was like talking to a butcher about Lent', while in West End Clubs and country houses 'you hear nothing but execration of Lloyd George and his budget.'[9] What aroused most antipathy among the aristocracy and gentry were the moves, inherent within the Budget, towards the valuation of land. Any valuation automatically opened up the prospect of far heavier taxes being raised in the future, based upon these assessments. As one

Conservative peer observed, 'It is not the Licence Duties, or the Super Tax, or the death duties that we mind so much, though they are bad enough, what we can't and won't stand for is the general valuation of land.'[10] More worryingly, not only did the new Land Value duties single out landowners for especially severe levels of taxation, there was also an ominous gap between the cost, estimated at £2,000,000, of the cumbersome valuation machinery and the meagre revenues expected.[11] To many landowners, this suggested that the new taxes were intended to be a punitive rather than a fiscal measure.

In the pages of the contemporary journal the *Nineteenth Century* the Liberal party was described as being neither a Liberal nor a Radical party, but a Liberal-Socialist party cosily allied with the Independent Labour Party. Thus, the Budget represented the realization of the Labour Party's campaign for the nationalization of land through the systematic and heavy taxation of landowners based on a detailed valuation of their property. This analysis received apparent confirmation when Lloyd George declared that 'state valuation must be the basis of all plans for communal purchase'.[12] The only way for landowners to counter this supposed socialist threat was for the aristocracy to take the people into partnership, a point recognized by Arthur Balfour in 1909. He said, 'I have always been one of those who have ardently desired to see . . . the ownership of agricultural land distributed in an incomparably greater number of hands than it now is'[13] which perhaps explains why Unionist opposition to the Small Holdings and Allotments legislation of 1907–8 was so muted. In practice, of course, the creation of such small holdings was frequently undermined by the deliberate obstruction of local landowners and farmers working in collusion in the County Council Chamber. Their intransigence, in the context of the People's Budget, was strongly criticized in the pages of the *Nineteenth Century*:

> Under Mr Asquith's Government . . . the process of taxing landowners out of their land has commenced. So far socialism has met with little resistance. Its success has been easy because there are only a few thousand big landowners to oppose its progress. Their single-handed resistance to the nationalization of the land will probably be as unsuccessful in the long run as was the opposition of their grand-fathers to the abolition of the Corn Laws . . . they [must therefore] take the people into partnership.[14]

As for those landlords who considered small holdings to be both damaging to the beauty of the countryside and to its sport, they were given very short shrift: 'Those landowners who oppose the creation of numerous freeholds . . . should ask themselves whether land exists chiefly to keep foxes and partridges, or to keep men?'[15] On the ground, in Suffolk, landlords were creating enough allotments to take the steam out the issue of land reform, hence the campaigns of the Land Nationalizers and the Single-Taxers in their little yellow and red vans were eventually suspended. But this still left the Budget, and how could landowners hope to stop it?

In the House of Commons the most active and vocal opponent of the Budget was the Suffolk landowner and MP, Colonel E. G. Pretyman. Having inherited the 18,500 acre Orwell Park estate, which was said to be twenty-two miles long by six wide with, in addition, a large urban estate in Felixstowe, from his cousin Colonel George Tomline in 1889, he was by 1909 the largest landowner in Suffolk.[16] He was also Chairman of the Land Union, which sought to represent the views of all property owners, not just large landowners such as himself.[17] Pretyman was particularly opposed to the duties on Unearned Increment and Undeveloped Land, which he considered were inherently flawed. In 1909, he stated:

> There are certain definite canons of finance which should be followed by every Chancellor of the Exchequer and by everyone who is concerned with the imposition of taxation. Every one of those considerations [is] . . . ignored or transgressed in this Budget. [For instance] . . . taxes should fall evenly upon all those in the country who pay them according to their ability to pay. The Right Hon Gentleman [Lloyd George] applauds that statement, but does he suggest that under his Budget a similar tax is levied upon the unearned increment of a man who has made thousands in the recent boom on the Stock Exchange as on that of a man who has invested his money in land?[18]

In Pretyman's opinion, land was being deliberately and unfairly discriminated against by a tax on what the Bill deemed to be the amount, if any, by which the value of a piece of land when sold, or following the death of its owner, exceeded its original site value.[19] Pretyman was equally critical of the proposed duties on what was referred to in the Bill as Undeveloped Land. Under Clause 7 of the Finance (1909–10) Bill, agricultural land had been exempted from Unearned Increment Duty, in accordance with the views expressed by Asquith: 'I believe we all agree that agricultural land . . . ought to be exempted from . . . tax of this kind.'[20] This exemption did not, however, extend to Undeveloped Land Duty.

Under the Act, the tax was to be levied on all agricultural land considered suitable for building or, as Pretyman described it, on all land which is not yet ripe for development but which has acquired a building value greater than its agricultural value. The difficulty this presented landowners with was highlighted by Lord Avebury, who, as mentioned previously, now had the lease to the Marquess of Bristol's London residence, No 6 St James's Square. He wrote that while Undeveloped Land Duty did not apply to agricultural land as such, this was merely a euphemism for land not built over. In other words, all agricultural land near towns and villages, being worth rather more than its agricultural value because sooner or later it would be built on, would be subject to the tax, although it was still agricultural land. In response, Pretyman tried, unsuccessfully, to amend the Act during its Committee stage, so that the tax could only be levied upon land when it had been *proved* to be required for building.[21]

Pretyman's greatest concern, however, centred, as did that of most landowners, on the issue of valuation. In order to levy the new duties on unearned increment and undeveloped land, between nine and a half and ten and a half million hereditaments, or separate units of tenure, had to be individually valued. This mandated, in effect, a new *Domesday Book*. The five land values to be ascertained were the *composite selling value* of the site and structures or gross value, from which mortgages and other charges were deducted to arrive at the *total value*; buildings and other improvements were then deducted to arrive at full *site value*. Another set of deductions, concerning improvements made to the site, reduced this to *assessable site value*. Owners were also allowed to substitute the original site value as it stood in 1909, for any higher value actually recorded in a transfer up to twenty years previously. This, in Offer's opinion, effectively neutralized the increment tax in many cases until values exceeded those of the previous boom in land prices. There was, finally, the *value of the land for agricultural purposes*.[22]

Thus, it's no surprise that when, in August 1910, a landowner received one of the Inland Revenue's infamous Form 4s asking him to provide these detailed particulars of the extent, income, use and tenure of his property, he had to turn to his solicitor for advice on how to fill them in. There was, in addition, only one month in which to return the completed form or face a fine. In mitigation, the Government argued that, 'Landowners have only to apply to the valuation officers and they will receive all possible help.' Colonel Pretyman caustically replied, 'To advise owners to consult them is much the same as telling one party in a law suit that he can consult his opponents' solicitor free of charge.'[23] When this form was returned, officials at the Inland Revenue would then issue a provisional valuation which the owner could test on appeal. Colonel Barnardiston, for example, objected to the valuation placed on his estate in Suffolk. [24]

However, allegations soon began to appear in opposition publications, such as the *Land Union Journal*, that the revenue authorities were in fact willing to decrease the written valuation of land in order to obtain higher increment duties. In the Commons, Pretyman was also highly sceptical of the valuers' true motives:

> There are two [key] taxes: Increment Value Duty which you impose upon land already built upon, and Undeveloped Land Duty which you impose upon land not yet built upon. It is in the interests of the Government to have land with houses valued low [as] . . . the State will get more if houses on their sites are valued low, because they will get Increment Duty at their sale. But on the other hand, if undeveloped land is valued high that is [also] in the interest of the State, because they will get Undeveloped Land Duty at a larger figure, and that is what has happened.[25]

Faced by the prospect of fines and penalties for non-compliance, landowners could only protest so far. Having received Colonel Barnardiston's objections to the valuation placed upon his estate, the District Valuer wrote back, 'I beg to acknowledge receipt of your notices of objection to the valuations [for Freckenham]. Although I am quite willing to endeavour to settle the valuations with you I may say at once that if you adhere to the amendments of site values of the cottages at 'Nil' I shall . . . discontinue any [further] negotiation.'[26]

Back at Westminster, the huge Liberal majority in the House of Commons ensured that, despite Pretyman's best efforts to highlight the inherent unfairness of the taxes themselves and the cost, delay and general inconvenience which would arise from their assessment, the Finance (1909–10) Bill duly passed through the Commons unamended.[27] It was then sent to the Lords where, unlike the Commons, the Tories held a massive majority. Conservative landowners in the Lords also shared Pretyman's concern over the probable implications of the Budget given what to them appeared to be its overtly socialist character. The Finance Bill was therefore vetoed on the grounds that it was 'unconstitutional to insert legislative proposals – the Land Clauses for instance, which [were] no fewer than twenty-eight in number and really a [socialist] Bill in themselves tacked onto the Budget Bill – in a measure which ought to be confined to finance.'[28] It was a view that echoed Pretyman's conviction that socialism rather than finance was at the 'foundation of this Budget'.[29] In response, the Government dissolved Parliament and went to the country. After two General Elections in 1910, the Liberals were returned to power and they immediately brought forward legislation to bring to an end the partisan interference of the House of Lords.

Under the Parliament Bill of 1911, the Lords were deprived of their powers to veto legislation. Significantly, following as it did in the wake of the Lords' willingness to veto the People's Budget, opposition to the Bill was surprisingly light. The Cabinet had outflanked their Lordships by securing a promise from George V to create some five hundred new Liberal peers should the Bill be rejected. In response, the Unionist leadership in the House of Lords had to capitulate and called for abstentions on the issue. Nevertheless, several diehard peers such as the fourth Marquess of Bristol, who succeeded his uncle the third Marquess in 1907, and the third Lord Tollemache, believed a stand had to be made. They therefore rejected the Marquess of Lansdowne's advice to abstain on this issue. When it came to the vote, a total of 112 peers voted against the Parliament Bill but their efforts were in vain as they were completely overwhelmed by a combination of Liberals and Unionists who 'feared a flood of new peers more than the immediate end to the prerogatives of their House'.[30] The years 1909 to 1911 have thus been considered to be a defining moment in the history of the great landed families. Indeed, it was widely assumed that the estates that now began to appear on the market were, in fact, put up for sale as a direct result of the Liberals' tax and legislative assaults on the landed aristocracy and gentry.

It could be argued, therefore, that it was in an atmosphere of apprehension and insecurity that many landowners began to sell off their estates in whole or in part at an increasing pace between the years 1909 and 1911.[31] In 1911, for example, the Board of Agriculture reported that 'an abnormal number of estates were being broken up and sold' due to the 'apprehension among owners as to the probable course of legislation and taxation in regard to land'.[32] On the other hand, this may have been no more than a convenient excuse employed by landowners seeking to justify selling-off outlying portions of an ancestral estate in order to rebalance their books or, at least, to reduce the size of their debts following the marked improvement in the price of agricultural land after 1910. In other words, as the price of agricultural land began to improve, financially embarrassed families could at last begin to cash in on their principal asset without running the risk of incurring negative equity. But whilst attention has inevitably focused on the level of sales after 1909, many families in Suffolk had already begun to sell off their estates in the 1880s and 1890s even though, at this time, the price of agricultural land had all but collapsed amid the 'general belief in the universality of depression in agriculture and despondency over its future.'[33]

These were forced sales, necessitated by a family's inability to cover the running costs of their estates and still meet their other expenses out of a greatly reduced income. According to Fox, there were 'several landowners who are getting absolutely nothing from their property after paying outgoings and family charges'. In the opinion of one agent, given their low incomes and high overheads, many landowners would have been 'considerably better off' if they had just given their estates away.[34] For these families, as Cannadine points out:

> With incomes between £1,000 and £10,000 a year – the chances of survival were . . . the least good. The pressure of debts was often at its greatest, the impact of depression and taxation was most marked, the alternative sources of non-agricultural wealth were least abundantly available, the room for financial manoeuvre was accordingly the least generous . . .[35]

It was against this background that, in 1884, the Sheppard family placed the 7,041 acre Campsea Ashe estate on the market after nearly 400 years of family ownership. Subsequently, in 1889, Lady Rokewode-Gage put the 6,210 acre Hengrave Hall estate up for sale. In the same year, the Oakes family sold around 490 acres of the Nowton Court estate. Further sales followed in the 1890s. In 1892, the 3,430 acres owned by the Tyrell family were sold, while the Bennet family were forced to sell the 3,949 acre Rougham Hall estate in 1893 for £81,000, despite the estate's having been valued in 1872 at £250,000. Clearly, families such as the Bennets were no longer in any position to go on trying to keep hold of their estates on what were, by the 1880s and 1890s, largely non-existent margins. For other better-off landowners such as Richard Berens, who sold the 10,000 acre Culford estate in 1889 (having inherited the property in 1883 from his uncle the Rev E. R. Benyon) to Earl Cadogan, or Sir Richard Wallace (the millionaire art collector and illegitimate son of the Marquess of Hertford) who sold the 11,200 acre Sudbourne Hall estate in 1884, the decision to sell was probably more a response to the fact that their estates were now useful merely as a home for game. [36]

What is most surprising, however, given the depressed state of agriculture in the 1880s and 1890s, is the fact that buyers were still forthcoming.

Hengrave, for example, was eventually sold in 1897 to Sir John Wood, an immensely wealthy cotton manufacturer from Glossop in Derbyshire. Sudbourne was purchased by the Liverpool banker Arthur Heywood, who resold the Hall in 1898 to A. E. Wood. He, in turn, sold it in 1904 to the cotton-rich Clark family. Meanwhile, the Rougham Hall estate, which had been sold for £80,000 to Edwin Johnston in 1893, was subsequently sold to Sir George Agnew, the son of Sir William Agnew, Chairman of the London publishers Bradbury, Agnew and Co Ltd. Interestingly, by the early 1900s, the supply of British tycoons was also being supplemented by American and South African ones. In 1902, the 2,913 acre Dalham Hall estate was sold by the Afflecks to Cecil Rhodes whilst the South African financier Adolph Goldschmidt (grandfather of Sir James Goldsmith) built Cavenham Hall near Mildenhall. Other buyers in the county included John Hargreaves who acquired the 1,105 acre Drinkstone Park estate in 1903 from the Powell family, and the actuary Sir Gerald Ryan who purchased the 3,612 Hintlesham Hall estate in 1909. In addition, Sir Edward Greene, the MP for Bury St Edmunds and Sir Cuthbert Quilter, the MP for South Suffolk, were both the owners of gentry-sized estates which had been put together farm by farm (the latter around Bawdsey Manor). Similarly, the Ogilvies eventually added 6,000 acres to the Sizewell Hall estate.[37] But what was the continuing attraction of buying land?

As we saw in the previous chapter, buyers, like hirers, were attracted by the enduring social position and the sport which came with the ownership of a landed estate. In the same way they wanted to be part of a landed society still studded with recognizably old names. Thus, when the 960 acre Coney Weston Manor estate was advertised for sale in the *Estates Gazette* in 1902, the principal selling point used to highlight the attractiveness of the property was the abundance of good sport in the neighbourhood, but even more particularly 'the social advantages of the district', which were 'well known'.[38] Blending new money into England's landed society and adopting its sporting pursuits are the keys to understanding the buyer's motivation. Land alone was no longer a guaranteed route into the House of Commons and thence to a title and a seat in the House of Lords that it once was. By the 1890s, and even more so in Edwardian England, it was money rather than land that increasingly held the key to the highest honours; land was often only added afterwards in a nod to the past. The size and number of the fortunes being created in the 1890s meant that new money had generated its own social momentum, enough so that, by the close of Queen Victoria's reign, aristocratic society had developed a 'new respect for money, especially for money not furnished by agricultural estates' and for those 'who made money in large scale enterprises'.[39]

For example, whilst the bulk of the established landed families were in mounting financial difficulty with the number of millionaire landlords falling from 118 in 1858–79 to 36 in 1880–99 and to 33 in 1900–19, the number of non-landed millionaires rose from 27 in 1860–79 to 60 in 1880–99 and to 101 in 1909–19. As Perkin recognized, the 1890s and early 1900s became the age of the millionaire. Given these changes and the fact that, by the 1890s, the middle classes had come to dominate the House of Commons, it was perhaps inevitable that the 'cream of industry and commerce' would also begin to assert themselves within the aristocracy.[40] After 1885, businessmen came to represent, on average, nearly a third of all new peers, compared to a tenth previously. Significantly, nearly a fifth had no noble or gentle antecedents. Their backgrounds were in railways, engineering, publications, newspapers, metallurgy, chemicals, shipping, textiles, building, mining, banking and brewing. Thus, whereas before 1885 the honours system had been essentially 'patrician, landed and limited', by 1914 honours were given out to those in almost every walk of national life. There was, however, strong public criticism of the 'adulteration of the peerage' through the granting of titles to individuals simply because they were very rich. [41]

For men such as the brewer Sir Edward Guinness, who left an estimated fortune of £11,000,000 in 1927, social recognition in the form of a peerage was practically guaranteed. Symbolically, it was only after he was created Lord Iveagh, in 1891, that he decided to acquire the Elveden estate, which was then considered to be one of the finest shoots in England.[42] It was certainly no longer a viable agricultural estate. As the magazine *Mayfair* noted, the estate was in effect a 'large game preserve' because 'the soil is poor . . . and does not repay cultivation.'[43] Of course, with a fortune based on the Guinness brewing empire, Iveagh was unlikely to be unduly bothered by either the negligible farm rents or the high costs attached to owning this or any other estate. What he wanted was the quintessentially English country gentleman's sporting estate.

The point to remember here is that, whilst those titled and non-titled landowners whose income was tied to agriculture were having a rough time of things, to those with fortunes tied to industry and commerce, the ownership of a great sporting estate in the Edwardian period was one long 'Indian Summer'. Thus it was during this period that sport really took over and assumed mammoth proportions. George Martelli reports that under Lord Iveagh, 70 men were employed in the Elveden game department. This figure included 24 liveried men, 30 warreners, and 16 horsemen and wire-fence-men. The shooting parties, usually of eight or nine guns, were driven to the first beat in shooting brakes. The beaters, a hundred strong, wore white smocks with red collars and chummy hats with red bands; the keepers, bowler hats, brown suits and leather gaiters. The whole array was then marshalled and directed in its operations by the head gamekeeper, riding a pony, signalling his orders by blasts of a German hunting horn.[44]

By 1907, the Breckland estates of Euston, Culford, Elveden, Barton and Ickworth (under the stewardship of the fourth Marquess) and the Rendlesham and Sudbourne estates on the light soils of the Suffolk Sandlings along the coast, were categorized together with the Thornham, Orwell, Easton, Benacre, Henham, Downham, Flixton, Heveningham and Sotterley estates on the heavier lands, as being 'some of the more noteworthy estates where most excellent sport is obtainable'.[45] Each drive on the Elveden estate had the precision of a military manoeuvre and the birds were concentrated for the kill with smooth efficiency. Each of the guns had his own attendant although, when Edward VII used to turn up, he was attended by two loaders, a cartridge boy and a private detective. It was considered to be a 'poor day' if fewer than a thousand head of game were killed, as 20,000 pheasants were reared every season. In 1899, therefore, the aggregate bag on the Elveden estate was 103,000 head of game including 21,000 pheasants! Killing on this scale was achieved thanks to the expansion of the pheasant laying pens, or pheasant 'mews' on the estate. Whole coverts, varying in size between 20 and 100 acres, were now enclosed to create massive laying pens from which pheasant eggs were collected twice a day or more from individual nests during the laying season. These eggs were then placed under broody hens or bantams in purpose built, enclosed hatching pens.

Significantly, among the names of the noteworthy sporting estates are several belonging to the leading aristocratic families in Suffolk. This would suggest a handy portfolio of shares was tucked away somewhere. The third Earl of Stradbroke, for example, despite having seen rents collapse on the estate, was still able to entertain the Prince of Wales in 1906, which also indicates that he was still resident at Henham Hall and that his household establishment had not been broken up. The household staff at Henham is reported to have included a housekeeper, a nurse, three ladies' maids, a cook, four housemaids, four laundry-maids, two still-room maids, a schoolroom maid, a nursery maid, two kitchen-maids, a scullery maid, three footmen and a butler.[46] The effort involved can be gauged from a letter sent by Lady Augusta Hervey to her son, the fourth Marquess, regarding the prospect of a similar visit being made by the King to Ickworth: 'There is no doubt that the King will want to shoot some day at Ickworth . . . The point uppermost with me is the physical exertion for you . . . [what with] the House, the staff [etc.] . . . Middle class entertaining won't do . . . nor really bad shooting.'[47]

Thus, among the aristocracy, especially those with cash salted away, there was generally a reluctance to give up their social position and their sport, and this ensured their continued presence in the county. Few, if any, Suffolk landowners followed the example of the second Lord Cranworth, who closed up Grundisburgh Hall and moved to Uganda, drawn by a love of big game shooting and a shortage of cash. Once in Uganda, he settled down to rearing cattle on two land grants totalling 30,000 acres. The result, given the lower cost of living, was 'a perfect life – aristocracy on the cheap'[48]; the only drawback was he was now living abroad. The decision to stay at home, however, did not preclude families better-placed from selling land. In 1912, the third Earl of Stradbroke sold off the 1,316 acre Darsham Hall estate in 19 lots. This sale, which included 12 farms as well as several small holdings and cottages, raised £25,200. Subsequently, in 1918, the Earl's 1,251 acre Bruisyard Hall estate: 'a compact agricultural and sporting estate . . . capable of holding a considerable head of game' was also put up for sale in 14 lots.[49] As Heather Clemenson states, for some, changes meant the total break-up or sale in one lot but, for many families, the heartland was retained while individual farm holdings on the periphery or secondary estates were sold. This was because, as in the case of the Earl of Stradbroke, funds were available from elsewhere. Reference to the Earl's portfolio can be found in the settlement made upon the marriage of Miss Helena Fraser to the Earl in 1898, in the form of two blocks of Madras Railway stock and Great Indian Peninsula Railway stock.[50]

Sir Savile Crossley (created Lord Somerleyton in 1916), having inherited a fortune of £800,000 and the chairmanship of his father's company, also sold outlying portions of the Somerleyton Hall estate totalling 804 acres in 1919. Similarly, the Tollemache family had to sell around 600 acres in Suffolk between 1884 and 1885, but that was all with which they needed to part. In 1888, three of Lord Tollemache's nine sons went into trade and bought the Ipswich brewery of Charles Cullingham for £100,000. Their father was apparently horrified and considered the whole enterprise degrading to the name of Tollemache. Nevertheless, the brewery was a great financial success and proved a 'blessing to the whole family'.[51] As a result, the Helmingham estate has remained intact and currently stands at 5,500 acres. But becoming involved in business ventures could have its downside, too. In 1894, the fifth Lord Thurlow, a director of eight joint-stock companies, appeared in the Bankruptcy Court with gross liabilities of £427,567. With total assets of only £29,890, he had to mortgage his estate in Suffolk for £43,200, which was said to be 'more than its actual value'. Subsequently, the estate had to be sold. Whilst still undischarged, he was again declared bankrupt in March 1910, with liabilities of £7,773.[52] It was far better to try and build up a share portfolio like the FitzRoys.

The FitzRoys were insulated from the effects of falling agricultural rents by a huge cash windfall which they received from the gradual redemption, between 1809 and 1857, of all the sinecure places and perpetual pensions conferred upon the first Duke of Grafton by Charles II. These comprised the 'prisage' and 'butlerage' of wine imported into England (estimated in 1797 at £7,500 a year), redeemed in 1809 and 1816 for a total of £135,568; the Receiver Generalship of the profits of the Seals in the Courts of Kings Bench and Common Pleas, abolished in 1845 for a pension of £843; an income of £7,194 charged on the Excise, redeemed in 1856 for £193,177; and an income of £3,384 charged on the Post Office, redeemed in 1857 for £91,181. Thus, by 1857, the FitzRoys had received a cash injection of £420,769. Shrewdly, £229,000 was invested in Government Stock, thanks, no doubt, to the financial advice proferred by Francis Baring, Lord Ashburton, following the marriage in 1858 of his daughter to William FitzRoy, who succeeded to the Dukedom in 1863. The family were therefore never under any direct financial pressure as a result of the agricultural depression. As a result, they did not need to raise cash by selling off the Euston Hall estate. The estate has in consequence remained around 11,000 acres.[53]

The third Marquess of Bristol, meanwhile, who had borrowed a further £62,000 in 1898 to cover his liabilities, was saved from having to dispose of Ickworth by his nephew, Captain Frederick Hervey RN, who had married Alice Wythes, the daughter and heiress of the hugely wealthy building contractor George Wythes of Copped Hall in Essex. Frederick was, in consequence, able to prevent the break up of the Ickworth estate by offering to clear his uncle's debts. In 1897, he wrote off around £5,000. In 1899, he signed an assignment exonerating his uncle from any personal liability for repaying the aforementioned sum of £62,000. Just as among the aristocracy, among the gentry too, heiresses were equally important sources of cash. Mark Schreiber, who became the life peer Lord Marlesford in 1991, recalls 'My grandfather married the Hon Margaret Henderson [the daughter of Lord Faringdon] in 1900, which restored the family fortune.'[54]

Back at Ickworth, Frederick's willingness to discharge his uncle's debts was far from being a purely philanthropic gesture. Under the terms of an agreement hammered out in 1897, in exchange first for discharging his uncle's liabilities and secondly 'taking upon himself, their gradual liquidation' and in the interim 'the payment of the interest', Frederick became heir to all his uncle's real and personal property. In addition, Lord Bristol also agreed 'not to put any further charges on the Estate either for improvement purposes or otherwise'[55] without his nephew's agreement, finally:

> All the rents [due from] . . . the Suffolk, Lincolnshire, Essex, Brighton and London properties [covered by the schedule] with the exception of Shotley [upon which had been placed a charge of £10,000, payable to Lady Bristol and a further charge of £8,000 payable to the Trustees of the Settled Estates] which had formerly been paid into the Estate Office, were now to be collected and paid into an Estate Account, at the National Provincial Bank, in Bury St Edmunds.[56]

In return, he still received the rents due from those parts of his estates not covered by the agreement and an annual sum of £5,000, which his nephew agreed to pay into his personal account in two separate half-yearly payments. Furthermore, any deficiency in making up the half yearly Estate Accounts to 30th June and 31st December was 'to be made good by Mr Frederick Hervey, such as not to exceed in any one year the sum of £10,000'.[57]

As a result, when an audit of the Bristol Estates Account was conducted by Francis Pixley in 1903, he found that, as of the half year ending 31st January 1902, the liabilities charged to the estate had been significantly reduced. For example, by 1902, Frederick or, more particularly, his wife had repaid two mortgages taken out with the Wythes Trustees amounting to £3,061 and £21,010 respectively, as well as improvement charges amounting to £6,834 owed to the Scottish Widows Fund and, 'other Associations'. In addition, they had also provided £9,000 for the half year to 'feed the Estate'. Taken as a whole, by the time Frederick inherited the Ickworth estate in 1907, nearly £200,000 had already been pumped into the estate. In so doing, they delayed the eventual break-up and sale of the Ickworth estate for another eighty-seven years.[58]

Across Suffolk, therefore, only one estate in excess of 10,000 acres imploded as a direct consequence of the forces at work during this period: the 19,869 acre Rendlesham Hall estate. Ironically, the Thellusson family, like the FitzRoys, had also been in receipt of a considerable cash windfall in the mid-nineteenth century. In complete contrast, however, by 1922, the Rendlesham Hall estate had been entirely broken-up and sold. The estate itself had been built up in the late eighteenth century by Peter Thellusson, an immensely rich and successful London merchant. In 1797, having bequeathed a large fortune to each member of his family, he had placed his remaining landed property (valued at £4,500 per annum) in trust together with his personal estate amounting to over £600,000. There both were to remain, or so he hoped, during the lifetimes of his three sons and their children, all the time gathering interest.

On the death of his last grandson, the vast accumulated sum was to be divided between the eldest male descendants of his three sons. Unsurprisingly, his heirs were keen to see the will set aside. In the end, despite having incurred massive legal bills, the will was pronounced valid by both the Lord Chancellor, Lord Loughborough in 1799, and by the House of Lords in 1805, at which point the estate was placed in the Court of Chancery. In 1856, following the death of Charles Thellusson, Peter's last surviving grandson, more litigation ensued, as the family sought to determine who was the eldest lineal male descendant? Did Peter mean his money to go to his oldest living male descendant on the death of his last grandson, or to the eldest living descendant of the eldest son to have had children? The matter was eventually brought before the House of Lords in 1859. There it was decided to divide his estate between his two surviving male representatives, namely Frederick William Brook Thellusson, fifth Baron Rendlesham and Charles Augustus Sabine Thellusson, of Brodsworth Hall in Yorkshire.[59]

No statement as to the amount actually received by Lord Rendlesham in 1859 exists within the public domain, although Sir William Holdsworth and G. E. Cokayne both suggest that 'owing to mismanagement and costs of litigation, [the Will] . . . realized a comparatively small amount'.[60] The damage that a protracted court case in Chancery could do to a family's fortunes was elegantly summed up by Charles Dickens, who wrote that the whole business was one that 'so exhausts finances, patience and courage, hope . . . so breaks the heart; that there is not an honourable man among its practitioners who would not give – who does not give – the warning, suffer any wrong that can be done to you, rather than come here.'[61] In 1875, the *Suffolk Mercury* speculated that after all the legal costs had been paid 'There was not much more money than Peter Thellusson originally devised in his Will.'[62]

This still represented a very sizeable sum, even after it was divided. Why then did the sixth Lord Rendlesham have to sell off land both before and after World War One? The answer would appear to lie in the fact that this windfall was simply frittered away, leaving the family dangerously exposed to falling rentals. In 1868, the fifth Lord Rendlesham rebuilt and refurnished Rendlesham Hall, at a cost of approximately £100,000. He was also engaged in massively expanding the Rendlesham estate by around 5,000 acres. Lord Rendlesham also charged the estate, in 1861, with the payment of a portion amounting to £10,000.[63] He then chose to improve the poor sandy soils of the Suffolk Sandlings, building up debts of £28,102 with the Lands Improvement Company, whilst at the same time turning Rendlesham into one of the best shoots in England. Unsurprisingly, once farm rents began to fall and with nearly 3,000 acres in hand by the early 1900s, problems began to emerge.[64] This would certainly explain why a mortgage was raised in 1896 for £17,100 and a further mortgage for £28,000 in 1904.[65]

It was at this juncture that the Thellussons also became one of the first victims of Lloyd George's decision to increase death duties. Following the death of the fifth Lord Rendlesham in 1911, the Rendlesham Hall estate was charged with the payment of £12,872, whilst the family's Hertfordshire property was charged with a further £9,479. Both these amounts were paid off in 1916. This was achieved by mortgaging 9,798 acres in Suffolk to the Clergy Mutual Life Office in 1916 and through the sale of land. Indeed, after 1911, the sixth Lord Rendlesham began to sell an ever increasing quantity of land to help clear his liabilities. As a result, by 1912–15 the estate had been reduced in size by 9,074 acres, down to 10,795 acres, from a peak of 19,869 in 1883. In 1914, for example, Lord Rendlesham sold a total of 5,857 outlying acres in 47 lots. Subsequently, during the summer of 1920, he sold a further 7,035 acres. Included in this sale was the Home Portion of the estate, which was broken up into 123 lots comprising 15 farms, 5,300 acres, 600 acres of woodland, the Hall and surrounding parkland and 140 cottages. Of these, 42 lots were eventually sold, realizing a total of £37,405.[66] But, whilst the Rendlesham Hall estate was by far the largest aristocratic estate to disappear in Suffolk amid the turbulence of the late nineteenth and early twentieth centuries, the sales made by the Thellusson family after 1918 were in fact only a small part of what was to become the largest redistribution of land seen in England since the Dissolution of the Monasteries.

Following the Allied victory in 1918, land began to pour onto the market in unprecedented quantities as the price of arable land rocketed amid the general agricultural bullishness of the times. Of the 12 greatest landowners in the county with estates in excess of 10,000 acres, seven were actively involved in selling land in the immediate post-war period.[67] Of these, the Earl of Stradbroke was merely taking advantage of the opportunity to sell off some of his unwanted outlying properties. Similarly, the Clark family, who bought the 11,224 acre Sudbourne Hall estate in 1904, being in little need of the cash broke up the estate in 1918, apparently bored with playing the role of the country squire. In 1920, the Adairs were forced to sell 2,800 acres to cover the payment of death duties. Meanwhile, in 1922, Lord de Saumarez also decided to sell 2,100 acres in 51 lots, presumably to help clear the liabilities charged to the estate by the will of Sir William Middleton.[68] More importantly, between 1918 and 1921, the Henniker-Majors, like the Thellussons, saw their chance to finally rebalance their books and so placed a large tranche of the Thornham Hall estate on the market. These sales, which included the Ashfield and Debenham portions of the estate, totalled 3,350 acres. In the mid-1990s, Lord Henniker disclosed that several thousand more acres were sold around this time; one presumes he was referring to the Oakley and Brome Hall estates which were sold in 1920 and 1921 'by order of mortgagees': these estates having passed to the family through the marriage in 1837 of John, fourth Lord Henniker, to the sister of Sir Edward Kerrison.[69]

Finally, in 1928, Lord Huntingfield was forced to sell the residue of the Heveningham Hall estate to his brother the Hon Andrew Vanneck. But this sale owed more to the negligence of the family than to the difficulties posed by low rentals. The family's fortune was not 'as buoyant as it had been in the eighteenth century'[70], nevertheless the third Lord Huntingfield, who died in 1897, left £130,698 in his will. What did for the family was the failure of the fourth Lord Huntingfield to leave a will. As a result, on succeeding to the title and the estate in 1915, the fifth Lord Huntingfield found himself assailed by twenty-four relatives claiming a share of his late uncle's estate! In the ensuing mêlée, he was able to retain the Hall, minus most of its contents, and also part of the estate – but not enough to support such a house. Hence the sale of what remained of the estate in 1928.[71]

But it should be apparent that the majority of the greatest aristocratic landowners in the county were, in fact, selling outlying properties rather than their heartlands. It was the members of the gentry, the owners of estates between 1,000 and 10,000 acres, with smaller incomes more vulnerable to falling rents, who provided the bulk of the estates which were sold in their entirety after 1918. For example, Herbert Leathes, having inherited the 1,433 acre Herringfleet Hall estate in 1915, placed the estate on the market in 1919. In the same year, the Rushbrooke family sold the 1,715 acre Rushbrooke Hall estate to Lord Islington, who later resold the estate to the Rothschilds. Previously, in 1918, the 1,825 acre Brettenham Park estate was sold by the Beale family. In that year, 1,050 acres of the Stoke Park estate were also sold in 21 lots by the executors of Lord Gwydyr. The residue of the estate, some 950 acres, was then sold in 1921. Again, in 1921, 1,260 acres of the 2,841 acre Assington Hall estate were sold in 18 lots by the Gurdon family. The following year, 525 acres of the Brent Eleigh estate were sold in 17 lots by the Elwes family. In 1923, the 1,694 acre Troston Hall estate was also sold, in 30 lots, by the Lofft family. Finally, in 1924, the 1,347 acre Hardwick House estate was sold in 28 lots by the Cullum family.[72]

Overall, these sales mark the culmination of a twenty-year process of retrenchment, involving the release of a vast amount of land onto the market by the landed gentry. *The Times,* for example, referring to the sharp upsurge in sales after World War One, famously declared that all England appeared to be changing hands. The frenzied selling which characterized this particular period was, of course, fed by land speculators. At the auction of the Home Portion of the Rendlesham estate, Lord Graham bought two farms for £18,250 in the morning; in the afternoon, Ash Abbey Farm plus four other lots were resold by Lord Graham for £19,700.[73] The cause of this speculation was the introduction of agricultural subsidies under the 1917 Corn Production Act. Indeed, it was these subsidies which enabled tenants to build a war chest to be ready to buy their farms, and helps explain the increased propensity for landlords to sell their estates in lots after World War One.

With the Act's repeal in 1922, the 'Great Betrayal', the price of wheat collapsed once again taking the price of land down with it, thereby bringing an end to the post-war land boom. This did not signal the end of all sales. There was still a considerable amount of slack that could be trimmed. The Henniker-Majors sold a further 5,541 acres after World War Two to clear the residue of their debts. According to the eighth Lord Henniker's agent, sales were made in order 'to eliminate all borrowings'.[74] But whilst the bulk of the great landed families sold land to balance their books, they were also, after 1894, subject to the payment of sometimes punitive death duties. As Lord Henniker's agent again revealed, 'Earlier sales were due to the payment of death duties.'[75]

In the opinion of Colonel Pretyman, the decision by Lloyd George to increase death duties to 15 per cent on estates over £1,000,000 constituted 'a mischievous and crushing burden' which would, in certain cases, 'owing to the accidents of life' prove to be unbearable.[76] Subsequently, in 1912, Pretyman made plain his belief that 'The sales of agricultural land, which are going on at the present time . . . have been most largely affected by the [increase in] Death Duties.'[77] Similarly, F. M. L. Thompson argues that the upsurge in sales after 1919 was prompted by the confiscatory Budget of

1919 which raised the level of death duties to 40 per cent on estates over £200,000. Death duties had, however, been a concern of landowners since their introduction by Sir William Harcourt in 1894. Speaking in 1894, one Suffolk squire looked upon them as a particularly 'cruel blow below the belt',[78] given the state of the gentry's agricultural incomes. As Wilson Fox noted:

> Landowners and agents unanimously asserted that the imposition of the death duties would prove a heavy burden on the land at a time when all available capital was required to prop up a tottering industry. It was said that their effect has already been shown in decreased expenditure, and that many proprietors would be unable to bear the burden of the payment. The smaller landowners, it is said, will particularly feel the imposition of these duties, particularly if their properties are subject to charges.[79]

Fear of having to pay death duties may well have prompted landed families to sell up, but were any sales actually caused by their payment before the Great War? This was certainly the case as regards the Rendlesham estate in 1911, but when the Ickworth estate was charged with the payment of £22,639 following the death of the third Marquess in 1907, this, as with all the other debts charged to the estate, was covered by the fourth Marquess of Bristol. Death duties only really began to bite among the Suffolk aristocracy after World War One. The deaths of the seventh, eighth and ninth Dukes of Grafton in quick succession, between 1918 and 1936, forced the FitzRoys to sell off their huge Wakefield Lodge estate in Northamptonshire. As Bernard Falk states, 'Payment of the successive death duties consequent on these swift changes in the dukedom meant great inroads being made into the FitzRoy fortune, [for] though the seventh Duke died worth a million pounds, meeting the charges necessitated the greater part of the Wakefield Lodge estate being sold.'[80] In so doing, the family were at least able to hold onto the Euston Hall estate. Nevertheless, the family's finances were left in a very parlous state. As the present Duke admitted:

> I was only 17 when my father unexpectedly inherited the Euston estate in Suffolk, which was then in a state of near bankruptcy, and faced a crippling bill for death duties, and I was quickly made conscious of the appalling problems which accompany the ownership of estates, large houses and collections. My father surmounted them, but only just, and everything was very nearly sold in 1938.[81]

The Adair family were, however, forced to sell up completely following the double blow they received as a result of the deaths in 1915 and 1949, of the fourth Baronet, Sir Frederick Adair (who succeeded his father Sir Hugh in 1902), and the fifth Baronet, Sir Shafto Adair. With regard to the former, the duties imposed on the death of Sir Frederick led to the sale of 15 outlying farms totalling 2,800 acres. The remainder of the Flixton Hall estate was then sold to pay the duties imposed on the death of Sir Shafto. As Lady Bridget Darrell recalled, 'My grandfather had the estate until he died at the end of the War . . . my father [the sixth Baronet] then sold it to pay death duties.'[82] Finally, the death of the third Earl of Stradbroke in 1947, followed by the death of the fourth Earl in 1983, led to a 'lot of land' being sold by the Rous family to pay off the estate or death duties charged to the estate. Nevertheless, the estate still covered an area of 3,900 acres in the mid-1990s and, whilst this is considerably less than the 12,200 acres covered in the 1880s, the heart of the estate remained in the hands of the Rous family.[83] The great aristocrats had the big advantage that, whatever befell them, most could release more than enough land to cover a pressing debt and still leave plenty besides. The gentry, on the other hand, were in a much more precarious position.

The Barnardistons are a good example of the problems facing the gentry. Following the death of Nathaniel Barnardiston in 1916, the net principal value of his property was assessed at £35,502. Based on this figure, the 6 per cent Estate and Settlement Duty levied on the estate left the family with a bill for £2,085. Given that their annual income was £1,433, the only way to pay these duties was through the sale of land. As a result, between 1917 and 1920, Freckenham Hall Farm, Alpheton Hall Farm, Little Chadacre Field Farm and Thorndon Hill Farm were all sold. Oak Hill was also ear-marked for sale as 'The net income from this property is very small, and when the time comes to pay the next death duties it will undoubtedly have to go.'[84] In other words, whilst the aristocracy could sell their outlying estates, the gentry had to sell the farms on their actual home estates. As Beckett states, 'It is clear that the greater owners with 10,000 acres or more of land had a better chance of survival than the more substantial gentry in the 3,000–10,000 acre bracket.'[85]

Of course, this presupposes that the gentry were entirely dependent on their farm rents. In 1893, the Trustees of Colonel Frederick Barne decided to purchase £3,133 New Zealand 3.5 per cent Stock and £3,613 Cape of Good Hope 3.5 per cent Consolidated Stock, with the money raised from the sale of the family's estate in Kent to the Bexley Heath Railway Company. As for the Barnardistons, they were in receipt of £1,078 per annum in dividends and mortgage interest in 1913–1914. [86] Foreign assets also proved useful. For example, in addition to the Bramford Hall estate, on marrying Frederica Broke, Sir Lambton Lorraine also acquired her uncle's property in Natal. Sir Lambton hoped to use the rents from this latter property to pay a heavy annuity owed to Lady Broke Middleton, which had been charged to the Bramford estate. [87]

But surely the key point is that *before* the First World War, when a member of the old landed gentry called it a day, there was a ready supply of new money waiting to fill their shoes. In so doing they were able to position themselves alongside the old gentry in the orbit of the estates of the Edwardian aristocracy and the great magnates, the Earl of Stradbroke, the Marquess of Bristol, the Duke of Grafton, the Earl of Iveagh, Lord Rendlesham, Sir Frederick Adair, Lord Huntingfield, Lord Henniker, Lord de Saumarez, Earl Cadogan, Sir Edward Bunbury, Lord Tollemache, Lord Somerleyton, and Sir Ernest Pretyman. Despite death duties, the 'People's Budget', agricultural depression, occasionally having the bailiffs at their door and being evicted from the House of Commons, the owners of these estates remained in situ. Indeed, 'What looks like unavoidable decline from one perspective appears very much like resilient adaptation from another.'[88] But what remained constant in all this was the aristocracy's colossal gravitational pull over the affairs of the English countryside. It was this, after all, that pulled new families into the countryside to further bolster the social influence that the aristocracy still possessed before the Great War.

CONCLUSION

Any survey of rural Suffolk in the Victorian period has to take into account its division into a three-tier social model of landowners, farmers and labourers, a division which was 'becoming clearer and harder as the century went on'.[1] This book makes the point that despite the near economic collapse of mixed arable and livestock farming in Suffolk, the social influence exerted by the landed aristocracy and gentry continued to be felt by both the labourer and the farmer, and thereby transcended both the reform of the House of Commons in 1884 and local government in 1886. Aristocrats and members of the local gentry were able to achieve this because, during the nineteenth century, they became the largest providers of affordable housing, complete with gardens or allotments or small holdings, prior to the appearance of Council housing. Chapter Four shows there was a close relationship between the labourer and the landowner in the estate villages, and in the villages close enough to experience the gravitational pull of the great estates. There was, also, an understanding among landlords of the labourers' economic position. Lord Francis Hervey in his critique of the small-holdings legislation highlighted the problems labourers would face were they to buy a small holding. Similarly, Lord Rendlesham in attacking the Repeal of the Corn Laws in 1846 used, as his main argument, the impact that repeal would have upon the wages of the agricultural labourer. In his opinion:

> The price of labour was regulated by the price of corn. When, in 1840, he inherited the estate he now held in Suffolk, the price of flour being 3s. per stone, the wages of the labourers were 12s. a week; when the price of flour fell to 2s. 6d. per stone, the wages fell to 11s. When corn declined further, the rate of remuneration to the labourer fell to 8s. per week. It would also be seen that the lower the price of corn, the smaller would be the surplus of wages left for the labourer after

purchasing the necessaries of life. The higher the price of corn, the more labourers would be employed on a farm.[2]

One could, of course, argue that it was a very convenient way to indirectly defend the interests of the aristocracy and the farmer by focusing on the impact repeal would have on the labourer. Surely, however, the key fact here is the degree of knowledge displayed by Lord Rendlesham with regard to the wages paid to his labourers. It was a closeness replicated in the desire of aristocratic landowners to keep possession of the cottages they built for their labourers rather than allow farmers to sub-let. Again, it can be countered, landowners only did this as part of their effort to build thrifty, hard-working communities on their estates. On the other hand, under these conditions the labourer and the landowner were in close enough proximity to one another's realms for Sir Edward Kerrison to observe, 'I, who am constantly among you, who am to be seen in this village and the surrounding villages almost every day among the labouring people, who speak to them, and who live among them . . . know more about them than I do about any other class around me.'[3]

Similarly, whilst 'there clearly developed a growing sense of solidarity among farmers, against labourers, but also against landlords, which created a clearer demarcation of farmers as a group'[4] the degree to which the farmer was *against* the landowner is open to interpretation; the issue of labourers' allotments for example did not provoke a conflict despite the farmers' considerable misgivings that allotments would distract labourers from their farm-work. The relationship between the landowner and the farmer, in Suffolk at least, was generally a close one. Lord Rendlesham again, in his speech in the Commons against the repeal of the Corn Laws, referred the House to:

> the opinion of a practical farmer in his district, who had told him that when he took the farms he held, forty years ago, the price of corn was higher, and he had been able to bring a larger average of light land into cultivation. Since good prices had declined, the land had not paid for itself for tillage. The cultivation of this land, had, however, answered his purpose, inasmuch as it had enabled him to employ a large number of labourers, men, women and children, who would otherwise have been paupers. The firm opinion of that farmer, however, was this – that if the present measure became the law of the country, this breadth of light land must be thrown out of culture entirely.[5]

Whilst this review of the opinion of farmers on the Rendlesham estate provides an interesting counterpoint to the position at Euston discussed in Chapter Two, it also demonstrates the degree to which landlords saw their interests and those of their tenants as inextricably intertwined – if one fell, they both fell. It was a similar line echoed by Sir Edward Kerrison during the 'Lock Out' when he explained that his moral duty 'to protect the labourer who occupies my house' was balanced by his duty to protect the interests of 'the tenant farmer who puts his capital on my land'.[6] The willingness of landlords, after 1846, to invest their money in improving the infrastructure of their farms in Suffolk, to enable their tenants to farm higher, underlined the landlord's duty of care towards the tenantry. Subsequently, during the late 1870s and 1880s as the agricultural depression progressively worsened, and landlords opted for partial reductions in rent, tensions inevitably arose. But once wholesale reductions were implemented, this animosity was dissipated – hence the disappearance of the Farmers Alliance.

The potential for farmers, especially the big farmers, to break away from their landlords, was always there. We can see it in the fear that farmers might become 'Red Republicans' because of the lack of legally enforced tenant-right or in Lord Rendlesham's conclusion that tenants 'in order to secure the proper representation of their own opinions in the House . . . would, at the next election, place one of themselves in the position of a candidate for their suffrages'.[7] Some farmers did stand. In 1880, the leading Suffolk farmer William Biddell, representing the Farmers Alliance, was elected as an Independent MP for the county. But this was also the same Biddell who, together with other leading farmers, had met with the Earl of Stradbroke to endorse the candidacy of John Henniker, the 'farmer's friend', in 1868. Clearly, whilst the dialogue between landowners and farmers in Suffolk could become strained, dialogue there was, and for the most part, before the First World War, farmers in the county were still prepared to stick with their landlords. Radicals were thus in a real dilemma in Southern England, for the harder they tried to prise the farmer away from their landlords, the more they risked estranging the labourer and *vice versa*. With the Liberal party caught between two stools, farmers continued to gravitate toward the Conservative party.[8]

By the mid-1890s, after nearly two decades of progressive rent reductions, there prevailed in Suffolk 'a most friendly feeling'[9] between farmers and landlords, indeed it was standing too close to their tenants that ensured many landlords went to the wall.[10] But not all landowners went to the wall between the commencement of the agricultural depression in 1874 and the outbreak of the First World War in 1914. Moreover, during these forty years, the relationships built up by landowners between themselves and the farmer and the labourer during the previous thirty-seven years, through farm improvements, cottage building and provision of allotments, were to prove invaluable in sustaining the aristocracy's leadership of rural society in Suffolk. Furthermore, because their hegemony over rural life in Suffolk survived, despite the catastrophic drop in revenue experienced by the owners of great estates in the county, it seems reasonable to assume that the aristocracy's social influence would have persisted across Southern England before the Great War. It was, after all, the ongoing social influence to be had as an English country squire that encouraged businessmen to become buyers rather than just hirers of sporting estates. The irony is that it was these hirers and buyers who in turn provided the last great boost to the aristocracy's leadership of rural society, prior to the real apocalypse of the Great War. However, writing in 1912, Arthur Ponsonby described the decline of the landed aristocracy in the following terms:

> The keynote of the transformation they are undergoing [is] the change from being able to hold the reins of government by special privilege and unquestioned tradition to a state of affairs in which privilege and tradition count for very little; [this] must alter materially the position, the prospects and the general outlook of the aristocrat.[11]

But did the loss of the reins of government materially affect their general outlook? What Ponsonby overlooks is that the ownership of land meant far more to the aristocracy than just political power. There was a reluctance to part with land, highlighted in Chapter One, that is still visible today. When questioned by the author in the 1990s about their motivations in holding onto their estates, those landowners surveyed came back with remarkably similar answers. Lord Tollemache retained Helmingham because in part the 'ownership goes back over several hundred years' and in part 'to see it handed to future generations'; Lord Cranworth cited his sense of 'family responsibility' in holding onto Grundisburgh Hall estate, while the Earl of Stradbroke held onto Henham in the hope 'the children may well take the place on'. Finally, with regard to the Thornham estate, Lord Henniker hoped to 'preserve it for the next generation'.[12] Clearly, a strong sense of family tradition persists as it would have done before the Great War. But before 1914, as you have seen, their ancestors' social influence in the English countryside was still immense, and as a result, in their localities, their prospects and general outlook remained unaltered. As the fifth Lord

Henniker observed in 1875, 'every owner of purely agricultural land would be a richer man by investing his capital in almost any other security' but land was preferred on account of the 'opportunity to lead a useful life, which its possession afforded beyond all other kinds of property'.[13] When all is said and done, up to the Great War there remained an unshakeable belief among the aristocracy and gentry in Suffolk that their usefulness was not yet at an end, although they were perhaps fortunate in that both the sporting and farming tenantry and their labourers continued to agree.

NOTES

Introduction
1 E. J. Hobsbawm, *Industry and Empire* (London, 1969), p. 198.
2 Kevin Cahill, *Who Owns Britain* (Edinburgh, 2001), p. 8.
3 G. E. Mingay, *The Gentry: The Rise and Fall of a Ruling Class* (London, 1976), p. 191.

Chapter One
1 F. M. L. Thompson, *English Landed Society in The Nineteenth Century* (London, 1963), pp. 32, 114–117; David Cannadine, *The Decline and Fall of the British Aristocracy* (London, 1990), p. 9; 'Return of Owners of Land (Suffolk)', *British Parliamentary Papers* LXXII, Part II (1874).
2 'Icklingham Hall', *Estates Gazette*, 29 January 1898, p. 836.
3 Arthur Oswald, 'Helmingham Hall, Suffolk, II', *Country Life*, 16 August 1956, p. 332; Arthur Oswald, 'Helmingham Hall, Suffolk, I', *Country Life*, 9 August 1956, p. 284; J. V. Beckett, *The Aristocracy in England 1660–1914* (Oxford, 1989), pp. 53–54; Arthur Oswald, 'Helmingham Hall, Suffolk, III', *Country Life*, 23 August 1956, p. 380.
4 H. J. Habakkuk, 'English landownership, 1680–1740', *Economic History Review* 1 (1940), p. 2; G. E. Mingay, *English Landed Society in the Eighteenth Century* (London, 1976), p. 50; Mingay, *Gentry*, p. 14.
5 Alan Mackley, 'An Economic History of Country House Building with Particular Reference to East Anglia and the East and West Ridings of Yorkshire, c.1660–1870', (University of East Anglia, Ph.D. 1993), p. 58; J. V. Beckett, 'English landownership in the later seventeenth and eighteenth centuries: The debate and the problems', *Economic History Review* 30 (1977), p. 569; C. Clay, 'Marriage, inheritance and the rise of large estates in England, 1660–1815', *Economic History Review* 21 (1968), pp. 503–519; C. Clay, 'Property settlements, financial provision for the family, and sale of land by the greater landowners 1660–1790', *Journal of British Studies* 21 (1981), pp. 18–38; B. A. Holderness, 'The English land market in the eighteenth century: The case of Lincolnshire', *Economic History Review* 27 (1974), pp. 557–577; F. M. L. Thompson, 'Landownership and economic growth in England in the eighteenth century', in E. L. Jones and S. J. Woolf (eds), *Agrarian Change and Economic Development: The Historical Problems* (Bungay, 1969), pp. 47–8.

6   Linda Colley, *Britons: Forging the Nation 1707–1837* (London, 1992), pp. 156–57; see also T. H. Hollingsworth, 'The demography of the British peerage', *Population Studies* XVIII (1964).

7   Clay, 'Marriage', pp. 510–11and 514.

8   Clay, 'Marriage', pp. 516 and 509.

9   Clay, 'Marriage', p. 517; Beckett, *Aristocracy*, p. 55.

10   Beckett, *Aristocracy,* p. 55

11   SRO (Ipswich) HA93/5/125; William Courthorpe (ed), *Debrett's Baronetage of England* (London, 1839), pp. 312 and 363; Robert P. Dod, *The Peerage, Baronetage and Knightage of Great Britain and Ireland* (London, 1863), p. 412; Robert H. Mair (ed), *Debrett's Baronetage and Knightage* (London, 1881), p. 333. William White, *History, Gazetteer and Directory of Suffolk* (London, 1885), pp. 139, 464, 507; Bernard Burke and Ashworth P. Burke (eds), *A Genealogical and Heraldic History of the Peerage and Baronetage* (London, 1912), p. 597.

12   G. E. Cokayne, *The Complete Peerage, Volume VI* (London, 1925), p. 46; White, *Suffolk*, p. 249; Bernard Falk, *The Royal FitzRoys: Dukes of Grafton Through Four Centuries* (London, 1950), pp. 14, 20; H. J. Habakkuk, 'The rise and fall of English landed families, 1600–1800', *Transactions of the Royal Historical Society* 29 (1979), p. 194.

13   Tom Williamson and Liz Bellamy, *Property and the Landscape* (London, 1987), p. 125.

14   David Dymond and Peter Northeast, *A History of Suffolk* (Chichester, 1995), p. 91.

15   G. E. Cokayne, *The Complete Peerage, Volume II* (London, 1912), p. 328.

16   Beckett, *Aristocracy*, p.104–5; Mingay, *Landed Society*, p. 32.

17   H. J. Habakkuk, *Marriage, Debt and the Estates System: English Landownership 1650–1950* (Oxford, 1994), p. 205.

18   Joan Thirsk (ed), *The Agrarian History of England and Wales, Volume V, Part II, 1640–1750: Agrarian Change* (Cambridge, 1985), pp. 193–6; Barbara English, *The Great Landowners of East Yorkshire, 1530–1910* (Hemel Hempstead, 1990), p. 93; SRO (Bury) HA507/4/35.

19   H. J. Habakkuk, 'Marriage settlements in the eighteenth century', *Transactions of the Royal Historical Society* 32 (1950), p. 24.

20   R. Trumbach, *The Rise of the Egalitarian Family* (London, 1978), p. 82.

21   SRO (Lowestoft) HA12/B3/11/6; G. E. Cokayne, *The Complete Peerage, Volume III* (London, 1913), p. 454.

22   G. D. Squibb, 'The end of the name and arms clause?', *Law Quarterly Review* 69 (1953), p. 220; Bernard Burke (ed), *A Genealogical and Heraldic History of the Landed Gentry, Volume II* (London, 1894), p. 1651. The grandson of George Pretyman-Tomline would later buy the Orwell Park estate in east Suffolk.

23   Sir Gerald Ryan and Lillian J. Redstone, *Timperley of Hintlesham: A Study of a Suffolk Family* (London, 1931), p. 125; Alun Howkins, 'Social, cultural and domestic life', in E. J. T. Collins (ed), *The Agrarian History of England and Wales, Volume VII* (Cambridge, 2000), p. 1358; Lawrence Stone and Jeanne C. Fawtier Stone, *An Open Elite? England 1540–1880* (Oxford, 1984), p. 401 and pp. 111–112; John Burke and John Bernard Burke (eds), *A Genealogical and Heraldic History of the Extinct and Dormant Baronetcies of England, Ireland and Scotland* (London, 1844), p. 182.

24 Arthur Oswald, 'Helmingham Hall, Suffolk, IV', *Country Life*, 27 September 1956, p. 657; Burke, *Peerage* (1912), pp. 672–674 and 1859; White, *Suffolk*, pp. 308–309.

25 Stone, *Open?*, p. 125, Beckett, *Aristocracy*, p. 87; Lawrence Stone, 'Spring back', *Albion* 17 (1985), p. 179; Eileen Spring and David Spring, 'The English landed elite, 1540–1879: A review', *Albion* 17 (1985), p. 160. The caveat here is that a failure in the male line, especially if it was unexpected, could lead to an estate falling into the hands of a tenant in tail with full powers to divest of the estate.

26 L. Crispin Warmington (ed), *Stephen's Commentaries on the laws of England, Volume I* (London, 1950), pp. 150–2 and 163; H. J. Habakkuk, 'England', in A. Goodwin (ed), *The European Nobility in the Eighteenth Century: Studies in the Nobilities of the Major European States in the Pre-Reform Era* (London, 1967), p. 2; H. J. Habakkuk, 'The English land market in the eighteenth century', in J. S. Bromley and E. H. Kossman (eds), *Britain and the Netherlands: Papers delivered to the Oxford-Netherlands Historical Conference, 1959* (London, 1960), pp. 161–2.

27 SRO (Ipswich) HA53/359/824. Philip Barne subsequently challenged the settlement as he had been 'under the impression that he would take £5,000' personally, SRO (Bury) HA507/4/34. The Hervey children received a reversionary interest in a part or share in £11,157 of reduced '£3 per cent annuities' purchased in 1863 out of funds held by the trustees of the Marquess's marriage settlement. SRO (Bury) HA507/4/44 and SRO (Bury) HA 507/4/45; Eileen Spring, 'The strict family settlement: Its role in family history', *Economic History Review* 41 (1988), p. 454; Lloyd Bonfield, 'Strict settlement and the family: A differing view', *Economic History Review* 41 (1988), p. 461; Eileen Spring, 'The family, strict settlement and historians', *Canadian Journal of History* 18 (1983), p. 379 and 'Law and the theory of the affective family', *Albion* 16 (1984) p. 1; J. P. Cooper, 'Patterns of inheritance and settlement by great landowners from the fifteenth to the eighteenth centuries' in Jack Goody, Joan Thirsk and E. P. Thompson (eds), *Family and Inheritance: Rural Society in Western Europe, 1200–1800* (Cambridge, 1976), pp. 220, 226–7.

28 Eileen Spring, 'The settlement of land in nineteenth century England', *The American Journal of Legal History* 8 (1964), p. 210.

29 Leslie Rutherford and Sheila Bone (eds), *Osborn's Concise Law Dictionary* (London, 1993), p. 247.

30 SRO (Ipswich) HA108/8/2.

31 Lloyd Bonfield, 'Marriage settlements and the "rise of great estates": The demographic aspects', *Economic History Review* 32 (1979), pp. 483 and 493; Habakkuk, 'England', p. 2.

32 Lloyd Bonfield, 'Marriage settlements, 1660–1740: The adoption of the strict settlement in Kent and Northamptonshire', in R. B. Outhwaite (ed), *Marriage and Society: Studies in the Social History of Marriage* (London, 1981), p. 101; Barbara English and John Savile, 'Family settlements and the "rise of great estates"', *Economic History Review* 33 (1980), p. 558; Lloyd Bonfield, 'Marriage settlements and the "rise of great estates": A rejoinder', *Economic History Review* 33 (1980), p. 559 see also Lloyd Bonfield, *Marriage Settlements 1601–1740: The Adoption of the Strict Settlement* (Cambridge, 1983); Habakkuk, 'Marriage settlements', pp. 15–31.

33 SRO (Bury) HA507/4/3a and HA507/4/34; SRO (Bury) HA507/4/55; SRO
    (Bury) HA507/3/825; SRO (Ipswich) HA53/359/850.
34 This figure comprised 2,355 acres in Lincolnshire, 1,126 acres in Essex and the
    1,129 acre Barrow Hall estate and the 1,803 acre Playford and Rushmere estates
    in Suffolk, SRO (Bury) HA 507/4/39; W. D. Rubinstein, 'New men of wealth
    and the purchase of land in nineteenth century Britain', *Past and Present* 92
    (1981), pp. 139–140; Beckett, 'Debate', p. 576.
35 SRO (Lowestoft) HA12/D3/4 and SRO (Ipswich) HA53/359/1043.
36 SRO (Ipswich) HA93/3/190.
37 SRO (Ipswich) HA53/359/688; SRO (Ipswich) HA53/359/688; *Public General
    Statutes* (London, 1856), p. 1121.
38 SRO (Ipswich) HA53/359/688 and *Public General Statutes* (London, 1850),
    pp. 350–351.
39 Cooper, 'Patterns', p. 233. By the late eighteenth century many families were in
    serious financial difficulty and were rescued only by resort to retrenchment and
    by the large rise in estate revenues, which accompanied the increasing prosperity
    of agriculture at this period, Mingay, *Landed Society*, p. 36; Holderness,
    'Lincolnshire', p. 573.
40 Mingay, *Landed Society*, p. 36. The development of the mortgage did give
    landowners more choice in the timing of the sale of land. H. J. Habakkuk, 'The
    rise and fall of English landed families, II', *Transactions of the Royal Historical
    Society* 30 (1980), p. 220.
41 Thompson, *Landed Society,* p. 69; Cooper, 'Patterns', p. 232; English, *East
    Yorkshire*, p. 125. Indeed, Johnson argues given 'the law can easily be evaded . . .
    it cannot be held that the accumulation of lands in the hands of a few is the *direct*
    result of our land laws'. Arthur H. Johnson, *The Disappearance of the Small
    Landowner* (Oxford, 1909), pp. 11–12.
42 G. E. Mingay, 'The size of farms in the eighteenth century', *Economic History
    Review* 14 (1962), pp. 469, 472 and 475; Habakkuk, 'Land market', pp. 155–8,
    160; Habakkuk, 'Families, II', p. 220 and 'The long-term rate of interest and
    the price of land in the seventeenth century', *Economic History Review* 5 (1952–
    3), pp. 26–30; Mingay, *Landed Society*, pp. 26 and 36–7; Arthur Oswald,
    'Hintlesham Hall, Suffolk', *Country Life* 18 August 1928, p. 238.
43 Thompson, 'Economic growth', pp. 49 and 51.
44 Tom Williamson, 'Shrubland before Barry: A house and its landscape, 1660–
    1880', in C. Harper-Bill, C. Rawcliffe and R. G. Wilson (eds), *East Anglia's
    History: Studies in Honour of Norman Scarfe* (Woodbridge, 2002), p. 196; Beckett,
    'Debate', p. 580.
45 Clive Paine (ed), *The Culford Estate 1780–1935* (Lavenham, 1993), p. 1–2; Richard
    Aldington, *Wellington* (London, 1946), p. 75; Mingay, *Landed Society,* p. 74.
46 Stone, *Open?*, p. 403; David and Eileen Spring, 'Social mobility and the English
    landed elite', *Canadian Journal of History* 21 (1986), p. 339; George Martelli, *The
    Elveden Enterprise: A Study of the Second Agricultural Revolution* (London, 1952), p. 41.
47 Arthur Oswald, 'Melford Hall, II, Suffolk', *Country Life*, 7 August 1937, p. 144;
    Hugh Montgomery-Massingberd (ed), *Burke's and Savills Guide to Country Houses,
    Volume III* (London, 1985), pp. 257 and 262–3; Bernard Burke (ed), *A
    Genealogical and Heraldic History of the Landed Gentry, Volume I* (London, 1894),
    pp. 91–2 and 137; White, *Suffolk,* pp. 228, 262,537, 562; SRO (Lowestoft)

HA12/E1/5/182; Thompson, *Landed Society*, p. 121; Jonathan Theobald, 'Estate stewards in Woodland High Suffolk, 1690–1820', in Harper-Bill et al., *East Anglia's History*, p. 246; Jonathan Theobald, 'Changing Landscapes, Changing Economies: Holdings in Woodland High Suffolk, 1600–1850', (University of East Anglia, Ph.D., 2000), pp. 207, 224 and 252; Daniel Defoe, *A Tour Through the Whole Island of Great Britain* (London, 1724, reprinted 1971), p. 84. The Crowfield Hall estate of Sir William Middleton was also considerably enlarged between 1750 and 1850. Wilson and Mackley suggest that Dalham Hall was sold to John Affleck, a Baltic merchant in 1707, Richard Wilson and Alan Mackley *Creating Paradise: The Building of the English Country House, 1660–1880* (London, 2000), p. 209.

48 Harold Perkin, *The Origins of Modern English Society, 1780–1880* (London, 1969), p. 57; Habakkuk, *Marriage*, p. 204; Beckett, *Aristocracy*, p. 66; S. Cornish Watkins, 'Heveningham Hall, Suffolk', *Country Life*, 25 April 1908, p. 599; R. G. Wilson, 'The Denisons and Milneses: Eighteenth century merchant landowners', in J. T. Ward and R. G. Wilson (eds), *Land and Industry: The Landed Estate and the Industrial Revolution* (Newton Abbot, 1971), p. 151; SRO (Ipswich) HB26/412/1758.

49 R. Porter, *London, A Social History* (London, 1994), p. 222; Paine (ed), *Culford*, p. 2; SRO (Ipswich) HA 408/C3/13. Whether or not the deflationary pressures of the 1820s prompted the sale of the Culford estate remains unclear. Edward Holland was the nephew of Edward John Holland, of the East India Co., who died unmarried in 1821 worth £600,000.

50 Beckett, *Aristocracy*, p. 61; Thompson, *Landed Society*, p. 121.

51 J. L. Smith-Dampier, *East Anglian Worthies* (Oxford, 1949), p. 9.

52 SRO (Lowestoft) SC/065/1; SRO (Ipswich) HA10/50/18/14.1(1–12).

53 F. M. L. Thompson, 'The land market in the nineteenth century', *Oxford Economic Papers* 9 (1957), pp. 290, 292 and 293–4; P. Barnes, 'The Economic History of Landed Estates in Norfolk Since 1880', (University of East Anglia, Ph.D. 1984), pp. 4–5; White, *Suffolk*, p. 489. By the nineteenth century, the term lesser gentry is applied to estates between 1,000 and 3,000 acres rather than as in the eighteenth century to estates with an annual value of between £250 and £1,000.

54 Large funds were suddenly available because the long legal wrangle surrounding the will of Peter Thellusson had finally come to an end, see Chapter Eight and SRO (Ipswich) HB 416/A2/14; SRO (Ipswich) HA1/F/29/66; SRO (Ipswich) HA1/F/31/43a; SRO (Ipswich) HA1/F/32/7; SRO (Ipswich) HA1/F/33/9; SRO (Lowestoft) HA12/D3/4; SRO (Ipswich) HB26/412/1602 and HB26/412/1603 and 1604; Tollemache Letters, (B.S.) D.S. Manuscript 21, Thetford Library; woods account, day book, (references to farms bought can be found in the front cover), SRO (Bury) HA507/3/501; SRO (Ipswich) HA11/C4/10–11, listed as HA11/C4/9; HA11/C8/4 and SRO (Ipswich) HB26/412/1603.

55 Thompson, *Landed Society*, pp. 120–1 and p. 122; Thompson, 'Land market', p. 294.

56 Rubinstein, 'Wealth', p. 129–131 and p. 134.

57 Rubinstein, 'Wealth', p. 127.

58 Rubinstein, 'Wealth', p. 138; Beckett, *Aristocracy*, p. 79; W. D. Rubinstein, 'Cutting-up rich: A reply to F. M. L. Thompson', *Economic History Review* 45 (1992), p. 354 & W. D. Rubinstein, 'Businessmen into landowners: The question revisited', in Negley Harte and Roland Quinault (eds), *Land and Society*

in Britain, 1700–1914: Essays in Honour of F. M. L. Thompson (Manchester 1996) p. 101.

59 David and Eileen Spring, 'Social mobility', pp. 336–7.

60 F. M. L. Thompson, 'Life after death: How successful nineteenth century businessmen disposed of their fortunes', *Economic History Review* 43 (1990), p. 43.

61 F. M. L. Thompson, 'Stitching it together again', *Economic History Review* 45 (1992), pp. 362 and 364–5; Mark Girouard, *The Victorian Country House* (London, 1979), p. 7; Thompson, *Landed Society*, pp. 119, 293, 297; White, *Suffolk*, pp. 264, 560 and 558; Mark Girouard, 'A town built on carpets', *Country Life* 24 September 1970, p. 759; John Bateman, *The Acre-Ocracy of England* (London, 1876), pp. 50, 80, 128; John Bateman, *The Great Landowners of Great Britain and Ireland* (London, 1883), p. 412; *Burke's Genealogical and Heraldic History of the Landed Gentry, Volume II* (London, 1965), p. 205; *Burke's and Savills, III*, p. 262; B. Crump and Gertrude Ghorbal, *History of the Huddersfield Woollen Industry* (Huddersfield, 1935), p. 128.

62 Thompson quoted in Rubinstein: 'Wealth', p. 126.

Chapter Two

1 G. E. Mingay (ed), *The Agricultural Revolution: Changes in Agriculture, 1650–1880* (London, 1977), p. 270.

2 Jonathan Brown and H. A. Beecham, 'Arable farming, farming practices', in G. E. Mingay (ed), *The Agrarian History of England and Wales, 1750–1850, Volume VI* (Cambridge, 1989), pp. 279–80; E. L. Jones, 'The changing basis of English agricultural prosperity 1853–1873', *Agricultural History Review* 10 (1962), pp. 104–5; Susanna Wade Martins and Tom Williamson, *Roots of Change: Farming and the Landscape in East Anglia, c. 1700–1870* (Exeter, 1999), pp. 132 & 152; G. E. Mingay (ed), *Arthur Young and His Times* (London, 1975), p. 58.

3 E. J. T. Collins and E. L. Jones, 'Sectoral advance in English agriculture, 1850–1880', *Agricultural History Review* 15 (1967), p. 67. The term 'Breckland' was coined by W. G. Clarke in 1895. According to William Marshall and R. R. Clarke a 'breck' was a newly made enclosure consisting of a tract of heathland that was broken up for cultivation from time to time, and then allowed to revert back to waste. Brecks were a characteristic feature of the heathlands of north-west Suffolk up to the late eighteenth century. As Mark Bailey states 'the region is actually named after a system for cropping the land as opposed to some unique physical characteristic'. Mark Bailey, *A Marginal Economy? East Anglian Breckland in the Later Middle Ages* (Cambridge, 1989), pp. 27–28; Edward Martin, 'The soil regions of Suffolk', in David Dymond and Edward Martin (eds), *An Historical Atlas of Suffolk* (Ipswich, 1988), p. 14. 'Report from the Select Committee on Agricultural Customs (1848)', *British Parliamentary Papers* VI (1866), p. 177.

4 The clayland parishes of Woodland High Suffolk had to be comprehensively under-drained in order to make them viable to plough: Theobald, 'Changing Landscapes', p. 254; Wade Martins and Williamson, *Roots*, p. 142; William and Hugh Raynbird, *On the Agriculture of Suffolk* (London, 1849), p. 7; James Caird, *English Agriculture, 1850–1851* (London, 1852. Reprinted 1968), p. 160–1; Jonathan Theobald, 'Agricultural productivity in Woodland High Suffolk, 1600–1850', *Agricultural History Review* 50 (2002), pp. 3 & 10; Paul Brassley,

'Arable systems: light land farming', in E. J. T. Collins (ed), *The Agrarian History of England and Wales, Volume VII* (Cambridge, 2000), pp. 461–2.

5   Joan Thirsk and Jean Imray (eds), *Suffolk Farming in the Nineteenth Century* (Ipswich, 1958); Raynbird, *Suffolk*, p. 9; J. D. Chambers and G. E. Mingay, *The Agricultural Revolution, 1750–1880* (London, 1978), p. 176. Sturgess argues that there was a significant increase in the output of livestock and livestock products on the English clays during the 1850s and 1860s. A view strongly disputed by Collins and Jones. R. W. Sturgess, 'The Agricultural Revolution on the English clays', *Agricultural History Review* 14 (1966), pp. 104–5; Collins and Jones, 'Sectoral advance', pp. 67–8; A. D. M. Phillips, 'Underdraining on the English claylands, 1850–1880: A review', *Agricultural History Review* 17 (1969), p. 55; R. W. Sturgess, 'The Agricultural Revolution on the English clays: A rejoinder', *Agricultural History Review* 15 (1967), pp. 82–87.

6   Caird, *English Agriculture*, p. 504; E. L. Jones, *The Development of English Agriculture, 1815–1873* (London, 1973), pp. 26–7; B. A. Holderness, 'Investment, accumulation and agricultural credit', in E. J. T. Collins (ed), *The Agrarian History of England and Wales, Volume VII* (Cambridge, 2000), p. 890.

7   *Hansard's Parliamentary Debates, Volume LXXXVII* (London, 1846), p. 544; G. Kitson Clark, 'The repeal of the Corn Laws and the politics of the Forties', *Economic History Review* 4 (1951), p. 1; Arthur Oswald, 'Helmingham Hall, Suffolk, V', *Country Life*, 4 October 1956, p. 715. The Marquess of Bristol by contrast supported Robert Peel, Cokayne, *Peerage, II*, p. 327; P. J. O. Trist, *A Survey of the Agriculture of Suffolk*, (London, 1971), p. 319.

8   *Hansard's (1846)*, p. 962; Wade Martins & Williamson, *Roots*, p. 152.

9   Thirsk, *Suffolk Farming*, pp. 96–7 and p. 27.

10 Caird, *English Agriculture*, p. 145.

11 Caird, *English Agriculture*, p. 491.

12 Chambers and Mingay, *Agricultural Revolution*, p. 177. Chambers and Mingay suggest that the effect of free trade between 1850 and 1870 was to 'bring the world price of wheat up to the British level and to make it more stable, rather than to severely depress the home price', pp. 158–9.

13 E. J. T. Collins, 'Rural and agricultural change', in E. J. T. Collins (ed), *The Agrarian History of England and Wales, Volume VII* (Cambridge, 2000), pp. 72–3.

14 Richard Perren, *Agriculture in Depression 1870–1940* (Cambridge, 1995), p. 4; SRO (Ipswich) HA11/C46/55–7.

15 Wade Martins and Williamson, *Roots*, pp. 142–3; 'Agricultural Customs', (1866), p.177; A. D. M. Phillips, 'Landlord investment in farm buildings in the English Midlands in the mid-nineteenth century', in B. A. Holderness and Michael Turner (eds), *Land, Labour and Agriculture, 1700–1920* (London, 1991), p. 191; SRO (Ipswich) HA93/3/459. In total, 234,964 pipes were laid across 176 acres in the parishes of Stonham Apsall, Creeting St Mary, Crowfield, Baylham and Barking, 'Royal Commission on Agricultural Depression: Minutes of evidence taken before Her Majesty's Commissioner's on Agriculture, Volume III', *British Parliamentary Papers* XIV (1882), p.179. Draining was the only improvement for which tenants customarily paid direct interest to their landlords. Jones, *Development*, p. 30.

16 Caird in Mingay, *Changes*, p. 271; SRO (Bury) 449/3/13; Phillips, 'Landlord investment', p. 201; 'Agricultural Customs', (1866), p. 181; George Ewart

Evans, *Where Beards Wag All: The Relevance of the Oral Tradition* (London, 1970), p.117; Theobald, 'Changing Landscapes', p. 250 also pp. 190 and 198.

17 SRO (Bury) 449/3/13.

18 B. A. Holderness, 'Landlord's capital formation in East Anglia, 1750 – 1870', *Economic History Review* 25 (1972), p. 445; SRO (Ipswich) HA93/3/227; SRO (Bury) HA507/3/730; SRO (Bury) HA507/3/823.

19 Mingay, *Young*, p. 59; M. R. Postgate, 'The field systems of Breckland', *Agricultural History Review* 10 (1962), p. 87 and p. 94; Arthur Young, *General View of the Agriculture of the County of Suffolk* (London, 1813), p. 169; D. P. Dymond, 'The Suffolk landscape', in Lionel M. Munby (ed), *East Anglian Studies* (Cambridge, 1968), p. 25; Martelli, *Elveden*, p. 35; SRO (Bury) 941/83/4; Michael Turner, *Enclosures in Britain, 1750–1830* (London, 1984), p. 36. In parishes where the landlord was the sole proprietor as on the Euston and Hengrave estates, there was no need for an act: David Dymond, 'Enclosure and reclamation', in David Dymond and Edward Martin (eds), *An Historical Atlas of Suffolk* (Ipswich, 1988), p. 100. As regards investment on the clay land estates see references to Henniker, Tollemache and Middleton in Theobald, 'Changing Landscapes', pp. 243 and 247–8.

20 Holderness, 'Capital formation', p. 442.

21 A. D. M. Phillips, *The Underdraining of Farmland in England During the Nineteenth Century* (Cambridge, 1989), pp. 63–65 and pp. 53–6. The Baylham and Crowfield estates were drained using loans, but improvements to field drainage on the Oakley Park and Brome Hall estates were paid for by the landlord out of income. Susanna Wade Martins and Tom Williamson, 'The development of the lease and its role in agricultural improvement in East Anglia, 1660–1870', *Agricultural History Review* 46 (1998), p. 136.

22 SRO (Bury) HA507/3/828; SRO (Lowestoft) HA12/D3/7; a further £2,100 was borrowed to build six new cottages on the Flixton estate, SRO (Lowestoft) HA12/D7/1/1; SRO (Bury), HA507/3/749.

23 SRO (Ipswich) HA1/HB6/4/8; 'Royal Commission', (1882), p. 179; Chambers and Mingay, *Agricultural Revolution*, pp. 159 and 176–7.

24 Chambers and Mingay, *Agricultural Revolution*, p. 163 Jones, *Development*, p. 30; SRO (Lowestoft) HA12/A8/1/2 and 11. This letter refers to the payment of £203 in interest, which on £5,470 works out at around 4 per cent. Chambers and Mingay, *Agricultural Revolution*, p. 163; Michael Turner, 'Cost, finance and parliamentary enclosure', *Economic History Review* 34 (1981), p. 245; Jones, *Development*, pp. 29–30.

25 B. A. Holderness, 'The Victorian farmer', in G. E. Mingay (ed), *The Victorian Countryside Volume I* (London, 1981), p. 233.

26 'Royal Commission', (1882), p. 179.

27 Philip S. Bagwell and G. E. Mingay, *Britain and America 1850–1939: A Study of Economic Change* (London, 1970), pp. 75 and 81; P. J. Perry, *British Farming in the Great Depression 1870–1914: An Historical Geography* (Newton Abbot, 1974), p. 51.

28 Lord Ernle, 'The Great Depression and recovery, 1874–1914', in P. J. Perry (ed), *British Agriculture 1875–1914* (Bungay, 1973), p. 1.

29 Cormac O'Grada, 'Agricultural decline, 1860–1914', in R. Floud and D. McCloskey (eds), *The Economic History of Britain Since 1700: Volume II, 1860 to*

the 1970s (Cambridge, 1981), p. 186; thereby catastrophically delaying the shift over to livestock and dairy production. Perry, *British Farming*, p. 59; P. J. Perry and R. J. Johnston, 'The temporal and spatial incidence of agricultural depression in Dorset, 1868–1902', *Journal of Interdisciplinary History* 2 (1972), p. 302.

30 'Royal Commission', (1882), p. 177; B. A. Holderness, 'The origins of high farming', in Holderness and Turner, *Land*, p. 151.

31 SRO (Lowestoft) HA12/D6/1/18 (Part I); C. S. Orwin and E. H. Whetham, *History of British Agriculture, 1846–1914* (Newton Abbot, 1971)), pp. 242–3; George Ewart Evans, *Ask the Fellows Who Cut the Hay* (London, 1956), p. 104.

32 SRO (Ipswich) HA53/359/57.

33 SRO (Bury) 941/30/109; T. W. Beastall, 'A South Yorkshire estate in the late nineteenth century', *Agricultural History Review* 14 (1966), p. 42.

34 'Royal Commission', (1882), p. 179.

35 SRO (Ipswich) HA11/C3/27. Interestingly, this document only refers to 10,333 acres. Given that Bateman records that the Henham estate covered an area of 12,203 acres in 1883, was the difference the land left unsettled? See also SRO (Lowestoft) HA12/D7/1/6, this document only refers to 9,078 acres of the Flixton estate. Of the remaining 1,852 acres references were found to six farms totalling 847 acres. Of these, only one farm had had its rent reduced. SRO (Lowestoft) HA12/D7/1/7.

36 'Royal Commission', (1882), p. 179.

37 SRO (Lowestoft) HA12/D7/1/6.

38 SRO (Bury) HA507/3/839; 'Royal Commission', (1882), p. 188; SRO (Bury) HA 507/3/749. In the same year £1,073 was borrowed to restore the navigation waterway on the River Lark. SRO (Bury) HA 507/3/749; SRO (Bury) 941/83/4; SRO (Bury) HA507/3/755; SRO (Lowestoft) HA12/D7/1/5; Perren, *Agriculture in Depression*, p. 6.

39 SRO (Bury) HA507/6/20.

40 R. C. K. Ensor, *England, 1870–1914*, (Oxford, 1936), p. 284.

41 T. W. Fletcher, 'Lancashire livestock farming during the Great Depression', *Agricultural History Review* 9 (1961), p. 17.

42 'Royal Commission on Agriculture: Report by Mr Wilson Fox (Assistant Commissioner) on the county of Suffolk', *British Parliamentary Papers* XVI (1895), p. 341 and pp. 344 and 416.

43 'Suffolk', (1895), p. 341; Brassley, 'Light land', pp. 459–460. In 1907, J. E. Vincent wrote, 'it may be suspected that some of the famous warrens of Norfolk and Suffolk [would] pay better in rabbits for the London market in these days than they would pay under crops'. J. E. Vincent, *Through East Anglia in a Motor Car* (London, 1907), p. 16. So long as the land was kept in tilth it provided a home for game, the shooting rights to which could be let.

44 H. Rider Haggard, *Rural England: Being An Account of Agricultural and Social Researches Carried Out in the Years 1901–1902, Volume II*, (London, 1902), p. 384.

45 'Suffolk', (1895), p. 359; SRO (Bury) HA507/3/536 and 538; SRO (Lowestoft) HA12/D9/1 and HA12/B3/9/7; G. E. Cokayne, *The Complete Peerage, Volume XII, Part II* (London, 1959), p. 435. Hugh succeeded to the Baronetcy, the peerage however became extinct; Perry, *British Farming*, pp. 42–44.

46 R. J. Thompson, 'An enquiry into the rent of agricultural land', in W. E.

Minchinton (ed), *Essays in Agrarian History, Volume II* (Newton Abbot, 1968), p.72; 'Suffolk', (1895), p. 351 and pp. 409–410; SRO (Bury), HA507/3/347, 348 and 349; Haggard, *Rural England*, p. 394.

47   Charles Wilson, 'Economy and society in late Victorian Britain', *Economic History Review* 18 (1965), p. 193; Fletcher, 'Lancashire', p. 37; T.W. Fletcher, 'The Great Depression of English agriculture, 1873–1896', *Economic History Review* 13 (1961), p. 419; Richard Perren, 'The North American beef and cattle trade with Great Britain, 1870–1914', *Economic History Review* 24 (1971), pp. 430–431; Perry, *British Farming*, p. 51; S. B. Saul, *The Myth of the Great Depression 1873–1896* (London, 1985), p. 35.

48   Jones, 'Changing basis', p. 109.

49   Jones, *Development*, p. 22.

50   SRO (Lowestoft) HA12/D3/7.

51   SRO (Lowestoft), HA12/D3/7.

52   SRO (Lowestoft) HA12/D3/7.

53   'Royal Commission', (1882), p. 179.

54   SRO (Lowestoft) HA12/D6/1/18.

55   'Agricultural Returns of Great Britain', *British Parliamentary Papers* 76 (1880), p. 680; Orwin and Whetham, *British Agriculture* p. 265; J. T. Coppock, 'Agricultural changes in the Chilterns 1875–1900', *Agricultural History Review* 9 (1961), pp. 5–12; Pamela Horn, *The Changing Countryside in Victorian and Edwardian England and Wales* (London, 1984), p. 33.

56   Richard Perren, 'The landlord and agricultural transformation, 1870–1900', *Agricultural History Review* 18 (1970), p. 37; Jean Marchand (ed), *A Frenchman in England, 1784: Being the Mélanges sur l'Angleterre of François de la Rochefoucauld,* (Cambridge, 1933); J. A. Chartres, 'Trends in the home market, the marketing of agricultural produce 1640–1750', in J. A. Chartres (ed), *Agricultural Markets and Trade, 1500–1750: Chapters from the Agrarian History of England and Wales, 1500–1750, Volume IV* (Cambridge, 1990), p. 197; J. Thirsk, 'The farming regions of England, East Anglia, Norfolk and Suffolk', in J. Thirsk (ed), *The Agrarian History of England and Wales, Volume I, 1500–1640* (Cambridge, 1967), p. 47; B. A. Holderness, *Pre-industrial England: Economy and Society 1500–1750* (London, 1976), p. 53; Holderness, 'Capital formation', pp. 211, 231; E. Kerridge, *The Farmers of Old England* (London, 1973), p. 86; Defoe, *Tour*, pp. 53–60; Raynbird, *Suffolk*, p. 118; Susanna Wade Martins, *A Great Estate at Work: The Holkham Estate and its Inhabitants in the Nineteenth Century* (Cambridge, 1980), p. 30.

57   Caird, *English Agriculture*, pp. 488–9; 'Suffolk', (1895), p. 411.

58   'Royal Commission on the Housing of the Working Classes. First Report of Her Majesty's Commissioners: Minutes of evidence', *British Parliamentary Papers* XXX (1884–1885), Question No. 15,058, p. 656.

59   'Suffolk', (1895), p. 356 and p. 411. Interestingly, the divergent fortunes of the Henham and Helmingham Hall estates within a predominantly cereal producing county like Suffolk highlight Perry's criticism of the Fletcher model as too crude. See F. M. L. Thompson, 'An anatomy of English agriculture, 1870–1914', in Holderness and Turner, *Land,* p. 221.

60   'Suffolk', (1895), p. 379; Thirsk, *Suffolk Farming*, p. 36.

61   W. D. Rubinstein, *Men of Property* (London, 1981), pp. 197–8. It was the

Guinness empire which enabled the second Earl of Iveagh to improve the Elveden estate during the agriculturally depressed 1920s. 'Suffolk', (1895), p. 410. Overall income for the year was £9,747. In the early 1870s, George Tomline had enjoyed an income of around £20,000 a year, gross. Unlike Fox, Bateman records that in 1883 the estate covered an area of 18,473 acres, 'Suffolk', (1895), pp. 409–10.

62 By 1930, the size of the dairy herd in Suffolk had increased by nearly a third. David Taylor, 'Growth and structural change in the English dairy industry c.1860–1930', *Agricultural History Review* 35 (1987), p. 62 and p. 47. The transition to livestock and dairy farming occurred under the most extreme of economic conditions. The implications for overall agricultural output are discussed in Thompson, 'Anatomy', p. 220 and Michael Turner, 'Output and prices in UK agriculture, 1867–1914', *Agricultural History Review* 40 (1992), p. 50.

63 Collins, 'Rural change', p. 221.

64 Perren, 'Agricultural transformation', p. 50; Cormac O'Grada, 'The landlord and agricultural transformation, 1870–1900: A comment on Richard Perren's hypothesis', *Agricultural History Review* 27 (1979), pp. 40–42; Richard Perren, 'The landlord and agricultural transformation 1870–1900: A rejoinder', *Agricultural History Review* 27 (1979), pp. 43–46.

65 'Suffolk', (1895), p. 355.

66 'Suffolk', (1895), pp. 352 and 355 and O'Grada, 'Agricultural decline', p. 188.

67 Charles H. Feinstein and Sidney Pollard (eds), *Studies in Capital Formation in the United Kingdom, 1750–1920*, (Oxford, 1988), p. 270; Thompson, *Landed Society*, p. 315.

68 'Suffolk', (1895), p. 348.

69 Holderness, 'Investment', p. 929.

70 E. H. Hunt and S. J. Pam, 'Responding to agricultural depression, 1873–1896: Managerial success, entrepreneurial failure?', *Agricultural History Review* 50 (2002), p. 238.

71 Herman Biddell, 'Agriculture' in William Page (ed), *The Victoria County History of Suffolk, Volume II* (London, 1907), p. 389.

72 Haggard, *Rural England*, p. 438.

Chapter Three

1 George Veitch, *The Genesis of Parliamentary Reform* (London, 1965), p. 11; Norman Scarfe (ed), *A Frenchman's Year in Suffolk: French Impressions of Suffolk Life in 1784* (Suffolk Records Society, 30, 1988), p. 24; Sir Lewis Namier and John Brooke, *The House of Commons 1754–1790* (London, 1964), p. 378.

2 O. F. Christie, *The Transition from Aristocracy 1832–1867* (London, 1927), pp. 29–30.

3 Asa Briggs (ed), *Gladstone's Boswell: Late Victorian Conversations by Lionel A. Tollemache and other Documents* (Brighton, 1984), p. x; J. Gibson and C. Rogers (eds), *Poll Books c. 1696–1872* (Oxford, 1989), pp. 5 and 7.

4 SRO (Bury) E18/750/10; Charles R. Dod, *Electoral Facts: From 1832 to 1853, Impartially Stated* (London, 1853), pp. 298–9; Namier and Brooke, *Commons*, pp. 378–9, 381–2; J. Holladay Philbin, *Parliamentary Representation 1832, England and Wales* (New Haven, 1965), pp. 174–179; Norman Gash, *Politics in the Age of Peel* (London,1966), pp. 159–164.

5 Howard Newby, *Green and Pleasant Land: Social Change in Rural England* (London, 1979), p. 33; John Langton Sanford and Meredith Townsend, *The Great Governing Families of England, Volume I* (Edinburgh, 1865), p. 3; Michael Brock, *The Great Reform Act* (London, 1973), p. 329.

6 Harold Perkin, *The Age of the Railway* (Newton Abbot, 1971), p. 151.

7 *Public Men of Ipswich and East Suffolk: A Series of Personal Sketches Reprinted from the Suffolk Mercury* (Ipswich, 1875), pp. 37 and 262.

8 Sanford and Townsend, *Governing Families*, p. 7.

9 Maurice Cowling, *1867, Disraeli, Gladstone and Revolution: The Passing of the Second Reform Bill* (Cambridge, 1967), pp. 26 and 29; Derek Beales, *From Castlereagh to Gladstone, 1815–1885* ((London, 1969), pp. 117 and 202; T. A. Jenkins, *Gladstone, Whiggery and the Liberal Party, 1874–1886* (Oxford, 1988), pp. 3–4.

10 D. C. Moore, *The Politics of Deference: A Study of the Mid-Nineteenth Century Political System* (Hassocks, 1976), p. 349.

11 F.M.L. Thompson, 'Land and politics in England in the nineteenth century', *Transactions of the Royal Historical Society* 15 (1965), p. 38.

12 A. V. Dicey, 'The paradox of the land law', *Law Quarterly Review* 21 (1905), p. 227.

13 C. Unwin and B. Villiers, *The Land Hunger: Life Under Monopoly. Descriptive Letters and Other Testimonials From Those Who Have Suffered* (London, 1913), p. 14.

14 Unwin and Villiers, *Monopoly*, p. 23.

15 Frederic Impey, *Three Acres and Cow: Successful Small Holdings and Peasant Proprietors* (London, 1885), p. 20.

16 Avner Offer, *Property and Politics, 1870–1914: Landownership, Law, Ideology and Urban Development in England* (Cambridge, 1981), p. 153.

17 *Public Men of East Suffolk,* pp. 11–12 and 17.

18 Perkin, *Railway*, p. 152; Thompson, *Landed Society*, p. 270; Cowling, *Second Reform Bill*, pp. 64 and 186.

19 *Public Men of East Suffolk,* pp. 117–119; J. Vincent and M. Stenton (eds), *McCalmont's Parliamentary Poll Book: British Election Results, 1832–1918* (London, 1971), p. 281.

20 'Return of Owners of Land, England & Wales (exclusive of the Metropolis), 1872–3', *British Parliamentary Papers* LXXII (1874), pp. 3–4; *Census of England and Wales, 1861* (London, 1863), p. xxxv; E. A. Wrigley and R. S. Schofield, *The Population History of England, 1541–187: A Reconstruction* (Cambridge, 1989), p. 595.

21 David Spring, 'Introduction', in John Bateman, *The Great Landowners of Great Britain and Ireland* (London, 1883. Reprinted, Leicester, 1971), pp. 11–12; Beckett, *Aristocracy,* p. 51.

22 George C. Broderick, *English Land and English Landlords: An Enquiry into the Origin and Character of the English Land System, with Proposals for Its Reform* (London, 1881), p.112. It was also argued that entails and primogeniture left estates in the hands of financially embarrassed owners to the disadvantage of the consumer. William Bear, 'The public interest in agricultural reform', *Nineteenth Century* June 1889, p. 1089.

23 Broderick, *English Landlords*, pp. 152–3.

24 Joseph Kay, *Free Trade in Land* (London, 1879), pp. 20–1; Broderick, *English Landlords*, pp. 152–153.

25 F. Barham Zincke, *Wherstead: Some materials for Its History, Territorial, Manorial and the Events Between,* (London, 1893), p. 130 also pp. 126 and 364.

26 'Discussions upon the land laws', *The Economist*, 27 September 1879, p. 1103; Kay, *Free Trade*, p. 28.

27 'The English Land Question', *The Economist*, 18 June 1881, p. 755.

28 A. Howkins, 'Peasants, servants, labourers: The marginal workforce in British agriculture *c*.1870–1914', *Agricultural History Review* 42 (1994), p. 49; P. G. Craigie, 'The size and distribution of agricultural holdings in England and abroad', *Journal of the Royal Statistical Society* L (1887); 'Board of Agriculture Returns as to the number and size of agricultural holdings in Great Britain, 1895', *British Parliamentary Papers* LXVII (1896); Johnson, *Small Landowner*, p. 128; Mark Freeman, 'The agricultural labourer and the "Hodge" stereotype *c*.1850–1914', *Agricultural History Review* 49 (2001), pp. 172–186.

29 W. L. Guttsman, 'The changing social structure of the British political elite, 1886–1935', *British Journal of Sociology* 2 (1951), p. 126.

30 Peter Clarke, '"Hodge's" politics: The agricultural labourers and the Third Reform Act in Suffolk', in Negley Harte and Roland Quinault (eds), *Land and Society in Britain, 1700–1914* (Manchester, 1996), p. 119.

31 For more discussion of Liberal Unionism in the county see Clarke, 'Reform Act', pp. 131–3.

32 Clarke, 'Reform Act', p. 127.

33 Clarke, 'Reform Act', p. 121.

34 *McCalmont's Poll Book,* pp. 230, 280–2; Michael Stenton and Stephen Lees, *Who's Who of British Members of Parliament, Volume II, 1886–1918: A Biographical Dictionary of the House of Commons* (Hassocks, 1978), p. 339; John R. Fisher, 'Agrarian politics', in E. J. T. Collins (ed), *The Agrarian History of England and Wales, Volume VII* (Cambridge, 2000), p. 355.

35 *McCalmont's Poll Book*, pp. 229–30. Graham, having married the daughter of the Duke of Hamilton in 1906 – the Duke owned a shooting estate at Easton Park near Wickham Market. *Suffolk County Handbook and Official Directory for 1917* (London, 1917), p. 71.

36 Flora Thompson, *Lark Rise to Candleford* (reprinted, Oxford, 1954), p. 320. Patricia Lynch suggests that what attracted rural, working class voters to the Liberal party was its continuing adherence to defending hard-working rural communities against aristocratic and clerical privilege. Patricia Lynch, *The Liberal Party in Rural England, 1885–1910: Radicalism and Community* (Oxford, 2003), p.220.

37 Clarke, 'Reform Act', p. 121.

38 'The creation of a peasant propriety', *The Economist*, 17 January 1885, p. 62.

39 Charles W. Boyd (ed), *Mr Chamberlain's Speeches* (London, 1914), pp. 146–9.

40 Boyd, *Speeches,* pp. 141–2 and 149.

41 Impey, *Three Acres*, p. 25 Fisher, 'Agrarian politics', p. 351.

42 Ralph E. Pumphrey, 'The introduction of industrialists into the British peerage: A study in the adaption of a social institution', *American Historical Review* LXV (1959), p. 13.

43 Pumphrey, 'Industrialists', p. 13; Beckett, *Aristocracy*, p. 128.

44 F. M. L. Thompson, 'Private property and public policy', in Lord Blake and Hugh Cecil (eds), *Salisbury: The Man and His Policies* (London, 1987), p. 252.

45 Micheal W. McCahill, *Order and Equipoise: The Peerage and the House of Lords, 1783–1806* (London, 1978), pp. 181–2.

46 Christie, *Transition*, p. 18.
47 Arthur Ponsonby, *The Decline of Aristocracy* (London, 1912), p. 16.
48 SRO (Bury) 941/71/9.
49 Thompson, 'Property', p. 252; *Suffolk County Handbook*, pp. 255–9.
50 *McCalmont's Poll Book*, p. 29. Guinness having stood unsuccessfully for the seat of North-West Suffolk in 1906, SRO (Bury) 941/71/9.
51 SRO (Bury) 941/71/9.
52 SRO (Bury) 941/71/9.
53 SRO (Bury) 941/71/9.
54 SRO (Bury) 941/71/9.
55 Christie, *Transition*, p. 107.
56 Clarke, 'Reform Act', p. 121 and pp.129–131.
57 Clarke, 'Reform Act', p. 131.
58 Ian Packer, *Lloyd George, Liberalism and the Land: The Land Issue and Party Politics in England, 1906–1914* (Woodbridge, 2001), p. 16.
59 F. M. L. Thompson, *The Rise of Respectable Society: A Social History of Victorian Britain, 1830–1900* (London, 1988), p. 342.
60 Packer, *Liberalism*, p. 18.
61 Fisher, 'Agrarian politics', p. 355; Lynch, *Rural England*, p. 130.
62 Clarke, 'Reform Act', p. 134.
63 SRO (Ipswich) HA53/359/57; Offer, *Property and Politics*, p. 352. Although, according to Pelling, there was very little contemporary evidence for the view that the slogan 'three acres and a cow' won votes for the Liberals given the unyielding influence of large landowners and the apathy of the labourers. H. M. Pelling, *Social Geography of British Elections, 1885–1914* (Aldershot, 1967), pp. 16 and 428. It is also worth remembering landlords were in a position to soak up any labourers who wanted an allotment by offering them one of the allotments available on their estates.
64 Robert Taylor, *Lord Salisbury* (London, 1975), p. 124; J. Enoch Powell, *Joseph Chamberlain* (London, 1977), p. 76; Michael Bentley, *Politics Without Democracy, 1815–1914: Perception and Preoccupation in British Government* (London, 1989), p. 245.
65 Or was it Chamberlain, by carrying over to the Tories the ideas of Cobden and Bright, who acted as the catalyst? Harold Perkin, *The Rise of Professional Society, England Since 1880*, (London, 1989), pp. 151–2.
66 Offer, *Property and Politics*, pp. 41, 150, 152–3, 352–3, 354 and 357; Alfred Russell Wallace, *Land Nationalization, Its Necessity and Its Aims: Being a Comparison of the System of Landlord and Tenant with that of Occupying Ownership in their Influence on the Well-Being of the People* (London, 1882), p.134; Roy Douglas, *Land, People and Politics: A History of the Land Question in the United Kingdom, 1878–1952* (London, 1976), p. 46. Salisbury can therefore be said to have laid the foundation stones of the Conservative party's ideal of a property-owning democracy. As to the Liberals 1906 and 1907 legislation, experience soon showed that it had been a mistake to allow County Councils to carry the Act into effect as most Conservative County Councils ignored it. J. Ellis Barker, 'The land, the landlords and the people', *Nineteenth Century*, October 1909, p. 560.
67 Michael Barker, *Gladstone and Radicalism: The Reconstruction of Liberal Policy in Britain, 1885–1894* (Brighton, 1975), p. 222.

68   *Hansard's Parliamentary Debates, Volume III* (London, 1892), p. 1210; Perkin, *Professional Society*, p. 152; Offer *Property and Politics*, p. 353. To the Radical mind, English farmers were being beaten by their competitors in the USA and laying off labourers, who were then forced to leave the land. To reverse this trend labourers had to given the opportunity to 'become in some form owners or permanent occupiers of the land they till'. Fisher, 'Agrarian politics', p. 347.

69   *Hansard's* (1892), pp. 1218–1219.

70   *Public General Acts* (London, 1892), p. 287.

71   Powell, *Chamberlain*, pp. 84–85.

72   *Hansard's Parliamentary Debates,Volume CCCXVIII* (London, 1887), p. 290.

73   *Hansard's* (1887), p. 291.

74   *Hansard's Parliamentary Debates, Volume CCCXXXVII* (London, 1889), p. 678.

75   Sir Arthur Underhill, *A Concise Explanation of Lord Birkenhead's Act, The Law of Property Act 1922, in Plain Language* (London, 1922), p. 58; Arthur Underhill, 'Property', *Law Quarterly Review* 51 (1935), p. 226; H. W. Elphinstone, 'The transfer of land', *Law Quarterly Review* 2 (1886), p. 18.

76   *Hansard's* (1889), pp. 679–80.

77   Life interests, entails and primogeniture were finally abolished by Lord Birkenhead's Act of 1922: 'Thus perished primogeniture, almost unnoticed, and the historian must wonder what all the fuss was about'. Thompson, 'Land and politics', pp. 31–2, but then the period after the Great War was a whole different kettle of fish. *Hansard's* (1889), pp. 679–80 and 688. Note the echoes of John Bright in Salisbury's argument. H. J. Leach (ed), *The Public Letters of the Right Hon. John Bright* (London, 1895), p. 187.

78   Frederick Clifford, *The Agricultural Lock-Out of 1874: With Notes Upon Farming and the Farm Labourer in the Eastern Counties* (London, 1874), pp. 186, 203 and 207; SRO (Bury) HA507/3/375 and HA507/3/365; SRO (Ipswich) HA11/C9/67, 68 and 69, HA11/C43/1/1. A number of allotments were also sub-let by Lord Stradbroke in 1861, to the Rev W. C. Safford who agreed 'to hire of the Earl [4 acres] lately purchased by his Lordship' and to 'allot the same to poor persons'. SRO (Ipswich) HA11/C11/1/8.

79   'Return of the number of instances in which County Councils under the provisions of the Allotments Acts, 1887 and 1890, have acquired land for allotments', *British Parliamentary Papers* LXVIII (1892), p. 70.

80   G. R. Searle, *The Liberal Party: Triumph and Disintegration, 1886–1929* (London, 2001), p. 41; Neal Blewett, 'The franchise in the United Kingdom, 1855–1918', *Past and Present* 32 (1965), p. 28; Beckett, *Aristocracy*, p. 128; David Spring, 'English landed society in the eighteenth and nineteenth centuries', *Economic History Review* 17 (1964), p. 152. The relationship between the gentry and the rural middle classes is less clear cut, see Chapter Four and J. R. Fisher, 'The limits of deference: Agricultural communities in a mid-nineteenth century election campaign', *Journal of British Studies* 21 (1981), p. 91; Moore, *Deference*, pp. 12–13; Packer, *Liberalism*, p.13.

81   Lynch, *Rural England*, p. 130; Thompson, *Respectable*, p. 342; Packer, *Liberalism*, p. 25. Until the Tories' disastrous flirtation with Tariff Reform left the labourer angered by the thought of higher bread prices benefiting their employers, the farmer. See Fisher, 'Agrarian politics', pp. 352–3.

Chapter Four

1 Thompson, *Respectable*, pp. 342–3; J. P. D. Dunbabin, *Rural Discontent in Nineteenth Century Britain* (London, 1974), p. 13.

2 'Royal Commission', (1882) p. 179.

3 'Report to the Poor Law Board of the Laws of Settlement, and Removal of the Poor: Report of G.A. à Beckett, Esq. to the Poor Law Board on the operation of the Laws of Settlement and Removal of the Poor in the counties of Suffolk, Norfolk and Essex and the Reading Union in Berkshire', *British Parliamentary Papers* XXVII (1850), p. 255.

4 'Poor Law Board', (1850), p. 242; Edward Twisleton, an Assistant Poor Law Commissioner having visited Suffolk in 1840, as part of his *Inquiry into the Dwellings of the Labouring Classes in Norfolk and Suffolk*, was also impressed by the fifty or so cottages built by the millionaire and landowner Richard Benyon de Beavoir in the parish of Culford. Each two-storey cottage costing between £85 and £170 was built of brick and had four rooms. Paine (ed), *Culford*, p. 69; B. A. Holderness, '"Open" and "close" parishes in England in the eighteenth and nineteenth centuries', *Agricultural History Review* 20 (1972), p. 127 and pp. 132–3.

5 Andrew Charlesworth (ed), *An Atlas of Rural Protest in Britain 1548–1900* (London, 1983) p. 137.

6 Mingay (ed), *Changes in Agriculture*, pp. 242–5; E. J. T. Collins, 'The rationality of surplus agricultural labour', *Agricultural History Review* 35 (1987), p. 40.

7 SRO, (Bury) HA507/3/747; Caird, *English Agriculture*, p. 161; SRO (Ipswich) HA11/B1/23/9 and HA11/B1/23/18.

8 Alun Howkins, 'Types of rural communities', in E. J. T. Collins (ed), *The Agrarian History of England and Wales, Volume VII* (Cambridge, 2000), p. 1320.

9 Thirsk, *Suffolk Farming* p. 32; Mingay (ed), *Changes in Agriculture*, p. 244; Howard Newby, *Country Life: A Social History of Rural England* (London, 1987), p. 85.

10 Paine (ed), *Culford*, pp. 69–70; SRO (Bury) 423/982.

11 'Royal Commission on the Employment of Children, Young Persons, and Women in Agriculture (1867): Report by the Rev James Fraser', *British Parliamentary Papers* XVII (1867–1868), p. 99.

12 SRO (Bury) 423/982; 'Fraser', (1867–8), p. 99.

13 'Fraser', (1867–8), p. 99.

14 'Evidence of Mr Frederic Impey to Her Majesty's Commissioners for Inquiry into the Housing of the Working Classes', *British Parliamentary Papers* XXX (1884–5), p. 651; Michael Havinden, 'The model village', in G. E. Mingay (ed), *The Victorian Countryside II* (London, 1981), p. 415.

15 SRO (Bury) HA507/3/749; 'First Report into Housing', p. 720; M. A. Havinden, *Estate and Villages: A Study of the BerkshireVillages of Ardington and East Lockinge* (London, 1966), p. 25.

16 SRO (Bury), HA507/3/747.

17 'First Report into Housing', (1884–5), p. 722.

18 'Royal Commission on Labour. The Agricultural Labourer: Report by Mr Wilson Fox on the Poor Law Union of Thingoe', *British Parliamentary Papers* XXXV (1893–4), p. 351; 'Royal Commission on Labour. The Agricultural Labourer: Summary Report', *British Parliamentary Papers* XXXV (1893–4), p. 332; Clifford, *Lock-Out*, pp. 203 and 207; SRO (Ipswich) HA11/C46/58 and HA11/

C46/61/1–3, HA11/B1/23/23, HA11/C3/25 and HA11/C6/25; 'First Report into Housing', (1884–5), p. 651.

19 SRO (Bury) 423/982.
20 SRO (Bury) 423/982.
21 'Summary Report', (1893–4), p. 335; Holderness, 'Parishes', pp. 131–2; 'Thingoe', (1893–4), p. 352.
22 'Royal Commission on Labour. The Agricultural Labourer: Report by Mr Arthur Wilson Fox (Assistant Commissioner) upon the Poor Law Union of Swaffham', *British Parliamentary Papers* XXXV (1893–1894), p. 386; 'Suffolk', (1895), p. 327.
23 Alan Armstrong, *Farmworkers: A Social and Economic History, 1770–1980* (London, 1988), p. 105.
24 'Thingoe', (1893–4), p. 352.
25 *The Land: The Report of the Land Enquiry Committee, Volume I, Rural* (London, 1913), p. 144.
26 James Caird, *The Landed Interest and the Supply of Food* (Fifth Edition, London, 1967), p. 57; Evans, *Where Beards Wag All*, p. 120.
27 'Summary Report', (1893–4), p. 332; Paine (ed), *Culford*, p. 2.
28 'Thingoe', (1893–4), p. 351.
29 SRO (Bury) HA507/3/749; H. Rider Haggard in David Rubinstein, (ed), *Victorian Homes* (Newton Abbot, 1974), p. 239; SRO (Bury) HA507/5/367; 'First Report into Housing', (1884–85), p. 722.
30 'Royal Commission', (1882), p. 179. The Marquess of Bristol's arrears averaged 22 per cent per annum between 1892 and 1905, SRO (Bury) HA507/3/367; Paine, (ed), *Culford*, p. 71; Martelli, *Elveden*, p. 48.
31 Clifford, *Lock-Out*, pp. 13–14; W. Hasbach, *A History of the English Agricultural Labourer* (London, 1908) p. 285; Nigel Scotland, *Methodism and the Revolt of the Field: A study of the Methodist Contribution to Agricultural Trade Unions in East Anglia, 1872–1896* (Gloucester, 1981), pp. 13–15; Pamela Horn, 'Agricultural trade unionism in Oxfordshire', in Dunbabin (ed), *Rural Discontent*, pp. 85–129.
32 Clifford, *Lock-Out*, pp. 56, 82 and 83; Hasbach, *Labourer*, p. 285.
33 Thirsk, *Suffolk Farming*, p. 143–4; SRO (Ipswich) HA11/A14/4.
34 SRO (Ipswich) HA11/A14/4.
35 J. H. Bettey, *Estates and the English Countryside* (London, 1993) p. 109. Lady Warwick for example, viewed rural society as 'a small select aristocracy born booted and spurred to ride, and a large dim mass born saddled bridled to be ridden'. J. F. C. Harrison, *Late Victorian Britain 1875–1901* (London, 1990), p. 41.
36 SRO (Ipswich) HA11/A14/4; Thirsk, *Suffolk Farming*, pp. 142–44.
37 Another letter sent to Her Ladyship dated April 24th also blamed the dispute on 'paid agitators'. SRO (Ipswich) HA11/A14/4; Evans, *Where Beards Wag All*, p. 209. In 1833, William Downes calculated that 'on a very considerable estate under my care' at least five per cent of the gross rental was given each year in donations to the 'parishes in which the estate was situated, for the clothing of the poor and coals, and various institutions'. 'Report to the Select Committee on Agriculture, 1833', *British Parliamentary Papers* V (1833), p. 88. The Duke of Grafton's disbursements for example, just for the care of the elderly on the Euston estate, totalled £84. 2s. 10d. in 1858, SRO (Bury) HA513/6 /190. Meanwhile, at New Year's in 1865, the Earl of Stradbroke gave two to 3 shillings

to each child living in the villages of Henham and Bulcamp, SRO (Ipswich) HA11/B27/3.

38 SRO (Ipswich) HA11/A14/4; Thompson, *Respectable*, p. 342. Writing of her experiences growing up in late Victorian Oxfordshire, Flora Thompson records that labouring families would however often take pride 'in their rich and powerful country-house neighbours, especially when titled' and would refer to the 'old Earl in the next parish' as 'our Earl' and when he was in residence they could say 'I see our family's at home again'. Thompson, *Lark Rise*, p. 320.

39 Thirsk, *Suffolk Farming*, p. 156.

40 Clifford, *Lock-Out*, p.103; Pamela Horn, *Labouring Life in the Victorian Countryside* (Bristol, 1976), p. 7.

41 Clifford, *Lock-Out*, pp. 19, 102–104; Thirsk, *Suffolk Farming*, p. 146.

42 Clifford, *Lock-Out*, pp. 103 and 105.

43 Clifford, *Lock-Out*, p. 108; F. E. Green, *A History of the English Agricultural Labourer* (London, 1920), p. 62.

44 Thirsk, *Suffolk Farming*, p. 146.

45 Thirsk, *Suffolk Farming*, pp. 152–5. By 1888, the Society had 377 members, SRO (Ipswich) HA11/B13/2 and 3.

46 Thirsk, *Suffolk Farming*, p. 144. The Duke of Marlborough, for example, deliberately made over the cottages and allotments on his estates in Oxfordshire to his tenants so that they could evict Union members.

47 Clifford, *Lock-Out*, p. 128. Lord Walsingham chided farmers for trying to stamp out the Union and had called on them as reasonable men not to deny labourers their 'right of combination'.

48 Green, *Labourer*, pp. 54 and 62.

49 Green, *Labourer*, p. 62.

50 Clifford, *Lock-Out*, pp. 117, 121 and 124.

51 Clifford, *Lock-Out*, p. 57. Lady Stradbroke was also commended by one farmer for the 'noble, energetic, bold and fearless defence' of the farmers in her neighbourhood. SRO (Ipswich) HA11/A14/4.

52 'Impey', (1884–5), p. 651; G. E. Fussell, *The English Rural Labourer* (London, 1949), pp. 108–9.

53 'Fraser', (1867–8), p. 426.

54 Jeremy Burchardt, *The Allotment Movement in England, 1793–1873* (Woodbridge, 2002), p. 174.

55 'Returns showing which Sanitary Authorities acquired land under the Acts of 1887 and 1890', *British Parliamentary Papers* LXVIII (1892), p. 70.

56 Hasbach, *Labourer*, p. 212.

57 Lord Ernle, *Whippingham to Westminster: Reminiscences of Lord Ernle* (London, 1938), p. 233.

58 'Fraser', (1867–8), p. 426; Alun Howkins, *Poor Labouring Men: Rural Radicalism in Norfolk 1872–1923* (London, 1985), p. 81.

59 John Glyde, *Suffolk in the Nineteenth Century: Physical, Social, Moral, Religious and Industrial* (London, 1856), pp. 352–3.

60 Evans, *Beards*, p. 131, see also Howkins, 'Rural communities', pp. 1321 and 1322.

61 Glyde, *Suffolk*, pp. 352–3; 'Fraser', (1867–8), p. 422.

62 Haggard, *Rural England*, p. 418.

63 Newby, *Country Life*, p. 149.

64 Geoffrey Searle. *The Liberal Party: Triumph and Disintegration, 1886–1929* (London, 2001), p. 40. Additionally, was land reform about the 're-colonization' of the countryside from the city or about rural regeneration?

Chapter Five

1 G. D. Phillips, *The Diehards: Aristocratic Society and Politics in Edwardian England* (London,1979), p. 57.

2 Beckett, *Aristocracy*, p. 362.

3 Beckett, *Aristocracy*, pp. 124, 378, 402; Roy Perrot, *The Aristocrats: A Portrait of Britain's Nobility and Their Way of Life Today* (London, 1968), pp. 184–5; Thompson, *Landed Society*, p. 109; 'Return giving the names and professions of all Justices of the Peace for the counties of England and Wales on the first day of June 1887', *British Parliamentary Papers* LXXXII (1888), pp. 329–332; Carl Zangerl, 'The social composition of the county magistracy in England and Wales, 1831–1887', *Journal of British Studies* 11 (1971), p. 116. Of the 256 individuals listed on the Commission of the Peace for Suffolk for 1853, only 219 or 86 per cent actually chose to take their oath of commission, 'Abstract of Return, 14th March 1853: Returns of the number of Justices in England and Wales', *British Parliamentary Papers* LXXVIII (1852–3), p. 329.

4 Norman Gash, *Aristocracy and People: Britain 1815–1865* (London, 1979), p. 347.

5 SRO (Ipswich) HA53/359/57; R. J. Olney, 'The politics of land', in G. E. Mingay (ed), *The Victorian Countryside, Volume I* (London, 1981), p. 58. Despite abolishing the purchase of commissions in 1871, 40 per cent of all officers in 1912 were drawn from the aristocracy and gentry; meanwhile in Suffolk, landowners controlled 107 livings, *Suffolk County Handbook* (London, 1917), pp. 150–161 and Becket, *Aristocracy*, p. 409. For more details of the gentry's ecclesiastical patronage see SRO (Lowestoft) HA12/A9/2 (a) c–I, HA12/A9/3 (a) b and c, HA12/A9/4 and HA12/A8/1/2. In Suffolk, Quarter Sessions were held at Ipswich and Bury St Edmunds, the county having been divided into the administrative divisions of Eastern and Western Suffolk since the Middle Ages. The Petty Sessional Divisions were Beccles, Blackbourn, Blything, Bosmere and Claydon, Boxford, Bungay, Framlingham, Hadleigh, Hartismere, Hoxne, Lackford, Lowestoft, Melford, Newmarket, Risbridge, Samford, Stowmarket, Thingoe and Thedwestry and Woodbridge. White, *Suffolk*, pp. 13–16.

6 *Public Men of East Suffolk*, pp. 202–3.

7 Michael Alexander and Sushila Anand, *Queen Victoria's Maharajah, Duleep Singh, 1838–1893* (London, 1980), p. 129.

8 *Public General Statutes* (London, 1862), pp. 1337–8; Paine (ed), *Culford*, p. 61.

9 F. M. L. Thompson, 'Landowners and the rural community', in G. E. Mingay (ed), *The Victorian Countryside, Volume II* (London, 1981), p. 460.

10 Russell M. Garnier, *History of the Landed Interest, the Customs, Laws, and Agriculture, Volume II* (London, 1908), pp. 470–1.

11 Newby, *Country Life*, p. 64.

12 SRO (Lowestoft) HA12/A6/2; Beckett, *Aristocracy*, p. 393. The establishment of elective Boards also opened the way for more farmers and tradesmen, who were poorly represented on the Bench, to become involved in local affairs.

13 *Public Men of East Suffolk*, pp. 94–95.

14 *Public Men of East Suffolk*, pp. 143 and 147.

15 *Burke's Genealogical and Heraldic History of the Peerage, Baronetage and Knightage*
    (London, 1970), p. 1311; *Kelly's Handbook to the Titled Landed and Official Classes*
    (London, 1904), pp. 122, 940 and 1236; *Kelly's Directory of Suffolk* (London,
    1904), pp. 18–19.

16 John France, 'Salisbury and the Unionist alliance', in Lord Blake and Hugh Cecil
    (eds), *Salisbury: The Man and his Policies* (London, 1987), p. 236; B. Keith-Lucas,
    The English Local Government Franchise (Oxford, 1952), pp. 105–106.

17 *Hansard's Parliamentary Debates, 2 July to 19 July, Volume CCCXXVIII* (London,
    1888), pp. 1286–7.

18 *Public Men of East Suffolk*, p. 257.

19 *Hansard's, 2 July to 19 July* (1888), pp. 1289–90.

20 *Hansard's, 2 July to 19 July* (1888), p. 1290 and Statements Shewing the
    Financial Effect on East and West Suffolk of a Complete Dissolution of the
    Partial Union of the Administrative Counties of East and West Suffolk. February
    1898. Tables A, B1, B2 and C. SRO (Ipswich) HA11/B4/5 and Accounts of
    Eastern Division of the County of Suffolk, Michaelmas 1887 to March 1889.
    SRO (Ipswich) HA11/B3/21.

21 *Hansard's, 2 July to 19 July* (1888), pp. 1290–1 and 1288.

22 *Hansard's Parliamentary Debates, 20 July to 7 August, Volume CCCXXIX* (London,
    1888), pp. 1663–5 and pp. 1667–8.

23 *Hansard's, 20 July to 7 August* (1888), p. 1667; SRO (Bury) 941/69/1 and 3;
    David Dymond and Peter Northeast, *A History of Suffolk* (Oxford, 1985), p. 112;
    Celia Jennings, *The Identity of Suffolk* (Bury St Edmunds, 1980), p. 3. Support
    for the Marquess of Bristol also came from Lord Thurlow who recognized 'the
    strong claims of West Suffolk to individual county machinery'.

24 *Hansard's, 20 July to 7 August* (1888), p. 1663.

25 Taylor, *Salisbury*, p. 126; Cannadine, *Decline and Fall*, p. 157; Beckett, *Aristocracy*,
    p. 393.

26 East Suffolk County Council. First meeting at Shirehall, Ipswich. Taken from a
    report in the *Suffolk Chronicle*, SRO (Ipswich) HA11/B4/4; Cannadine, *Decline
    and Fall*, p. 158–9; Beckett, *Aristocracy*, p. 395; J. P. D. Dunbabin, 'Expectations
    of the new county councils and their realization', *Historical Journal* 8 (1965),
    pp. 376–7; J. P. D. Dunbabin, 'British local government reform', *English
    Historical Review* October (1977), p. 794; 'Return for each administrative county
    in England and Wales, 1889', *British Parliamentary Papers* LXV (1889), pp. 29–
    30; F. R. Parker, *The Election of County Councils* (London, 1888), p. 179.

27 Cannadine, *Decline and Fall*, p. 163; Phillips, *Diehards*, pp. 70–71.

28 SRO (Ipswich) HA11/B4/3. Justices of the Peace also continued to sit as *ex-officio*
    Poor Law Guardians, while control of the police force was placed under a joint
    standing committee of the County Council and Quarter Sessions. Beckett,
    Aristocracy, p. 395.

29 Phillips, *Diehards*, p. 68; Beckett, *Aristocracy*, p. 395; Christie, *Aristocracy*, p. 31.

30 Evans, *Where Beards Wag All*, pp. 185–6.

31 Evans, *Where Beards Wag All*, pp. 185–6. Cannadine, *Decline and Fall*, p. 157.

32 Phillips, *Diehards*, p. 72; SRO (Ipswich) HA11/A15/4.

33 'Return showing in each county the number of magistrates who have been
    placed on the Bench by virtue of their election as Chairman of District Councils',
    British Parliamentary Papers LXXXI (1895), p. 461; Phillips, *Diehards*, p. 67.

34 SRO (Ipswich) HA11/A15/4.

35 Cannadine, *Decline and Fall*, p. 155; J. M. Lee, *Social Leaders and Public Persons* (Oxford, 1963), p. 15.

36 SRO (Bury) 941/65/4; 'Return of names of Lord Lieutenants of counties of England and Wales, as the same stood on the 1st day of January 1875', *British Parliamentary Papers* LX (1875), p. 644; *Public Men of East Suffolk*, pp. 22, 23 and 26; SRO (Ipswich) HA11/B2/40.

37 SRO (Bury) 941/65/4.

38 Cannadine, *Decline and Fall*, p. 155 see also newspaper cutting, dated January 5th 1883, SRO (Ipswich) HA11/B3/20. Radicals called for the office itself to be democratized and opened up to all regardless of wealth or birth. J. Redlich and F.W. Hirst, *Local Government in England* (London, 1903), p. 204.

39 'Royal Commission on the Selection of Justices of the Peace, 1910', *British Parliamentary Papers* XXXVII (1911) p. 8; Phillips, *Diehards*, p. 65.

40 Phillips, *Diehards*, p. 65.

41 Lee, *Social Leaders*, p. 15; Cannadine, *Decline and Fall*, p. 154 and p. 156; 'Return giving the name and profession of all Justices of the Peace for the counties of England and Wales, 1892', *British Parliamentary Papers* LXXIV, Part I (1893–4), pp. 415–418.

42 'Return of all magistrates appointed between 1892 and 1894', *British Parliamentary Papers* LXXXI (1895), pp. 381–2.

43 Phillips, *Diehards*, pp. 67–8.

44 SRO (Ipswich) 107/4/1, signature unclear. Lord Gorrell, who was a High Court Judge, owned the 214 acre Stratford Hills estate, SRO (Ipswich) HA108/9/13; Boulge Hall was formerly the seat of the Purcell-Fitzgeralds, from whom it was purchased by the White family some time between 1885 and 1904.

45 Phillips, *Diehards*, p. 62; SRO (Ipswich) 107/4/2. The remaining magistrates the meeting were F. W. French of Depper Hall, representing the Hoxne Bench, R. C. Mann representing Bungay, L. J. Peto representing Metford and Lothingland and General H. P. Phillips of Barham Hall who represented the Bosmere and Claydon Bench.

46 Orwin and Whetham, *History of British Agriculture*, p. 44; *Public Persons of East Suffolk*, p. 203.

47 Anthony Brundage, 'The landed interest and the New Poor Law: A reappraisal of the revolution in government', *English Historical Review* 87 (1972), p. 29; Peter Dunkley, 'The landed interest and the New Poor Law: A critical note', *English Historical Review* 88 (1973), p. 837; Anthony Brundage, *The Making of the New Poor Law* (London, 1978), pp. 183–4; SRO (Bury) HA507/3/815 and 816; Anthony Brundage, 'The landed interest and the New Poor Law: A reply', *English Historical Review* 90 (1975), pp. 347–8.

48 P. F. Ashcroft and Herbert Preston-Thomas, *The English Poor Laws System: Past and Present* (London, 1902), p. 218; 'Report from the Select Committee on Poor Law Guardians', *British Parliamentary Papers* XVII (1878), pp. 309–10.

49 Dunkley, 'Critical note', p. 838.

50 SRO (Bury) HA507/3/815.

51 Brundage, 'Reappraisal', pp. 29–30; Brundage, *Poor Law*, p. 184. The maximum number of votes available to a resident landowner was increased to 12 by

Graham's Act of 1844 (7 and 8 Vict., c.101) which assimilated the ratepayer's franchise with the owner's franchise.

52 Dunkley, 'Critical note', pp. 838–840.

53 Brundage, 'Reply', p. 350; Digby quoted in George R. Boyer, *An Economic History of the English Poor Law, 1750–1850* (Cambridge, 1990), p. 201; Dunkley, 'Critical note', p. 838; Beckett, *Aristocracy*, p. 391.

54 SRO (Ipswich) HA11/B5/21. The Chairmen of the Wangford and Bosmere and Claydon Boards were magistrates. White, *Suffolk*, pp. 19–34.

55 Anthony Brundage, 'The English Poor Law', *Agricultural History* 48 (1974), p. 408; although see Peter Dunkley, 'The "Hungry Forties" and the New Poor Law', *Historical Journal* 17 (1974), p. 329.

56 Brundage, *Poor Law*, p. 120.

57 Anthony Brundage, 'Reform of the Poor Law electoral system, 1834–1894', *Albion* 7 (1975), p. 213.

58 Keith-Lucas, *Local Government*, p. 106; Brundage, *Poor Law*, p. 185.

59 Perrot, *Aristocrats*, p. 184; Cannadine, *Decline and Fall*, pp. 356–7.

60 SRO (Ipswich) HA11/B4/2.

Chapter Six

1 E. A. Goodwyn, *A Suffolk Town in Mid-Victorian England: Beccles in the 1860s* (Ipswich, 1960), p. 44; James Caird, *The Landed Interest and the Supply of Food* (London, 1878), p. 58; Mingay (ed), *Changes*, p. 54; 'Suffolk', (1895), pp. 395, 401; SRO (Ipswich) HA11/A13/4/8.

2 Orwin and Whetham, *British Agriculture*, p. 152.

3 G. E. Mingay, *Rural Life in Victorian England* (London, 1977), pp. 130–1; 'Suffolk' (1895), p. 329.

4 W. Bence Jones, 'Landowning as a business', *Nineteenth Century*, March 1882, pp. 346–7; Mingay, *Rural Life*, p. 130.

5 Fisher, 'Agrarian politics', pp. 334 and 332.

6 'Landlord and tenant, money abatements of rent', *The Economist*, 24 September 1853, p. 1075.

7 J. A. Perkins, 'Tenure, tenant right and agricultural progress in Lindsey, 1780–1850', *Agricultural History Review* 23 (1975), p. 4. It had been taken as axiomatic since at least the mid-eighteenth century that everything possible had to be done to avoid farms falling into hand. G. E. Mingay, *A Social History of the English Countryside* (London, 1991), p. 51.

8 David Low, *On Landed Property and the Economy of Estates* (London, 1848), p. 9; Arthur Young wrote 'If a man really means to be a good farmer, it can never answer to him to enter a farm with a shorter lease than twenty-one years', Broderick, *English Landlords*, p. 203.

9 Raynbird, *Suffolk*, p. 150.

10 Evidence of J. G. Cooper, a farmer and valuer in East Suffolk, 'Agricultural Customs', (1866), p. 81; Lord Ernle, *English Farming Past and Present* (London, 1961), p. 200.

11 'Agriculture, social status and tenant-farmers', *The Economist*, 18 November 1884, p. 1263.

12 'Agriculture, long leases and large farms', *The Economist*, 2 February 1856, p. 115.

13 SRO (Bury) 449/3/13; T. W. Beastall, 'Landlords and tenants', in G.E. Mingay (ed), *The Victorian Countryside, Volume II* (London, 1981), p. 430.

14 Raynbird, *Suffolk*, p.149.

15 SRO (Lowestoft) HA12/D3/11, the majority of the old leasehold agreements had expired in the early 1870s, many tenants having opted for 14 year leases in the late 1850s, SRO (Lowestoft) HA12/D8/5/1–10, HA12/D8/6/1–8 and HA12/D8/7/1–2; SRO (Ipswich) HA61/436/896; 'Agricultural Customs', (1866), p. 175; Raynbird, *Suffolk*, p. 149; Orwin & Whetham, *British Agriculture*, p. 159; SRO (Bury) HA507/4/55, HA507/3/580 (a.); SRO (Ipswich) HA11/C11/1/9 and HA11/C11/1/4.

16 Biddell, 'Agriculture', p. 389.

17 Caird, *English Agriculture*, p.504; SRO (Bury) 449/3/13; G. E. Mingay, *Land and Society in England, 1750–1980* (London, 1994), p. 67; Perkins, 'Tenure', p. 7.

18 John Glyde, *Suffolk in the Nineteenth Century: Physical, Social, Moral, Religious and Industrial* (London, 1856), p. 340. For example, in 1872, George Hope, despite being a highly respected practitioner of high farming and having succeeded his father and his grandfather as a tenant on his landlord's estate, was asked to leave. This was because in 1864 he had stood as a Liberal candidate against Lord Elcho, a close friend of his landlord.

19 SRO (Ipswich) HA11/C11/1/3; SRO (Bury) HA507/3/580(a); 'Agriculture and farmer's capital in England', *The Economist*, 9 March 1872, p. 16; Raynbird, *Suffolk*, p. 151; Orwin and Whetham, *British Agriculture*, pp. 153 and 155; William Shaw and Henry Corbet, *Digest of Evidence Taken Before a Committee of the House of Commons Appointed to Inquire into the Agricultural Customs of England and Wales in Respect to Tenant-Right* (London, 1849), pp. 39–40.

20 'Suffolk', (1895), p. 335.

21 'Suffolk', (1895), p. 334.

22 SRO (Ipswich) HA11/B1/23/49.

23 'Agricultural Customs', (1866), p. 82; Raynbird, *Suffolk*, p.151.

24 'Agricultural Customs', (1866), p. 82.

25 Orwin and Whetham, *British Agriculture*, p. 157; Eric Richards, 'The Leviathan of wealth: West-Midland agriculture, 1800–1850', *Agricultural History Review* 22 (1974), p. 115.

26 F. M. L. Thompson, 'The second Agricultural Revolution, 1815–1880', *Economic History Review* 21 (1968), p. 68; R. J. Olney, *Lincolnshire Politics, 1832–1885* (Oxford, 1973), p. 41; David Grigg, *The Agricultural Revolution in South Lincolnshire* (Cambridge, 1966), p. 134; Joan Thirsk, *English Peasant Farming: The Agrarian History of Lincolnshire from Tudor to Recent Times* (London, 1957), p. 266; A. W. Jones, 'Glamorgan custom and tenant right', *Agricultural History Review* 31 (1983), p. 6.

27 'Agricultural Customs', (1866), p. 82.

28 'Agricultural Customs', (1866), p. 178; SRO (Ipswich) HA11/C3/26.

29 SRO (Ipswich) HA11/C11/1/4.

30 Richards, 'Leviathan', p. 116.

31 J. R. Fisher, 'Landowners and English tenant right, 1845–1852', *Agricultural History Review* 31 (1983), p. 25; B. A. Holderness, 'The Victorian farmer', in G. E. Mingay (ed), *The Victorian Countryside, Volume I* (London, 1981), p. 233.

32 SRO (Bury) 449/3/13.

33 SRO (Ipswich) HA11/B1/23/49; Julian R. McQuiston, 'Tenant-right: Farmer against landlord in Victorian England, 1847–1883', *Agricultural History* XLVII (1973), p. 109. The efforts made by these richer tenants were highlighted by Caird who complained that while on one side of the hedge might be seen well-drained, well-fertilized soil tilled by modern equipment, on the other, there persisted waterlogged, infertile clays, antiquated implements and crops harvested by the sickle, Mingay, *Rural Life*, p. 63.

34 David Spring, *The English Landed Estate in the Nineteenth Century: Its Administration* (Maryland, 1963), p. 2.

35 Biddell, 'Agriculture', p. 388.

36 SRO (Ipswich) HA11/B1/23/49, sadly the Earl's letter has yet to be traced.

37 G. E. Mingay, 'The farmer', in E. J. T. Collins (ed), *The Agrarian History of England and Wales, Volume VII* (Cambridge, 2000), pp. 766–7.

38 A. H. H. Matthews, *Fifty Years of Agricultural Politics: Being the History of the Central Chamber of Agriculture 1865–1915* (London, 1915), pp. 16 and 179; J. R. Fisher, *Clare Sewell Read, 1826–1905: A Farmer's Spokesman of the Late Nineteenth Century* (Hull, 1975), p. 4; SRO (Bury) 941/30/101; Fisher, 'Agrarian politics', p. 334.

39 *Hansard's Parliamentary Debates, Volume CCXXIII* (London, 1875), p. 936.

40 *Public Men of East Suffolk*, p. 122.

41 *Hansard's* (1875), pp. 936–7.

42 *Hansard's* (1875), pp. 937–8.

43 *Hansard's* (1875), p. 938.

44 *Hansard's* (1875), p. 938.

45 Leech, (ed), *Bright*, pp. 196–7.

46 J. R. Fisher, 'The Farmer's Alliance: An agricultural protest movement of the 1880s', *Agricultural History Review* 26 (1978), p. 17.

47 Fisher, 'Agrarian politics', p. 333; Dunbabin, *Rural Discontent*, p. 174.

48 Evans, *Ask the Fellows,* p. 104; SRO (Bury), 449/3/13 and J. H. Porter, 'Tenant-right: Devonshire and the 1880 Ground Game Act', *Agricultural History Review* 34 (1986).

49 Nicholas Everitt, 'Shooting', in William Page (ed), *The Victoria County History of Suffolk, Volume II* (London, 1907), p. 366.

50 SRO (Ipswich) HA1/HB6/4/8.

51 Everitt, 'Shooting' p. 365. To avoid any arguments with farmers about shooting over his land the Earl of Iveagh simply bought out his tenants on the Elveden estate and replaced them with bailiffs who kept the land in cultivation as a home for game! Martelli, *Elveden*, p. 49. .

52 SRO (Ipswich) HA11/B1/23/49; McQuiston, 'Tenant-right', p. 105.

53 William Bear, 'The public interest in agricultural reform', *Nineteenth Century*, June 1879, pp. 1088–9; 'Tenant right in Great Britain', *The Economist*, 24 September 1881, p. 1182.

54 SRO (Bury) HA507/3/669.

55 'Royal Commission', (1882), p. 179; SRO (Ipswich) HA61/436/920; SRO (Lowestoft) HA/D6/2.

56 William Bear, 'Tenant right' in C. F. Dowsett (ed), *Land: Its Attractions and Riches: By Fifty-Seven Writers* (London, 1892), p. 380.

57 'Royal Commission on Agriculture: Report by Mr Wilson Fox (Assistant

Commissioner) on the county of Cambridge', *British Parliamentary Papers* XVII (1895), p. 170.

58 'Suffolk', (1895), p. 334.

59 'Suffolk', (1895), pp. 329–30; Mingay, 'Farmer', p. 802.

60 'Suffolk', (1895), pp. 328 and 330.

61 Biddell, 'Agriculture', p. 388.

62 Mingay, *Rural Life*, p. 63, which was why tenant-right was such an issue with the more entrepreneurial farmers, McQuiston, 'Tenant-right', p. 109.

63 *The Land: The Report of the Land Enquiry Committee, Volume I, Rural* (London, 1913), p. 313; 'Suffolk', (1895), p. 177; P. J. Perry, 'High farming in Victorian Britain: The financial foundations', *Agricultural History* 52 (1978), p. 373. Although as G. Shaw Lefevre noted, no reform of tenure could prove a remedy for a bad harvest, G. Shaw Lefevre, *Agrarian Tenures: A Survey of the Laws and Customs Relating to the Holding of Land in England, Ireland and Scotland of the Reforms Therein During Recent Years* (London, 1893), p. vi.

64 E. J. T. Collins, 'Rural and agricultural change: The Great Depression, 1875–1896', in E. J. T. Collins (ed), *The Agrarian History of England and Wales, Volume VII* (Cambridge, 2000), p. 205.

65 'Final Report of Her Majesty's Commissioners appointed to inquire into the subject of agricultural depression. Royal Commission on Agriculture', *British Parliamentary Papers* XV (1897), p. 96.

66 Mingay, 'Farmer', p. 801. The 1919 Agricultural Land Sales (Restriction of Notices to Quit) Act also invalidated a notice to quit if the landlord subsequently contracted to sell the holding.

67 Alastair Mutch, 'Farmers organizations and agricultural depression in Lancashire, 1890–1900', *Agricultural History Review* 31 (1983), pp. 33–4; C. S. Orwin, *A History of English Farming* (London, 1949), p. 118; Alun Howkins, 'Social cultural and domestic life: The farmers', in E. J. T. Collins (ed), *The Agrarian History of England and Wales, Volume VII* (Cambridge, 2000), pp. 1377–8; Fisher, 'Agrarian politics', p. 335 and 343.

68 Fisher, 'Agrarian politics', p. 344; Dunbabin, *Rural Discontent,* p.174; G. E. Mingay, *The Transformation of Britain, 1830–1939* (London, 1986), pp. 114–5.

69 Howkins, 'The farmers', p. 1377.

70 Fisher, 'Agrarian politics', p. 356; Packer, *Liberalism*, p. 13. Farmers were also unhappy at the thought of labourers having allotments because they believed they would increase the labourers' independence and distract them from tilling their fields.

Chapter Seven

1 Habakkuk, *Marriage*, p. 94; Oswald, 'Helmingham, III', p. 380.

2 Douglas, *Land,* p. 17.

3 David Spring, 'English landownership in the nineteenth century: A critical note', *Economic History Review* IX (1957), p. 476; David Spring, 'The Earls of Durham and the great northern coalfield, 1830–1880', *Canadian Historical Review* XXXIII (1952), p. 249; Clay, 'Property settlements', p. 18.

4 Spring, 'Critical note', p. 475; Habakkuk, *Marriage,* p. 134.

5 SRO (Bury) HA507/4/39; *Burke's Peerage* (1970), p. 356; no appropriate dates for Lady Mary; F. M. L. Thompson, 'The end of a great estate', *Economic History Review* VIII (1955), pp. 43–4.

6 Namely, Lady Augusta Seymour and Lady Georgiana Grey, SRO (Bury) HA507/4/39.

7 Thompson, 'End', p. 43. Although portions continued to be provided.

8 Wilson and Mackley, *Creating Paradise*, p. 297; Spring, 'Critical note', p. 477 and pp. 474–5.

9 Christopher Hussey, 'Ickworth Park, Suffolk', *Country Life*, 10 March 1955, p. 680.

10 Wilson and Mackley, *Creating Paradise*, p. 288.

11 SRO (Ipswich) HB26/412/1854; Anthony Dale, *James Wyatt* (Oxford, 1956), pp. 33–5; White, *Suffolk*, pp. 315–6; *Burke's and Savills, III*, pp. 243–5; the grounds were landscaped by Capability Brown who also redesigned Euston Park, Norman Scarfe, *The Suffolk Landscape* (London, 1972), pp. 226–7. As regards Euston Hall, between 1750 and 1756, the exterior was remodelled at a cost of £6,000 'for an eighteenth century Duke this was modest indeed', Wilson and Mackley, *Creating Paradise*, p. 275.

12 Mackley, 'Country House Building' p. 58 and pp. 21–59; H. Colvin and J. Harris (eds), *The Country Seat* (London, 1970), pp. 164 and 168. This evidence is also illustrative of the fact, as Clay noted in Chapter One, that many large landowners bought as well as sold land; furthermore as Trumbach pointed out, also in Chapter One, not all marriage portions were used to purchase land.

13 John Martin Robinson, *The Wyatts: An Architectural Dynasty* (Oxford, 1979), p. 87; Wilson and Mackley, *Creating Paradise*, p. 213.

14 Thompson, 'End', p. 51; White, *Suffolk*, pp. 326 and 537; *Burke's and Savills, III*, pp. 254, 256–7 and 265; Robinson, *The Wyatts*, p. 87; Wilson and Mackley, *Creating Paradise*, pp. 213 and 279.

15 SRO (Bury) HA513/5/22.

16 SRO (Bury) HA513/5/23, HA513/5/22 aand HA513/5/19. A similar policy was followed in the case of Sir John Blois, when Cockfield Hall together with all his real and personal property was assigned to trustees until he could settle his debts; Mackley, 'Country House Building', p. 265.

17 SRO (Bury) HA513/5/19.

18 SRO (Bury) HA513/5/24.

19 SRO (Bury) HA513/5/25.

20 SRO (Bury) HA513/5/25.

21 SRO (Bury) HA513/5/27. The amount owed was around £1,000 SRO (Bury) HA513/5/26.

22 SRO (Bury) HA513/5/27.

23 SRO (Bury) HA513/5/27.

24 SRO (Bury) HA513/5/28.

25 David Spring, 'The English landed estate in the age of coal and iron: 1830–1880', *Journal of Economic History* XI (1951), p. 15.

26 SRO (Ipswich) HB26/412/1854. This was in accordance with the arrangements laid out in the settlement dated 2nd March 1839, made on the marriage of his eldest son Charles.

27 David Cannadine, 'Aristocratic indebtedness in the nineteenth century: The case re-opened', *Economic History Review* XXX (1977), p. 645 and pp. 624–5.

28 SRO (Bury) HA507/4/39.

29 SRO (Bury) HA507/4/39.

30 SRO (Bury) HA507/4/39. This is inclusive of the £400 owed in mortgage

interest, which has itself been deducted and added to the Suffolk mortgages to give a total figure for the money owing of £1,691.

31 SRO (Bury) HA 507/4/39.

32 Although Spring counters 'if non-agricultural income rose impressively, as it often though not invariably did, why not use it to pay off debt?' This is however wholly inapplicable to the finances of the third Marquess of Bristol whose income, save for £273 from his urban property in Brighton, was entirely agricultural. David Spring, 'Aristocratic indebtedness in the nineteenth century: A comment', *Economic History Review* XXXIII (1980), p. 566.

33 SRO (Ipswich) HA108/8/2 (item10); SRO (Ipswich) HA93/5/125.

34 1871, £619, rent-charge £43; 1875, £2,446, rent-charge £147; 1881, £1,380, rent-charge £80; 1885, £1,923 rent-charge £108; 1884, £923, rent-charge £52; 1892, £354, rent-charge £22; 1892 £1,073, rent-charge £68, SRO (Bury) HA507/3/749; SRO (Bury) 941/71/4; SRO (Lowestoft) HA12/D7/1/5.

35 This, and a bill for general repairs for £1,273, was paid in July 1859, SRO (Bury) 941/30/61 and 62. Further repairs totalled £1,674. SRO (Bury) 941/30/ 75, 81, 71 and 114. Cannadine, 'Indebtedness: Re-opened', p. 639; Mark Girouard, *The Victorian Country House* (London, 1979), pp. 8–9; Lawrence and Jeanne C. Fawtier Stone, 'Country houses and their owners in Hertfordshire, 1540–1879', in W.O. Aydelotte, A. C. Beque and R.W. Fogel (eds), *The Dimensions of Quantitative Research in History* (London, 1972); Nicklaus Pevsner, *Suffolk* (London, 1974); M. W. Flinn, *Origins of the Industrial Revolution* (London, 1966), p. 48; Spring, 'Indebtedness: A comment', p. 566; Wilson and Mackley, *Creating Paradise*, p. 232 and p. 171.

36 Dale, *Wyatt* p. 68 and Colvin and Harris (eds), *The Country Seat*, p. 168; proposed plans drawn up by Edward Barry, SRO (Ipswich) HA11/C46/2/1 & 2 and HA11/C46/3, 4 and 5/1–5. Regretfully no building accounts appear to have been deposited in the archives.

37 *Burke's and Savills, III,* pp. 232–4; Wilson and Mackley, *Creating Paradise*, p. 217.

38 G. E. Cokayne, *The Complete Peerage, Volume X* (London, 1945) p. 767; *Burke's and Savills, III,* p. 258; SRO (Lowestoft) SC/335/1; White, *Suffolk,* p. 540.

39 Cannadine, 'Indebtedness: Re-opened', pp. 639–40; Cokayne, *Peerage, X*, p. 767; SRO (Lowestoft) SC/335/1. Between c.1830 and 1871 Lord Rendlesham presumably resided on his estate in Hertfordshire. Wilson and Mackley, *Creating Paradise*, p. 27.

40 SRO (Lowestoft) HA12/B3/14/17. The sale being sanctioned under a settlement dated 23rd September 1844. Nevertheless, the estate remained subject to various debts, see below.

41 Michael I. Wilson, *The English Country House and its Furnishings* (London, 1977), pp. 161–2; Heather Clemenson, *English Country Houses and Landed Estates* (London, 1992), pp. 46–47; Olive Cooke, *The English Country House As Art and a Way of Life* (London, 1974), pp. 228–9; White, *Suffolk*, pp. 140, 560; *Burke's and Savills, III,* p. 218 and 262; Wilson and Mackley also suggest that Brandeston Hall was purchased in the 1830s rather than 1842.

42 Girouard, *Victorian Country House*, pp. 7 and 9.

43 F. M. L. Thompson, 'Landowners and the rural community', in G. E. Mingay (ed), *The Victorian Countryside, Volume II* (London, 1981), p. 459.

44   Cannadine, *Decline and Fall*, p. 16.

45   Everitt, 'Shooting', p. 367.

46   Alexander and Anand, *Maharajah,* pp. 110 and 112.

47   Everitt, 'Shooting', p. 367.

48   Corrance quoted in Everitt, 'Shooting', p. 367. Essentially, wild eggs were gathered and put under hens.

49   Following the lead of Lord Rendlesham, Duleep Singh also tried to introduce red grouse to the heathlands of Breckland.

50   Alexander and Anand, *Maharajah,* pp. 111 and 133; Goodwyn, *Beccles*, p. 44; SRO (Bury) HA 513/16/1–20; Cokayne, *Peerage, X*, p. 768.

51   SRO (Lowestoft) HA12/B3/14/3; HA12/A8/1/12; HA12/A8/1/6; HA12/A8/1/ 7; SRO (Ipswich) HA108/8/2 (item 10).

52   Cannadine, 'Indebtedness: Re-opened', p. 645.

53   David Cannadine, 'Aristocratic indebtedness in the nineteenth century: A restatement', *Economic History Review* XXXIII (1980), p. 571. Indeed, if, as Spring suggests, the aristocracy had in fact 'reduced' or even 'removed' the debts charged to their estates, 'One is bound to ask what all the fuss was about'. These figures are exclusive of £680 in urban rents from the Marquess' Brighton property; outgoings on this property totalled £250. SRO (Bury) 941/71/4.

54   SRO (Bury) HA507/3/756.

55   SRO (Bury) HA507/3/756. Presumably Pixley was referring to the capital monies in the hands of the Trustees of the Settlement of 1862. (£8,189), SRO (Bury) HA507/4/55 p. 53.

56   Case No. 1563, SRO (Bury) HA507/6/21.

57   SRO (Bury) HA507/3/837; SRO (Bury) 941/71/4.

58   Charles Adeane and Edwin Savill, *The Land Retort: A Study of the Land Question with an Answer to the Report of the Secret Enquiry Committee* (London, 1914), p. 80; SRO (Bury) 941/74/12; SRO (Bury) 941/71/4; SRO (Bury) HA507/3/323; SRO (Bury) 941/71/4.

59   Author's correspondence with Lord Henniker 21/9/1994.

60   'Suffolk', (1895), p. 355.

61   Bramford, Hall, SRO (Ipswich) HA61/436/870–872; Broke Hall, SRO (Ipswich) HA93/3/37–38; Bosmere Hall, SRO (Ipswich) HA93/3/361–2; Wilson and Mackley, *Creating Paradise*, p. 350.

62   Horn, *Changing Countryside*, p. 47; J. Harris, *The Design of the English Country House 1620–1920* (London, 1985), p. 9; White, *Suffolk*, pp. 312, 318, 538; *Kelly's Directory of Suffolk* (London, 1888), pp. 997, 998, 1000, 1078 and 1104.

63   Thompson, *English Landed Society*, p. 303.

64   Girouard, *English Country House*, p. 302.

65   Presumably the sport was better than at Hintlesham Hall. SRO (Ipswich) HA93/3/39; SRO (Ipswich) HA93/3/40. Sir George's niece, Lady Louisa Broke-Lorraine, let Bramford Hall to Major General J. C. Russell in 1896, SRO (Ipswich) HA51/436/1171.

66   Everitt, 'Shooting', p. 364.

67   'Suffolk', (1895), p. 348.

68   Everitt, 'Shooting', p. 365; Haggard, *Rural England*, pp. 383–4. As a result, estates on the Brecklands still fetched a good price, 'not on account of their agricultural value [which given the low price of wheat and the heavy inputs

required to boost fertility was almost nil] but because it was splendid game country'.

69 Wilson and Mackley, *Creating Paradise*, p. 351.

70 Haggard, *Rural England*, p. 383.

71 Haggard, *Rural England*, p. 384.

72 Everitt, 'Shooting', p. 366; my thanks also to Harvey Osborne.

73 Kenneth Clark, *Another Part of the Wood: A Self-Portrait* (London, 1974), pp. 4 and 14.

Chapter Eight

1 Roy Jenkins, *Mr Balfour's Poodle: An Account of the Struggle Between the House of Lords and the Government of Mr Asquith* (London, 1954), p. 12.

2 Geoffrey Searle, *The Liberal Party: Triumph and Disintegration, 1886–1929* (London, 1992), p. 36; Jenkins, *Poodle*, p. 12; After 1886, members of land-owning families also tended to be concentrated on one side of the House of Commons as either Tories or Liberal Unionists, F. M. L. Thompson, 'Britain', in David Spring (ed), *European Landed Elites in the Nineteenth Century* (London, 1977), p. 24. Neal Blewett has calculated that in the early 1900s approximately one-third of those sitting on the Unionist side of the House of Commons were still drawn from among the landed elite. Neal Blewett, *The Peers, The Parties and the People: The General Elections of the 1910* (London, 1972), pp. 68–9.

3 Searle, *Liberal*, p. 32.

4 Douglas, *Land*, p. 114.

5 J. Enoch Powell, *Joseph Chamberlain* (London, 1975) p. 85.

6 Powell, *Chamberlain*, pp. 97–9.

7 Harold Perkin, *The Rise of Professional Society: England Since 1880* (London, 1989) p. 47; Bentley, *Democracy*, p. 293.

8 Jenkins, *Poodle*, p. 17. Note the restraint shown by the Lords when dealing with such contentious issues as the establishment of County Councils by the Marquess of Salisbury.

9 Blewett, *Peers*, pp. 76 and 70.

10 Blewett, *Peers*, p. 76.

11 Offer, *Property and Politics,* p. 363.

12 Offer, *Property and Politics*, p. 363; J. Ellis Barker, 'Unionist or socialist land reform?', *Nineteenth Century*, December 1909, p. 1092.

13 Offer, *Property and Politics*, p.357; Barker, 'Unionist', p. 1097; J. Ellis Barker, 'The land, the landlords and the people', *Nineteenth Century*, October 1909, p. 566. The concept of a property owning democracy.

14 Barker, 'Land', p. 566. As Lord Ernle noted, 'The comparative failure of the Act was due to the unattractive terms which it was offered to rural workers', Lord Ernle, *Whippingham to Westminster: Reminiscences of Lord Ernle* (London, 1938), p. 233.

15 Barker, 'Land', p. 564.

16 Burke, *Gentry, II,* (1894), p. 1651; Bateman, *Great Landowners,* p. 443; Offer *Property and Politics*, p. 367. This was because Lord Rendlesham was already in the process of breaking up his estate. Between 1895 and 1906 Pretyman sat for the Woodbridge Division. From 1908 he sat for Chelmsford.

17 Offer, *Property and Politics*, p. 367; Edward Bristow, 'The Liberty and Property Defence League and individualism', *Historical Journal* XVIII (1975), p. 764.

18 *Hansard's Parliamentary Debates, Volume IV* (London, 1910), pp. 516–7; *Hansard's Parliamentary Debates, Volume IV* (London, 1909), p. 915.

19 Avner Offer, 'The origins of the Law of Property Act, 1910–1925', *The Modern Law Review* 40 (1977), p. 507.

20 Lord Avebury, 'The Finance Bill', *Nineteenth Century*, November 1909, p. 745. 'Not out of deference to Dukes, but out of deference to facts' which were that in the previous twenty-eight years, agricultural rents had fallen continuously, as had the selling or capital value of agricultural land, W. H. Mallock, 'An inquiry into the actual amount of the annual increment of land values', *Nineteenth Century*, November 1909, p. 758.

21 *Hansard's Parliamentary Debates, Volume IX* (London, 1909), pp. 83–4 and p. 118; Avebury, 'Finance Bill', p. 745.

22 Offer, *Property and Politics,* pp. 363–4.

23 Charles Newton-Robinson, 'The blight of the Land Taxes', *Nineteenth Century*, September 1910, p. 397; *Hansard's Parliamentary Debates, Volume V* (London, 1910), p. 1653.

24 SRO (Bury) Ac. 613/813/1.

25 *Hansard's Parliamentary Debates, Volume V* (London, 1911), p. 2034; Offer, *Property and Politics*, p. 364.

26 SRO (Bury) Ac. 613/184; *Hansard's Parliamentary Debates, Volume VII* (London, 1909), pp. 39–41.

27 The House of Commons in 1906 contained 399 Liberals, 156 'Unionists' and 29 Labour members. F. W. S. Craig (ed), *British Electoral Facts, 1832–1980* (London, 1981), p. 28.

28 Avebury, 'Finance Bill', pp. 752–3.

29 *Hansard, IV* (1909), p. 908.

30 G. D. Phillips, *The Diehards: Aristocratic Society and Politics in Edwardian England* (London, 1979), pp. 1, 163 and 173–5; A. Wilson Fox, *The Earl of Halsbury: Lord High Chancellor 1823–1921* (London, 1929), pp. 236–7; Jenkins, *Poodle*, p. 171; George Dangerfield, *The Strange Death of Liberal England* (New York, 1935), pp. 22, 42–3; The Earl of Winterton, *Pre-War* (London, 1932), p. 177; Harry Jones, *Liberalism and the House of Lords* (London, 1912), pp. 151–152; Thompson, *English Landed Society*, p. 314; Peter Fraser, 'The Unionist debacle of 1911 and Balfour's retirement', *The Journal of Modern History XXXV* (1963), pp. 354–5.

31 Offer, *Property and Politics*, p. 378. A situation compounded by Lloyd George who embarked upon a renewed land campaign in 1912.

32 F. M. L. Thompson, 'The land market in the nineteenth century', *Oxford Economic Papers* IX (1957), p. 306.

33 Thompson, *English Landed Society*, p. 318.

34 'Suffolk', (1895), p. 348.

35 Cannadine, *Decline and Fall*, p. 126.

36 White, *Suffolk*, pp. 201 and 595; Nowton Hall estate, SRO (Bury) HA535/5/71; Hengrave Hall Estate, SRO (Bury) Ac. 449/3/14 and 'Hengrave Hall', *Estates Gazette*, June 1889, pp. 444–5; Alan Armstrong, *Farmworkers: A Social and Economic History, 1770–1980* (London, 1988), p.135; Thompson, *English Landed Society*, p. 320; H. Auvray Tipping, 'Hengrave Hall, Suffolk', *Country Life*, 16 April 1910, p. 566; 'Tyrell Estates', *Estates Gazette*, May 1892, p. 521; 'Sudbourne Hall, Suffolk', *Country Life*, 23 February 1901, p. 242; G. E.

Cokayne, *The Complete Peerage, Volume VI* (London, 1926), p. 514; *Debrett's Baronetage and Knightage* (London, 1881), p. 489; Paine, (ed), *Culford* p. 2. Other aristocratic buyers included the brother of the third Earl of Lonsdale, the Hon William Lowther, who purchased the Campsea Ashe estate in 1883, White, *Suffolk*, (1885), p. 201; *Walford's County Families* (London, 1919), p. 839; and *Burke's Genealogical and Heraldic History of the Peerage, Baronetage and Knightage* (London, 1970), p. 2693. His son was created Viscount Ullswater in 1921.

37   Alexander Ogilvie having bought Sizewell Hall in 1859, R. A. Whitehead, *The Beloved Coast and Suffolk Sandlings* (Lavenham, 1991), p. 3; *Kelly's Directory of Suffolk* (London, 1888), p. 887; *Kelly's Directory of Suffolk* (London, 1904), p. 38; White, *Suffolk*, pp. 111; *Burke's and Savills, III*, pp. 215, 221–2, 229 and 264; Ryan, *Hintlesham*, pp. 123–5; Arthur Oswald, 'Hintlesham Hall, Suffolk', *Country Life*, 18 August 1928; *Walford's*, p. 1171; R. G. Wilson, *Greene King: A Business and Family History* (London, 1983), pp. 148 and 163; Hengrave Estate, SRO (Bury) Ac. 382/1–3; 'Sudbourne', (1901), p. 242; *Kelly's Handbook to the Titled, Landed and Official Classes* (London, 1904), pp. 695 and 737. Subsequently, in 1918, the Sudbourne estate was broken up and sold in 158 separate lots, SRO (Ipswich) SC400/1; Mark Girouard, *Life in the English Country House: A Social and Architectural History* (Yale, 1978), p. 301; Jill Franklin, 'The Victorian country house', in G. E. Mingay (ed), *The Victorian Countryside, Volume II* (London, 1981), p. 411.

38   'Coney Weston Manor', *Estates Gazette*, July 1902, p. 799, see also the reference, in Chapter One, to the sale of the Icklingham Hall estate in 1898. Other sporting estates on offer included the 2,854 acre Brandon Park estate, *Estates Gazette*, January 1898, p. 1079 and the Depperhaugh estate, *Estates Gazette*, September 1894, p. 349.

39   Thompson, *English Landed Society*, p. 302.

40   H. J. Hanham, 'The sale of honours in late Victorian England', *Victorian Studies* 3 (1959/1960), p. 279; Perkin, *Professional Society*, p. 63.

41   Cannadine, *Decline and Fall*, p. 299; Jamie Camplin, *The Rise of the Plutocrats* (London, 1978) p. 125; Ralph E. Pumphrey, 'The introduction of industrialists into the British peerage: A study in the adaptation of a social institution', *American Historical Review* LXV (1959), pp. 11 and 14.

42   He was subsequently created Viscount Iveagh in 1905, and Viscount Elveden and Earl of Iveagh in 1919. Originally, he had sought to acquire the Savernake estate in Wiltshire for £750,000, from the deeply indebted fourth Marquess of Ailesbury. This sale was blocked by Ailesbury's uncle, Lord Henry, who refused to see 800 years of family history sold to that 'mere upstart merchant . . . nouveau-riche Irishman'. A comment which suggests Lord Henry was more than a little jealous of the wealth of the newer and far richer peers created after 1885 especially as he himself was Chairman of Meux & Co Brewers Ltd. G. E. Cokayne, *The Complete Peerage, Volume VII* (London, 1929), p. 78; G. E. Cokayne, *Complete Peerage, Volume I* (London, 1910), p. 66; Thompson, *English Landed Society*, p. 314, Camplin, *Plutocrats*, p. 220. Guinness having acquired Elveden in 1894 also acquired the neighbouring Icklingham Hall estate.

43   Martelli, *Elveden*, pp. 50–51 and pp. 53–54; Camplin, *Plutocrats*, p. 222.

44   Martelli, *Elveden*, p. 49.

45   Everitt, 'Shooting', p. 365. The Earl of Cadogan, who purchased Culford in

1889, owed his wealth to his ground rents from Cadogan Square and Sloane Square. Paine (ed), *Culford*, p. 2; Porter, *London*, p. 120; David Cannadine, *Lords and Landlords: The Aristocracy and the Towns, 1774 – 1967* (Leicester, 1980), p. 426; D. Spring, 'Land and politics in Edwardian England', *Agricultural History* 58 (1984), pp. 19–20. Subsequently, in 1919, part of the central London property was sold off, while the Culford estate was broken up and sold in 145 separate lots by the sixth Earl in 1934 raising £105,569, SRO (Ipswich) SC/124/1; W. D. Rubinstein, *Men of Property* (London, 1981), p. 202.

46 SRO (Ipswich) HA11/A15/7; SRO (Ipswich) HA11/C47/16/4. The household at Euston was equally impressive, SRO (Bury) HA513/7/8; Andrew Adonis, *Making Aristocracy Work* (Oxford, 1993), p. 244; Girouard, *English Country House*, p. 300.

47 Pamela Horn, *High Society: The English Social Elite, 1880–1914* (Stroud, 1992), p. 134. The Marquess subsequently modernized Ickworth in 1908, even putting in squash courts, SRO (Bury) 941/30/113. Weekend guests at Orwell Park, meanwhile, included Lord and Lady Stradbroke, Lord and Lady Graham, the Walter Guinnesses and Sir Savile Crossley. Sir Austen Chamberlain, *Politics from the Inside* (London, 1936), p. 167.

48 Cannadine, *Decline and Fall*, p. 438.

49 SRO (Ipswich) HA11/C8/13; SRO (Ipswich) HA11/C8/13. The Earl of Ashburnham whose heartland was in Sussex, broke up and sold for £55,616 the Barking Hall estate in 1917, SRO (Ipswich) HA1/HB4/6–7. The outlying portions of this estate had already been sold in 1914 for £6,620. Similarly, the Duke of Hamilton sold the bulk of the Easton Park estate in 1919 for £58,000, the residue being sold in 1922. SRO (Ipswich) SC/142/5 and SC/142/10.

50 SRO (Ipswich) HA11/C5/17; Heather Clemenson, *English Country Houses and Landed Estates* (London, 1982), p. 111. There were also aristocratic buyers. The Earl of Cranbrook purchased the Great Glemham estate in 1914 from the Meinatzagen family. Author's correspondence with the Countess of Cranbrook, 12/2/1997.

51 T. R. Gourvish and R. G. Wilson, *The British Brewing Industry 1830–1980* (Cambridge, 1994), p. 241; D. H. Tollemache, *The Tollemaches of Helmingham and Ham* (Ipswich, 1949). Subsequently, the Tollemaches amalgamated the brewery with that of the Cobbolds to create 'Tolly Cobbolds'; SRO (Ipswich) SC313/2; SRO (Lowestoft) HA236/2/132, HA236/2/162 and HA236/2/133; H. L. Malchow, *Gentlemen Capitalists* (London, 1991), p. 320; author's correspondence with Lord Somerleyton 13/2/1996. The estate in the mid-1990s covered an area of 4,620 acres.

52 G. E. Cokayne, *The Complete Peerage, Volume XII, Part I* (London, 1953), pp. 733–4; author's correspondence with Lord Tollemache 6/9/1994.

53 Author's correspondence with the Duke of Grafton, 26/7/1994. For example, in 1919 the Duke of Grafton let rather than sold the Bradfield Hall estate, together with shooting rights over 1,000 acres, SRO (Bury) HA513/21/56; G. E. Cokayne, *The Complete Peerage, VI* (London, 1926), p. 49; Falk, *The Fitzroys*, p. 20. The family were, however, forced to sell the Wakefield Lodge estate in Northamptonshire to pay death duties.

54 Author's correspondence with Lord Marlesford, 15/2/1997; SRO (Bury) HA507/6/24; *Walford's*, p. 164; SRO (Bury) HA507/4/53.

55 SRO (Bury) 941/71/4.

56 SRO (Bury) 941/71/4.

57 SRO (Bury) 941/71/4.

58 When owing to the debts incurred by the seventh Marquess of Bristol (suc: 1985), who spent over £7,000,000 on a life of Regency style excess, the Ickworth estate was gradually broken up until, finally, the last vestiges of the original nineteenth century estate, some 2,200 acres, were sold off in 1994 for £3.5 million. Subsequently the contents of the East Wing, valued at approximately £1 million, were also auctioned-off by Sotheby's in 1996. the Hall itself having been handed over to the National Trust in the 1950s by the late Marchioness of Bristol after it and many of its more notable contents were accepted by the Treasury, together with a large capital endowment in lieu of death duties, on the proviso that all future heirs could remain in the East Wing. *Burke's and Savills, III*, p. 248; *Eastern Daily Press*, 3 June 1994; *Eastern Daily Press*, 7 June 1996; *Debrett's Peerage and Baronetage* (London, 1995), p. 162; Christopher Hussey, 'Ickworth Park, Suffolk', *Country Life*, 10 March (1955), p. 678. The Marquess was thus merely 'the latest in a long and not particularly honourable line of aristocrats who have blown the fruits of centuries of careful accumulation in a single generation', *Country Life*, 31 March (1994), p. 67; SRO (Bury) 941/71/8; SRO (Bury) HA507/3/756a.

59 *Debrett's Peerage, Baronetage, Knightage and Companionage* (London, 1912), pp. 742–3; G. E. Cokayne, *The Complete Peerage, Volume X* (London, 1945) p. 766 and *Public Men of East Suffolk* pp. 133–5. The government, meanwhile, was so concerned at the thought of private individuals inheriting such vast sums of money that it passed an Act in 1800, commonly known as the Thellusson Act, prohibiting a testator from devising property to accumulate for more than twenty years. In 1857 the Thellusson Estate consisted of 8,429 acres in Yorkshire, 801 acres in Durham, 3,955 acres in Hertfordshire, 1,492 acres in Warwickshire, 294 acres in Norfolk and 14,965 acres in Suffolk, SRO (Ipswich) HB416/A2/14. For more details see Patrick Polden, *Peter Thellusson's Will of 1797 and its Consequences for Chancery Law* (Lampeter, 2002).

60 Cokayne, *Peerage, X*, p. 766; Sir William Holdsworth, *A History of English Law, Volume VII* (London, 1925), p. 230.

61 Charles Dickens, *Bleak House* (London, 1868), p. 10.

62 Cokayne, *Peerage, X*, p. 767.

63 SRO (Ipswich) HB416/A2/20.

64 SRO (Ipswich) HB416/A2/20; SRO (Ipswich) HB416/A2/19; SRO (Lowestoft) SC/335/1, p. 3.

65 SRO (Ipswich) HB416/A2/20.

66 *The East Anglian*, 28 May 1920 in SRO (Lowestoft) SC/335/1. What remained of the estate was sold between 1922 and 1925. Author's correspondence with Lord Rendlesham 25/7/1994; SRO (Ipswich) SC/335/4–5; *Burke's and Savills, III*, p. 258; SRO (Ipswich) HB416/A2/20; SRO (Ipswich) HB416/A2/22; SRO (Ipswich) SC/335/1 and /2 and /3. The Hall, which failed to find a bidder, was demolished in 1949.

67 Saumarez's combined estates totalled 13,500 acres. 'Suffolk', (1895), p. 351.

68 Crowfield Estate, SRO (Ipswich) SC/123/2. The Baylham and Darmsden portions of the estate (2,600 acres, in 40 lots) was sold in 1941, SRO (Ipswich) SC/033/1.

69   Oakley Park, (7,400 acres in 41 lots) SRO (Ipswich) SC/230/3 and (1,296 acres in 34 lots), SC/230/4; author's correspondence with Lord Henniker, 21/9/1994; outlying portions (2,000 acres), SRO (Ipswich) SC/394/4; Debenham and Ashfield (1,350 acres in 19 lots), SRO (Ipswich) SC/011/6; *Burke's Peerage* (1970), p. 1311.

70   J. Cornforth, 'The future of Heveningham', *Country Life*, 18 September 1969, p. 671; G. E. Cokayne, *The Complete Peerage, Volume VI* (London, 1945), p. 674.

71   'Heveningham: The path to disaster', *Country Life*, 11 February 1988, p. 74; H. Auvray Tipping, 'Heveningham Hall, III, Suffolk', *Country Life*, 3 October 1925, p. 514; SRO (Ipswich) SC/213/9. When the Hon Andrew Vanneck died in 1965 his decision to leave the Hall as a discretionary settlement to his family left the family open to the 1965 Finance Act, which made discretionary settlements subject to Capital Gains Tax. This tax was liable on the capital appreciation of underlying assets every fifteen years. In other words, if Heveningham was said to be worth £250,000 when the deed of settlement was made (in this case in 1955), if it were held that this sum had doubled during the 15 year period, the Trustees would find themselves liable for £75,000, or 30 per cent of the gain. In these circumstances, and with Capital Gains Tax set to be levied in 1969, the family felt compelled to place the Hall on the market. Beckett, *Aristocracy*, pp. 477–8.

72   Troston Hall Estate, SRO (Ipswich) SC/424/2; Brent Eleigh Hall Estate SRO (Ipswich) SC/069/1; Assington Hall Estate, Outlying Portions, SRO (Ipswich) SC/014/3, the residue of the estate, some 2,108 acres, was sold in 60 lots in 1938, SRO (Ipswich) SC/014/4; Stoke Park Estate, SRO (Ipswich) SC/242/86 and 87; SRO (Ipswich) SC/175/1; Brandeston Hall Estate, SRO (Ipswich) SC/065/2; Brettenham Park Estate SRO (Ipswich) SC/158/1; Hardwick House Estate, SRO (Ipswich) SC/201/1; the Stowlangtoft estate was sold by the Wilson family in 1915 in 18 lots, SRO (Ipswich) SC/391/2; *Burke's Genealogical and Heraldic History of the Landed Gentry, Volume III* (London, 1965), pp. 236, 260, 525. The Earl of Guildford meanwhile, sold a secondary estate, the 2,864 acre Glemham Hall estate, to the Cobbolds, the Ipswich brewers, in the 1920s.

73   SRO (Lowestoft) SC/335/1.

74   Author's correspondence with Lord Henniker 21/9/1994. Outlying portions (37 farms, 64 cottages and 4,553 acres) in 101 lots, SRO (Ipswich) HA116/22 and SC/412/3; Reydon Estate, (5 farms, 18 cottages and 988 acres) SRO (Ipswich) HA116/23; the remainder of the Brome Hall estate sold in 1953 for £25,965, SRO (Ipswich) SC/074/2. E. H. Whetham, 'The Agriculture Act, 1920 and its Repeal', *Agricultural History Review* 22 (1974), p. 36; E. G. Strutt, *British Agriculture* (London, 1917), p. 27

75   Author's correspondence with Lord Henniker 21/9/1994.

76   *Hansard's, V* (1911), pp. 2026–7; *Hansard's Parliamentary Debates, Volume VIII* (London, 1912), pp. 626–7.

77   *Hansard's, VIII* (1912), p. 625.

78   'Suffolk', (1895), p. 391; Thompson, *English Landed Society*, p. 330; Beckett, *Aristocracy*, p. 477.

79   'Suffolk', (1895), p. 391.

80   Falk, *FitzRoys*, p. 239; Marcus Binney, 'Wakefield Lodge, Northamptonshire', *Country Life*, 2 August 1973, p. 301; SRO (Bury) HA507/4/55.

81 Lawrence Rich, *Inherit the Land: Landowners in the Eighties* (London, 1987), p. 6.

82 Author's correspondence with Lady Darrell, 16/2/1997. The family were also weakened by the redemption in the early 1900s of several of the mortgages charged to the estate. SRO (Lowestoft) HA12/A8/1/6, 7, 8 and 12. Flixton Hall Estate, SRO (Ipswich) HA11/CS/14; *Burke's Peerage* (1970), p. 24. The estate itself (inclusive of both the Trust Estate and Alexander Adair's Trust) covered 13,726 acres in 1913, SRO (Lowestoft) HA12/D3/11.

83 Author's correspondence, Earl of Stradbroke, 14/9/1994.

84 SRO (Bury) Ac. 613/813; SRO (Bury) Ac. 613/813.9; SRO (Bury) Ac. 613/16.

85 Beckett, *Aristocracy*, p. 476.

86 SRO (Bury) Ac. 613/16; SRO (Ipswich) HA53/359/824 and 825; SRO (Bury) HA519/109–126; see also the mortgage portfolio of the Bence family of Kentwell Hall, SRO (Bury) HA505/7/25,/26,/27 and /28; SRO (Bury) HA505/7/86; SRO(Bury) HA505/7/84; SRO (Bury) HA505/7/82.

87 SRO (Ipswich) HA436/1266–9.

88 Cannadine, *Decline and Fall,* p. 706.

Conlusion

1 Alun Howkins, 'Social, cultural and domestic life', in E. J. T. Collins (ed), *The Agrarian History of England and Wales, Volume VII* (Cambridge, 2000), p. 1356.

2 *Hansard's Parliamentary Debates, Volume LXXXV* (London, 1846), p. 99.

3 Clifford, *Lock-Out*, pp. 19, 102–104; Thirsk, *Suffolk Farming*, p. 146.

4 Howkins, 'Domestic Life', p. 1356.

5 *Hansard's, LXXXV* (1846), p. 100.

6 Clifford, *Lock-Out*, p. 103; Pamela Horn, *Labouring Life in the Victorian Countryside* (Bristol, 1976), p. 7.

7 *Hansard, LXXXV* (1846), p. 100.

8 Geoffrey Searle, *The Liberal Party: Triumph and Disintegration, 1886–1929* (London, 2001), p.41. In Wales, the Radical strategy of uniting the farmer and the labourer in an assault on the privileges of landowners worked much better, as their economic and social ties were much closer and both felt more alienated from an 'Anglican' landed elite.

9 E. J. T. Collins, 'Rural and agricultural change', in E. J. T. Collins (ed), *The Agrarian History of England and Wales, Volume VII* (Cambridge, 2000), p. 178.

10 Howkins, 'Domestic life', p. 1356. Significantly, after the War, many estates were broken up into lots to give tenants a chance to buy their own farms.

11 Arthur Ponsonby, *The Decline of Aristocracy* (London, 1912), p. 99.

12 Author's correspondence with Lords Cranworth, Henniker, Tollemache and the Earl of Stradbroke.

13 *Hansard's Parliamentary Debates, Volume CCXXIII* (London, 1875), p. 938.

APPENDIX: THE GREAT LANDOWNERS OF LATE VICTORIAN SUFFOLK

Name	Suffolk Acreage	Total Acreage	County in which largest acreage is situated
Lord Rendlesham	19,869	24,028	Suffolk
George Tomline	18,473	26,914	Suffolk
Maharajah Duleep Singh	17,210	17,210	Suffolk
Marquess of Bristol	16,981	32,014	Suffolk
Lord Huntingfield	16,869	16,869	Suffolk
Earl of Stradbroke	12,203	12,203	Suffolk
Sir Richard Wallace Bt	11,224	72,307	County Antrim
Duke of Grafton	11,124	25,773	Northamptonshire
Lord Waveney	10,930	19,252	Suffolk
Lord Henniker	10,910	11,040	Suffolk
Rev Edward Benyon	10,060	10, 664	Suffolk
Sir Edward Kerrison Bt	9,955	11,861	Suffolk
Sir Charles Bunbury Bt	9,831	9,831	Suffolk
Sir George Broke-Middleton Bt	9,500	9,500	Suffolk
William Mackenzie	8,300	27,750	Suffolk
Sir Charles Rowley Bt	7,324	8,616	Suffolk
Sir Alfred Gooch Bt	7,186	7,186	Suffolk
John Shepherd	7,041	7,041	Suffolk
Lord Tollemache	7,010	35,726	Cheshire
Frederick Barne	6,424	7,642	Suffolk
Lady Rokewode-Gage	6,210	6,210	Suffolk
Sir John Blois Bt	6,057	6,307	Suffolk
George Holt-Wilson	5,466	6,249	Suffolk
William Henry Smith	5,150	6,777	Suffolk
Arthur Maitland Wilson	5,016	5,016	Suffolk
Duke of Hamilton	4,939	157,386	Bute
William Gilstrap	4,880	4,880	Suffolk
John Berners	4,815	4,815	Suffolk

Earl Howe	4,695	33,669	Nottinghamshire
Frederick Vernon-Wentworth	4,161	22,930	Perthshire
Phillip Bennet	3,949	3,949	Suffolk
Thomas Thornhill	3,718	6,263	Suffolk
John Lloyd-Anstruther	3,612	3,612	Suffolk
Sir William Parker Bt	3,482	3,482	Suffolk
Charles Tyrell	3,462	3,462	Suffolk
Earl of Ashburnham	3,372	24,489	Sussex
Charles Dashwood	3,218	3,218	Suffolk
Sir Savile Crossley Bt	3,613	3,294	Suffolk
Charles Austin	3,134	3,134	Suffolk
R. E. Lofft	2,919	2,919	Suffolk
Sir Robert Affleck Bt	2,913	3,764	Suffolk
Earl of Guildford	2,864	10,929	Kent
William Long	2,850	3,634	Suffolk
Philip Gurdon	2,841	2,841	Suffolk
James Oakes	2,840	2,840	Suffolk
E. R. S. Bence	2,795	2,795	Suffolk
Mrs Weller-Poley	2,749	2,749	Suffolk
Miss Broke	2,737	3,550	Suffolk
Mrs Bence	2,625	3,929	Suffolk
R. H. M. Elwes	2,578	3,441	Suffolk
George Frere	2,574	4,512	Suffolk
R. J. Pettiward	2,475	2,475	Suffolk
Nathanial Barnardiston	2,474	2,932	Suffolk
T. R. Mills	2,460	2,460	Suffolk
J. G. Barclay	2,383	3,816	Suffolk
Rev Edmund Holland	2,349	4,243	Suffolk
Rev James Holden	2,327	2,327	Suffolk
Rev C R Cooke	2,326	2,326	Suffolk
J. G. Weller-Poley	2,312	2,312	Suffolk
F. Hayward	2,298	2,479	Suffolk
W. T. Brown	2,278	2,278	Suffolk
W. R. G. Farmer	2,160	9,495	Montgomeryshire
H. B. Mackworth-Praed	2,138	2,198	Suffolk
Sir Thomas Western Bt	2,134	10,009	Essex
Mrs Sheriffe	2,133	2,133	Suffolk
Mrs Shuldham	2,099	2,099	Suffolk
F. C. Brooke	2,063	2,063	Suffolk
Henry Waddington	2,041	2,934	Suffolk
Mrs Pike-Scrivener	2,039	2,039	Suffolk
Henry Lowry-Corry	1,987	1,987	Suffolk
Rev R. Gwilt	1,925	1,925	Suffolk
Trustees of G. Parkyns	1,914	1,914	Suffolk
J. L. Garden	1,845	1,845	Suffolk
Henry Micklethwait	1,839	10,579	Norfolk
T. B. Beale	1,825	1,825	Suffolk
F. S. Corrance	1,805	1,805	Suffolk
Rev R. W. Cobbold	1,781	1,781	Suffolk

Robert Cartwright	1,779	1,779	Suffolk
Robert Rushbrooke	1,715	1,715	Suffolk
C. W. Robinson	1,670	4,066	Cambridgeshire
Duke of Rutland	1,591	70,137	Leicestershire
Trustees of Mr Davers	1,546	1,546	Suffolk
Executers of J. C. Cobbold	1,539	1,539	Suffolk
Lady Rose	1,537	1,537	Suffolk
Lord Thurlow	1,529	13,894	Elgin
Robert Simpson	1,491	1,491	Suffolk
J. K. Brooke	1,462	1,462	Suffolk
W. A. Deane	1,438	1,438	Suffolk
H. M. Leathes	1,433	2,125	Suffolk
Charles Gwilt	1,430	1,430	Suffolk
R. C. Fowler	1,412	1,412	Suffolk
H. J. Wilkinson	1,362	1,362	Suffolk
E. Ruck-Keene	1,327	6,246	Oxfordshire
R. Barthorpe	1,326	1,326	Suffolk
Trustees of the Denston Hall estate	1,298	1,298	Suffolk
Colonel W. Parker	1,291	2,049	Suffolk
C. N. Ware	1,254	1,254	Suffolk
Miss Tatlock	1,242	1,242	Suffolk
Robert Gurdon	1,221	11,034	Northumberland
Lord Gwydyr	1,218	2,000	Suffolk
Trustees of Mrs Leach	1,187	1,187	Suffolk
H. H. Howard-Vyse	1,171	3,288	Northamptonshire
C. E. Gibbs	1,170	1,170	Suffolk
William Manfield	1,144	1,144	Suffolk
Robert Walford	1,134	1,134	Suffolk
T. P. Hale	1,120	1,120	Suffolk
Thomas Harcourt Powell	1,105	4,640	Pembrokeshire
Rev T. A. Cooke	1,102	1,102	Suffolk
Robert Josselyn	1,091·	1,091	Suffolk
B. H. Tooke	1,084	1,084	Suffolk
Rev C. F. Norman	1,079	3,266	Essex
Rev R. A. Arnold	1,075	1,075	Suffolk
Lord Walsingham	1,075	19,148	Norfolk
H. M. Doughty	1,073	1,073	Suffolk
H. J. Gurdon-Rebow	1,072	4,209	Essex
T. Waller	1,034	1,034	Suffolk
W. P. T. Phillips	1,032	1,032	Suffolk
Trustees of S. Bagnold	1,024	1,024	Suffolk
T. Woodward	1,021	1,021	Suffolk
Rev J. White	1,018	1,018	Suffolk
Miss Soame	1,014	1,014	Suffolk
Total	456,004	751,733	

(Source: John Bateman, *The Great Landowners of Great Britain and Ireland* [London, 1883] and 'Return of Owners of Land (Suffolk)', *British Parliamentary Papers* LXXII, Part II [1874]).

BIBLIOGRAPHY

Family Papers:
Adair Collection
Austin Collection
Ashburnham Collection
Barnardiston Collection
Barne Collection
Bence Collection
Crossley Collection
Gage Collection
Grafton Collection
Grafton Family Papers
Hervey Collection
Hervey Family Papers
Lorraine Collection
Oakes Collection
Rendlesham Collection
Rous Collection
Rowley Collection
De Saumarez Collection
Vanneck Family Papers

Reference works:
P. Barnes, 'The Economic History of Landed Estates in Norfolk Since 1880',
(University of East Anglia, Ph.D., 1984).
Alan Mackley, 'An Economic History of Country House Building with Particular
Reference to East Anglia and the East and West Ridings of Yorkshire, c.1660–
1870', (University of East Anglia, Ph.D., 1993).
Jonathan Theobald, 'Changing Landscapes, Changing Economies: Holdings in
Woodland High Suffolk, 1600–1850', (University of East Anglia, Ph.D.,
2000).
John Bateman, *The Acre-Ocracy of England* (London, 1876).
——*The Great Landowners of Great Britain and Ireland* (London, 1883).
Bernard Burke (ed), *A Genealogical and Heraldic History of the Landed Gentry, Volumes I
and II* (London, 1894).

Bernard Burke and Ashworth P. Burke, (eds), *A Genealogical and Heraldic History of the Peerage and Baronetage* (London, 1912).

John Burke and John Bernard Burke (eds), *A Genealogical and Heraldic History of the Extinct and Dormant Baronetcies of England, Ireland and Scotland* (London, 1844).

Burke's Genealogical and Heraldic History of the Landed Gentry, Volumes II and III (London, 1965).

Burke's Genealogical and Heraldic History of the Peerage, Baronetage and Knightage (London, 1970).

G. E. Cokayne, *The Complete Peerage, Volume I* (London, 1910); *Volume II* (London, 1912); *Volume III* (London, 1913); *Volume VI* (London, 1925); *Volume VII* (London, 1929); *Volume X* (London, 1945); *Volume XII, Part I* (London, 1953); *Volume XII, Part II* (London, 1959).

William Courthorpe (ed), *Debrett's Baronetage of England* (London, 1839).

F. W. S. Craig (ed), *British Electoral Facts, 1832–1980* (London, 1981).

Debrett's Baronetage and Knightage (London, 1881).

Debrett's Peerage, Baronetage, Knightage and Companionage (London, 1912)

Debrett's Peerage and Baronetage (London, 1995).

Charles R. Dod, *Electoral Facts: From 1832 to 1853, Impartially Stated* (London, 1853).

Robert P. Dod, *The Peerage, Baronetage and Knightage of Great Britain and Ireland* (London, 1863).

J. Gibson and C. Rogers (ed), *Poll Books c. 1696–1872* (Oxford, 1989).

Hansard's Parliamentary Debates, Volume LXXXVII (London, 1846); *Volume CCXXIII* (London, 1875); *Volume CCCXVIII* (London, 1887); *Volume CCCXXVIII* (London, 1888); *Volume CCCXXIX* (London, 1888); *Volume CCCXXXVII* (London, 1889); *Volume III* (London, 1892); *Volume IV* (London, 1909); *Volume VII* (London, 1909); *Volume IX* (London, 1909); *Volume IV* (London, 1910); *Volume V* (London, 1910); *Volume V* (London, 1911); *Volume VIII* (London, 1912).

Kelly's Directory of Suffolk (London, 1888); (London, 1904).

Kelly's Handbook to the Titled, Landed and Official Classes (London, 1904).

Robert H. Mair (ed), *Debrett's Baronetage and Knightage* (London, 1881).

Hugh Montgomery-Massingberd (ed), *Burke's and Savills Guide to Country Houses Volume III* (London, 1985).

——*Public General Statutes* (London, 1850); (London, 1856); (London, 1862); (London, 1892).

Leslie Rutherford and Sheila Bone (eds), *Osborn's Concise Law Dictionary* (London, 1993).

Michael Stenton and Stephen Lees, *Who's Who of British Members of Parliament, Volume II, 1886–1918: A Biographical Dictionary of the House of Commons* (Hassocks, 1978).

Suffolk County Handbook and Official Directory for 1917 (London, 1917)

J. Vincent and M. Stenton (eds), *McCalmont's Parliamentary Poll Book: British Election Results, 1832–1918* (London, 1971).

Walford's County Families (London, 1919).

L. Crispin Warmington (ed), *Stephen's Commentaries on the laws of England, Volume I* (London, 1950).

William White, *History, Gazetteer and Directory of Suffolk* (London, 1885).

British Parliamentary Papers:

'Abstract of Return, 14th March 1853: Returns of the number of Justices in England and Wales', *British Parliamentary Papers* LXXVIII (1852–3).

'Agricultural Returns of Great Britain', *British Parliamentary Papers* 76 (1880).

'Board of Agriculture Returns as to the number and size of agricultural holdings in Great Britain, 1895', *British Parliamentary Papers* LXVII (1896).

'Evidence of Mr Frederic Impey to Her Majesty's Commissioners for Inquiry into the Housing of the Working Classes', *British Parliamentary Papers* XXX (1884–5).

'Final Report of Her Majesty's Commissioners appointed to inquire into the subject of agricultural depression. Royal Commission on Agriculture', *British Parliamentary Papers* XV (1897).

'Report to the Select Committee on Agriculture, 1833', *British Parliamentary Papers* V (1833).

'Report to the Poor Law Board of the Laws of Settlement and Removal of the Poor: Report of G.A. à Beckett, Esq. to the Poor Law Board on the operation of the Laws of Settlement and Removal of the Poor in the counties of Suffolk, Norfolk and Essex and the Reading Union in Berkshire', *British Parliamentary Papers* XXVII (1850).

'Report from the Select Committee on Agricultural Customs', *British Parliamentary Papers* VI (1866).

'Report from the Select Committee on Poor Law Guardians', *British Parliamentary Papers* XVII (1878).

'Return of Owners of Land, England & Wales (exclusive of the Metropolis), 1872–3', *British Parliamentary Papers* LXXII (1874).

'Return of Owners of Land (Suffolk)', *British Parliamentary Papers* LXXII, Part II (1874).

'Return of names of Lord Lieutenants of counties of England and Wales, as the same stood on the 1st day of January 1875', *British Parliamentary Papers* LX (1875).

'Return giving the names and professions of all Justices of the Peace for the counties of England and Wales on the first day of June 1887', *British Parliamentary Papers* LXXXII (1888).

'Return for each administrative county in England and Wales, 1889', *British Parliamentary Papers* LXV (1889).

'Return of the number of instances in which County Councils, under the provisions of the Allotments Acts, 1887 and 1890, have acquired land for allotments', *British Parliamentary Papers* LXVIII (1892).

'Return giving the name and profession of all Justices of the Peace for the counties of England and Wales, 1892', *British Parliamentary Papers* LXXIV, Part I (1893–4).

'Return of all magistrates appointed between 1892 and 1894', *British Parliamentary Papers* LXXXI (1895).

'Return showing in each county the number of magistrates who have been placed on the Bench by virtue of their election as Chairman of District Councils', *British Parliamentary Papers* LXXXI (1895).

'Returns of the number of convictions under the Game Laws in separate counties in England and Wales for the year 1869', *British Parliamentary Papers* LVII (1870).

'Returns showing which Sanitary Authorities acquired land under the Acts of 1887 and 1890', *British Parliamentary Papers* LXVIII (1892).

'Royal Commission on the Employment of Children, Young Persons and Women in Agriculture (1867): Report by the Rev James Fraser', *British Parliamentary Papers* XVII (1867–1868).

'Royal Commission on Agricultural Depression: Minutes of evidence taken before Her Majesty's Commissioner's on Agriculture, Volume III', *British Parliamentary Papers* XIV (1882).

'Royal Commission on the Housing of the Working Classes. First Report of Her Majesty's Commissioners: Minutes of evidence', *British Parliamentary Papers* XXX (1884–1885).

'Royal Commission on Labour. The Agricultural Labourer: Report by Mr Wilson Fox on the Poor Law Union of Thingoe', *British Parliamentary Papers* XXXV (1893–4).

'Royal Commission on Labour. The Agricultural Labourer: Summary Report', *British Parliamentary Papers* XXXV (1893–4).

'Royal Commission on Labour. The Agricultural Labourer: Report by Mr Arthur Wilson Fox (Assistant Commissioner) upon the Poor Law Union of Swaffham', *British Parliamentary Papers* XXXV (1893–1894).

'Royal Commission on Agriculture: Report by Mr Wilson Fox (Assistant Commissioner) on the county of Cambridge', *British Parliamentary Papers* XVII (1895).

'Royal Commission on Agriculture: Report by Mr Wilson Fox (Assistant Commissioner) on the county of Suffolk', *British Parliamentary Papers* XVI (1895).

'Royal Commission on the selection of Justices of the Peace, 1910', *British Parliamentary Papers* XXXVII (1911).

Secondary Sources:

Charles Adeane and Edwin Savill, *The Land Retort: A Study of the Land Question with an Answer to the Report of the Secret Enquiry Committee* (London, 1914).

Andrew Adonis, *Making Aristocracy Work* (Oxford, 1993).

'Agriculture, long leases and large farms', *The Economist*, 2 February 1856.

'Agriculture and farmer's capital in England', *The Economist*, 9 March 1872.

'Agriculture, social status and tenant-farmers', *The Economist*, 18 November 1884.

Aldington, Richard, *Wellington* (London, 1946).

Michael Alexander and Sushila Anand, *Queen Victoria's Maharajah, Duleep Singh, 1838–1893* (London, 1980).

Alan Armstrong, *Farmworkers: A Social and Economic History, 1770–1980* (London, 1988).

P. F. Ashcroft and Herbert Preston-Thomas, *The English Poor Laws System: Past and Present* (London, 1902).

H. Auvray Tipping, 'Hengrave Hall, Suffolk', *Country Life*, 16 April 1910.

'Heveningham Hall, III, Suffolk', *Country Life*, 3 October 1925.

Lord Avebury, 'The Finance Bill', *Nineteenth Century*, November 1909.

Philip S. Bagwell & G. E. Mingay, *Britain and America 1850–1939: A Study of Economic Change,* (London, 1970).

Mark Bailey, *A Marginal Economy? East Anglian Breckland in the Later Middle Ages* (Cambridge, 1989).

Michael Barker, *Gladstone and Radicalism: The Reconstruction of Liberal Policy in Britain, 1885–1894* (Brighton, 1975).

Derek Beales, *From Castlereagh to Gladstone, 1815–1885* ((London, 1969).

William Bear, 'The public interest in agricultural reform', *Nineteenth Century*, June 1879.

——'Tenant right', in C. F. Dowsett (ed), *Land: Its Attractions and Riches: By Fifty-Seven Writers* (London, 1892).

T. W. Beastall, 'A South Yorkshire estate in the late nineteenth century', *Agricultural History Review* 14 (1966).

——'Landlords and tenants', in G. E. Mingay (ed), *The Victorian Countryside, Volume II* (London, 1981).

J. V. Beckett, 'English landownership in the later seventeenth and eighteenth centuries: the debate and the problems', *Economic History Review* 30 (1977).

——*The Aristocracy in England 1660–1914* (Oxford, 1989).

W. Bence Jones, 'Landowning as a business', *Nineteenth Century*, March 1882.

Michael Bentley, *Politics Without Democracy, 1815–1914: Perception and Preoccupation in British Government* (London, 1989).

J. H. Bettey, *Estates and the English Countryside* (London, 1993).

Herman Biddell, 'Agriculture', in William Page (ed), *The Victoria County History of Suffolk, Volume II* (London, 1907).

Marcus Binney, 'Wakefield Lodge, Northamptonshire', *Country Life*, 2 August 1973.

Neal Blewett, 'The franchise in the United Kingdom, 1855–1918', *Past and Present* 32 (1965).

——*The Peers, The Parties and the People: The General Elections of the 1910* (London, 1972).

Lloyd Bonfield, 'Marriage settlements and the "rise of great estates": the demographic aspects', *Economic History Review* 32 (1979).

——'Marriage settlements and the "rise of great estates": A rejoinder', *Economic History Review* 33 (1980).

——'Marriage settlements, 1660–1740: The adoption of the strict settlement in Kent and Northamptonshire', in R. B. Outhwaite (ed), *Marriage and Society: Studies in the Social History of Marriage* (London, 1981).

——'Strict settlement and the family: A differing view', *Economic History Review* 41 (1988).

Charles W. Boyd (ed), *Mr Chamberlain's Speeches* (London, 1914).

George R. Boyer, *An Economic History of the English Poor Law, 1750–1850* (Cambridge, 1990).

'Brandon Park estate', *Estates Gazette*, January 1898.

Paul Brassley, 'Arable systems: Light land farming', in E. J. T. Collins (ed), *The Agrarian History of England and Wales, Volume VII* (Cambridge, 2000).

Asa Briggs (ed), *Gladstone's Boswell: Late Victorian Conversations by Lionel A. Tollemache and other Documents* (Brighton, 1984).

Edward Bristow, 'The Liberty and Property Defence League and individualism', *Historical Journal* XVIII (1975).

Michael Brock, *The Great Reform Act* (London, 1973).

George C. Broderick, *English Land and English Landlords: An Enquiry into the Origin and Character of the English Land System, with Proposals for Its Reform* (London, 1881).

Jonathan Brown & H. A. Beecham, 'Arable farming, farming practices', in G. E. Mingay (ed), *The Agrarian History of England and Wales, 1750–1850, Volume VI* (Cambridge, 1989).

Anthony Brundage, 'The Landed Interest and the New Poor Law: A reappraisal of the revolution in government', *English Historical Review* 87 (1972).

——'The English Poor Law', *Agricultural History* 48 (1974).

——'The Landed Interest and the New Poor Law: A reply', *English Historical Review* 90 (1975).

——'Reform of the Poor Law electoral system, 1834–1894', *Albion* 7 (1975).

——*The Making of the New Poor Law* (London, 1978).

Jeremy Burchardt, *The Allotment Movement in England, 1793–1873* (Woodbridge, 2002).

Kevin Cahill, *Who Owns Britain* (Edinburgh, 2001).

James Caird, *English Agriculture, 1850–1851* (London, 1852. Reprinted 1968).

——*The Landed Interest and the Supply of Food* (London, 1878).

Jamie Camplin, *The Rise of the Plutocrats* (London, 1978).

David Cannadine, 'Aristocratic indebtedness in the nineteenth century: The case re-opened', *Economic History Review* XXX (1977).

——'Aristocratic indebtedness in the nineteenth century: A restatement', *Economic History Review* XXXIII (1980).

——*Lords and Landlords: The Aristocracy and the Towns, 1774–1967* (Leicester, 1980).

——*The Decline and Fall of the British Aristocracy* (London, 1990).

Sir Austen Chamberlain, *Politics from the Inside* (London, 1936).

J. D. Chambers and G. E. Mingay, *The Agricultural Revolution, 1750–1880* (London, 1978).

Andrew Charlesworth (ed), *An Atlas of Rural Protest in Britain 1548–1900* (London, 1983).

J. A. Chartres, 'Trends in the home market, the marketing of agricultural produce 1640–1750', in J. A. Chartres (ed), *Agricultural Markets and Trade, 1500–1750. Chapters from the Agrarian History of England and Wales, 1500–1750, Volume IV* (Cambridge, 1990).

O. F. Christie, *The Transition from Aristocracy 1832–1867* (London, 1927).

Kenneth Clark, *Another Part of the Wood: A Self-Portrait* (London, 1974).

Peter Clarke, '"Hodge's" politics: The agricultural labourers and the Third Reform Act in Suffolk', in Negley Harte and Roland Quinault (eds), *Land and Society in Britain, 1700–1914: Essays in Honour of F. M. L. Thompson* (Manchester, 1996).

C. Clay, 'Marriage, inheritance and the rise of large estates in England, 1660–1815', *Economic History Review* 21 (1968).

——'Property settlements, financial provision for the family, and sale of land by the greater landowners 1660–1790', *Journal of British Studies* 21 (1981).

Heather Clemenson, *English Country Houses and Landed Estates* (London, 1982).

Frederick Clifford, *The Agricultural Lock-Out of 1874: With Notes Upon Farming and the Farm Labourer in the Eastern Counties* (London, 1874).

Linda Colley, *Britons, Forging the Nation 1707–1837* (London, 1992).

E. J. T. Collins, 'The rationality of surplus agricultural labour', *Agricultural History Review* 35 (1987).

——'Rural and agricultural change: The Great Depression, 1875–1896', in E. J. T. Collins (ed), *The Agrarian History of England and Wales, Volume VII* (Cambridge, 2000).

E. J. T. Collins and E. L. Jones, 'Sectoral advance in English agriculture, 1850–1880', *Agricultural History Review* 15 (1967).

H. Colvin and J. Harris (eds), *The Country Seat* (London, 1970).

'Coney Weston Manor', *Estates Gazette*, July 1902.

Olive Cooke, *The English Country House As Art and a Way of Life* (London, 1974).

J. P. Cooper, 'Patterns of inheritance and settlement by great landowners from the fifteenth to the eighteenth centuries', in Jack Goody, Joan Thirsk and E. P. Thompson (eds), *Family and Inheritance: Rural Society in Western Europe, 1200–1800* (Cambridge, 1976).

J. T. Coppock, 'Agricultural changes in the Chilterns 1875–1900', *Agricultural History Review* 9 (1961).

J. Cornforth, 'The future of Heveningham', *Country Life* 18 September 1969.

S. Cornish Watkins, 'Heveningham Hall, Suffolk', *Country Life*, 25 April 1908.

Maurice Cowling, *1867, Disraeli, Gladstone and Revolution: The Passing of the Second Reform Bill* (Cambridge, 1967).

B. Crump and Gertrude Ghorbal, *History of the Huddersfield Woollen Industry* (Huddersfield, 1935).

Anthony Dale, *James Wyatt* (Oxford, 1956).

George Dangerfield, *The Strange Death of Liberal England* (New York, 1935).

Daniel Defoe, *A Tour Through the Whole Island of Great Britain* (London, 1724, reprinted 1971).

'Depperhaugh estate', *Estates Gazette*, September 1894.

A. V. Dicey, 'The paradox of the Land Law', *Law Quarterly Review* 21 (1905).

Charles Dickens, *Bleak House* (London, 1868).

'Discussions upon the land laws', *The Economist*, 27 September 1879.

Roy Douglas, *Land, People and Politics: A History of the Land Question in the United Kingdom, 1878–1952* (London, 1976).

J. P. D. Dunbabin, 'Expectations of the new County Councils and their realization', *Historical Journal* 8 (1965).

——*Rural Discontent in Nineteenth Century Britain* (London, 1974).

——'British local government reform', *English Historical Review* October (1977).

Peter Dunkley, 'The Landed Interest and the New Poor Law: A critical note', *English Historical Review* 88 (1973).

——'The "Hungry Forties" and the New Poor Law', *Historical Journal* 17 (1974).

David Dymond, 'The Suffolk landscape', in Lionel M. Munby (ed), *East Anglian Studies* (Cambridge, 1968).

——'Enclosure and reclamation', in David Dymond and Edward Martin (eds), *An Historical Atlas of Suffolk* (Ipswich, 1988).

David Dymond and Peter Northeast, *A History of Suffolk* (Oxford, 1985).

J. Ellis Barker, 'The land, the landlords and the people', *Nineteenth Century*, October 1909.

——'Unionist or socialist land reform?', *Nineteenth Century*, December 1909.

H. W. Elphinstone, 'The transfer of land', *Law Quarterly Review* 2 (1886).

Barbara English, *The Great Landowners of East Yorkshire, 1530–1910* (Hemel Hempstead, 1990).

Barbara English and John Savile, 'Family settlements and the "rise of great estates"', *Economic History Review* 33 (1980).

R. C. K. Ensor, *England, 1870–1914*, (Oxford, 1936).

Lord Ernle, *Whippingham to Westminster: Reminiscences of Lord Ernle* (London, 1938).

——*English Farming Past and Present* (London, 1961).

——'The Great Depression and recovery, 1874–1914', in P. J. Perry (ed), *British Agriculture 1875–1914* (Bungay, 1973).

George Ewart Evans, *Ask the Fellows Who Cut the Hay* (London, 1956).

——*Where Beards Wag All: The Relevance of the Oral Tradition* (London, 1970).

Nicholas Everitt, 'Shooting', in William Page (ed), *The Victoria County History of Suffolk, Volume II* (London, 1907).

Bernard Falk, *The Royal FitzRoys: Dukes of Grafton Through Four Centuries* (London, 1950).

Charles H. Feinstein and Sidney Pollard (eds), *Studies in Capital Formation in the United Kingdom, 1750–1920,* (Oxford, 1988).

J. R. Fisher, *Clare Sewell Read, 1826–1905: A Farmer's Spokesman of the Late Nineteenth Century* (Hull, 1975).

——'The Farmer's Alliance: An agricultural protest movement of the 1880s', *Agricultural History Review* 26 (1978).

——'The limits of deference: Agricultural communities in a mid-nineteenth century election campaign', *Journal of British Studies* 21 (1981).

——'Landowners and English tenant right, 1845–1852', *Agricultural History Review* 31 (1983).

——'Agrarian politics', in E. J. T. Collins (ed), *The Agrarian History of England and Wales, Volume VII* (Cambridge, 2000).

T. W. Fletcher, 'Lancashire livestock farming during the Great Depression', *Agricultural History Review* 9 (1961).

——'The Great Depression of English agriculture, 1873–1896', *Economic History Review* 13 (1961).

M. W. Flinn, *Origins of the Industrial Revolution* (London, 1966).

A. Wilson Fox, *The Earl of Halsbury, Lord High Chancellor 1823–1921* (London, 1929).

John France, 'Salisbury and the Unionist alliance', in Lord Blake and Hugh Cecil (eds), *Salisbury: The Man and his Policies* (London, 1987).

Jill Franklin, 'The Victorian country house', in G. E. Mingay (ed), *The Victorian Countryside, Volume II* (London, 1981).

Peter Fraser, 'The Unionist debacle of 1911 and Balfour's retirement', *The Journal of Modern History* XXXV (1963).

Mark Freeman, 'The agricultural labourer and the "Hodge" stereotype c.1850–1914', *Agricultural History Review* 49 (2001).

G. E. Fussell, *The English Rural Labourer* (London, 1949).

Russell M. Garnier, *History of the Landed Interest, the Customs, Laws, and Agriculture, Volume II* (London, 1908).

Norman Gash, *Politics in the Age of Peel* (London, 1966).

——*Aristocracy and People, Britain 1815–1865* (London, 1979).

Mark Girouard, 'A town built on carpets', *Country Life* 24 September 1970.

——*Life in the English Country House: A Social and Architectural History* (Yale, 1978).

——*The Victorian Country House* (London, 1979).

John Glyde, *Suffolk in the Nineteenth Century: Physical, Social, Moral, Religious and Industrial* (London, 1856).

E. A. Goodwyn, *A Suffolk Town in Mid-Victorian England: Beccles in the 1860s* (Ipswich, 1960).

T. R. Gourvish and R. G. Wilson, *The British Brewing Industry 1830–1980* (Cambridge, 1994).

F. E. Green, *A History of the English Agricultural Labourer* (London, 1920).

David Grigg, *The Agricultural Revolution in South Lincolnshire* (Cambridge, 1966).

W. L. Guttsman, 'The changing social structure of the British political elite, 1886–1935', *British Journal of Sociology* 2 (1951).

H. J. Habakkuk, 'English landownership, 1680–1740', *Economic History Review* 1 (1940).

———'Marriage settlements in the eighteenth century', *Transactions of the Royal Historical Society* 32 (1950).

———'The long-term rate of interest and the price of land in the seventeenth century', *Economic History Review* 5 (1952–3).

———'The English land market in the eighteenth century', in J. S. Bromley and E. H. Kossman (eds), *Britain and the Netherlands: Papers delivered to the Oxford-Netherlands Historical Conference, 1959* (London, 1960).

———'England', in A. Goodwin (ed), *The European Nobility in the Eighteenth Century: Studies in the Nobilities of the Major European States in the Pre-Reform Era* (London, 1967).

———'The rise and fall of English landed families, 1600–1800', *Transactions of the Royal Historical Society* 29 (1979).

———'The rise and fall of English landed families, II', *Transactions of the Royal Historical Society* 30 (1980).

———*Marriage, Debt and the Estates System: English Landownership 1650–1950* (Oxford, 1994).

H. Rider Haggard, *Rural England: Being An Account of the Agricultural and Social Researches Carried Out in the Years 1901 and 1902, Volume II* (London, 1902).

H. J. Hanham, 'The sale of honours in late Victorian England', *Victorian Studies* 3 (1959/1960).

J. Harris, *The Design of the English Country House 1620–1920* (London, 1985).

J. F. C. Harrison, *Late Victorian Britain 1875–1901* (London, 1990).

W. Hasbach, *A History of the English Agricultural Labourer* (London, 1908).

Michael Havinden, *Estate and Villages: A Study of the Berkshire Villages of Ardington and East Lockinge* (London, 1966).

———'The model village', in G. E. Mingay (ed), *The Victorian Countryside II,* (London, 1981)

———'Hengrave Hall', *Estates Gazette*, June 1889.

———'Heveningham: The path to disaster', *Country Life*, 11 February 1988.

E. J. Hobsbawm, *Industry and Empire* (London, 1969).

B. A. Holderness, 'Landlord's capital formation in East Anglia, 1750 – 1870', *Economic History Review* 25 (1972).

———'"Open" and "Close" Parishes in England in the Eighteenth and Nineteenth Centuries', *Agricultural History Review* 20 (1972).

———'The English land market in the eighteenth century: The case of Lincolnshire', *Economic History Review* 27 (1974).

———*Pre-industrial England: Economy and Society 1500–1750* (London, 1976).

———'The Victorian farmer', in G. E. Mingay (ed), *The Victorian Countryside, Volume I* (London, 1981).

———'The origins of high farming', in B. A. Holderness and Michael Turner (eds), *Land, Labour and Agriculture, 1700–1920* (London, 1991).

———'Investment, accumulation and agricultural credit', in E. J. T. Collins (ed), *The Agrarian History of England and Wales, Volume VII* (Cambridge, 2000).

Sir William Holdsworth, *A History of English Law, Volume VII* (London, 1925).

Pamela Horn, *Labouring Life in the Victorian Countryside* (Bristol, 1976).

———'Agricultural trade unionism in Oxfordshire', in J. P. D. Dunbabin (ed), *Rural Rural Discontent in Nineteenth Century Britain* (London, 1974).

——*The Changing Countryside in Victorian and Edwardian England and Wales* (London, 1984).

——*High Society: The English Social Elite, 1880–1914* (Stroud, 1992).

Alun Howkins, *Poor Labouring Men: Rural Radicalism in Norfolk 1872–1923* (London, 1985).

——'Peasants, servants, labourers: The marginal workforce in British agriculture c. 1870–1914', *Agricultural History Review* 42 (1994).

——'Social cultural and domestic life: The farmers', in E. J. T. Collins (ed), *The Agrarian History of England and Wales, Volume VII* (Cambridge, 2000).

——'Types of rural communities', in E. J. T. Collins (ed), *The Agrarian History of England and Wales, Volume VII* (Cambridge, 2000).

E. H. Hunt and S. J. Pam, 'Responding to agricultural depression, 1873–1896: Managerial success, entrepreneurial failure?', *Agricultural History Review* 50 (2002).

Christopher Hussey, 'Ickworth Park, Suffolk', *Country Life*, 10 March 1955.

——'Icklingham Hall', *Estates Gazette*, 29 January 1898.

Frederic Impey, *Three Acres and Cow: Successful Small Holdings and Peasant Proprietors* (London, 1885).

Roy Jenkins, *Mr Balfour's Poodle: An Account of the Struggle Between the House of Lords and the Government of Mr Asquith* (London, 1954).

T. A. Jenkins, *Gladstone, Whiggery and the Liberal Party, 1874–1886* (Oxford, 1988).

Celia Jennings, *The Identity of Suffolk* (Bury St Edmunds, 1980).

A. H. Johnson, *The Disappearance of the Small Landowner, Ford Lectures, 1909* (Oxford, 1909).

A. W. Jones, 'Glamorgan custom and tenant right', *Agricultural History Review* 31 (1983).

E. L. Jones, 'The changing basis of English agricultural prosperity 1853–1873', *Agricultural History Review* 10 (1962).

——*The Development of English Agriculture, 1815–1873* (London, 1973).

Harry Jones, *Liberalism and the House of Lords* (London, 1912).

Joseph Kay, *Free Trade in Land* (London, 1879).

B. Keith-Lucas, *The English Local Government Franchise* (Oxford, 1952).

E. Kerridge, *The Farmers of Old England* (London, 1973).

G. Kitson Clark, 'The repeal of the Corn Laws and the politics of the Forties', *Economic History Review*, 4 (1951).

'Landlord and tenant, money abatements of rent', *The Economist*, 24 September 1853.

The Land: The Report of the Land Enquiry Committee, Volume I, Rural (London, 1913).

H. J. Leach (ed), *The Public Letters of the Right Hon John Bright* (London, 1895).

J. M. Lee, Social Leaders and Public Persons (Oxford, 1963).

G. Shaw Lefevre, *Agrarian Tenures: A Survey of the Laws and Customs Relating to the Holding of Land in England, Ireland and Scotland of the Reforms Therein During Recent Years* (London, 1893).

David Low, *On Landed Property and the Economy of Estates* (London, 1848).

Patricia Lynch, *The Liberal Party in Rural England, 1885–1910: Radicalism and Community* (Oxford, 2003).

H. L. Malchow, *Gentlemen Capitalists* (London, 1991).

W. H. Mallock, 'An inquiry into the actual amount of the annual increment of land values', *Nineteenth Century*, November 1909.

Jean Marchand (ed), *A Frenchman in England, 1784: Being the Mélanges sur l'Angleterre of François de la Rochefoucauld,* (Cambridge, 1933).

George Martelli, *The Elveden Enterprise: A Study of the Second Agricultural Revolution* (London, 1952).

Edward Martin, 'The soil regions of Suffolk', in David Dymond and Edward Martin (eds), *An Historical Atlas of Suffolk* (Ipswich, 1988).

A. H. H. Matthews, *Fifty Years of Agricultural Politics: Being the History of the Central Chamber of Agriculture 1865–1915* (London, 1915).

Michael W. McCahill, *Order and Equipoise: The Peerage and the House of Lords, 1783–1806* (London, 1978).

Julian R. McQuiston, 'Tenant-right: Farmer against landlord in Victorian England, 1847–1883', *Agricultural History* XLVII (1973).

G. E. Mingay, 'The size of farms in the eighteenth century', *Economic History Review* 14 (1962).

——*Arthur Young and His Times* (London, 1975).

——*English Landed Society in the Eighteenth Century* (London, 1976).

——*The Gentry: The Rise and Fall of a Ruling Class* (London, 1976).

——*The Agricultural Revolution: Changes in Agriculture, 1650–1880* (London, 1977).

——*Rural Life in Victorian England* (London, 1977).

——*The Transformation of Britain, 1830–1939* (London, 1986).

——*A Social History of the English Countryside* (London, 1991).

——*Land and Society in England, 1750–1980* (London, 1994).

——'The farmer', in E. J. T. Collins (ed), *The Agrarian History of England and Wales, Volume Seven* (Cambridge, 2000).

D. C. Moore, *The Politics of Deference: A Study of the Mid-Nineteenth Century Political System* (Hassocks, 1976).

Alastair Mutch, 'Farmers organizations and agricultural depression in Lancashire, 1890–1900', *Agricultural History Review* 31 (1983).

Sir Lewis Namier and John Brooke, *The House of Commons 1754–1790* (London, 1964).

Howard Newby, *Green and Pleasant Land: Social Change in Rural England* (London, 1979)

——*Country Life: A Social History of Rural England* (London, 1987).

Charles Newton-Robinson, 'The blight of the Land Taxes', *Nineteenth Century*, September 1910.

Avner Offer, 'The origins of the Law of Property Act, 1910–1925', *The Modern Law Review* 40 (1977).

——*Property and Politics, 1870–1914: Landownership, Law, Ideology and Urban Development in England* (Cambridge, 1981).

Cormac O'Grada, 'The landlord and agricultural transformation, 1870–1900: A comment on Richard Perren's Hypothesis', *Agricultural History Review*, 27 (1979).

——'Agricultural decline, 1860–1914', in R. Floud and D. McCloskey (eds), *The Economic History of Britain Since 1700. Volume II, 1860 to the 1970s* (Cambridge, 1981).

R. J. Olney, *Lincolnshire Politics, 1832–1885* (Oxford, 1973).

——'The politics of land', in G. E. Mingay (ed), *The Victorian Countryside, Volume I* (London, 1981).

C. S. Orwin, *A History of English Farming* (London, 1949).

C. S. Orwin and E. H. Whetham, *History of British Agriculture, 1846–1914* (Newton Abbot, 1971).

Arthur Oswald, 'Hintlesham Hall, Suffolk', *Country Life*, 18 August 1928.

——'Melford Hall, II, Suffolk', *Country Life*, 7 August 1937.

——'Helmingham Hall, Suffolk, I', *Country Life,* 9 August 1956.

——'Helmingham Hall, Suffolk, II', *Country Life*, 16 August 1956.

——'Helmingham Hall, Suffolk, III', *Country Life*, 23 August 1956.

——'Helmingham Hall, Suffolk, IV', *Country Life*, 27 September 1956.

——'Helmingham Hall, Suffolk, V', *Country Life*, 4 October 1956.

Ian Packer, *Lloyd George, Liberalism and the Land: The Land Issue and Party Politics in England, 1906–1914* (Woodbridge, 2001).

Clive Paine (ed), *The Culford Estate 1780–1935* (Lavenham, 1993).

F. R. Parker, *The Election of County Councils* (London, 1888).

H. M. Pelling, *Social Geography of British Elections, 1885–1914* (Aldershot, 1967).

Harold Perkin, *The Origins of Modern English Society, 1780–1880* (London, 1969).

——*The Age of the Railway* (Newton Abbot, 1971).

——*The Rise of Professional Society: England Since 1880* (London, 1989)

J. A. Perkins, 'Tenure, tenant right and agricultural progress in Lindsey, 1780–1850', *Agricultural History Review* 23 (1975).

Richard Perren, 'The landlord and agricultural transformation, 1870–1900', *Agricultural History Review* 18 (1970).

——'The North American beef and cattle trade with Great Britain, 1870–1914', *Economic History Review* 24 (1971).

——'The landlord and agricultural transformation 1870–1900: A rejoinder', *Agricultural History Review* 27 (1979).

——*Agriculture in Depression 1870–1940* (Cambridge, 1995).

Roy Perrot, *The Aristocrats: A Portrait of Britain's Nobility and Their Way of Life Today* (London, 1968).

P. J. Perry, *British Farming in the Great Depression 1870–1914: An Historical Geography*, (Newton Abbot, 1974).

——'High farming in Victorian Britain: The financial foundations', *Agricultural History* 52 (1978).

P. J. Perry and R. J. Johnston, 'The temporal and spatial incidence of agricultural depression in Dorset, 1868–1902', *Journal of Interdisciplinary History* 2 (1972).

Nicklaus Pevsner, *Suffolk* (London, 1974).

J. Holladay Philbin, *Parliamentary Representation 1832, England and Wales* (New Haven, 1965).

A. D. M. Phillips, 'Underdraining on the English claylands, 1850–1880: A review', *Agricultural History Review* 17 (1969).

——*The Underdraining of Farmland in England During the Nineteenth Century* (Cambridge, 1989).

——'Landlord investment in farm buildings in the English Midlands in the mid-nineteenth century', in B. A. Holderness and Michael Turner (eds), *Land, Labour and Agriculture, 1700–1920* (London, 1991).

G. D. Phillips, *The Diehards: Aristocratic Society and Politics in Edwardian England* (London, 1979).

Arthur Ponsonby, *The Decline of Aristocracy* (London, 1912).

J. H. Porter, 'Tenant-right: Devonshire and the 1880 Ground Game Act', *Agricultural History Review* 34 (1986).

R. Porter, *London: A Social History* (London, 1994).

M. R. Postgate, 'The field systems of Breckland', *Agricultural History Review* 10 (1962).

J. Enoch Powell, *Joseph Chamberlain* (London, 1975).

Public Men of Ipswich and East Suffolk: A Series of Personal Sketches Reprinted from the Suffolk Mercury (Ipswich, 1875)

Ralph E. Pumphrey, 'The introduction of industrialists into the British peerage: A study in the adaptation of a social institution', *American Historical Review* LXV (1959).

William and Hugh Raynbird, *On the Agriculture of Suffolk* (London, 1849).

J. Redlich and F. W. Hirst, *Local Government in England* (London, 1903).

Lawrence Rich, *Inherit the Land, Landowners in the Eighties* (London, 1987).

Eric Richards, 'The Leviathan of wealth: West-Midland agriculture, 1800–1850', *Agricultural History Review* 22 (1974).

John Martin Robinson, *The Wyatts: An Architectural Dynasty* (Oxford, 1979).

David Rubinstein, (ed), *Victorian Homes* (Newton Abbot, 1974).

W. D. Rubinstein, *Men of Property* (London, 1981).

——'New men of wealth and the purchase of land in nineteenth century Britain', *Past and Present* 92 (1981).

——'Cutting-up rich: A reply to F. M. L. Thompson', *Economic History Review* 45 (1992).

——'Businessmen into landowners: The question revisited', in Negley Harte and Roland Quinault (eds), *Land and Society in Britain, 1700–1914: Essays in Honour of F. M. L. Thompson* (Manchester 1996).

Sir Gerald Ryan and Lillian J. Redstone, *Timperley of Hintlesham A Study of a Suffolk Family* (London, 1931).

John Langton Sanford and Meredith Townsend, *The Great Governing Families of England, Volume I* (Edinburgh, 1865).

S. B. Saul, *The Myth of the Great Depression 1873–1896* (London, 1985).

Norman Scarfe, *The Suffolk Landscape* (London, 1972).

——*A Frenchman's Year in Suffolk: French Impressions of Suffolk Life in 1784* (Suffolk Records Society, 30, 1988).

Nigel Scotland, *Methodism and the Revolt of the Field: A study of the Methodist Contribution to Agricultural Trade Unions in East Anglia, 1872–1896* (Gloucester, 1981).

Searle, Geoffrey, *The Liberal Party: Triumph and Disintegration, 1886–1929* (London, 2001).

William Shaw and Henry Corbet, *Digest of Evidence Taken Before a Committee of the House of Commons Appointed to Inquire into the Agricultural Customs of England and Wales in Respect to Tenant-Right* (London, 1849).

J. L. Smith-Dampier, *East Anglian Worthies* (Oxford, 1949).

David Spring, 'The English landed estate in the age of coal and iron: 1830–1880', *Journal of Economic History* XI (1951).

——'The Earls of Durham and the great northern coalfield, 1830–1880', *Canadian Historical Review* XXXIII (1952).

——'English landownership in the nineteenth century: A critical note', *Economic History Review* IX (1957).

——*The English Landed Estate in the Nineteenth Century: Its Administration* (Maryland, 1963).

——'English landed society in the eighteenth and nineteenth centuries', *Economic History Review* 17 (1964).

——'Introduction', in John Bateman's, *The Great Landowners of Great Britain and Ireland* (London, 1883. Reprinted, Leicester, 1971).

——'Aristocratic indebtedness in the nineteenth century: A comment', *Economic History Review* XXXIII (1980).

——'Land and politics in Edwardian England', *Agricultural History* 58 (1984).

David and Eileen Spring, 'Social mobility and the English landed elite', *Canadian Journal of History* 21 (1986).

Eileen Spring, 'The settlement of land in nineteenth century England', *The American Journal of Legal History* 8 (1964).

——'The family, strict settlement and historians', *Canadian Journal of History* 18 (1983).

——'Law and the theory of the affective family', *Albion* 16 (1984).

——'The strict family settlement: Its role in family history', *Economic History Review* 41 (1988).

Eileen Spring and David Spring, 'The English landed elite, 1540–1879: A review', *Albion* 17 (1985).

G. D. Squibb, 'The end of the name and arms clause?', *Law Quarterly Review* 69 (1953).

Lawrence Stone, 'Spring back', *Albion* 17 (1985).

Lawrence and Jeanne C. Fawtier Stone, 'Country houses and their owners in Hertfordshire, 1540–1879', in W. O. Aydelotte, A. C. Beque and R.W. Fogel (eds), *The Dimensions of Quantitative Research in History* (London, 1972).

——*An Open Elite? England 1540–1880* (Oxford, 1984).

E. G. Strutt, *British Agriculture* (London, 1917)

R. W. Sturgess, 'The Agricultural Revolution on the English clays', *Agricultural History Review* 14 (1966).

——'The Agricultural Revolution on the English clays: A rejoinder', *Agricultural History Review* 15 (1967).

——'Sudbourne Hall, Suffolk', *Country Life*, 23 February 1901.

David Taylor, 'Growth and structural change in the English dairy industry c.1860–1930', *Agricultural History Review* 35 (1987).

Robert Taylor, *Lord Salisbury* (London, 1975).

'Tenant right in Great Britain', *The Economist*, 24 September 1881.

'The English Land Question', *The Economist*, 18 June 1881.

'The creation of a peasant propriety', *The Economist*, 17 January 1885.

Jonathan Theobald, 'Agricultural productivity in Woodland High Suffolk, 1600–1850', *Agricultural History Review*, 50 (2002).

——'Estate stewards in Woodland High Suffolk, 1690–1820', in C. Harper-Bill, C. Rawcliffe and R. G. Wilson (eds), *East Anglia's History: Studies in Honour of Norman Scarfe* (Woodbridge, 2002).

Joan Thirsk, *English Peasant Farming: The Agrarian History of Lincolnshire from Tudor to Recent Times* (London, 1957).

——'The farming regions of England, East Anglia, Norfolk and Suffolk' in J. Thirsk (ed), *The Agrarian History of England and Wales, Volume IV. 1500–1640* (Cambridge, 1967).

——*The Agrarian History of England and Wales, Volume V, Part II, 1640–1750: Agrarian Change* (Cambridge, 1985).

Joan Thirsk and Jean Imray (eds), *Suffolk Farming in the Nineteenth Century* (Ipswich, 1958).

F. M. L. Thompson, 'The end of a great estate', *Economic History Review* VIII (1955).

——'The Land Market in the Nineteenth Century', *Oxford Economic Papers* IX (1957).

—— *English Landed Society in the Nineteenth Century* (London, 1963).

——'Land and politics in England in the nineteenth century', *Transactions of the Royal Historical Society* 15 (1965).

——'The Second Agricultural Revolution, 1815–1880', *Economic History Review Second* 21 (1968).

——'Landownership and economic growth in England in the eighteenth century', in E. L. Jones and S. J. Woolf (eds), *Agrarian Change and Economic Development: The Historical Problems* (Bungay, 1969).

——'Britain' in David Spring (ed), *European Landed Elites in the Nineteenth Century* (London, 1977).

——'Landowners and the rural community', in G. E. Mingay (ed), *The Victorian Countryside, Volume II* (London, 1981).

——'Private property and public policy', in Lord Blake and Hugh Cecil (eds), *Salisbury: The Man and His Policies* (London, 1987).

—— *The Rise of Respectable Society: A Social History of Victorian Britain, 1830–1900* (London, 1988).

——'Life after death: How successful nineteenth century businessmen disposed of their fortunes', *Economic History Review* 43 (1990).

——'An anatomy of English agriculture, 1870–1914', in B. A. Holderness and Michael Turner (eds), *Land, Labour and Agriculture, 1700–1920* (London, 1991).

——'Stitching it together again', *Economic History Review* 45 (1992).

Flora Thompson, *Lark Rise to Candleford* (Reprinted, Oxford, 1954).

R. J. Thompson, 'An enquiry into the rent of agricultural land', in W. E. Minchinton (ed), *Essays in Agrarian History, Volume II* (Newton Abbot, 1968).

D. H. Tollemache, *The Tollemaches of Helmingham and Ham* (Ipswich, 1949).

P. J. O. Trist, *A Survey of the Agriculture of Suffolk,* (London, 1971).

R. Trumbach, *The Rise of the Egalitarian Family* (London, 1978).

Michael Turner, 'Cost, finance and parliamentary enclosure', *Economic History Review* 34 (1981).

—— *Enclosures in Britain, 1750–1830* (London, 1984).

——'Output and prices in UK agriculture, 1867–1914', *Agricultural History Review* 40 (1992).

'Tyrell Estates', *Estates Gazette*, May 1892.

Sir Arthur Underhill, *A Concise Explanation of Lord Birkenhead's Act, The Law of Property Act 1922, in Plain Language* (London, 1922).

——'Property' *Law Quarterly Review* 51 (1935).

C. Unwin and B. Villiers, *The Land Hunger: Life Under Monopoly. Descriptive Letters and Other Testimonials From Those Who Have Suffered* (London, 1913).

George Veitch, *The Genesis of Parliamentary Reform* (London, 1965).

J. E. Vincent, *Through East Anglia in a Motor Car* (London, 1907)

Susanna Wade Martins, *A Great Estate at Work: The Holkham Estate and its Inhabitants in the Nineteenth Century* (Cambridge, 1980).

Susanna Wade Martins and Tom Williamson, 'The development of the lease and its role in agricultural improvement in East Anglia, 1660–1870', *Agricultural History Review* 46 (1998).

—— *Roots of Change: Farming and the Landscape in East Anglia, c. 1700–1870* (Exeter, 1999).

Alfred Russell Wallace, *Land Nationalization, Its Necessity and Its Aims: Being a Comparison of the System of Landlord and Tenant with that of Occupying Ownership in their Influence on the Well-Being of the People* (London, 1882)

E. H. Whetham, 'The Agriculture Act, 1920 and its repeal', *Agricultural History Review* 22 (1974).

R. A. Whitehead, *The Beloved Coast and Suffolk Sandlings* (Lavenham, 1991).

Tom Williamson, 'Shrubland before Barry: A house and its landscape, 1660–1880', in C. Harper-Bill, C. Rawcliffe and R. G. Wilson (eds), *East Anglia's History, Studies in Honour of Norman Scarfe* (Woodbridge, 2002).

Tom Williamson and Liz Bellamy, *Property and the Landscape* (London, 1987).

Charles Wilson, 'Economy and society in late Victorian Britain', *Economic History Review* 18 (1965).

R. G. Wilson, 'The Denisons and Milneses: Eighteenth century merchant landowners', in J. T. Ward and R. G. Wilson (eds), *Land and Industry: The Landed Estate and the Industrial Revolution* (Newton Abbot, 1971).

R. G. Wilson, *Greene King: A Business and Family History* (London, 1983).

Richard Wilson and Alan Mackley, *Creating Paradise: The Building of the English Country House, 1660–1880* (London, 2000).

Michael I. Wilson, *The English Country House and its Furnishings* (London, 1977).

The Earl of Winterton, *Pre-War* (London, 1932).

E. A. Wrigley and R. S. Schofield, *The Population History of England, 1541–1871: A Reconstruction* (Cambridge, 1989).

Arthur Young, *General View of the Agriculture of the County of Suffolk* (London, 1813)

Carl Zangerl, 'The social composition of the county magistracy in England and Wales, 1831–1887', *Journal of British Studies* 11 (1971).

F. Barham Zincke, *Wherstead: Some materials for Its History, Territorial, Manorial and the Events Between*, (London, 1893).

INDEX